The Mystical

City of God

The Life of the Virgin Mother of God

The Mystical

CITY OF GOD

The Life of the Virgin Mother of God

A New Abridgement

by

Walter R. Blados

ZONON BOOKS
Cincinnati, Ohio

ISBN: 978-0-9978975-2-4

ZONON BOOKS; Cincinnati, OH
United States of America
www.ZononBooks.com

I dedicate this effort to the loving memory of Kay, my wife of 52 years. Kay was devoted to the Blessed Mother, and I know she would have approved of this final result.

ABOUT THE AUTHOR

Walter Blados was born in 1931, in the small town of Southold, New York, located on the end of the north fork of Long Island. He was enrolled at Fordham University, on the Bronx, New York campus, from 1949-1952, and then decided to study for the priesthood. He joined the Maryknoll Fathers, and studied with them until 1956.

He thereupon decided to enlist in the United States Navy, and was commissioned as an Ensign in 1957. In the same year, he married his wonderful wife Katherine Anne Tarpey, from Brookline, Massachusetts. Walt and wife Kay managed to bring into this world, six sons and one daughters—a lot of work; but a lot of fun.

The first few years of his Naval career were spent in Key West, Bermuda, and Puerto Rico. He then switched his naval career toward intelligence related occupations.

After retiring from the Navy in 1974, he was recruited by the Navy to serve as a civilian and worked in the intelligence field until 1976.

He then left the intelligence field, to begin working with the U.S. Air Force at Andrews Air Force Base, and subsequently transferred to the Pentagon. He served as the U.S. Air Force Scientific and Technical Information Program Manager, as well as the U.S. Delegate to the NATO Advisory Group for Aerospace Research and Development Technical Information Panel.

He retired from the U.S. Civil Service in 1991, but continued work as a consultant to NASA, U.S. Geological Survey, and the Defense Technical Information Center. He is currently living in Glendale, a quiet suburb of Cincinnati, Ohio.

NOTE TO THE READER

On the bottom left of each page there is a notation which will serve as a reference point for those wishing to examine or study a particular topic in more depth.

For example, a page listing B1C4 will refer you to Book 1, Chapter 4 of the current popular abridged version of The Mystical City of God.

http://www.ecatholic2000.com/agreda/mystical/city.shtml provides an online copy of the current popular abridgement of The Mystical City of God. This source was current as of the publication date.

TABLE OF CONTENTS

PREFACE

"The Mystical City of God: Life of the Virgin Mother of God", was manifested and recorded by the Venerable Mother Mary of Jesus in the small town of Agreda near Tarazona in Spain. The book was completed in 1665; it is a monumental four-volume, 2,676 page history of the life of the Blessed Virgin Mary, as revealed to her in ecstasy by Heaven itself.

A popular abridgement of the four volume work was compiled by Fiscar Marison (Reverend George J. Blatter). He began the translation from the original authorized Spanish edition on the Feast of the Assumption 1902, and it was completed in 1912. The purpose of this popular abridgement was to bring to an even wider readership the sublime truths found in "The Mystical City of God"

The abridged version, as well as the original document, was difficult to read, but after completing the reading and study of "The Mystical City of God", I remain humbled and overwhelmed by the beauty and sublimity of the contents. I cannot find words to describe how enriched I felt and feel after reading the book. I am an elderly born-and-bred Catholic, but had never been introduced to such a rich history of the entire life of the Blessed Mother.

My contemplative life has been immensely enriched. I now see Blessed Mary in a whole new light. I can marvel at the various aspects of Mary: Her deep sense of humility, Her charitable works, Her interactions with Our Lord and the Trinity, as well as Her influence and involvement with the Apostles.

Certain sections of the book provide excellent topics for study and contemplation; my meditations during the recitation of the mysteries of the rosary now have more meaning. Certain sections of Mary's life can bring absolute chills, certain sections can bring sorrow, certain sections can bring an abundance of joy; all sections portray a magnificent Woman.

After rereading and contemplating the various books and chapters of the abridged version, I knew it would be difficult to entice and encourage my family and friends to read the book. I wondered if there was some way I could make it easier and more interesting for my children, grandchildren, my extended family, and others to read and appreciate this wonderful work, and thus increase their knowledge of Blessed Mary and Our Lord Jesus Christ.

Herewith, then, is my attempt to even further abridge and condense the contents of both the original and the abridged versions of "The Mystical City of God". My aim is to make it easier to read by providing the facts and details of the many chapters in a more narrative form, liberally copying from the book, and omitting the many long and beautiful prayers. Hopefully as individuals progress in their reading, they might be inspired to delve further into the more complete books for more definitive information.

I am publishing this condensation as part of my legacy to my extended family in the hopes that it will inspire them to make an attempt to read it, thereby expanding their knowledge and appreciation of the Mother of God and Our Lord Jesus Christ; and to learn to know the life of a most remarkable and extraordinary Woman. I hope they will enjoy reading it as much as I have had in condensing it.

Walter R. Blados,
5 January 2017

Ad Maiorem Dei Gloriam

ACKNOWLEDGEMENTS

I wish to acknowledge and thank the following individuals who provided support and assistance in developing, providing editorial tasks, and organizing the final layout of this new abridgement of The Mystical City of God.

FATHER DAVID FAY—*Pastor, Saint Gabriel Church, Glendale, Ohio, for his encouragement and pastoral support.*

MR. GENE M. OSTENKAMP—*Music Director and Organist, Saint Gabriel Church, Glendale, Ohio, for his guidance and assistance in sharing his know-how in the many steps to prepare the final manuscript for publication.*

MS. KELLY RHOADES—*a freelance individual who did so many of the myriad tasks involved in bringing this labor of love to fruition.*

The Mystical

City of God

The Life of the Virgin Mother of God

Chapter One

Chapter One

CREATION AND FALL OF MAN
ADAM AND EVE

When the Most High formed and created Adam, he created him at the age of thirty-three years - this being the age in which Christ was to suffer death. Adam, with regard to his body, was so like unto Christ, that scarcely any difference existed. Also, according to the soul, Adam was similar to Christ. From Adam God formed Eve so similar to the Blessed Virgin, that she was like unto Her in personal appearance and in figure.

God looked upon these two creations with the highest pleasure and benevolence, and on account of their similarities to Christ and Mary, He heaped many blessings upon them. But the happy state in which God had created the parents of the human race lasted only a very short while.

Although Lucifer (Satan) had witnessed the creation of all other things, he was not permitted to witness the formation of Adam and Eve; for the Lord did not choose to manifest to him the creation of man, nor the formation of Eve from a rib; all these things were concealed from him for a space of time until both of them were joined. And here Lucifer was also deceived; for the Lord had from the beginning mysteriously manifested to him, that the Word (Christ) was to assume human nature in the womb of the most holy Mary, but not how and when; and thus He also concealed the creation of Adam and the formation of Eve, in order that Lucifer might from the beginning labor under his ignorance concerning the mystery and the time of the Incarnation.

The envy of Lucifer was immediately aroused against them; he had been patiently awaiting their creation, and no sooner were they created, than his hatred became active against them.

When the demon saw the admirable composition of the human nature, perfect beyond that of any creature, and the beauty of the souls and bodies of Adam and Eve; when he saw the paternal love with which the Lord regarded them, and how He made them the lords of all creation; and when he saw that He gave them hope of eternal life, the wrath of the dragon was lashed to fury, and no tongue can describe the rage with which that beast was filled, nor how great was his envy and his desire to take the life of these two beings.

Like an enraged lion he certainly would have done so, if he had not known that a superior force would prevent him. Nevertheless he studied and plotted out some means, which would suffice to deprive them of the grace of the Most High and make them God's enemies.

As his wrath and his watchfulness had thus been so signally forestalled in regard to Christ and Mary, he suspected that Adam had come forth from Eve, and that She was the Mother and Adam the incarnate Word. His suspicions grew, when he felt the divine power, which prevented him from harming the life of these creatures. On the other hand, he soon became aware of the precepts of God, for these did not remain concealed from him, since he heard their conversation in regard to them.

Being freed more and more from his doubt as he listened to the words of the first parents and sized up their natural gifts, he began to follow them like a roaring lion seeking an entrance through those inclinations, which he found in each of them. Nevertheless, until he was undeceived in the course of the Redemption, he continued to hesitate between his wrath against Christ and Mary and the dread of being overcome by Them. Most of all he dreaded the confusion of being conquered by the Queen of heaven, who was to be a mere creature and not God.

Lucifer entered with all his energy upon the work of entrapping them and of opposing and hindering the execution of the divine Will. He first approached the woman, and not the man, because he knew her to be by nature more frail and weak, and because in tempting her he would be more certain that it was not Christ whom he was encountering. Against her also he was more enraged ever since he had seen the sign in the heaven and since the threat, which God had made in it against him.

[NOTE: When God created the angels, they were told that the being of God was one in substance, trine in person – the good angels agreed to adore and reverence Him as their Creator and highest Lord. Lucifer, with his following, did not so agree.]

When the angels were informed that God was to create a human nature and reasoning creatures lower than themselves, in order that they too should love, fear and reverence God, as their Author and eternal Good, they agreed. But Lucifer, full of envy and pride, resisted and induced his followers to resist.

When the angels were informed that they were to submit to the Mother of the Incarnate Word conjointly with Him; a Woman, in whose womb the Only begotten of the Father was to assume flesh and that this Woman was to be the Queen and Mistress of all the creatures, the good angels freely subjected themselves by obeying this command of the Lord.

But Lucifer shouted that he would persecute and destroy this human nature which the Lord looked upon with so much love and favored so highly. This proud boast so aroused the indignation of the Lord that in order to humble it, He spoke to Lucifer: "This Woman whom thou refusest to honor, shall crush thy head and by Her shalt thou be vanquished and annihilated"

Before he showed himself to her, however, he aroused her in many disturbing thoughts or imaginations, in order to approach her in a state of excitement and pre-occupation. He took upon himself the form of a serpent, and thus speaking to Eve drew her into a conversation, which she should not have permitted. Listening to him and answering, she began to believe him; then she violated the command of God, and finally persuaded her husband likewise to transgress the precept. Thus ruin overtook them and all the rest: for themselves and for us they lost the happy position in which God had placed them.

When Lucifer saw the two fallen, and their interior beauty and grace and original justice changed into the ugliness of sin, he celebrated his triumph with incredible joy. But he soon fell from his proud boasting, when he saw, contrary to his expectations, how kindly the merciful love of God dealt with the delinquents, and how He offered them a chance of doing penance by giving them hope of pardon and return of grace. Moreover he saw how they were disposing themselves toward this forgiveness by sorrow and contrition, and how the beauty of grace was restored to them. When the demons perceived the effect of contrition, all hell was again in confusion.

His consternation grew, when he heard the sentence, which God pronounced against the guilty ones, in which he himself was implicated. More especially and above all was he tormented by the repetition of that threat: "The Woman shall crush thy head" which he had already heard in heaven.

Notwithstanding all this the Most High, in his ineffable kindness, gave our first parents his benediction, in order that the human race might grow and multiply. The most high Providence permitted that Eve, in the birth of Cain, should bring forth a type of the evil fruits of sin, and in the birth of Abel, the type of Christ our Lord both in figure and in imitation. For in the just one the law and doctrine of Christ began to exert its effects. All the rest of the just were to follow it, suffering for justice sake, hated and persecuted by the sinners and the reprobate and by their own brothers.

Accordingly, patience, humility and meekness began to appear in Abel, and in Cain, envy and all wickedness, for the benefit of the just and for his own perdition. The wicked triumph and the good suffer, exhibiting the spectacle, which the world in its progress shows to this day, namely, the Jerusalem of the godfearing and the Babylon of the godforsaken, each with its own leader and head.

The offspring of Eve multiplied after the fall and so arose the distinction and the multiplication of the good and the bad, the elect and the reprobate, the ones following Christ the Redeemer, and the others following Satan. The elect cling to their Leader by faith, humility, charity, patience and all the virtues, and in order to obtain victory, they are assisted, helped and beautified by the divine grace and the gifts which the Redeemer and Lord of all merited for them.

But the reprobate, without receiving any such benefits from their false leader, or earning any other reward than the eternal pain and the confusion of hell, follow him in pride, presumption, obscenity and wickedness, being led into these disorders by the father of lies and the originator of sin.

The Most High also wished that the first Adam should be the type of the second in the manner of their creation; for, just as before the creation of the first, He created and ordered for him the republic of all the beings, of which he was to be the lord and head; so before the appearance of his Onlybegotten, the Most High allowed many ages to pass by, in order that his Son might find prepared for Himself a people, of which He was to be the Head, the Teacher, and the King. As the world progressed in course, in order that the Word might descend from the bosom of the Father and clothe Itself in our mortality, God selected and prepared a chosen and most noble people, the most admirable of past and future times.

Within it also He constituted a most illustrious and holy race, from which He was to descend according to the flesh, and the mysteries and holy Sacraments, which He entrusted to it, as was afterwards made manifest through his holy Church.

He reared most holy Prophets and Patriarchs, who in figures and prophecies announced to us from far off, that, which we have now in possession. He wishes us to venerate them, knowing how they esteemed the law of grace and how earnestly they yearned and prayed for it.

To this people God manifested his immutable Essence by many revelations, and they again transmitted these revelations to us by the Holy Scriptures, containing immense mysteries, which we grasp and learn to know by faith. All of them, however, are brought to perfection and are made certain by the incarnate Word, who transmitted to us the secure rule of faith and the nourishment of the sacred Scriptures in his Church.

Although the Prophets and the just ones of that people were not so far favored as to see Christ in his body, they nevertheless experienced the liberality of the Lord, who manifested Himself to them by prophecies and who moved their hearts to pray for his coming and for the Redemption of the whole human race.

The consonance and harmony of all these prophecies, mysteries and aspirations of the ancient fathers, were a sweet music to the Most High, which resounded in the secret recesses of the Divinity and which regarded and shortened the time (to speak in a human manner) until He should descend to converse with man.

At this juncture, the Most High directed his attention to the attribute of his mercy; He counterbalanced the weight of his incomprehensible justice with the law of clemency, and chose to yield more to his own goodness. He chose to listen to the clamors and faithful services of the just and the prophets of his people, rather than to his indignation at the wickedness and sins of all the rest of mankind. He resolved to pledge the day of grace, sending into the world two most bright luminaries to announce the approaching dawn of the Son of Justice, Christ our Salvation. These were Saints Joachim and Anne, prepared and created by especial decree according to his own heart.

SAINTS JOACHIM AND ANNE

Joachim had his home, his family and relations in Nazareth, a town of Galilee. He, always a just and holy man and illumined by especial grace and light from on high, had a knowledge of many mysteries of the Holy Scriptures and of the olden Prophets. In continual and fervent prayer he asked God to fulfill his promises, and his faith and charity penetrated the heavens. He was a man most humble and pure, leading a most holy and sincere life, yet he was most grave and earnest, and incomparably modest and honest.

The most fortunate Anne had a house in Bethlehem and was a most chaste, humble and beautiful maiden. From her childhood she led a most virtuous, holy and retired life, enjoying great and continual enlightenment in exalted contemplation. Withal she was most diligent and industrious, thus attaining perfection in both the active and contemplative life. This woman also prayed most fervently that the Almighty deign to procure for her in matrimony a husband, who should help her to observe the ancient law and testament, and to be perfect in the fulfillment of all its precepts.

At the moment in which Saint Anne thus prayed to the Lord, his Providence ordained that Saint Joachim make the same petition: both prayers were made at the same time before the tribunal of the holy Trinity, where they were heard and fulfilled, it being then and there divinely disposed, that Joachim and Anne unite in marriage and become the parents of Her, who was to be the Mother of the incarnate God.

In furtherance of this divine decree the Archangel Gabriel was sent to announce it to them both. To Saint Anne he appeared in visible form, while she was engaged in fervent prayer.

The angel did not then manifest this great sacrament to Saint Anne; but he said to her: "The Most High give thee his blessing, servant of God, and be thy salvation. His Majesty has heard thy petitions and He wishes thee to persevere therein and that thou continue to clamor for the coming of the Redeemer. It is his will, that thou accept Joachim as the spouse, for he is a man of upright heart and acceptable to the Lord: in his company thou wilt be able to persevere in the observance of his law and in his service.

To Saint Joachim the Archangel did not appear in a corporeal manner, but he spoke to the man of God in sleep as follows: "Joachim, be thou blessed by the right hand of the Most High! Persevere in thy desires and live according to rectitude and perfection. It is the will of the Almighty, that thou receive Saint Anne as thy spouse, for her the Lord has visited with his blessing. Take care of her and esteem her as a pledge of the Most High and give thanks to his Majesty, because he has given her in thy charge."

In consequence of this divine message Saint Joachim immediately asked for the hand of the most chaste Anne and, in joint obedience to the divine ordainment, they espoused each other. The two holy spouses lived in Nazareth, continuing to walk in the justification of the Lord. In rectitude and sincerity they practiced all virtue in their works. The rents and incomes of their estate they divided each year into three parts. The first one they offered to the temple of Jerusalem for the worship of the Lord; the second they distributed to the poor, and the third they retained for decent sustenance of themselves and family. God augmented their temporal goods on account of their generosity and charity.

They themselves lived with each other in undisturbed peace and union of heart, without quarrel or shadow of a grudge. The most humble Anne subjected herself and conformed herself in all things to the will of Joachim: and that man of God, with equal emulation of humility, sought to know the desires of holy Anne, confiding in her with his whole heart. Thus they lived together in such perfect charity, that during their whole life they never experienced a time, during which one ceased to seek the same thing as the other.

This fortunate couple passed twenty years of their married life without bearing any children. In those times, and among the people of the Jews, this was held to be the greatest misfortune and disgrace. On this account they had to bear much reproach and insult from their neighbors and acquaintances, for all those that were childless, were considered as excluded from the benefits of the Messiah. They continued in most fervent prayers from the bottom of their hearts, and made an express vow to the Lord, that if He should give them issue, they would consecrate It to his service in the temple of Jerusalem.

Having, at the command of the Lord, persevered a whole year in fervent petitions, it happened by divine inspiration and ordainment, that Joachim was in the temple of Jerusalem offering prayers and sacrifices for the coming of the Messiah. Arriving with others of his town to offer the common gifts and contributions in the presence of the high priest, Isachar, an inferior priest, harshly reprehended the old and venerable Joachim, for presuming to come with the other people to make offerings in spite of his being childless.

Among other things he said to him: "Why dost thou, Joachim, come with thy offerings and sacrifices, which are not pleasing in the eyes of God, since thou art a useless man? Leave this company and depart; do not annoy God with thy offerings and sacrifices, which are not acceptable to Him." Joachim hastened away from the temple full of sorrow to a farm or storehouse which he possessed, and there in solitude he prayed and for some days called upon the Lord to bless them with a child.

While Joachim was making these petitions in his retirement, the holy angel manifested to holy Anne, that her prayer for an issue, was pleasing to the Almighty. Having thus recognized the will of God and of her husband Joachim, she prayed with humble subjection and confidence that it be fulfilled.

The petitions of the most holy Joachim and Anne reached the throne of the holy Trinity, where they were accepted. The three divine Persons spoke to them as follows: "We have in our condescension resolved, that the person of the Word shall assume human flesh and that through Him all the race of mortals shall find a remedy. .... and above all have We before our eyes Her, who is to be the chosen One, who is to be acceptable above all creatures and singled out for our delight and pleasure; because She is to conceive the person of the Word in her womb and clothe Him with human flesh.... Joachim and Anne have found grace in our eyes; We look upon them with pleasure and shall enrich them with choicest gifts and graces."

From the throne an intellectual voice proceeded saying: "Gabriel, enlighten, vivify and console Joachim and Anne, our servants, and tell them, that their prayers have come to our presence and their petitions are heard in clemency. Promise them, that by the favor of our right hand they will receive the Fruit of benediction, and that Anne shall conceive a Daughter, to whom We give the name of MARY."

With this mandate of the Most High, Gabriel appeared to holy Joachim, while he was in prayer, saying to him: "Just and upright man, the Almighty from his sovereign throne has taken notice of thy desires and has heard thy sighs and prayers, and has made thee fortunate on earth. Thy spouse Anne shall conceive and bear a Daughter, who shall be blessed among women. The nations shall know Her as the Blessed. He wishes to enrich thy house and thy family with a Daughter, whom Anne shall conceive; the Lord himself has chosen for Her the name of MARY. From her childhood let Her be consecrated to the temple, and in it to God, as thou hast promised. She shall be elected, exalted, powerful and full of the Holy Ghost; on account of the sterility of Anne her conception shall be miraculous; She shall be a Daughter wonderful in all her doings and in all her life. Thou shalt go to give thanks in the temple of Jerusalem and in testimony of the truth of this joyful message, thou shalt meet, in the Golden Gate, thy sister Anne, who is coming to the temple for the same purpose."

The Angel appeared to Anne saying: "The humility, faith and the alms of Joachim and of thyself have come before the throne of the Most High and now He sends me, his angel, in order to give thee news full of joy for thy heart: His Majesty wishes, that thou be most fortunate and blessed. He chooses thee to be the mother of Her who is to conceive and bring forth the Onlybegotten of the Father. Thou shalt bring forth a Daughter, who by divine disposition shall be called MARY. She shall be blessed among women and full of the Holy Ghost.

Know also that I have announced to Joachim, that he shall have a Daughter who shall be blessed and fortunate: but the full knowledge of the mystery is not given him by the Lord, for he does not know, that She is to be the Mother of the Messiah. Go now to the temple to give thanks to the Most High for having been so highly favored by his powerful right hand.

In the Golden Gate thou shalt meet Joachim, where thou wilt confer with him about this tiding. Thou art the one, who art especially blessed of the Lord and whom He wishes to visit and enrich with more singular blessings. In solitude He will speak to thy heart and there give a beginning to the law of grace, since in thy womb He will give being to Her, who is to vest the Immortal with mortal flesh and human form. In this humanity, united with the Word, will be written, as with his own blood, the true law of Mercy."

Anne heard it and received it with magnanimity and incomparable joy. Immediately arising she hastened to the temple of Jerusalem, and there found Saint Joachim, as the angel had foretold to them both. Together they gave thanks to the Almighty for this wonderful blessing and offered special gifts and sacrifices. They were enlightened anew by the grace of the Holy Spirit, and, full of divine consolation, they returned to their home. Joyfully they conversed about the favors which they had received from the Almighty. Anew they made the vow to offer Her to the temple and that each year on this day they would come to the temple to offer special gifts, spend the day in praise and thanksgiving, and give many alms. This vow they fulfilled to the end of their lives.

The prudent matron Anne never disclosed the secret that her Daughter was to be the Mother of the Messiah, neither to Joachim nor to any other creature. Nor did that holy parent in the course of his life know any more than that She was to be a grand and mysterious woman. However, in the last moments of his life the Almighty made the secret known to him.

THE IMMACULATE CONCEPTION

Knowing that the opportune and preordained time had arrived, the three divine Persons conferred with each other saying: "Now is the time to begin the work of our pleasure and to call into existence that pure Creature and that Soul, which is to find grace in our eyes above all the rest. Let Us furnish Her with richest gifts and let Us deposit in Her the great treasures of our grace".

"Let Us create a soul according to our pleasure, a fruit of our attributes, a marvel of our infinite power, without touch or blemish of the sin of Adam. Let Her be a most special image and likeness of our Divinity and let Her be in our presence for all eternity the culmination of our goodwill and pleasure."

"We will set Her apart from the ordinary law, by which the rest of the mortals are brought into existence, for in Her the seed of the serpent shall have no part. I will descend from heaven into her womb and in it vest Myself from her substance with human nature."

"The Word (Christ) which is to become man, being the Redeemer and Teacher of men, must lay the foundation of the most perfect law of grace, and must teach through it, that the father and mother are to be obeyed and honoured as the secondary causes of the natural existence of man."

'The law is first to be fulfilled by the divine Word by honoring Her as his chosen Mother, by exalting Her with a powerful arm, and lavishing upon Her the most admirable, most holy and most excellent of all graces and gifts. Among these shall be that most singular honor and blessing of not subjecting Her to our enemy, nor to his malice; and therefore She shall be free from the death of sin."

"On earth the Word shall have a Mother without a father, as in heaven He has a Father without a mother. And in order that there may be the proper correspondence in calling God his Father and this Woman his Mother, We desire that the highest correspondence and approach possible between a creature and its God be established."

"The human flesh, from which He is to assume form, must be free from sin. Since He is to redeem in it the sinners, He must not be under the necessity of redeeming his own flesh, like that of sinners. Being united to the Divinity his humanity is to be the price of Redemption. We wish that for all eternities the Word should be glorified through this tabernacle and habitation of the human nature."

"And since the incarnate Word is to be the Teacher of humility and holiness, and for this end is to endure labors, confounding the vanity and deceitful fallacies of mortals by choosing for Himself sufferings as the treasure most estimable in our eyes. We wish that She, who is to be his Mother, experience the same labors and difficulties, that She be singularly distinguished in patience, admirable in sufferings, and that She, in union with the Only-begotten, offer the acceptable sacrifices of sorrow to Us for her greater glory."

"Let now the prophecies of our servants and the promises made to them, that We would send a Savior to redeem them, be fulfilled. And in order that all may be executed according to our good pleasure, and that We may give a beginning to the mystery hidden since the constitution of the world, We select for the formation of our beloved Mary the womb of our servant Anne; in her be She conceived and in her let that most blessed Soul be created. Although her generation and formation shall proceed according to the usual order of natural propagation, it shall be different in the order of grace, according to the ordainment of our Almighty power."

Then the Most High chose and appointed those who were to be occupied in the exalted service (the guardianship of Mary) from each of the nine choirs of angels. He selected one hundred, being nine hundred in all.

Moreover he assigned twelve others who should in a special manner assist Mary in corporeal and visible forms. Besides these the Lord assigned eighteen other angels, selected from the highest ranks, who were to ascend and descend by that mystical stairs of Jacob with the message of the Queen to his Majesty and those of the Lord to Her.

In addition to all these holy angels the Almighty assigned and appointed seventy seraphim in order that they might communicate and converse with this Princess of heaven in the same way as they themselves interact with each other, and as the higher communicate with the lower ones.

In order that this invincible warrior–troop might be well appointed, Saint Michael, the prince of the heavenly militia was placed at their head, and although not always in the company of the Queen, he was nevertheless often near Her and often showed Himself to Her. The Almighty destined him as a special ambassador of Christ our Lord and to act in some of the mysteries as the defender of his most holy Mother.

In a like manner the holy prince Gabriel was appointed to act as legate and minister of the eternal Father in the affairs of the Princess of heaven. Thus did the most holy Trinity provide for the custody and the defense of the Mother of God.

In the formation of the body of the most holy Mary the wisdom and power of the Almighty proceeded so cautiously that the quantities of the four natural elements of the human body, the sanguine, melancholic, phlegmatic and choleric, were compounded in exact proportion and measure; this wonderfully composed temperament was afterwards the source and the cause, which in its own way made possible the serenity and peace that reigned in the powers and faculties of the Queen of heaven during all her life.

Then the Almighty created the soul of his Mother and infused it into the body; and thus entered into the world that pure Creature, more holy, perfect and agreeable to His eyes than all those He had created, or will create to the end of the world, or through the eternities.

She was possessed of the most perfect justice, superior to that of Adam and Eve in their first formation. To Her was also concealed the most perfect use of the light of reason, corresponding to the gifts of grace, which She had received. Not for one instant was She to remain idle, but to engage in works most admirable and pleasing to her Maker.

Although She was endowed with all perfections and with the whole range of infused virtues, it was not necessary that She should exercise all of them at once, it being sufficient that She exercise those, which were befitting her state in the womb of her mother.

Among the first thus exercised were the three theological virtues, faith, hope and charity, which relate immediately to God. These she at once practiced in the most exalted manner recognizing by a most sublime faith the Divinity with all its perfections and its infinite attributes, and the Trinity with its distinction of Persons.

She exercised also the virtue of hope, seeing in God the object of her happiness and her ultimate end. In the virtue of charity it was seeing in God the infinite and highest Good, and conceiving such an intense appreciation of the Divinity.

She had an infused knowledge and habit of all the virtues and of all the natural arts, so that She knew and was conversant with the whole natural and supernatural order of things. Hence from her first instant in the womb of her mother, She was wiser, more prudent, more enlightened, and more capable of comprehending

God and all his works, than all the creatures have been or ever will be in eternity, excepting of course her most holy Son.

THE BLESSED BIRTH OF IMMACULATE MARY

Holy Anne passed the days of her pregnancy altogether spiritualized by the divine operations and by the sweet workings of the Holy Ghost. Divine Providence, however, in order to direct her course to greater merit and reward, ordained that the weight of trouble be not wanting, for without it, the cargo of grace and love is scarcely ever secure. In order to understand better for what happened to this holy woman, it must be remembered that Satan, after he was hurled with the other bad angels from heaven into the infernal torments, never ceased, during the reign of the old Law, to search through the earth hovering with lurking vigilance above the women of distinguished holiness, in order to find Her, whose sign he had seen and whose heel was to bruise and crush his head.

Filled with malice and astuteness, he observed closely the exceeding great holiness of the excellent matron Anne; and although he could not estimate the richness of the Treasure which was enclosed in her blessed womb, yet he felt a powerful influence proceeding from her. The fact that he could not penetrate into the source of this activity, threw him at times into greater fury and rage. At other times he quieted himself with the thought that this pregnancy arose from the same causes as others in the course of nature, and that there was no special cause for alarm.

Nevertheless the whole event was a source of great misgiving to this perverse spirit, when he saw how quietly her pregnancy took its course and especially, when he saw, that many angels stood in attendance. Above all he was enraged at his weakness in resisting the force which proceeded from the blessed Anne, and he suspected that it was not She alone who was the cause of it.

Filled with this mistrust, the dragon determined, if possible, to take the life of the most felicitous Anne; or, if that was impossible, to see that she should obtain little satisfaction from her pregnancy. Audaciously therefore, he set himself to tempt holy Anne, with many suggestions, misgivings, doubts and diffidence about the truth of her pregnancy, alleging her protracted years. All this the demon attempted in order to test the virtue of the saint, and to see, whether these temptations would not afford some opening for the perversion of her will.

But the invincible matron resisted these onslaughts with humble fortitude, patience, continued prayer and vivid faith in the Lord. Nevertheless, in his insatiable malice, the enemy did not desist on that account; he sought human aid. Having tried to overthrow the dwelling of saint Joachim and Anne, in order that she might be frightened and excited by the shock of its fall, and not being able to succeed, he incited against saint Anne one of the foolish women of her acquaintance to quarrel with her.

This the woman did with great fury, insolently attacking Saint Anne with reproach and scorn; she did not hesitate to make mockery of her pregnancy, saying, that she was the sport of the demon in being thus found pregnant at the end of so many years and at so great an age.

The blessed Anne did not permit herself to be disturbed by this attack, but in all meekness and humility bore the injuries and treated her assailants with kindness. From that time on she looked with greater love upon these women and lavished upon them so much the greater benefits. But their wrath was not immediately pacified, for the demon had taken possession of them, filling them with hate against the saint; and he incited these miserable dupes to plot even against the person and life of Saint Anne.

But they could not put their plots into execution, because divine power interfered to foil their natural womanly weakness. They were not only powerless against the saint, but they were overcome by her admonitions and brought to the knowledge and amendment of their evil course by her prayers.

The dragon was repulsed, but not vanquished; for he immediately availed himself of a servant, who lived in the house with Joachim and Anne, and exasperated her against the holy matron. Through her he created even a greater annoyance than through the other women, for she was a domestic enemy and more stubborn and dangerous than the others. But with the help of God, Saint Anne won a more glorious victory than before; for the Lord put to ignominious flight Satan and his followers.

The day destined for the parturition of Saint Anne had arrived: a day most fortunate for the world. This birth happened on the eighth day of September, fully nine months having elapsed since the Conception of the soul of our most holy Queen and Lady.

Saint Anne was prepared by an interior voice of the Lord, informing her, that the hour of her parturition had come. Full of the joy of the Holy Spirit at this information, she prostrated herself before the Lord and besought the assistance of his grace and his protection for a happy deliverance. The most blessed child Mary was at the same time by divine providence and power ravished into a most high ecstasy. Hence Mary was born into the world without perceiving it by her senses, for their operations and faculties were held in suspense.

She was born pure and stainless, beautiful and full of grace, thereby demonstrating, that She was free from the law and the tribute of sin. Although She was born substantially like other daughters of Adam, yet her birth was accompanied by such circumstances and conditions of grace that it was the most wonderful and miraculous birth in all creation and will eternally redound to the praise of her Maker.

At twelve o'clock in the night, this divine Luminary issued forth, dividing the night of the ancient Law and its pristine darkness from the new day of grace, which now was about to break into dawn. She was clothed, handled, dressed and treated like other infants. Her mother did not allow Her to be touched by other hands than her own, but she herself wrapped Her in swaddling clothes, and in this Saint Anne was not hindered by her present state of childbirth; for she was free from the toils and labours, which other mothers usually endure in such circumstances.

Saint Anne received in her arms her, who was her Daughter, but at the same time the most exquisite Treasure of the entire universe, inferior only to God and superior to all other creatures. With fervent tears of joy she offered this Treasure to his Majesty, and asked Him to guide her in the handling of her daughter.

The Lord answered that she was to treat her heavenly Child outwardly as mothers treat their daughters, without any demonstration of reverence; but to retain this reverence inwardly, fulfilling the laws of a true mother toward Her, and rearing Her with all motherly love and solicitude. All this the happy mother complied with; making use of this permission and her mother's rights without losing her reverence, she regaled herself with her most holy Daughter, embracing and caressing Her in the same way as other mothers do with their daughters. But it was always done with a proper reverence and consciousness of the hidden and divine sacrament known only to the mother and Daughter.

At the moment of the birth of Mary, the Most High sent the archangel Gabriel as an envoy to bring this joyful news to the holy Fathers in limbo. Immediately the heavenly ambassador descended, illumining that deep cavern and rejoicing the just who were detained therein. He told them that already the dawn of eternal felicity had commenced and that the reparation of man, which was so earnestly desired and expected by the holy Patriarchs and foretold by the Prophets, had been begun, since She, who was to be the Mother of the Messiah, had now been born; soon they would see the salvation and glory of the Most High.

The holy prince gave them an understanding of the excellence of the most holy Mary and of what the Omnipotent had begun to work in Her, in order that they might better comprehend the happy beginning of the mystery, which was to end their prolonged

B1C7

imprisonment. Then all the holy Patriarchs and Prophets and the rest of the just in limbo rejoiced in spirit and in new canticles praised the Lord for this benefit.

All these happenings at the birth of our Queen succeeded each other in a short space of time. The first exercise of her senses was to recognize her parents and other creatures. The arms of the Most High began to work new wonders in Her far above all conceptions of men, and the first and most stupendous one was to send innumerable angels to bring the Mother of the eternal Word body and soul into the empyrean heaven for the fulfilling of his further intentions regarding Her. The holy princes obeyed the divine mandate, and receiving the child Mary from the arms of her holy Mother Anne, they arranged a new and solemn procession bearing heavenward to rest in the temple of the King of kings. This was the second step, which most holy Mary made in her life, namely, from this earth to the highest heaven.

Borne by the hands of the angels the child Mary entered the empyrean heaven where She prostrated Herself before the royal throne in the presence of the Most High. Then the Most High arose from his throne, received her with honour and reverence, and seated her at his side as queen. New graces and gifts were bestowed upon Her, by which her faculties were correspondingly elevated. Her powers of mind, besides being illumined and prepared by new grace and light, were raised and proportioned to the divine manifestation, and the Divinity displayed Itself in the new light. This was the first time in which the most holy soul of Mary saw the blessed Trinity in unveiled beatific vision.

In this divine consistory and tribunal of the most holy Trinity it was determined to give a name to the Child Queen. The Lord himself wishing to give and impose Her name in heaven, revealed to the angelic spirits that the three divine Persons had decreed and formed the sweet names of Jesus and Mary for the Son and Mother from the beginning before the ages.

B1C7

The holy angels heard a voice from the throne speaking in the person of the Father: "Our chosen One shall be called MARY, and this name is to be powerful and magnificent. Those that shall invoke it with devout affection shall receive most abundant graces; those that shall honor it and pronounce it with reverence shall be consoled and vivified, and will find in it the remedy of their evils, the treasures for their enrichment, the light which shall guide them to heaven. It shall be terrible against the power of hell, it shall crush the head of the serpent and it shall win glorious victories over the princes of hell."

The Lord commanded the angelic spirits to announce this glorious name to saint Anne, so that what was decreed in heaven might be executed on earth. The heavenly Child, lovingly prostrate before the throne, rendered most acceptable and human thanks to the eternal Being; and She received the name with most admirable and sweet jubilation. In the meanwhile the infant Queen remained ignorant of the real cause of all that She thus experienced, for her dignity of Mother of the incarnate Word was not revealed to Her till the time of the Incarnation.

With reverential jubilee the angels returned to replace Her into the arms of holy Anne, to whom this event remained a secret, as was also the absence of her Daughter; for a guardian angel, assuming an aerial body, supplied her place for this very purpose.

On the eighth day after the birth of the great Queen multitudes of most beautiful angels in splendid array descended from on high bearing an escutcheon on which the name of MARY was engraved and shone forth in great brilliancy. Appearing to the blessed mother Anne, they told her, that the name of her daughter was to be MARY, which name they had brought from heaven, and which divine Providence had selected and now ordained to be given to their child by Joachim and herself.

The Saint called for her husband and they conferred with each other about this disposition of God in regard to the name of their Daughter. The more than happy father accepted the name with joy and devout affection. They decided to call their relatives and a priest and then, with much solemnity and festivity, they imposed the name of MARY on their Child.

HER CHILDHOOD YEARS

The sovereign Child was treated like other children of her age. Her nourishment was of the usual kind, though less in quantity; and so was her sleep, although her parents were solicitous that She take more sleep. She was not troublesome, but was most amiable and caused no trouble to anyone.

She maintained, even in her infancy, a pleasant countenance, yet mixed with gravity and a peculiar Majesty, never showing any childishness. She sometimes permitted Herself to be caressed, though, by a secret influence and a certain outward austerity; She knew how to repress the imperfections connected with such endearments. Her prudent mother Anne treated her Child with incomparable solicitude and caressing tenderness; her father Joachim loved Her as a father and as a saint, although he was ignorant of the mystery at that time.

The Child on Her part showed a special love toward him, as one whom She knew for her father, and one much beloved of God. Although She permitted more tender caresses from her father than from others, yet God inspired the father as well as all others, with such an extraordinary reverence and modesty towards Her, that even his pure and fatherly affection was outwardly manifested only with the greatest moderation and reserve.

In all things the infant Queen was most gracious, perfect and admirable. Though She passed her infancy subject to the common laws of nature, yet this did not hinder the influx of grace. During her sleep her interior acts of love, and all other exercises of her faculties which were not dependent on the exterior senses, were never interrupted.

The silence of other children in their first years, and the slow evolution of their intellect and their power of speech arising from natural weakness, was a heroic virtue in the infant Queen. She was in perfect possession of all her faculties since her Conception, so the fact of her not speaking as soon as She was born did not arise from the want of ability, but because She did not wish to make use of her power. Her not speaking was a virtue and great perfection, which opportunely concealed her science and grace, and evaded the astonishment naturally caused by one speaking in infancy.

It was ordained by the Most High, that the sovereign Child should voluntarily keep this silence during the time in which ordinarily other children are unable to speak. The only exception made was in regard to the conversation held with the angels of her guard, or when She addressed Herself in vocal prayer to the Lord. For in regard to interaction with God and the holy angels, this reason for maintaining silence did not hold good: on the contrary it was befitting, that, since there was no impediment, She should pray with her lips and her tongue; for it would not be proper to keep them unemployed for so long a time.

But her mother never heard Her, nor did she know of her being able to speak during that period; and from this it can be better seen, what perfection it required in Her to pass that year and a half of her infancy in total silence. But during that time, whenever her mother freed her arms and hands, the child Mary immediately grasped the hands of her parents and kissed them with great submission and reverent humility, and in this practice She continued as long as her parents lived.

She also sought to make them understand during that period of her age, that She desired their blessing, speaking more by the affection of her heart than by word of mouth. So great was her reverence for them, that never did She fail in the least point concerning the honor and obedience to them. Nor did She cause them any trouble or annoyance, since She knew beforehand all their thoughts and was anxious to fulfill them before they were made manifest.

When She reached the age of two years She began to exercise her special pity and charity toward the poor. She solicited alms for them of Saint Anne, and the kind–hearted mother readily granted her petitions, both for the sake of the poor and to satisfy the tender charity of her most holy Daughter, at the same time encouraging Her who was the Mistress of mercy and charity, to love and esteem the poor. She gave to the poor not as if conferring a benefit upon them, but rather as paying a debt due in justice, saying in her heart: this is my brother and master who deserves what he needs and what I possess. In giving alms She kissed the hands of the poor; never did She give alms to the poor without conferring still greater favors on their souls by interceding for them, and thus dismissing them relieved in body and soul.

Not less admirable were the humility and obedience of the most holy Child in permitting Herself to be taught to read and to do other things as other children in that time of life. She was instructed in reading and other arts by her parents and She submitted, though She had infused knowledge of all things created.

Her holy mother Anne observed with rapture the heavenly Princess and blessed the Most High in Her. As the time for presenting Her in the temple approached, she began to dread the approaching end of the three years set by the Almighty and the consciousness, that the terms of her vow must punctually be fulfilled.

Therefore the child Mary began to prepare and dispose her mother, manifesting to her, six months before, her ardent desire of living in the temple. She recounted the benefits which they had received at the hands of the Lord, how much they were obliged to seek His greater pleasure, and how, when She should be dedicated to God in the temple, She would be more her Daughter than in their own house.

The holy Anne heard the discreet arguments of her child Mary; and was resigned to the divine will and wished to fulfill her promise of offering up her beloved Daughter. Full of grief she said to the Child: "My beloved Daughter, for many years I have longed for Thee and only for a few years do I merit to have thy company; but thus let the will of God be fulfilled; I do not wish to be unfaithful to my promise of sending Thee to the temple, but there is yet time left for fulfilling it; have patience until the day arrives for the accomplishment of thy wishes."

A few days before most holy Mary reached the age of three years, She was favored with an abstract vision of the Divinity, in which it was made known to Her that the time of her departure for the temple ordained by God, had arrived, and that there She was to live dedicated and consecrated to His service.

At the same time Saint Anne had a vision, in which the Lord enjoined her to fulfill her promise by presenting her Daughter in the temple on the very day on which the third year of her age should be complete. Saint

Joachim also had a vision of the Lord at this time, receiving the same command as Saint Anne.

Having conferred with each other and taking account of the will of the Lord, they resolved to fulfill it with humble submission and appointed the day on which the Child was to be brought to the temple. Great was the grief of this holy old man, though not quite as great as that of Saint Anne, for the high mystery of her being the future Mother of God was yet concealed from him.

Chapter Two

HER PRESENTATION IN THE TEMPLE

The three years time decreed by the Lord having been completed, Joachim and Anne set out from Nazareth, accompanied by a few kindred and bringing with them the most holy Mary, in order to deposit Her in the holy temple of Jerusalem. This humble procession was scarcely noticed by earthly creatures, but it was invisibly accompanied by the angelic spirits, who, in order to celebrate this event, had hastened from heaven in greater numbers than ordinary as her bodyguard, and were singing in heavenly strains the glory and praise of the Most High. The Princess of heaven heard and saw them as She hastened her beautiful steps along in the sight of the highest and the True Lord.

They arrived at the holy temple, and the blessed Anne on entering took her Daughter by the hand, and accompanied and assisted by Saint Joachim they offered a devout and fervent prayer to the Lord; the parents offering to God their Daughter, and the most holy Child offering up Herself.

She alone perceived that the Most High received and accepted Her. Having offered their prayers, they rose and betook themselves to the priest. The parents consigned their Child into the hands of the priest and he gave them his blessing. Together they conducted Her to the portion of the temple buildings, where many young girls lived to be brought up in retirement and in virtuous habits, until old enough to assume the state of matrimony. It was a place of retirement especially selected for the first–born daughters of the royal tribe of Juda and the sacerdotal tribe of Levi.

Fifteen stairs led up to the entrance of these apartments. Other priests came down these stairs to welcome the blessed child Mary. The one that had received them placed Her on the first step. Mary, with his permission, turned and kneeling down before Joachim and Anne, asked their blessing and kissed their hands, recommending herself to their prayers before God. The holy parents in tenderest tears gave Her their blessing; whereupon She ascended the fifteen stairs without any assistance. She hastened upward with incomparable fervor and joy, neither turning back, nor shedding tears, nor showing any childish regret at parting from her parents.

The priests received Her among the rest of the maidens, and Saint Simeon consigned Her to the teachers, one of whom was the prophetess Anne. This holy matron had been prepared by the Lord by especial grace and enlightenment, so that She joyfully took charge of this Child of Joachim and Anne.

Sorrowfully her parents Joachim and Anne retraced their journey to Nazareth, now poor and deprived of the rich Treasure of their house. But the Most High consoled and comforted them in their affliction.

The holy priest Simeon, although he did not at this time know of the mystery enshrined in the child Mary, obtained great light as to her sanctity and her special selection by the Lord; also the other priests looked upon Her with great reverence and esteem. In ascending the fifteen stairs the Child brought to fulfillment, that, which Jacob saw happening in sleep; for here too were angels ascending and descending: the ones accompanying, the others meeting their Queen as She hastened up; whereas at the top God was waiting to welcome Her as his Daughter and Spouse.

The child Mary, when brought to her teacher, knelt in profound humility before her and asked her blessing. She begged to be admitted among those under her direction, obedience and counsel, and asked her kind forbearance in the labor and trouble, which She would occasion. The prophetess Anne, her teacher, received Her with pleasure, and said to Her: "My Daughter, Thou shalt find in me a helpful mother and I will take care of Thee and of thy education with all possible solicitude."

B2C1

Then the holy Child proceeded to address Herself with the same humility to all the maidens which were then present; each one She greeted and embraced, offering Herself as their servant and requesting them, as older and more advanced than She in the duties of their position, to instruct and command Her. She also gave them thanks, that without her merit they admitted Her to their company.

Her teacher assigned to Her a place among the rest of the maidens, each of whom occupied a large alcove or little room. The Princess of heaven prostrated Herself on the pavement, and, remembering that it was holy ground and part of the temple, She kissed it. In humble adoration She gave thanks to the Lord for this new benefit, and She thanked even the earth for supporting Her and allowing Her to stand in this holy place; for She held Herself unworthy of treading and remaining upon it.

Then She turned toward her holy angels and said to them: "Celestial princes, Messengers of the Almighty, I beseech you with all the powers of my soul to remain with me in this holy temple of my Lord, and remind me of all that I should do; instructing me and directing me as the teachers and guides of my actions, so that I may fulfill in all things the perfect will of the Most High, give pleasure to the holy priests and obey my teacher and my companions."

Mary continued with the others in heavenly conversation. She began to feel a supernal influence, spiritualizing Her and elevating Her in burning ecstasy, and immediately the Most High commanded the Seraphim to assist in illumining and preparing her most holy soul. Instantly

She was filled with a divine light and force, which perfected and proportioned her faculties in accordance with the mysteries now to be manifested to Her. Thus prepared and accompanied by her holy angels and many others, the celestial Child was raised body and

B2C1

soul to the empyrean heaven, where She was received by the holy Trinity.

She prostrated Herself in the presence of the most Mighty and high Lord, and adored Him in profound reverence and humility. Then She was further transformed by new workings of divine light, so that She saw, intuitively and face to face, the Divinity itself. This was the second time that It manifested Itself to Her in this intuitive manner during the first three years of her life.

The Person of the Father spoke to the future Mother of his Son, and said: "My Dove, my beloved One, I desire thee to see the treasures of my immutable being and of my infinite perfections, and also to perceive the hidden gifts destined for the souls, whom I have chosen as heirs of my glory and who are rescued by the life—blood of the Lamb."

"Behold, my Daughter, how liberal I am toward my creatures, that know and love Me; how true in my words, how faithful in my promises, how powerful and admirable in my works. Take notice, my Spouse, how ineffably true it is, that he who follows Me does not walk in darkness."

"I desire that thou, as my chosen One, be an eye—witness of the treasures which I hold in reserve for raising up the humble, enriching the poor, exalting the downtrodden, and for rewarding all that the mortals shall do and suffer for my name."

The most holy Mary answered the Lord and said: "Most high, supreme and eternal God, incomprehensible Thou art in thy magnificence what shall my littleness begin to do at the sight of thy magnificence? I acknowledge myself unworthy to look upon thy greatness, yet I am in great need of being regarded by it."

"What shall I thy servant do, who am but dust? Fulfill in me all thy desire and thy pleasure; and if trouble and persecutions suffered by mortals in patience, if humility and meekness are so precious in thy eyes, do not consent, O my Beloved, that I be deprived of such a rich treasure and pledge of thy love. But as the rewards of these tribulations, give them to thy servants and friends, who deserve them better than I, for I have not yet labored in thy service and pleasure."

The Most High was much pleased with the petition of the heavenly Child and He gave Her to understand that He would admit Her to suffering and labor for his love in the course of her life, without at the time revealing to Her the order and the manner in which He was to dispense them.

The Princess of heaven gave thanks for this blessing and favor of being chosen to labor and suffer for the glory of God's name. Burning with desire of securing such favor, She asked of his Majesty to be allowed to make four vows in his presence: of chastity, of poverty, of obedience, and of perpetual enclosure in the temple whither He had called Her.

To this petition the Lord answered and said to Her: "My Spouse, my thoughts rise above all that is created, and thou, my chosen one, dost not yet know what is to happen to thee in the course of thy life, and thou dost not yet understand why it is impossible to fulfill thy fervent desires altogether in the manner in which thou now dost imagine. The vow of chastity I permit and I desire that thou make it; I wish that from this moment thou renounce earthly riches. It is also my will that as far as possible thou observe whatever pertains to the other vows, just as if thou hadst made them all"

The most holy Child then made the vow of chastity and as for the rest, She renounced all affection for terrestrial and created things. She moreover resolved to obey all creatures for the sake of God. In the fulfillment of these promises She was more punctual, fervent and faithful than any who have ever made these vows or ever will make them.

B2C1

Forthwith the clear and intuitive vision of the Divinity ceased, but She was not immediately restored to the earth: She enjoyed another, an imaginary vision of the Lord in a lower state of ecstasy, so that in connection with it, She saw other mysteries.

In this secondary and imaginary vision some of the seraphim closest to the Lord approached Her and by his command adorned and clothed Her in the following manner; all her senses were illumined with an effulgent light, which filled them with grace and beauty.

The attention of all the angelic spirits was drawn toward the Most High and a voice proceeded from the throne of the blessed Trinity, which, addressing the most holy Mary, spoke to Her: "Thou shalt be our Spouse, our beloved and chosen One among all creatures for all eternity; the angels shall serve thee and all the nations and generations shall call thee blessed."

The sovereign Child then celebrated a more glorious and marvelous espousal than ever could enter the mind of the highest cherubim and seraphim; for the Most High accepted Her as his sole and only Spouse and conferred upon Her the highest dignity which can befall a creature; He deposited within Her his own Divinity in the person of the Word and with it all the treasures of grace befitting such eminence.

Meanwhile the most Humble among the humble was lost in the abyss of love and wonder which these benefits and favors caused in Her , and in the presence of the Lord She spoke: "I accept Thee, O my King and my Lord, as my Spouse and I offer myself as thy slave. Let not my understanding attend to any other object, nor my memory hold any other image, nor my will seek other object or pleasure than Thee, my highest Good, my true and only Love. Let not my eyes look upon human creature, nor my faculties and senses attend upon anything beside Thee and whatever thy Majesty shall direct. Thou alone for thy spouse, my Beloved, and She for Thee only, who art the immutable and eternal Good."

The Most High received with ineffable pleasure this consent of the sovereign Princess to enter into the new espousal with her most holy soul. The most humble Dove at once proceeded to beseech the Lord with the most burning charity, to send His Onlybegotten to the world as a remedy for mortals; that all men be called to the true knowledge of his Divinity; that her natural parents, Joachim and Anne, receive an increase of the loving gifts of his right hand; that the poor and afflicted be consoled and comforted in their troubles; and that in Herself be fulfilled the pleasure of the divine will.

These were some of the more express petitions addressed by the new Spouse on this occasion to the blessed Trinity. And all the angelic host sang new songs of admiration in praise of the Most High, while those appointed by his Majesty, midst heavenly music, bore back the holy Child from the empyrean heaven to the place in the temple, from which they had brought Her.

In order to commence at once to put in practice what She had promised in the presence of the Lord, She betook Herself to her instructress and offered all that her mother had left for her comfort and sustenance, with the exception of a few books and clothes. She requested her to give it to the poor or use it for any other purpose according to her pleasure, and that she command and direct Her what She was to do.

The discreet matron, by divine impulse, accepted and approved of the offering of the beautiful Child and dismissed Her entirely poor and stripped of everything except the garments which She wore. She resolved to take care of Her in a special manner as one destitute and poor; for the other maidens each possessed their spending money and a certain sum assigned and destined for their wearing apparel and for other necessities according to their inclinations.

The holy matron, having first consulted the high priest, also gave to the sweetest Child a rule of life. By thus despoiling and resigning Herself the Queen and Mistress of creation obtained a complete freedom and detachment from all creatures and from her own Self, neither possessing nor desiring anything except only the most ardent love of God and her own abasement and humiliation.

HER FIRST YEARS IN THE TEMPLE

After the vision of the Divinity, and after She had offered Herself entirely to the Lord and delivered up to her instructress all that She possessed, being thus deprived of all, entirely bound over to obedience, and hiding, beneath the veil of these virtues, treasures of grace and wisdom greater than that of the seraphim, She requested the priest and her teacher to prescribe for Her an order of life and to direct Her in the occupations, which She was to assume.

The priest spoke to Her and said: "My Daughter, as a very young Child the Lord has drawn Thee to his house and holy temple; be thankful for this favor and seek to profit by it by striving hard to serve Him in truth and with an upright heart. Acquire all the virtues, in order that thou mayest return from this holy place prepared and fortified against the troubles and the dangers of this world. Obey thy Mistress Anne and commence early to bear the sweet yoke of virtue, in order that thou mayest find it more easy to bear during the rest of thy life."

The sovereign Child answered: "I thou, my master, who art the minister and priest of God; and holdest his place, and thou my Mistress together with him, command and instruct me in whatever I am to do that I may not commit any fault: this I beg of you, wishing to obey you in all things."

The priest and her instructress, having together considered her petition with the aid of a special enlightenment from on high and desiring to regulate from now on the exercises of this heavenly Child of only three years, called Her to their presence. The Princess of heaven remained kneeling before them during this interview and, although they bade Her rise, She begged most humbly be allowed to remain in this reverent position in the presence of the minister and priest of the Most High and her teacher, on account of their office and dignity.

The priest and her teacher Anne felt within themselves a great enlightenment and a divine impulse to attend especially to this heavenly Child and to care for Her more than the other maidens. Conferring with themselves about this great esteem, with which they had been inspired, though ignorant of the mystery by which it came to them, they resolved to devote particular attention to her guidance and assistance.

But as their care could extend only to the exterior and visible actions, they were far from suspecting the interior acts and inspirations of her heart, for over these the Most High watched with singular protection and favor. Thus the pure heart of the Princess of heaven remained free to advance and grow in interior vision, without losing one instant, in which She did not reach what is highest and most excellent in virtue.

The priest also gave Her a rule for her occupations and said: "My Daughter thou wilt assist at the exercises of divine praise and song in honor of the Lord with all reverence and devotion, and always pray to the Most High for the necessities of his holy temple and of his people, and for the coming of the Messiah. At eight o'clock thou wilt retire for sleep and at the beginning of dawn thou wilt arise in order to praise the Lord until the third hour (our nine o'clock in the morning).

From the third hour until evening thou wilt occupy thyself in some manual works, in order that thou mayest be instructed in all things. At meals, of which thou wilt partake after thy exercise, observe befitting moderation. Then thou wilt go to hear the instructions of thy teacher; the rest of the day thou wilt engage thyself in the reading of holy Scriptures, and in all things be humble, affable, and obedient to the commands of thy instructress,"

The most holy Child remained on her knees, while She listened to the words of the priest and then asked his blessing; having kissed his hand and the hand of her mistress, She proposed in her heart to observe the order of life assigned Her during her stay in the temple and as long as they should not command her otherwise.

And She, who was the Mistress of sanctity, fulfilled their orders as if She were the least of all the scholars. Her desires and her most ardent love impelled Her to many other external exercises, which they had not included in their orders; but with regard to these She subjected Herself to the minister of the Lord, preferring the sacrifice of perfect and holy obedience to the high dictates of her own fervor.

In the performance of works not commanded Her, our Queen and Lady distinguished Herself from other maidens by asking her teacher to be allowed to serve them all and be engaged in the humble occupation of scrubbing and cleaning the rooms and of washing the dishes.

Although this seemed extraordinary, especially in one of the firstborn children, who were treated with greater consideration and respect, yet the incomparable humility of the heavenly Princess could not be restrained or confined by any consideration of what was due to her position, but reached out for the most humble occupations. With such an eager humility She knew how to gain time and opportunity for doing such work, that She was beforehand in assuming the tasks of others.

The sovereign Princess was so docile, so sweet and friendly in her actions, so ready to serve and so eager and diligent in humbling Herself, so anxious to show kindness and esteem toward all the maidens in the temple, obeying them as if each had been Her Mistress, that She ravished all the hearts. By Her ineffable and heavenly prudence She proceeded in all her actions in such a manner, that She never lost an occasion for engaging in lowly work, in humble service of her companions, and in the fulfillment of the divine pleasure.

She divided her time and applied it with rare prudence so as to give to each of her actions and occupations its proper share. She read much in the sacred writings of the ancients and, by means of her infused science, She was so well versed in them and in all their profound mysteries, that none of them was unfamiliar to Her; for the Most High made known to Her all their mysteries and sacraments; She treated and conversed about them in her conferences with the holy angels of her guard, familiarizing Herself with them and asking about them with incomparable intelligence and great acuteness. If this sovereign Mistress had written what She understood, we would have many other additions to the sacred Scriptures; and we would be able to draw out of them a perfect understanding of those writings and the deep meanings and mysteries of all those preserved in the Church.

THE TRIALS OF THE QUEEN IN THE TEMPLE
THE DEATH OF HER PARENTS

The Lord appeared to Mary and told her to take notice, that according to divine ordainment, Her father Joachim must pass from this mortal to the eternal and immortal life. His death would happen shortly and He would pass in peace and placed among the saints in limbo, to await the Redemption of the human race.

This announcement did not disturb the royal heart of the blessed Mary; but as the love of children for their parents is a just debt of nature, and as in this most holy Child this love had attained its highest perfection, the natural sorrow for the loss of her father Joachim could not be wanting, for She loved him with a holy love. She offered an ardent prayer for her father. She besought the Lord to give him grace to depend upon Him as his powerful and true God in his transit through a blessed death; and asked Him to defend Joachim against the demon, preserve him for and constitute him among the number of the elect.

The Lord accepted Her petition and consoled the heavenly Child by assuring Her that He would assist her father as a most merciful and kind Rewarder of those that love and serve Him, and that He would place him among the Patriarchs Abraham, Isaac and Jacob. At the same time He prepared Her anew for the acceptance and endurance of troubles. Eight days before the death of the Patriarch Joachim the most holy Mary received another notice from the Lord, advising Her of the day and hour in which He was to die. His death took place only six months after Her entrance into the temple.

Having received this notice from the Lord, for the last hours of his life, She sent all the angels of her guard asking the Lord to make them visible to him for his greater consolation. God conceded this favor and confirmed all the wishes of Mary; and the great patriarch, most happy Joachim, saw the thousand angels which guarded Mary. In response to her prayer and wishes, the Almighty allowed his graces to overflow, commanding the angels to address Joachim as follows:

"Man of God, may the Most High and powerful Lord be thy eternal salvation and may He send thee from his holy place the necessary and opportune help for thy soul. Mary thy Daughter has sent us in order to assist thee in this hour, in which thou must pay the debt of mortality to thy Creator."

"Although his Majesty has not as yet revealed the sacraments and dignity in which He shall invest thy Daughter, He wishes thee to know it now in order that thou mayest magnify and praise Him, and in order that the pain and sorrow of natural death may be relieved by the joy of thy spirit at this news. Mary, thy Daughter, is chosen and ordained by the Almighty as the One in whom the divine Word shall vest Himself with human flesh and form."

"She is to be the happy Mother of the Messiah and the Blessed among women, the most exalted among all creatures, and only inferior to God himself..... Since thou leavest to the world a Daughter, through whom God will restore it and prepare a full remedy, do thou part from it in the joy of thy soul, and may the Lord bless thee from Sion and constitute thee in the inheritance of the saints and bring thee to the vision and enjoyment of the blessed Jerusalem."

During these words of the holy angels to Joachim, his spouse, holy Anne, stood at the head of his bed and by divine disposition She heard and understood what they said. In the same moment the holy patriarch lost the use of speech and, treading into the path common to all flesh, he commenced his agony in a marvellous struggle between his joy at this message and the pain of death. In this conflict of the interior powers of his soul he made many fervent acts of divine love, of faith, of admiration, of praise, of thanksgiving, of humility and heroic acts of many other virtues.

B2C6

Thus absorbed in the knowledge of so divine a mystery, he arrived at the term of his natural life and died the precious death of the saints. His holy soul was carried by the angels to the limbo of the Patriarchs and just souls and, for a new consolation and light in the protracted night in which they lived, the Most High sent the soul of Joachim as the last messenger and legate of the Lord to announce to the whole congregation of the just that the dawn of the eternal day was at hand; that the morning light was breaking upon the world in most holy Mary, Daughter of Joachim and Anne; that from Her was to be brought forth the Sun of the Divinity, Christ, the Redeemer of all the human race. This great news the holy fathers and the just in limbo heard and received with jubilee and in their exultation they sang many hymns of thanksgiving to the Most High.

The first affliction which our Princess suffered was that the Lord suspended the continual visions, which He had so far vouchsafed Her. Also the holy angels concealed themselves from Her, that most pure Soul seemed to Herself entirely forsaken and left alone in the dark night occasioned by the absence of her Beloved.

It was a great surprise; for the Lord, though He had in general prepared Her for the coming of tribulations, had not specified their nature. And as the innocent heart of the Mary harbored no thoughts, and entertained no practical conclusions except such as were conformable to her humility and incomparable love, She explained all according to this same light.

In her humility She began to think, that She had not merited the further presence and possession of the lost Good on account of her ingratitude; and in her inflamed love She sighed and yearned after It with such great and loving affection and sorrow, that there are no words to express them. She turned with her whole soul to the Lord in this new state and prayed to Him.

Meanwhile, Satan, the dragon, though seeing her courage and constancy, and though feeling the force of the divine assistance, knew nothing of the hidden wisdom and prudence of our sovereign Queen. Nevertheless he persisted in his pride and besieged the City of God in diverse ways and several kinds of warfare. Our Princess was that strong woman on whom the heart of her husband confidently relied, without the least anxiety lest his desires should be frustrated in Her.

The unclean and proud serpent could not look upon this Creature without being blinded anew in the fury of his confusion; therefore he resolved to take away her life, and the horde of malignant spirits began to exert their utmost powers toward this end. In this attempt they spent some time.

After the most holy Virgin had successfully fought these secret temptations and battles, the serpent instituted a new conflict by means of creatures. For this purpose he secretly kindled the sparks of envy and emulation against the most holy Mary in the hearts of her maiden companions of the temple. This contagion was much the harder to counteract, as it arose from the punctuality with which our heavenly Princess distinguished Herself in the practice of all virtues, growing in wisdom and grace before God and man. For where the prodding of ambition is, the very light of virtue darkens and blinds the judgment, and at last enkindles the flames of envy.

The dragon through his secret suggestions persuaded these simple maidens, that the light of this sun, most holy Mary, would obscure them and cause them to be little noticed; that on her account their own negligences were more clearly apparent to the priests and their teacher; and that Mary alone was preferred in the estimation and judgment of all.

The maidens allowed the devil to sow this bad seed in their bosoms; for they were heedless and little experienced in spiritual ways. They allowed it to increase until it grew into a sort of interior abhorrence of the most pure Mary, and this into anger. Filled with this anger, they began to look upon and treat Her with hatred, not being able to endure her modesty. For the dragon had incited them and had already imbued the incautious girls with some of his own wrath. The temptation continuing, its effects became manifest and the temple maidens began to plot among themselves.

They agreed among themselves to molest and persecute her until She should be forced to leave the temple. Accordingly they called Her aside and spoke to Her very sharp words, treating Her at the same time very haughtily. They called Her a hypocrite and reproached Her with scheming to obtain the favor of the priests and of their teacher, while seeking to discredit all the other girls by her complaints and her exaggerations of their faults, whereas She was the most useless of them all and therefore deserved their hatred as an enemy.

These contumelies and many other accusations the most prudent Virgin bore without disturbance and with equable humility. She answered: "My friends and my mistresses, you are right no doubt in saying, that I am the least and the most imperfect among you; but then you, my sisters, being better informed, must pardon me my faults and must teach me in my ignorance. Direct me therefore, that I may succeed in doing better and act according to your pleasure. I beseech you, my friends, not to deny me your good will, which, though I am so imperfect, I sincerely wish to merit; for I love you and reverence you as a servant, and I will obey you in all things, in which you desire to make a trial of my good will. Command me then, and tell me what you wish of me."

These humble and sweet reasonings of the most humble Mary did not soften the hardened hearts of her associates and companions, for they were infected by the poisonous fury of the dragon against Her. For many days this persecution continued, during which the heavenly Lady sought in vain to appease the hate of her companions by her humility, patience, modesty and tolerance.

On the contrary the demon was emboldened to inspire them many thoughts full of temerity, urging them to lay violent hands on the most humble lamb and maltreat Her, even so far as to take away her life. But the Lord did not permit the execution of such sacrilegious suggestions and the farthest which they were allowed to proceed, was to insult Her by words or to inflict some blows.

This quarrelling remained concealed from the teacher of the maidens and from the priests, and during this time most holy Mary gained incomparable merits in the sight of the Almighty, because She took occasion to exercise all the virtues, as well in regard to God as also in regard the creatures, which were persecuting and hating Her. She performed heroic acts of charity and humility, yielding good for evil, blessings for curses, prayers for blasphemies. Before the Lord She exercised the most exalted virtues, by praying for his creatures who were persecuting Her; and She excited the admiration of the angels.

It happened one day, that, impelled by the diabolical suggestions, these girls brought Mary to a retired room, where they could act with more safety. Here they began to heap unmeasured injuries and insults upon Her, to excite Her to weakness or anger and to entrap modesty into some hasty action.

But as the Queen of virtues could not even for a moment be subject to vice, She showed Herself immovable, and She answered them with great kindness and sweetness. Being enraged beyond bounds on account of not succeeding in their purpose, her companions raised their voices in discordant strife, so that they were heard in the temple and by such unwonted noise caused great astonishment and confusion.

The priests and the teacher hastened to the place whence the noise proceeded, and the Lord permitted a new humiliation of his Spouse, for they asked with severity, what was the cause of this strife.

While the most meek Dove remained silent, the other maidens angrily answered and said: "Mary of Nazareth brings us all into strife and quarreling by her horrid conduct: for in your absence, She irritates and provokes us in such a manner, that if She does not leave the temple, it will be impossible to keep any peace with Her. When we allow Her her own way, She becomes overbearing; if we reprehend Her, She makes fun of all of us by prostrating Herself at our feet with feigned humility, and afterwards She quarrels anew and throws all into uproar."

The priests and the instructress brought the Mistress of the world into another room, and there they severely reprehended Her, giving full credit at that time to all the accusations of her companions, and, having exhorted Her to reform and behave as one living in the house of God, they threatened to expel Her from the temple, if She would not mend Her conduct. This threat was the most severe punishment, which they could have given Her, even if She had been guilty: so much the more severe was it, when She was altogether innocent of any of the faults imputed to Her.

Mary answered with words full of sweetest innocence and modesty; and therewith the instructress and the priests dismissed Her, enjoining anew upon Her that doctrine, of which She herself was the most wise Teacher.

Immediately She betook Herself to her companions, and prostrating Herself at their feet, She asked them pardon. They received Her this time with more good will, because they thought that her tears were the effect of the punishment and the warning of the priests and the instructress, whom they had induced to act thus in pursuance of their badly governed passions.

The dragon, who was secretly contriving this entanglement, urged the incautious hearts of all these girls to still greater haughtiness and presumption, and as they had now made headway in the estimation of the priests themselves, they proceeded to greater audacity in discrediting and lowering the good name of the most pure Virgin.

Accordingly by instigation of the devil, they fabricated new accusations and lies; but the Most High never permitted them to say anything very grave and dishonorable of Her. He merely allowed the indignation and deceit of the maidens go so far as to exaggerate very much some small faults, which were even in themselves altogether fictitious, but which they accused Her of.

Moreover they were permitted to practice many feminine intrigues, to which their own restlessness drove them. In these different ways and in the reprehensions of her instructress and of the priests our most humble Lady Mary found many occasions of exercising virtues, of increasing the gifts of the Most High, and of exalting Her merit.

The Lord did not sleep, nor did He slumber during the clamors of his beloved spouse Mary, although He pretended not to hear them, delighting in the prolonged exercise of her sufferings, which occasioned so many glorious triumphs and the admirations and praises of the supernal spirits. But when the opportune time arrived for putting an end to the blind envy and jealousy of those ensnared maidens, and in order that their petulance might not altogether discredit Her, the Lord spoke to the priest in his sleep and said to Him "My servant Mary is pleasing in my eyes, and She is my perfect and my chosen One: She is entirely innocent of anything of which She is accused." The same revelation was given to Anne, the instructress of the maidens.

That morning the priest and the instructress conferred with each other about the message, which both had received. Being now certain, they repented of the deceit, into which they had been led, and called the Princess Mary, asking her pardon for having given credit to the false report of the girls and offering Her all the reparation necessary to defend Her from the persecution and the sufferings consequent upon it.

She, after listening to their words, answered the priest and the instructress "My superiors, I am the one that deserves your reprehensions and I beseech you do not hold me unworthy of undergoing them, since I ask for them as most necessary to me. The interactions with my sisters, the other maidens, is most highly prized by me, and I do not wish to be deprived of it through my fault, since I owe them so much for having borne with me and as a return for that benefit, I desire to serve them more faithfully; nevertheless if you command me anything else, I stand prepared to obey your will."

This answer of the most holy Mary still more comforted and consoled the priest and the instructress; and they approved of her humble petition, but from that time on they attended to Her and observed Her with new reverence and affection.

The most humble Maiden begged to kiss the hand of the priest and of the matron, asking for their blessing according to her custom; with this they dismissed Her. The enlightenment of the priests and the instructress concerning Mary abated the persecutions of the maidens. The Lord also restrained them and prevented the demon from inciting them thereafter.

The time during which He absented Himself and during which He hid Himself from this heavenly spouse, lasted ten years; although the Most High interrupted this absence a few times by allowing the veil to fall from his face for the relief of his Beloved; but it was not often that He dispensed this favor during that time, and He did it with less lavishness and tenderness than in the first years of her childhood.

This absence of the Lord was ordained for our Queen in order She might, by actual exercise of all perfection, be made worthy for the dignity to which She was destined by the Most High.

But during this retirement and absence of the Lord, although most holy Mary missed the intuitive and abstractive visions of the divine Essence and of the angels as mentioned above, her most holy soul and her faculties enjoyed more gifts of grace and more supernatural enlightenment, than all the saints ever attained or received. For in regard to this the hand of God never withdrew from Her.

B2C6

But in comparison with the frequent visitations of the Lord in her first years, there was an absence and withdrawal of the Lord. It commenced eight days before the death of her father, and afterwards the persecution of hell began, followed by the persecutions on the part of creatures.

They lasted until our Princess reached the age of twelve years. Having passed this age, the holy angels on a certain day, without manifesting themselves, spoke to Her as follows: "Mary, the end of the life of thy holy mother Anne as ordained by the Most High, is now about to arrive, and his Majesty has resolved to free her from the prison of her mortal body and bring her labors to a happy fulfillment."

At this unexpected and sorrowful message the heart of the affectionate Daughter was filled with compassion. Prostrating Herself in the presence of the Most High, She poured forth a fervent prayer to the Lord for the happy death of her mother saint Anne.

The Lord did not respond expressly in words to this petition; but his answer was a marvelous favor, shown to Her and to her mother, Saint Anne. During that night his Majesty commanded the guardian angels of the most holy Mary to carry Her bodily to the sickbed of her mother and one of them to remain in her stead, assuming for this purpose an aerial body a substitute for hers.

The holy angels obeyed the mandate of God and they carried Mary to the house and to the room of her holy mother Anne. Being thus brought to the presence of her mother, Mary kissed her hand and said to her: "My mother and mistress, may the Most High be thy light and thy strength, and may He be blessed, since He has in his condescension not permitted me in my necessity to remain without the benefit of thy last blessing: may I then receive it, my mother, from thy hand."

Holy Anne gave her last blessing to Mary and with overflowing heart also thanked the Lord for the great favor thus conferred upon Herself. For She knew the sacrament of her Daughter and Queen, and she did not forget to express her gratitude for the love, which Mary had shown her on this occasion.

In the midst of such exalted and heavenly colloquies the blessed mother saint Anne felt the throes of death approaching and, reclining upon the throne of grace, that is, in the arms of her most holy Daughter Mary, she rendered her most pure soul to her Creator. Having closed the eyes of her mother, as Saint Anne had requested, and leaving the sacred body in position for burial, the Queen Mary was again taken up by the holy angels and restored to her place in the temple.

The Most High did not impede the force of her filial love, which naturally would cause a great and tender sorrow at the death of her mother and a sense of loneliness at being deprived of her assistance. But these sorrows were most holy and perfect in our Queen, governed by the graces of her most prudent innocence and purity.

In the midst of them She gave praise to the Most High for the infinite mercies, which He had shown to her mother both in life and in death, while her sweet and loving complaints on account of the absence of the Lord continued unabated.

HER WONDERFUL ESPOUSAL WITH SAINT JOSEPH

At the age of thirteen and a half years, having grown considerably for her age, most pure Mary had another abstractive vision of the Divinity. In this vision something happened similar to that which the holy Scriptures relate of Abraham, when God commanded him to sacrifice his beloved son Isaac. God tempted Abraham trying and probing the promptness of his obedience in order to reward it. We can say the same thing of our great Lady, that God tried Her in this vision, by commanding Her to enter the state of matrimony.

Thence we can understand the truth of the words: How inscrutable are the judgments of the Lord and how exalted are his ways and thoughts above our own. As distant as heaven is from earth, were the thoughts of most holy Mary from the plans which the Most High now made known to Her, commanding Her to accept a husband for her protection and company; for as far as depended upon her will, She had desired and resolved during all her life not to have a husband and She had often repeated and renewed the vow of chastity, which She had taken at such a premature age.

Nevertheless at this unexpected command the most prudent Virgin suspended her judgment, and preserved the calmness of her hope and belief more perfectly than Abraham. Hoping against hope, She made answer to the Lord saying: "Thou canst dispose of me according to thy pleasure, without making me fail in that which I have promised to Thee; and if it be not displeasing to Thee, I confirm and ratify anew my desire to remain chaste during all my life and to have Thee for my Lord; and since my only duty as a creature is to obey Thee, see Thou to it, that according to thy Providence I may escape from this predicament in which thy holy love places me."

There was, however, some uneasiness in the most chaste maiden Mary, as far as her inferior nature was concerned, though She felt some sadness, it did not hinder Her from practicing the most heroic obedience which until then had fallen to her lot, and She resigned Herself entirely into the hand of the Lord. His Majesty answered her: "Mary, let not thy heart be disturbed, for thy resignation is acceptable to Me and my powerful arm is not subject to laws; by my disposition that will happen, which is most proper for Thee."

Consoled only by this vague promise of the Lord, most holy Mary recovered from her vision and returned to her ordinary state. Left between doubt and hope by the divine command and promise, She was full of solicitude, for the Lord intended that She should multiply Her tearful sentiments of love and confidence, of faith, humility, of obedience, of purest chastity and of other virtues, impossible to enumerate.

In the meanwhile, while our great Lady applied Herself to vigilant prayer, and to her resigned and prudent sighs and solicitude, God spoke in sleep to the high priest, Saint Simeon, and commanded him to arrange for the marriage of Mary, the daughter of Joachim and Anne of Nazareth; since He regarded Her with special care and love.

The holy priest answered, asking what was his will in regard to the person whom the maiden Mary was to marry, and to whom She was to give Herself as Spouse. The Lord instructed Him to call together the other priests and learned persons and to tell them that this Maiden was left alone and an orphan, and that She did not desire to be married; but that, as it was a custom for the firstborn maidens not to leave the temple without being provided for, it was proper She should be married to whomever it seemed good to them.

The most prudent Virgin, with a countenance betokening virginal modesty, answered the priest with great composure and humility: "Sir, as far as my inclinations are concerned, I desire to preserve perpetual chastity during all my life; for I wished to dedicate myself to God in the service of this holy temple in return for the great blessings which I have received in it. I never had the intention or the desire to enter the state of matrimony, since I consider myself incapable of fulfilling the duties connected with it. This was my inclination, but thou, my Master, who art to me in place of God, wilt teach me what is according to his holy Will,"

"My Daughter," answered the priest, "thy holy desires are acceptable to the Lord; but remember, that no maiden of Israel abstains from marriage as long as we expect the coming of the Messiah conformably to the divine prophecies. Therefore all who obtain issue of children among our people esteem themselves happy and blessed. In the matrimonial state, Thou canst serve God truly and in great perfection; and in order that Thou mayest obtain a companion according to the heart of God and who will be conformable to thy wishes, we will pray to the Lord, as I have told Thee, asking Him to single out a husband for Thee, who shall be pleasing to Him and of the line of David; do Thou also pray continually for the same favor, in order that the Most High may favor Thee and may direct us all."

This happened nine days before the one appointed for the execution and realization of their resolve. During this time the most holy Virgin multiplied her prayers, beseeching the Lord with incessant tears and sighs, to fulfill his divine pleasure in that which She had so much at heart.

On one of those nine days the Lord appeared to Her and said to Her: "My Spouse and my Dove, let thy afflicted heart expand and let it not be disturbed or sad; I will attend to thy yearnings and to thy requests, I will direct all things, and will govern the priests by my enlightenment; I will give Thee a spouse selected by Myself, and one who will put no hindrance to thy holy desires, but who, by my grace will prosper Thee in them. I will find for Thee a perfect man conformable to my heart and I will choose him from the number of my servants; my power is infinite, and my protection and aid shall never fail Thee."

On the day on which Mary completed the fourteenth year of her life, the men, who at that time in the city of Jerusalem were descendants of the tribe of Judah and of the race of David, gathered together in the temple. The sovereign Lady was also of that lineage. Among the number was Joseph, a native of Nazareth and living in Jerusalem; for he was one of the descendants of the royal race of David.

He was then thirty–three years of age, of handsome person and pleasing countenance, but also of incomparable modesty and gravity; above all he was most chaste in thought and conduct, and most saintly in all his inclinations. From his twelfth year he had made and kept the vow of chastity. He was related to the Virgin Mary in the third degree, and was known for the utmost purity of his life, holy and irreprehensible in the eyes of God and of men.

All these unmarried men gathered in the temple and prayed to the Lord conjointly with the priests. In order to be governed by the Holy Spirit in what they were about to do. The Most High spoke to the heart of the high priest, inspiring him to place into the hands of each one of the young men a dry stick, with the command that each ask his Majesty with a lively faith, to single out the one whom He had chosen as the spouse of Mary. And as the sweet odor of her virtue and nobility, the fame of her beauty, her possessions and her modesty, and her position as being the firstborn in her family was known to all of them, each one coveted the happiness of meriting Her as a spouse.

Among them all only the humble and most upright Joseph thought himself unworthy of such a great blessing; and remembering the vow of chastity which he had made and resolving anew its perpetual observance, he resigned himself to God's will, leaving it all to his disposal and being filled at the same time with a veneration and esteem greater than that of any of the others for the most noble maiden Mary.

While they were thus engaged in prayer the staff which Joseph held was seen to blossom and at the same time a dove of purest white and resplendent with admirable light, was seen to descend and rest upon the head of the Saint, while in the interior of his heart God spoke: "Joseph, my servant, Mary shall be thy Spouse; accept Her with attentive reverence, for She is acceptable in my eyes, just and most pure in soul and body, and thou shalt do all that She shall say to Thee."

At this manifestation and token from heaven the priests declared Saint Joseph as the spouse selected by God himself for the maiden Mary. Calling Her forth for Her espousal, the Chosen one issued forth like the sun, more resplendent than the moon, and She entered into the presence of all with a countenance more beautiful than that of an angel, incomparable in the charm of her beauty, nobility and grace; and the priests espoused Her to the most chaste and holy of men, saint Joseph.

The heavenly Princess, more pure than the stars of the firmament, with tearful and sorrowful countenance and as the Queen of majesty, most humble yet uniting all perfections within Herself, took leave of the priests, asking their blessing, and of her instructress and her companions, begging their pardon. She gave thanks to all of them for the favors received at their hands during her stay in the temple. She took leave of the temple not without great grief on account of the sacrifice of her inclinations and desires.

In the company of attendants who were some of the more distinguished laymen in the service of the temple, She betook Herself with her spouse Joseph to Nazareth, the native city of this most fortunate married couple. Joseph, although he had been born in that place, had, by the providential disposition of circumstances, decided to live for some time in Jerusalem. Thus it happened that he so improved his fortune as to become the spouse of Her, whom God had chosen to be his own Mother.

Having arrived at their home in Nazareth, where the Mary had inherited the possessions and estates of her blessed parents, they were welcomed and visited by their friends and relatives with the joyful congratulations customary on such occasions.

After they had in a most holy manner complied with the natural duties of friendship and politeness, and satisfied the worldly obligations connected with the conversation and interaction with their fellowmen, the two most holy spouses, Joseph and Mary, were left at leisure and to their own counsel in their house.

Custom had introduced the practice among the Hebrews, that for the first few days of their married state the husband and wife should enter upon a sort of study or trial of each others' habits and temperament, in order that afterwards they might be able to make reciprocal allowance in their conduct one toward the other.

During this time Saint Joseph said to his spouse Mary: "My spouse and Lady, I give thanks to the Lord God for the favor of having designed me as your husband, though I judged myself unworthy even of thy company. But his Majesty, who can raise up the lowly whenever He wishes, showed this mercy to me. I desire and hope, relying on thy discretion and virtue, that Thou help me to make a proper return in serving Him with an upright heart. Hold me, therefore, as thy servant, and by the true love which I have for thee, I beg of thee to supply my deficiencies in the fulfillment of the domestic duties and of other things, which as a worthy husband, I should know how to perform. Tell me, Lady, what is thy pleasure, in order that I may fulfill it."

The heavenly Spouse heard these words with an humble heart, and yet also with a serene earnestness, and She answered the Saint: "My master, I am fortunate, that the Most High, in order to place me in this state of life, has chosen thee for my husband and that He has given me such evident manifestation of his will, that I serve thee; but if thou givest me leave I will speak of my thoughts and intentions, which I wish to manifest to thee for this purpose." The Most High forestalled the sincere and upright heart of Saint

Joseph with his grace and inflamed it anew with divine love through the word of most holy Mary, and he answered Her, saying: "Speak, Lady, thy servant hears."

On this occasion the Mistress of the world was surrounded by the thousand angels of her guard, in visible form. She had asked them to be present in that manner, because the Lord had permitted her to feel the respect and reverence with which She was bound to speak to her husband, and left her to the natural shyness and dread which She always felt in speaking to men alone; for She had never done this, except perhaps by accident with the high priest.

The holy angels obeyed their Queen and, visible only to Her, stood in attendance. In this glorious company She spoke to her spouse Saint Joseph, and said to him: "My Lord, it is just that we give praise and glory with all reverence to our God and Creator... I acknowledge myself among all creatures as more beholden and indebted to Him than all others, and more than all of them together; for, meriting less. I have received from his liberal hand more than they. At a tender age I consecrated myself to God by a perpetual vow of chastity in body and soul; His I am, and Him I acknowledge as my Spouse and Lord, with fixed resolve to preserve for Him my chastity. I beseech thee, my master, to help me in fulfilling this vow, while in all other things I will be thy servant, willing to work for the comfort of thy life as long as mine shall last. Yield, my spouse, to this resolve and make a like resolve, in order that, offering ourselves as an acceptable sacrifice to our eternal God, He may receive us in the odor of sweetness and bestow on us the eternal goods for which we hope."

The most chaste spouse Joseph, full of interior joy at the words of his heavenly Spouse, answered Her: "My Mistress, in making known to me thy chaste and welcome sentiments, thou hast penetrated and dilated my heart. I have not opened my thoughts to Thee before knowing thy own.

I also acknowledge myself under greater obligation to the Lord of creation than other men; for very early He has called me by his true enlightenment to love Him with an upright heart; and I desire Thee to know, Lady, that at the age of twelve years I also made a promise to serve the Most High in perpetual chastity.

On this account I now gladly ratify this vow in order not to impede thy own. In the presence of his Majesty I promise to aid Thee, as far as in me lies, in serving Him and loving Him according to thy full desires. I will be, with the divine grace, thy most faithful servant and companion, and I pray Thee accept my chaste love and hold me as thy brother, without ever entertaining any other kind of love, outside the one which Thou owest to God and after God to me.

In this conversation the Most High confirmed anew the virtue of chastity in the heart of Saint Joseph, and the pure and holy love due to his most holy spouse Mary. This love the saint already had in an eminent degree, and the Lady herself augmented it sweetly, dilating his heart by her most prudent discourse.

By divine operation the two most holy and chaste Spouses felt an incomparable joy and consolation. The heavenly Princess, as one who is the Mistress of all virtues and who in all things pursued the highest perfection of all virtues, lovingly corresponded to the desires of saint Joseph. The Most High also gave to saint Joseph new purity and complete command over his natural inclinations, so that without hindrance or any trace of sensual desires, but with admirable and new grace, he might serve his spouse Mary, and in Her, execute his will and pleasure.

They immediately set about dividing the property inherited from Saint Joachim and Anne, the parents of the most holy Virgin; one part they offered to the temple, where She had stayed, another they destined for the poor, and the third was left in the hands of the holy spouse Saint Joseph to be disposed of according to his judgment.

Our Queen reserved for Herself only the privilege of serving Him and of attending to the household duties. For from intercourse with outsiders and from the management of property, buying or selling, the most prudent Virgin always kept aloof, as I will mention farther on.

In his former life Saint Joseph had learnt the trade of carpentering as being a respectable and proper way of earning the sustenance in life. He was poor in earthly possessions. He therefore asked his most holy Spouse, whether it was agreeable to Her, that he should exercise his trade in order to be able to serve Her and to gain something for distribution among the poor, since it was necessary to do some work and not to remain idle. The most prudent Virgin approved of this resolve, saying that the Lord did not wish them to be rich, but poor and lovers of the poor, desirous of helping them in as far as their means would allow.

Then arose, between the two Spouses, a holy contest: who should obey the other as superior. But She, who among the humble was the most humble, won in this contest of humility; for as the man is the head of the family, She would not permit this natural order to be inverted. She desired in all things to obey her spouse saint Joseph, asking him solely for permission to help the poor, which the saint gladly gave.

Saint Joseph during these days by divine enlightenment learned to know more and more the qualities of his spouse Mary, her rare prudence, humility, purity and all her other virtues exceeding by far his thoughts and estimates. He was seized with ever new admiration and, in great joy of spirit, continued to praise and thank the Lord again and again for having given him a Companion and Spouse so far above his merits.

And in order that this work of the Most High might be entirely perfect (for it was the beginning of the greatest, which He was to execute by his Omnipotence) He ordained that the Princess of heaven, by her mere presence and interactions, should infuse into the heart of her spouse a holy fear and reverence greater than words could ever suffice to describe. This effect was wrought upon Saint Joseph by an effulgence or reflection of the divine light, which shone from the face of our Queen and which was mingled with an ineffable and always visible majesty.

Chapter Three

THE NOVENA BEFORE THE INCARNATION

The Most High had placed upon our Queen and Mistress the duties of a spouse of Saint Joseph, which was a position requiring more interaction with her neighbors. The heavenly Mistress, finding Herself in this new estate, was filled with exalted thoughts and sentiments in the fulfillment of her duties, and ordered all the activities of her life with such wisdom, that She was an object of admirable emulation to the angelic spirits and an unparalleled example for men.

Few knew Her and still fewer had interaction with Her: but these happy ones were so filled with that celestial influence of Mary, that with a wonderful joy they sought to express and manifest the light which illumined their hearts and which they knew came from Her.

The most prudent Queen was not unaware of these operations of the Most High but neither was it yet time, nor would her most profound humility as yet consent to their becoming known to the world. She continually besought the Lord to hide them from men, to make all the favors of his right hand redound solely to his praise, and to permit Her to be ignored and despised by all the mortals, in as far as his infinite goodness would not be offended thereby.

Mary busied Herself during the six months and seventeen days which intervened between her espousal and the Incarnation of the Word. By her sanctity and merits, God felt Himself obliged and compelled, to hasten His steps to bring about the Incarnation of the Onlybegotten of the Father in the virginal womb of this Lady.

In order to proceed with a dignity befitting Himself, God prepared most holy Mary in a singular manner during the nine days immediately preceding this mystery. On the first day of this most blessed novena, the heavenly Princess Mary, left her couch at midnight and, prostrate in the presence of the Most High, commenced her accustomed prayer and holy exercises.

In this vision Mary learned most high secrets of the Divinity and of its perfections, and especially of God's communications in the work of creation. She saw that it originated in the goodness and liberality of God. Many sacraments and secrets were manifested to our Queen, which neither can nor should be made known to all. She besought the eternal Father with heart aflame, that He send his Onlybegotten into the world and give salvation to men.

On the first day therefore, He manifested to Her all that He had made on the first day of the creation of the world, as it is recorded in Genesis, and She perceived all with greater clearness and comprehension, than if She had been an eye–witness; for She knew them first as they are in God, and then as they are in themselves.

She perceived and understood, how the Lord in the beginning created heaven and earth; how the darkness was over the face of the abyss; how at the divine command, light was made, and how, after the darkness was divided, it was called night and the light day, and how the first day was made.

The rebellion of the bad angels was revealed to Her, their fall and the occasion and the cause of that fall, though the Lord always concealed from Her that which concerned Herself. She understood the punishment and the effects of sin in the demons, and at the conclusion of the first day, the Lord showed to Her, how She too was formed of this lowly earthly material and endowed with the same nature as all those, who return to the dust: He did not, however, say that She would again return to it.

This whole vision and all its effects the Most High arranged in such a way as to open up in the heart of Mary the deep trenches that were required for the foundations of the edifice, which He wished to erect in Her. When the Princess of heaven had finished this vision, She returned to her ordinary and more natural state.

On the second day, at the same hour of midnight, Mary was visited in the same way. The divine power raised Her up to prepare Her for the visions of the Divinity. He manifested Himself again in an abstractive manner as on the first day, and She was shown the works performed on the second day of the creation. She learnt how and when God divided the waters, establishing the firmament.

In the most prudent Virgin this knowledge did not lay idle, nor remain sterile; for immediately the most clear light of the Divinity overflowed in Her, and inflamed and emblazoned Her with admiration, praise, and love of the goodness and power of God.

And as in the preceding first day, God made Her a participant of his wisdom, so on this second day He made Her in corresponding measure, a participant in the divine Omnipotence, and gave Her power over the influences of the heavens, of the planets and elements, commanding them all to obey Her. Thus was this great Queen raised to Sovereignty over the sea, the earth, the elements, and the celestial orbs, with all the creatures which are contained therein.

On the third day She was informed of the works of creation as they happened on the third day. She learned when and how the waters flowed together in one place, disclosing the dry land, which the Lord called earth, while He called the waters the sea. She was taught the greatness of the sea, its depth and its divisions, its correspondence with the streams and the fountains; the different plants and herbs, the flowers, trees, roots, fruits and seeds; She perceived how all and each one of them serve for the use of man.

There is another special favor which the most holy Mary received for the benefit of the mortals on the third day; for during this vision God manifested to Her in a special way the desire of His divine love to come to the aid of men and to raise them up from all their miseries.

B3C1

In accordance with the knowledge of His infinite mercy and the object for which it was conceded, the Most High gave to Mary a certain kind of participation of his own attributes, in order that afterwards, as the Mother and Advocate of sinners, She might intercede for them.

Whatever all men have suffered from the beginning of the world till this hour, and whatever they will suffer till the end, would have been a small matter for the love of this most merciful Mother. Let therefore mortals and sinners understand what they owe to most holy Mary.

From that day on, the heavenly Lady continued to be the Mother of kindness and great mercy for two reasons: first, because from that moment She sought with an especial and anxious desire to communicate without envy the treasures of grace, which She had comprehended and received; and second, because this love of most holy Mary for the salvation of men was one of the principal dispositions required for conceiving the eternal Word in her virginal womb.

The Most High manifested to Her in this vision the new Law of grace which the Redeemer of the world was to establish, the Sacraments contained in it, the end for which He would leave them in his new Church of the Gospel, the gifts and blessings prepared for men, and his desire, that all should be saved and that all should reap the fruit of the Redemption.

And great was the wisdom which the most holy Mary drew from these visions, wherein She was taught by the highest Teacher and the Corrector of the wise. Her science was greater than that of all other men: for into the heart and mind of our Princess was emptied and exhausted the ocean of the Divinity, which the sins and the evil disposition of the creatures had confined, repressed and circumscribed. It was concealed within its own source until the proper time, which was no other than the hour in which She was chosen as Mother of the Onlybegotten of the Father.

The fifth day of the novena had arrived. Just as in the preceding days She was elevated to an abstractive vision of the Divinity. She discovered new mysteries during this day; for the preparations and enlightenments emitted ever stronger rays of light and divine graces, which flashed into Her most holy soul and emptied the treasures of infinity into Her faculties, assimilating and transforming the heavenly Lady more and more to a likeness of her God in order to make Her worthy of being his Mother.

Mary was instructed in the great mysteries regarding the number of the predestined and the reprobate, and also regarding the hindrances and impediments by which sinful men delayed the coming of the eternal Word as man into the world. She beheld the vision both of the infinite bounty and equity of the Creator and of the measureless iniquity and malice of men. It is impossible to describe the hidden secrets which most holy Mary then saw in the Lord; for She perceived in Him all the creatures of the past, present and the future, and the position of each one in creation, the good and bad actions and the final ending of each one.

Our Lady and Queen was asked, what was her name; and She said: "I am a daughter of Adam, formed by thy hands from the insignificant dust." And the Most High answered: "Henceforth Thou shalt be called: Chosen for the Mother of the Onlybegotten." But the latter part of this name was heard only by the courtiers of heaven, while to Her it was as yet hidden until the proper time.

She therefore heard only the word "Chosen. The whole blessed Trinity gave to Mary the explicit promise, that They would now send into the world the eternal Word made man. Filled with incomparable joy and exultation by this fiat, She asked and received the benediction of the Most High.

During this vision were also revealed the works of the fifth day of the creation in the manner in which they happened; She saw how, by the force of the divine command, were engendered and produced in the waters beneath the firmament, the imperfect reptiles, which creep upon the earth, the winged animals that course through the air, and the finny tribes that glide through the watery regions.

She knew the birds of heaven (for so we call the atmosphere), with the varied forms of each kind, their ornaments, feathers, their lightness; the innumerable fishes of the seas and the rivers, the differences between the whales, their forms, composition and qualities, their caverns and the foods furnished them by the sea, the ends which they serve, the use to which they can be put in the world.

And his Majesty especially commanded all these hosts of creatures to recognize and obey most holy Mary, giving Her the power to command all of them.

Having seen God in this vision She was immediately shown the works on the sixth day of the creation of the world. She witnessed, as if She Herself had been present, how at the command of the Lord the earth brought forth the living beings according to their kinds, as Moses says.. She saw and understood all the kinds and species of animals, which were created on this sixth day, and by what name they were called: some, beasts of burden, because they serve and assist man, others, wild beasts, as being more fierce and untamed; others, reptiles, because they do not raise themselves or very little from the earth. She knew and comprehended the qualities of all of them: their fury, their strength, the useful purposes which they serve, and all their distinctions and singularities.

Over all these She was invested with dominion and they were commanded to obey Her. Many times did some of these animals show their subjection to her commands, as when, at the birth of her most Holy Son, the ox and the ass prostrated themselves and by their breaths warmed the infant God at the command of his blessed Mother.

B3C1

After seeing the creation of all the irrational creatures, She became aware, how the most blessed Trinity, in order to complete and perfect the world, said: "Let us make man to our image and likeness" and how by virtue of this divine decree the first man was formed of the earth as the first parent of all the rest. She had a profound insight into the harmonious composition of the human body and soul and of their faculties, of the creation and infusion of the soul into the body and of its intimate union with the body.

The Lord manifested to Her also the happy state of original justice, in which He placed the first parents Adam and Eve; She understood their condition, beauty and perfection of innocence and grace; and for how short a time they persevered in it. She perceived how they were tempted and overcome by the astuteness of the serpent and what were the consequences of their sin; and how great were the fury and hate of the demon against the human race.

The seventh day of this mysterious preparation for the approaching sacrament arrived, and in the same hour as already mentioned, the heavenly Lady was called and elevated in spirit, but with this difference, that She was bodily raised by her holy angels to the empyrean heaven, while in her stead one of them remained to represent Her in corporeal appearance.

Placed into this highest heaven, She saw the Divinity by abstract vision as in other days; but always with new and more penetrating light, piercing to new and more profound mysteries, which God according to his free will can conceal or reveal. Presently She heard a voice proceeding from the royal throne, which said: "Our Spouse and chosen Dove, our gracious Friend, who hast been found pleasing in our eyes and hast been chosen among thousands: We wish to accept thee anew as our Bride, and therefore We wish to adorn and beautify thee in a manner worthy of our design."

B3C1

On hearing these words, the most Humble Mary abased and annihilated Herself in the presence of the Most High more than can be comprehended by human power. Entirely submissive to the divine pleasure and with entrancing modesty, She responded: "At thy feet, o Lord, lies the dust and abject worm, ready is thy poor slave for the fulfillment of all thy pleasure in her. Make use, o eternal Good, of this thy insignificant instrument according to thy desire, and dispose of it with thy right hand."

Presently the Most High commanded two seraphim, of those nearest to his throne and highest in dignity, to attend on this heavenly Virgin. Accompanied by others, they presented themselves in visible form before the throne, and there surrounded the most holy Mary, who was more inflamed with divine love than they.

The most holy Mary, had now attained such fullness of grace and beauty and the heart of God was so wounded by her tender affections and desires that He was irresistibly drawn to begin his flight from the bosom of the eternal Father to the bridal–chamber of her virginal womb and end the long delay of more than five thousand years.

Nevertheless, since this new wonder was to be executed in the plenitude of his wisdom and equity, the Lord arranged this event in such a way, that the Princess of the heavens Herself, being the worthy Mother of the incarnate Word, should at the same time be also the most powerful Mediatrix of his coming and the Redeemer of his people.

In order to put the last touch of preparing the most holy Mary, the Lord extended his powerful arm and expressly renewed the spirit and the faculties of the great Lady, giving Her new inclinations, habits and qualities, the greatness and excellence of which are inexpressible in terrestrial terms. It was the finishing act and the final retouching of the living image of God, in order to form, in it and of it, the very shape, into which the eternal Word, the essential image of the eternal Father and the figure of his substance was to be cast.

Thus the whole temple of most holy Mary, was covered with the purest gold of the Divinity inside and out, so that nowhere could be seen in Her any grossness of an earthly daughter of Adam. Her entire being was made to shine forth the Divinity; for since the divine Word was to issue from the bosom of the eternal Father to descend to that of Mary, He provided for the greatest possible similarity between the Mother and the Father.

B3C1

THE INCARNATION OF THE SON OF GOD

Thereupon his Majesty announced to all the other angels that the time of the Redemption had come and that He had commanded it to be brought to the world without delay; for already, in their own presence, the most holy Mary had been prepared and adorned to be his Mother, and had been exalted to the supreme dignity.

The heavenly spirits heard the voice of their Creator, and with incomparable joy and thanksgiving for the fulfillment of his eternal and perfect will, they intoned new canticles of praise, repeating therein that hymn of Sion: "Holy, holy, holy art thou, God and Lord Sabaoth. Just and powerful art Thou, Lord our God, who livest in the highest and lookest upon the lowly of the earth. Admirable are all thy works, most high and exalted in thy designs."

The supernal prince Gabriel, obeying with singular delight the divine command and accompanied by many thousands of most beautiful angels in visible forms, descended from the highest heaven. The appearance of the great prince and legate was that of a most handsome youth of rarest beauty; his face emitted resplendent rays of light, his bearing was grave and majestic, his advance measured, his motions composed, his words weighty and powerful, his whole presence displayed a pleasing, kindly gravity and more of godlike qualities than all the other angels until then seen in visible form by the heavenly Mistress.

He wore a diadem of exquisite splendor and his vestments glowed in various colors full of refulgent beauty. Enchased on his breast, he bore a most beautiful cross, disclosing the mystery of the Incarnation, which He had come to announce. All these circumstances were calculated to rivet the affectionate attention of the most prudent Queen.

The whole of this celestial army with their princely leader, Holy Gabriel, directed their flight to Nazareth, a town of the province of Galilee, to the dwelling place of most holy Mary. This was a humble cottage and her chamber was a narrow room, The heavenly Mistress was at this time fourteen years, six months and seventeen days of age; for her birthday anniversary fell on the eighth of September and six months seventeen days had passed since that date, when this greatest of all mysteries ever performed by God in this world, was enacted in Her.

The bodily shape of the heavenly Queen was well proportioned and taller than is usual with other maidens of her age; yet extremely elegant and perfect in all its parts. Her face was rather more oblong than round, gracious and beautiful, without leanness or grossness; its complexion clear, yet of a slightly brownish hue; her forehead spacious yet symmetrical; her eyebrows perfectly arched; her eyes large and serious, of incredible and ineffable beauty and dovelike sweetness, dark in color with a mixture tending toward green; her nose straight and well shaped; her mouth small, with red—colored lips, neither too thin nor too thick.

All the gifts of nature in Her were so symmetrical and beautiful, that no other human being ever had the like. To look upon Her caused feelings at the same time of joy and seriousness, love and reverential fear. She attracted the heart and yet restrained it in sweet reverence; her beauty impelled the tongue to sound her praise, and yet her grandeur and her overwhelming perfections and graces hushed it to silence. In all that approached Her, She caused divine effects not easily explained; She filled the heart with heavenly influences and divine operations, tending toward the Divinity.

Her garments were humble and poor, yet clean, of a dark silvery hue, somewhat like the color of ashes, and they were arranged and worn without pretense, but with the greatest modesty and propriety. At the time when, without her noticing it, the embassy of heaven drew nigh unto Her, She was engaged in the highest contemplation concerning the mysteries which the Lord had renewed in Her by so many favors during the nine receding days. And since, as we have said above, the Lord himself had assured Her that his Only begotten would soon descend to assume human form, this great Queen was full of fervent and joyful affection in the expectation of its execution and inflamed with humble love.

In order that the mystery of the Most High might be fulfilled, the holy archangel Gabriel, accompanied by innumerable angels in visible human forms and resplendent with incomparable beauty, entered into the chamber, where most holy Mary was praying.

It was on a Thursday at six o'clock in the evening and at the approach of night. The great modesty and restraint of the Princess of heaven did not permit Her to look at him more than was necessary to recognize him as an angel of the Lord. Recognizing him as such, She, in her usual humility, wished to do him reverence; the holy prince would not allow it; on the contrary he himself bowed profoundly as before his Queen and Mistress.

The holy archangel saluted our and his Queen and said: "Ave gratia plena, Dominus tecum, benedicta tu in mulieribus" (Hail, Full of Grace, Blessed art Thou among women). Hearing this new salutation of the angel, this most humble of all creatures was disturbed, but not confused in mind.

This disturbance arose from two causes: first, from her humility, for She thought herself the lowest of the creatures and thus in her humility, was taken unawares at hearing Herself saluted and called the "Blessed among women;" secondly, when She heard this salute and began to consider within Herself how She should receive it, She was interiorly made to understand by the Lord, that He chose Her for his Mother, and this caused a still greater perturbance.

On account of this perturbance, the angel proceeded to explain to Her the decree of the Lord, saying: "Do not fear, Mary, for thou hast found grace before the Lord; behold thou shalt conceive a Son in thy womb, and thou shalt give birth to Him, and thou shalt name Him Jesus; He shall be great, and He shall be called Son of the Most High."

Our most prudent and humble Queen alone, among all the creatures, was sufficiently intelligent and magnanimous to estimate at its true value such a new and unheard of sacrament; and in proportion as She realized its greatness, so She was also moved with admiration.

But She raised her humble heart to the Lord and asked new light and assistance by which to govern Herself in such an arduous transaction. She replied and said to holy Gabriel: "How shall this happen, that I conceive and bear, since I know not, nor can know, man?" At the same time She interiorly represented to the Lord the vow of chastity, which She had made and the espousal, which his Majesty had celebrated with Her.

The holy prince Gabriel replied "Lady, it is easy for the divine power to make Thee a Mother without the cooperation of man; the Holy Spirit shall remain with Thee by a new presence, and the virtue of the Most High shall overshadow Thee, so that the Holy of Holies can be born of Thee, who shall himself be called the Son of God. And behold, thy cousin Elisabeth has likewise conceived a son in her sterile years and this is the sixth month of her conception; for nothing is impossible with God. He that can make her conceive, who was sterile, can bring it about, that Thou, Lady, be his Mother, still preserving thy virginity and enhancing thy purity.

With these and many other words the ambassador of heaven instructed the most holy Mary, in order that, by the remembrance of the ancient promises and prophecies of holy Writ, by the reliance and trust in them and in the infinite power of the Most High, She might overcome her hesitancy at the heavenly message.

But as the Lady herself exceeded the angels in wisdom, prudence and in all sanctity, She withheld her answer, in order to be able to give it in accordance with the divine will, and that it might be worthy of the greatest of all the mysteries and sacraments of the divine power.

She reflected that upon her answer depended the pledge of the most blessed Trinity: the fulfillment of his promises and prophecies, the most pleasing and acceptable of all sacrifices, the opening of the gates of paradise, the victory and triumph over hell, the Redemption of all the human race, the satisfaction of the divine justice, the foundation of the new law of grace, the glorification of men, the rejoicing of the angels, and whatever was connected with the Incarnation of the Onlybegotten of the Father and his assuming the form of servant in her virginal womb.

A great wonder, indeed, that all these mysteries and whatever others they included, should be entrusted by the Almighty to a humble Maiden, and made dependent upon her fiat. But befittingly and securely He left them to the wise and strong decision of this courageous Woman since She would consider them with such magnanimity and nobility, that perforce his confidence in Her was not misplaced.

Therefore this great Lady considered and inspected profoundly this spacious field of the dignity of Mother of God in order to purchase it by her *fiat;* She clothed Herself in fortitude more than human, and She tasted and saw how profitable was this enterprise and commerce with the Divinity.

She comprehended the ways of his hidden benevolence and adorned Herself with fortitude and beauty. And having conferred with Herself and with the heavenly messenger Gabriel about the grandeur of these high and divine sacraments, and finding herself in excellent condition to receive the message sent to Her, her purest soul was absorbed and elevated in admiration, reverence and highest intensity of divine love.

By the intensity of these movements and supernal affections, her most pure heart, as it were by natural consequence, was contracted and compressed with such force, that it distilled three drops of her most pure blood, and these, finding their way to the natural place for the act of conception, were formed by the power of the divine and holy Spirit, into the body of Christ our Lord. Thus the matter, from which the most holy humanity of the Word for our Redemption is composed, was furnished and administered by the most pure heart of Mary and through the sheer force of her true love.

At the same moment, with a humility never sufficiently to be extolled, inclining slightly her head and joining her hands, She pronounced these words, which were the beginning of our salvation: "Fiat mihi secundum verbum tuum' (Let it be done unto me according to Thy word).

At the pronouncing of this "fiat," so sweet to the hearing of God and so fortunate for us, in one instant, four things happened. First, the most holy body of Christ our Lord was formed from the three drops of blood furnished by the heart of most holy Mary. Secondly, the most holy soul of the same Lord was created, just as the other souls. Thirdly, the soul and the body united in order to compose his perfect humanity. Fourthly, the Divinity united Itself in the Person of the Word with the humanity, which together became one composite being in hypostatical union; and thus was formed Christ true God and Man, our Lord and Redeemer.

This happened in springtime on the twenty–fifth of March, at break or dawning of the day, in the same hour, in which our first father Adam was made and in the year of the creation of the world 5199, which agrees also with the count of the Roman Church in her Martyrology under the guidance of the Holy Ghost.

Conformable to this, the world was created in the month of March, which corresponds to the beginning of creation. And as the works of the Most High are perfect and complete the plants and trees come forth from the hands of his Majesty bearing fruit, and they

B3C2

would have borne them continually without intermission, if sin had not changed the whole nature.

The divine Child began to grow in the natural manner in the recess of the womb, being nourished by the substance and the blood of its most holy Mother, just as other men; yet it was more free and exempt from the imperfections, to which other children of Adam are subject in that place and period. For from some of these, namely those that are accidental and unnecessary to the substance of the act of generation, being merely effects of sin, the Empress of heaven was free.

She was also free from the superfluities caused by sin, which in other women are common and happen naturally in the formation, sustenance, and growth of their children. For the necessary matter, which is proper to the infected nature of the descendants of Eve and which was wanting in Her, was supplied and administered in Her by the exercise of heroic acts of virtue and especially by charity.

By the fervor of her soul and her loving affections, the blood and humors of her body were changed and thereby divine Providence provided for the sustenance of the divine Child.

Thus in a natural manner the humanity of our Redeemer was nourished, while his Divinity was recreated and pleased with her heroic virtues. Most holy Mary furnished to the Holy Ghost, for the formation of this body, pure and limpid blood, free from sin and all its tendencies.

And whatever impure and imperfect matter is supplied by other mothers for the growth of their children, was administered by the Queen of heaven most pure and delicate in substance. For it was built up and supplied by the power of her loving affections and her other virtues. In a like manner was purified whatever served as food for the heavenly Queen. She knew that her nourishment was at the same time to sustain and nourish the Son of God, She partook of it with such heroic acts of virtue, that the angelic spirits wondered how such common human actions could be connected with such supernal heights of merit and perfection in the sight of God.

Thus adorned and deified by the Divinity and its gifts, the most holy soul of Christ our Lord proceeded in its operations in the following order: immediately it began to see and know the Divinity intuitively as It is in Itself and as It is united to his most holy humanity, loving It with the highest beatific love and perceiving the inferiority of the human nature in comparison with the essence of God.

The soul of Christ humiliated itself profoundly, and in this humility it gave thanks to the immutable being of God for having created it and for the benefit of the hypostatic union, by which, though remaining human, it was raised to the essence of God.

It also recognized that his most holy humanity was made capable of suffering, and was adapted for attaining the end of the Redemption. In this knowledge it offered itself as the Redeemer in sacrifice for the human race, accepting the state of suffering and giving thanks in his own name and in the name of mankind to the eternal Father.

He recognized the composition of his most holy humanity, the substance of which it was made, and how most holy Mary by the force of her charity and of her heroic virtues, furnished its substance. He took possession of this holy tabernacle and dwelling; rejoicing in its most exquisite beauty, and, well pleased, reserved as his own property the soul of this most perfect and most pure Creature for all eternity. He praised the eternal Father for having created Her and endowed Her with such vast graces and gifts: for having exempted Her and freed Her from the common law of sin, as his Daughter, while all the other descendants of Adam have incurred its guilt.

He prayed for the most pure Lady and for Saint Joseph, asking eternal salvation for them. All these acts, and many others, were most exalted and proceeded from Him as true God and Man. Not taking into account those that pertain to the beatific vision and love, these acts and each one by itself, were of such merit that they alone would have sufficed to redeem infinite worlds, if such could exist.

Even the act of obedience alone, by which the most holy humanity of the Word subjected itself to suffering and prevented the glory of his soul from being communicated to his body, was abundantly sufficient for our salvation.

But although this sufficed for our salvation, nothing would satisfy his immense love for men except the full limit of effective love, for this was the purpose of his life, that He should consume it in demonstrations and tokens of such intense love, that neither the understanding of men nor of angels was able to comprehend it.

And if in the first instant of his entrance into the world He enriched it so immeasurably, what treasures, what riches of merits must He have stored up for it, when He left it by his Passion and Death on the cross after thirty–three years of labor and activity all divine! O immense love! O charity without limit! O mercy without measure! O most generous kindness! and, on the other hand, O ingratitude and base forgetfulness of mortals in the face of such unheard of and such vast benefaction!

What would have become of us without Him? How much less could we do for this our Redeemer and Lord, even if He had conferred on us but small favors, while now we are scarcely moved and obliged by his doing for us all that He could? If we do not wish to treat as a Redeemer Him, who has given us eternal life and liberty, let us at least hear Him as our Teacher, let us follow Him as our Leader, as our guiding light, which shows us the way to our true happiness.

These operations of Christ our Lord in the first instant of his conception were followed by the beatific vision of the Divinity. In this vision the heavenly Lady perceived with clearness and distinction the mystery of the hypostatic union of the divine and the human natures in the person of the eternal Word, and the most holy Trinity confirmed Her in the title and the rights of Mother of God. This in all rigor of truth She was, since She was the natural Mother of a Son, who was eternal God with the same certainty and truth as He was man.

Although this great Lady did not directly cooperate in the union of the Divinity with the humanity, She did not on this account lose her right to be called the Mother of the true God; for She concurred by administering the material and by exerting her faculties, as far as it pertained to a true Mother, and to a greater extent than to ordinary mothers, since in Her the conception and the generation took place without the aid of a man.

Just as in other generations the agents, which bring them about in the natural course, are called father and mother, each furnishing that which is necessary, without however concurring directly in the creation of the soul, nor in its infusion into the body of the child; so also, and with greater reason, most holy Mary must be called, and did call Herself, Mother of God for She alone concurred in the generation of Christ, true God and Man, as a Mother, to the exclusion of any other natural cause; and only through this concurrence of Mary in the generation, Christ, the Man–God, was born.

But She was especially persistent and fervent in her prayer to obtain guidance of the Almighty for the worthy fulfillment of her office as Mother of the Onlybegotten of the Father. For this, before all other graces, Her humble heart urged Her to desire, and this was especially the subject of her solicitude, that She might be guided in all her actions as becomes the Mother of God. The Almighty answered Her: "My Dove, do not fear, for I will assist thee and guide thee, directing thee in all things necessary for the service of my onlybegotten Son."

With this promise She came to Herself and issued from her ecstasy. Restored to her faculties, her first action was to prostrate Herself on the earth and adore her holiest Son, God and Man, conceived in her virginal womb; for this She had not yet done with her external and bodily senses and faculties. Nothing that She could do in the service of her Creator, did this most prudent Mother leave undone.

From that time on She was conscious of feeling new and divine effects in her holiest soul and in her exterior and interior faculties. And although the whole tenor of her life had been most noble both as regards her body as her soul; yet on this day of the incarnation of the Word it rose to still greater nobility of spirit and was made more godlike by still higher reaches of grace and indescribable gifts.

Most Holy Mary Visits Elisabeth

"And Mary rising up in those days," says the sacred text, "went into the hill country with haste, into a city of Jude" .This rising up of our heavenly Queen signified not only her preparations and setting out from Nazareth on her journey, but it referred to the movement of her spirit and to the divine impulse and command which directed Her to arise from the humble retirement. Arising at the bidding of the Lord, She lovingly hastened to accomplish His most holy will: in procuring without delay the sanctification of the Precursor of the Incarnate Word, who was yet held prisoner in the womb of Elisabeth.

Leaving behind then the house of her father and forgetting her people, the most chaste spouses, Mary and Joseph, pursued their way to the house of Zacharias in mountainous Judea. It was twenty six leagues distant from Nazareth, and the greater part of the way was very rough and broken, unfit for such a delicate and tender Maiden. All the convenience at their disposal for the arduous undertaking was a humble beast, on which She began and pursued her journey.

Although it was intended solely for her comfort and service, yet Mary, the most humble and unpretentious of all creatures, many times dismounted and asked her spouse Saint Joseph to share with Her this commodity and to lighten the difficulties of the way by making use of the beast.

Her discreet spouse never accepted this offer; and in order to yield somewhat to the solicitations of the heavenly Lady, he permitted her now and then to walk with him part of the way, whenever it seemed to him that her delicate strength could sustain the exertion without too great fatigue.

But soon he would again ask Her, with great modesty and reverence, to accept of this slight alleviation and the celestial Queen would they obey and again proceed on her way seated in the saddle.

Thus alleviating their fatigue by humble and courteous contentions, the most holy Mary and Saint Joseph continued on their journey, making good use of each single moment. They proceeded alone, without accompaniment of any human creatures; but all the thousand angels, which were set to guard the most holy Mary, attended upon them.

Although the angels accompanied them in corporeal form, serving their great Queen and her most holy Son in her womb, they were visible only to Mary. Sometimes She conversed with the angels and, alternately with them, sang divine canticles concerning the different mysteries of the Divinity and the works of Creation and of the Incarnation.

In all this her spouse Saint Joseph contributed his share by maintaining a discreet silence, and by allowing his beloved Spouse to pursue the flights of her spirit; for, lost in highest contemplation, he was favored with some understanding as to what was passing within her soul.

At other times the two would converse with each other and speak about the salvation of souls and the mercies of the Lord, of the coming of the Redeemer, of the prophecies given to the ancient Fathers concerning Him, and of other mysteries and sacraments of the Most High.

Something happened on the way, which caused great wonder in her holy spouse Joseph: he loved his Spouse most tenderly with a chaste and holy love, such as had been ordained in Him by the special grace and dispensation of the divine love itself. In addition to this privilege, Saint Joseph was naturally of a most noble and courteous disposition, and his manners were most pleasing and charming; all this produced in him a most discreet and loving solicitude, which was yet increased by the great holiness, which he had seen from the beginning in his Spouse and which was ordained by heaven as the immediate object of all his privileges.

Therefore the saint anxiously attended upon most holy Mary and asked her many times, whether She was tired or fatigued, and in what He could serve Her on the journey. But as the Queen of heaven already carried within the virginal chamber the divine fire of the incarnate Word, Joseph, without fathoming the real cause, experienced in his soul new reactions, proceeding from the words and conversations of his beloved Spouse.

He felt himself so inflamed by divine love and imbued with such exalted knowledge of the mysteries touched upon in their conversations, that he was entirely renewed and spiritualized by this burning interior light.

The farther they proceeded and the more they conversed about these heavenly things, so much the stronger these affections grew, and he became aware, that it was the words of his Spouse, which thus filled his heart with love and inflamed his will with divine ardor.

Having pursued their journey four days, the most holy Mary and her spouse arrived at the town of Juda, where Zachary and Elisabeth then lived. In order to announce their visit, Saint Joseph hastened ahead of Mary and calling out saluted the inmate of the house, saying: "The Lord be with you and fill souls with divine grace."

Elisabeth was already forewarned, for the Lord himself had informed her in a vision that Mary of Nazareth had departed to visit her. She had also in this vision been made aware that the heavenly Lady was most pleasing in the eyes of the Most High; while the mystery of her being the Mother God was not revealed to her until the moment, when they both saluted each other in private.

B3C3

But saint Elisabeth immediately issued forth with a few of her family, in order to welcome most holy Mary, who, as the more humble and younger in years, hastened to salute her cousin, saying: "The Lord be with you, my dearest cousin, and Elisabeth answered : "The same Lord reward you for having come in order to afford me this pleasure

After the first salutation of Elisabeth by the most holy Mary, the two cousins retired. And immediately the Mother of grace saluted anew her cousin saying: "May God save thee, my dearest cousin, and may his divine light communicate to thee grace and life". At the sound of most holy Mary's voice, Saint Elisabeth was filled by the Holy Ghost and so enlightened interiorly, that in one instant she perceived most exalted mysteries and sacraments.

These emotions, and those that at the same time were felt by the child John in the womb of his mother, were caused by the presence of the Word made flesh in the bridal chamber of Mary's womb, for, making use of the voice of Mary as his instrument, He, as Redeemer, began from that place to use the power given to Him by the eternal Father.

And since He now operated as man, though as yet of the diminutive size of one conceived eight days before, He assumed, in admirable humility, the form and posture of one praying and beseeching the Father. He asked in earnest prayer for the justification of his future Precursor and obtained it at the hands of the blessed Trinity.

This happened before the most holy Mary had put her salutation into words. At the pronunciation of the words mentioned above, God looked upon the child in the womb of Saint Elisabeth, and gave it perfect use of reason, enlightening it with his divine light, in order that he might prepare himself by foreknowledge for the blessings which he was to receive.

Together with this preparation he was sanctified from original sin, made an adopted son of God, and filled with the most abundant graces of the Holy Ghost and with the plenitude of all his gifts; his faculties were sanctified, subjected and subordinated to reason, thus verifying in himself what the archangel Gabriel had said to Zacharias; that His son would be filled with the Holy Ghost from the womb of his mother.

At the same time the fortunate child, looking through the walls of the maternal womb as through clear glass upon the incarnate Word, and assuming a kneeling posture, adored his Redeemer and Creator, whom he beheld in most holy Mary as if enclosed in a chamber made of the purest crystal.

This was the movement of jubilation, which was felt by his mother Elisabeth as coming from the infant in her womb. Many other acts of virtue the child John performed during this interview, exercising faith, hope, charity, worship, gratitude, humility, devotion and all the other virtues possible to him there. From that moment he began to merit and grow in sanctity, without ever losing it and without ever ceasing to exercise it with all the vigor of grace.

Saint Elisabeth was instructed at the same time in the mystery of the Incarnation, the sanctification of her own son and the sacramental purpose of this new wonder. She also became aware of the virginal purity and of the dignity of the most holy Mary. On this occasion, the heavenly Queen, being absorbed in the vision of the Divinity and of the mysteries operated by it through her most holy Son, became entirely godlike, filled with the clear light of the divine gifts which She participated; and thus filled with majesty saint Elisabeth saw Her.

Filled with admiration at what She saw and heard in regard to these divine mysteries, saint Elisabeth was wrapt in the joy of the Holy Ghost; and, looking upon the Queen of the world and what was contained in Her, she burst forth in loud voice of praise, "Blessed are Thou among women and blessed is the fruit of thy womb. And whence is this to me, that the Mother of my Lord should come to me? For behold as soon as the voice of thy salutation sounded in my ears, the infant in my womb leaped for joy, and blessed art Thou, that has believed, because those things shall be accomplished, that were spoken to Thee by the Lord."

In these prophetic words saint Elisabeth rehearsed the noble privileges of most holy Mary, perceiving by the divine light what the power of the Lord had done in Her, what He now performed, and what He was to accomplish through Her in time to come.

All this also the child John perceived and understood, while listening to the words of his mother; for she was enlightened for the purpose of his sanctification, and since he could not from his place in the womb bless and thank her by word of mouth, She, both for herself and for her son, extolled the most holy Mary as being the instrument of their good fortune.

These words of praise, pronounced by Saint Elisabeth, referred to the Mother of the Creator; and Mary, in the sweetest and softest voice intoned the Magnificat:

My soul doth magnify the Lord;

And my spirit hath rejoiced in God my Saviour.

Because He hath regarded the humility of his handmaid; for behold from henceforth all generations shall call me blessed.

Because he that is mighty hath done great things to me and holy is his name.

And his mercy is from generation unto generation to them that fear him.

He hath showed might in his arm; He hath scattered the proud in the conceit of their heart.

He hath put down the mighty from their seat and hath exalted the humble.

B3C3

He hath filled the hungry with good things and the rich He hath sent empty away.

He hath received Israel, his servant, being mindful of his mercy;

As He spoke to our fathers, to Abraham and his seed forever."

Just as saint Elisabeth was the first one who heard this sweet canticle from the mouth of most holy Mary, so she was also the first one who understood it and, by means of her infused knowledge, commented upon it. She penetrated some of the great mysteries. which its Authoress expressed therein in so few sentences. The soul of most holy Mary magnified the Lord for the excellence of his infinite Essence; to Him She referred and yielded all glory and praise, both for the beginning and the accomplishment of her works.

She knew and confessed that in God alone every creature should glory and rejoice, since He alone is their entire happiness and salvation. She confessed also the equity and magnificence of the Most high in attending to the humble and in conferencing upon them his abundant spirit of divine love, She saw how worthy of mortals it is to perceive, understand and ponder the gifts that were conferred on the humility of Her, whom all nations were to call blessed, and how all the humble ones, each according to his degree, could share the same good fortune.

And as the mercies of the Most High overflowed from Mary's plenitude to the whole human race, and as She was the portal of heaven, through which they issued and continue to issue, and through which we are to enter into the participation of the Divinity; therefore She confessed, that the mercy of the Lord in regard Her is spread out over all the generations, communicating itself to them that fear Him. And just as the infinite mercies raise up the humble and seek out those that fear God; so also the powerful arm of divine justice scatters and destroys those who are proud in the mind of their heart, and hurls them from their thrones in order to set in their place the poor and lowly.

When it was time to come forth from their retirement, Saint Elisabeth offered herself and her whole family, and all her house for the service of the Queen of heaven. She asked Her to accept, as a quiet retreat, the room which she herself was accustomed to use for her prayers, and which was much retired and accommodated to that purpose.

The heavenly Princess accepted the chamber with humble thanks, and made use of it for recollecting Herself and sleeping therein, and no one ever entered it, except the two cousins. As for the rest She offered to serve and assist Elisabeth as a handmaid, for She said, that this was the purpose of visiting her and consoling her.

O what friendship is so true, so sweet and inseparable, as that which is formed by the great bond of the divine love! How admirable is the Lord in manifesting this great sacrament of the Incarnation to three women before He would make it known to any one else in the human race! For the first was Saint Anne, Her mother; the second one was her Daughter most holy Mary; the third was Saint Elisabeth, and conjointly with Her, her son, for he being yet in the womb of his mother, cannot be considered as distinct from her.

The most holy Mary and Elisabeth came forth from their retirement at nightfall, having passed a long time together; and the Queen saw Zacharias standing before her in his muteness. She asked him for his blessing as from a priest of the Lord, which the saint also gave to Her. Yet, although She tenderly pitied him for his affliction, She did not exert her power to cure him, because She knew the mysterious occasion of his dumbness; yet She offered a prayer for him.

Saint Elisabeth, who already knew the good fortune of the most chaste spouse Joseph, although he himself as yet was not aware of it, entertained and served him with great reverence and highest esteem. After staying three days in the house of Zacharias, however, he asked permission of his heavenly Spouse Mary to return to Nazareth and leave Her in the company of Saint Elisabeth in order to assist her in her pregnancy.

The holy husband left them with the understanding that he was to return in order to accompany the Queen home as soon as they should give him notice. Saint Elisabeth offered him some presents to take home with him; but he would take only a small part of them, yielding only to their earnest solicitations, for this man of God was not only a lover of poverty, but was possessed of a magnanimous and noble heart.

Therewith he pursued his way back to Nazareth, taking along with him the little beast of burden, which they had brought with them. At home, in the absence of his Spouse, he was served by a neighboring woman and cousin of his, who, also when most holy Mary was at home, was wont to come and go on necessary errands outside of the house.

Mary ordered all her occupations in the house of her cousin Elisabeth: She rose up at midnight in accordance with her former custom, spending the hours in the continued contemplation of the divine mysteries. In labor and repose She continued to receive new favors, illuminations, exaltation and caresses of the Lord.

During these three months She had many visions of the Divinity. More frequent still were the visions of the most holy humanity of the Word in its hypostatic union; for her virginal womb, in which She bore Him, served Her as her continual altar and sanctuary. She beheld the daily growth of that sacred body.

By this experience and by the sacraments, which every day were made manifest to Her in the boundless fields of the divine power and essence, the spirit of this exalted Lady expanded to vast proportions. To these occupations, which were concealed from all, She added those, which the service and consolation of her cousin

Elisabeth demanded, although She did not apply one moment more to them, than charity required. These fulfilled, She turned immediately to her solitude and recollection, where she could pour out the more freely her spirit before the Lord.

Not less solicitous was She to occupy Herself interiorly; She was engaged for many hours in manual occupations. And in all this the Precursor was so fortunate that the great Queen, with her own hands, sewed and prepared the swaddling clothes and coverlets in which he was to be wrapped and reared; for his mother Elisabeth, in her maternal solicitude and attention, had secured for saint John this good fortune humbly asking this favor of the heavenly Queen.

Mary with incredible love and subjection complied with her request in order to exercise Herself in obedience to her cousin, whom She wished to serve as the lowest handmaid. Although Saint Elisabeth sought to anticipate Her in much that belonged to her service, yet, in her rare prudence and wisdom, Mary knew how to forestall her cousin, always gaining the triumph of humility.

The hour for the rising of the morning star, which was to precede the clear Sun of justice and announce the wished—for day of the law of grace, had arrived The time was suitable to the Most High for the appearance of his Prophet in the world; and greater than a prophet was John, who pointing out with his finger the Lamb, was to prepare mankind for the salvation and sanctification of the world.

Before issuing from the maternal womb the Lord revealed to the blessed child the hour in which he was to commence his mortal career among men. The child had the perfect use of his reason, and of the divine science infused by the presence of the incarnate Word. He therefore knew that he was to arrive at the port of a cursed and dangerous land, and to walk upon a world full of evils and snares, where many are overtaken by ruin and perdition.

At the request of his mother the Queen received in her arms the newborn child and offered him as a new oblation to the eternal Father, and his Majesty, well pleased, accepted it as the first–fruits of the Incarnation and of the divine decrees. The most blessed child, full of the Holy Ghost, acknowledged his sovereign Queen, showing Her not only interior, but outward reverence by a secret inclination of his head, and again he adored the divine Word, which was manifested to him in her womb by an especial light.

And as he also was aware, that he was privileged before all men, the grateful child performed acts of fervent thanksgiving, humility, love and reverence of God and of his Virgin Mother. The heavenly Queen, in offering him to the eternal Father, pronounced this prayer for him: "Highest Lord and Father, all holy and powerful, accept in thy honor this offering and seasonable fruit of thy most holy Son and my Lord. He is sanctified by the Onlybegotten and rescued from the effects of sin and from the power of thy ancient enemies. Receive this morning's sacrifice, and infuse into this child the blessings of thy Holy Spirit, in order that he may be a faithful minister to Thee and to thy Onlybegotten."

This prayer of our Queen was efficacious in all respects, and She perceived how the Lord enriched this child, chosen as his Precursor; and She also felt within Herself the effects of these admirable blessings.

Then they bespoke of the arrangements for the circumcision of the child, for the time appointed by the law was approaching. Complying with the custom observed among the Jews, especially among the more distinguished, many relatives and other acquaintances of the house of Zacharias began to gather, in order to resolve upon the name to be given to the child; for, in addition to the ordinary preparations and consultations concerning the name to be given to a son, the high position of Zacharias and Elisabeth and the news of the miraculous fecundity of the mother naturally suggested the existence of some great mystery to the minds of all their relations.

B3C3

Zacharias was still dumb, and therefore it was necessary that Saint Elisabeth should preside at this meeting. Over and above the high esteem which she inspired, she now exhibited such evident signs of the exalted renewal and sanctification of her soul, which resulted from the knowledge of the mysteries and from her interactions with the Queen of heaven, that all her relatives and friends noticed the change. For even in her countenance she exhibited a kind of effulgence which made her mysteriously attractive and was the reflection of the Divinity, in whose presence she lived.

The relatives then appealed by signs to Zacharias, who, being unable to speak, asked for a pen and declared his will by writing upon the tablet: "Johannes est nomen ejus (John is his name)." At the same time most holy Mary, making use of her power over all nature, commanded the dumbness to leave him, his tongue to be loosened, as the moment had arrived when it should bless the Lord. At this heavenly command he found himself freed from his affliction, and, to the astonishment and fear of all present, he began to speak.

The voice of our Lady Mary was the instrument for the sanctification of the child John and his mother, so her secret mandate and her intercession had the effect of loosening the tongue of Zacharias, filling him with the holy Spirit and the gift of prophecy. Hence he broke forth in prayer, the Benedictus:

"Blessed be the Lord God of Israel; because He hath visited and wrought the redemption of his people:

And hath raised up a horn of salvation to us, in the house of David his servant:

And he hath spoken by the mouth of his holy prophets, who are from the beginning;

Salvation from our enemies, and from the hands of all that hate us:

To perform mercy to our fathers, and to remember his holy testament,

The oath, which he swore to Abraham our father, that he would grant to us,

That being delivered from the hand of our enemies, we may serve him without fear,

In holiness and justice before him, all our days.

And thou, child, shalt be called the prophet of the Highest: for thou shalt go before the face of the Lord to prepare his ways:

To give knowledge of salvation to his people: unto the remission of their sins:

Through the bowels of the mercy of our God, in which the Orient from on high hath visited us

To enlighten them that sit in darkness, and in the shadow of death: to direct our feet into the way of peace.

In the divine canticle of the Benedictus Zacharias embodied all of the highest mysteries, which the ancient prophets had foretold in a more profuse manner concerning the Divinity, Humanity and the Redemption of Christ, and in these few words he embraces many great sacraments. He also understood them by the grace and light, which filled his spirit, and which raised him up in the sight of all that had come to attend the circumcision of his son; for all of them were witnesses to the solving of his tongue and to his divine prophecies.

At the call of Elisabeth, the most fortunate of husbands, Saint Joseph, had come in order to attend most holy Mary on her return to her home in Nazareth. On arriving at the house of Zacharias he had been welcomed with indescribable reverence and devotion by saint Elisabeth and Zacharias; for now also the holy priest knew that he was the guardian of the sacramental treasures of heaven, though this was yet unknown to the great patriarch saint Joseph himself.

His heavenly Spouse received him in modest and discreet jubilation. and, kneeling before him, She, as usual, besought his blessing, and also his pardon, for having failed to serve him for nearly three months during her attendance upon her cousin Elisabeth. Though She had been guilty of no fault, nor even of an imperfection in thus devotedly fulfilling the will of God in conformity with the wishes of her spouse, yet, by this courteous and endearing act of humility, She wanted to repay her husband for the want of her consoling companionship. The holy Joseph answered that as he now again saw Her, and again enjoyed her delightful presence, he was relieved of the pain caused by her absence.

In the course of a few days they announced the day of their departure. Thereupon the princess Mary took leave of the priest Zacharias. As he had already been enlightened by the Lord concerning the dignity of the Virgin Mother, he addressed Her with the greatest reverence as the living sanctuary of the Divinity and humanity of the eternal Word.

The whole household of Zacharias had been sanctified by the presence of most holy Mary and of the incarnate Word in her womb; all its inmates had been edified by her example, instructed by her conversations and teachings, and sweetly affected by her intercourse and modest behavior. While She had drawn toward Herself all the hearts of that happy family, She also merited and obtained for them from her most holy Son the plenitude of celestial gifts.

Holy Joseph was held in high veneration by Zacharias, Elisabeth and John; for they had come to know his high dignity before he himself was yet aware of it, The blessed Patriarch, happy in his Treasure, the full value of which as yet he did not know, took leave of all and departed for Nazareth. But before they began their journey most holy Mary, on bended knees, besought saint Joseph to bless Her, as She was accustomed to do on such occasions, and after She had received his blessing, they betook themselves on their journey.

Chapter Four

Saint Joseph Resolves to Leave His Spouse

The divine pregnancy of the Princess of heaven had advanced to its fifth month when the most chaste Joseph, her husband, commenced to notice the condition of the Virgin; for on account of the natural elegance and perfection of her virginal body, any change could not long remain concealed and would so much the sooner be discovered.

One day, when Saint Joseph was full of anxious doubts and saw Her coming out of her oratory, he noticed more particularly this evident change, without being able to explain away what he saw so clearly with his eyes. The man of God was wounded to his inmost heart by an arrow of grief, unable to ward off the force of evidence, which at the same time wounded his soul.

The principal cause of his grief was the most chaste, and therefore the most intense love with which he cherished his most faithful Spouse, and in which he had from the beginning given over to Her his whole heart. Moreover, her charming graces and incomparable holiness had captured and bound to Her his inmost soul. As She was so perfect and accomplished in her modesty and humble reticence, Saint Joseph, besides his anxious solicitude to serve Her, naturally entertained the loving desire of meeting a response of his love from his Spouse. This was so ordained by the Lord, in order that by the desire for this interchange of affection he might be incited to love and serve Her more faithfully.

Besides all this was the certainty of his not having any part in this pregnancy, the effects of which were before his eyes; and there was the inevitable dishonor which would follow as soon as it would become public. This thought caused so much the greater anxiety in him, as he was of a most noble and honorable disposition, and in his great foresight he knew how to weigh the disgrace and shame of himself and his Spouse in each circumstances. The third and most intimate cause of his sorrow, and which gave him the deepest pain, was the dread of being obliged to deliver over his Spouse to the authorities to be stoned, for this was the punishment of an adulteress convicted of the crime.

The heart of Saint Joseph, filled with these painful considerations, found itself as it were exposed to the thrusts of many sharp–edged swords, without any other refuge than the full confidence which he had in his Spouse. But as all outward signs confirmed the correctness of his observations, there was no escape from these tormenting thoughts, and as he did not dare to communicate about his grievous affliction with anybody, be found himself surrounded by the sorrows of death, and he experienced in himself the saying of the Scriptures, that: "Jealousy is hard as hell."

In the midst of these tormenting anxieties the holy Spouse Joseph appealed to the tribunal of the Lord in prayer. Saint Joseph persevered in prayer, adding many more affectionate petitions; for even though he conjectured that there must be some mystery in the pregnancy of the most holy Mary hidden from him, he could not find assurance therein. This thought had no greater force to exculpate most holy Mary than the other reasons founded upon her holiness; and therefore the idea that the most holy Queen might be the Mother of the Messiah did not come to his mind.

If at times he drove away his conjectures, they would return in greater number and with more urgent force of evidence. Thus he was cast about on the turbulent waves of doubt. From sheer exhaustion he would at times fall into a condition of mind wherein he could find neither an anchor of certainty for his doubts, nor tranquillity for his heart, nor any standard by which he could direct his course. Yet his forebearance under this torment was so great that it is an evident proof of his great discretion and holiness, and that it made him worthy of the singular blessing which awaited him.

All that passed in the heart of Saint Joseph was known to the Princess of heaven, who penetrated into its interior by the light of her divine science. Although her soul was full of tenderness and compassion for the sufferings of her spouse, She said not a word in the matter; but She continued to serve him with all devotion and solicitude. The man of God watched Her without outward demonstration, yet with a greater anxiety than that of any man that ever lived.

The pregnancy of most holy Mary was not burdensome or painful to Her; but as the great Lady in serving him at table or any other domestic occupations, necessarily disclosed her state more and more openly, Saint Joseph noticed all these actions and movements and with deep affliction of soul verified all his observations.

Notwithstanding his being a holy and just man, he permitted himself to be respected and served by the most holy Virgin after their espousal, claiming in all things the position of head and husband of the family, though with rare humility and prudence. As long as he was ignorant of the mystery of his Spouse he judged it right, within befitting limits, to show his authority in imitation of the ancient Fathers and Patriarchs. For he knew that they demanded subjection and prompt obedience of their wives, and he did not wish to recede from their example. He would have been right in this course if most holy Mary, our Lady, had been no more than other women.

Yet although there was such a great difference, no woman ever existed or will exist who was or will be so obedient, humble and devoted to her husband as the most exalted Queen was toward her spouse. She served him with incomparable respect and promptitude; although She knew his troubled thoughts and observations concerning her pregnancy. She omitted no service due to him, nor did She try to conceal or palliate her state. For such evasion or duplicity would not have consorted with the angelic truthfulness and openness, nor with the nobility and magnanimity of her generous heart.

The great Lady could easily have asserted her entire innocence and referred to the testimony of Saint Elisabeth and Zacharias; for, if Saint Joseph had any suspicion of guilt in Her, he could naturally have supposed it to have been incurred during her stay with them. Hence, through them and by other references, She could have justified Herself and quieted the anxieties of Saint Joseph without disclosing the mystery.

The Mistress of prudence and humility did nothing of the kind; for these virtues did not allow Her to think of Herself, nor to trust the justification of her mysterious condition to her own explanation. With great wisdom She resigned the whole matter into the hands of divine Providence. Although her compassion for her spouse and her love for him made Her anxious to console and comfort him, She would not do it by clearing Herself or by concealing her pregnancy, but rather by serving him with more devoted demonstrations of love, and by trying to cheer him up, asking him what She could do for him and lovingly showing her devoted and submissive affection.

Many times She served him on her knees, and although this somewhat consoled Saint Joseph, yet on the other hand, it was also a cause for new grief. For thus he only saw the motives of love and esteem multiplied and still remained uncertain whether She had been untrue or not. The heavenly Lady offered up continual prayers for him and besought the Most High to look upon him and console him; as for the rest She submitted all to the will of his Majesty.

Saint Joseph could not entirely conceal his cruel sorrow, and therefore he often appeared to be in doubt and sad suspense. Sometimes, carried away by his grief, he spoke to his heavenly Spouse with some degree of severity, such as he had not shown before. This was the natural effect of the affliction of his heart not of anger or vengeful feelings; for these never entered his thoughts, as we shall see later.

The most prudent Lady, however, never lost the sweetness of her countenance, nor showed any feeling; but merely redoubled her efforts to relieve her husband. She served at table, offered him a seat, administered food and drink, and if, after all these services, which She performed with incomparable grace, Saint Joseph urged Her to sit down, and he could convince himself more and more of her pregnancy.

Yet although her sorrow exceeded all bounds, the capacity of her generous and magnanimous soul was much greater and therefore She could conceal her grief more completely, and occupy her faculties in the loving care of Saint Joseph, her spouse. Her sorrow therefore only incited Her to attend so much the more devotedly to his health and comfort. Nevertheless, as the inviolable rule of the actions of the most prudent Queen was to perform all in the fullness of wisdom and perfection.

She continued to conceal the mystery about the disclosure of which She had received no command. Though She alone could relieve her spouse by an explanation, She withheld it in reverence and faithfulness due to the sacrament of the heavenly King. As far as She herself was concerned, She exerted her utmost powers; She spoke to him about his health, She asked what She could do to serve him and afford him help in the weakness which so mastered him. She urged him to take some rest and recreation, since it was a duty to yield to necessity and repair the weakened strength, in order to be able to work for the Lord afterward.

The Princess of heaven, becoming aware of the resolve of her spouse Saint Joseph to leave Her and absent himself, turned in great sorrow to her holy angels and said to them: "Blessed spirits and ministers of the highest King, I beseech you, my friends, to present before God's clemency the afflictions of my spouse Joseph. Beseech the Lord to look upon him and console him as a true

Father. I pray, beseech and supplicate you, that without delay you assist and relieve my most faithful spouse in the affliction of his heart and drive from his mind and heart his resolve of leaving me."

The angels which the Queen selected for this purpose obeyed immediately and instilled into the heart of saint Joseph many holy thoughts, persuading him anew that his Spouse Mary was holy and most perfect, and that he could not believe anything wrong of Her; that God was incomprehensible in his works, and most hidden in his judgments, that He was always most faithful to those who confide in him, and that He would never despise or forsake them in tribulation.

By these and other holy inspirations the troubled spirit of saint Joseph was somewhat quieted, although he did not know whence they came; but as the cause of his sorrow was not removed, he soon relapsed, not finding anything to assure and soothe his soul, and he returned to his resolve of withdrawing and leaving his Spouse.

The heavenly Queen was aware of this and She concluded that it was necessary to avert this danger and to insist in earnest prayer on a remedy. She addressed Herself entirely to her most holy Son in her womb, and with most ardent affection of her soul She prayed: "Lord and God of my soul, with thy permission, I will speak in thy kingly presence and manifest to Thee my sighs, that cannot be hidden from Thee. It is my duty not to be remiss in assisting the spouse whom I have received from thy hand. ....to console thy servant Joseph and dispose him to assist me in the fulfillment of thy great works. It would not be well that I, thy servant, be left without a husband for a protection and guardian. Do not permit, my Lord and God, that he execute his resolve and withdraw from me."

The Most High answered Her: "My dearest Dove, I shall presently visit my servant Joseph with consolation; and after I shall have manifested to him by my angel the sacrament, which is unknown to him, thou mayest speak openly about all that I have done with thee, without the necessity of keeping silent thenceforward in these matters. I will fill him with my spirit and make him apt to perform his share in these mysteries. He will assist Thee in them and aid Thee in all that will happen."

With this promise of the Lord, most holy Mary was comforted and consoled, and She gave most fervent thanks to the same Lord, who disposes all things in admirable order, measure and weight. For besides the consolation, which the relief from this anxiety afforded Her, She also knew well how proper it was that the spirit of saint Joseph be tried and dilated by this tribulation before the great mysteries should be entrusted to his care.

In the meanwhile Saint Joseph was anxiously debating within himself concerning the proper course or action, for he had borne his tribulation already for two months; and now, overcome by the greatness of it, he argued with himself: "I do not find a better way out of these difficulties than to absent myself. I confess that my Spouse is most perfect and exhibits nothing but what shows Her a saint; but after all She is pregnant and of it I cannot fathom the mystery. I do not wish to injure Her reputation of holiness by involving Her in the punishment of the law; yet at the same time I cannot stand by and witness the consequences of her pregnancy. I will leave her now, and commit myself to the providence of the Lord, who governs me."

He then resolved to depart during that night, and in order to prepare for his journey he packed some clothes and other trifles into a small bundle. Having also claimed some wages due to him for his work, he retired to rest with the intention of leaving at midnight. But on account of the strangeness of his undertaking, and because he was in the habit of commending his intentions to God in prayer, after he had come to this resolve he spoke to the Lord: "Highest and eternal God of our fathers Abraham, Isaac and Jacob, the grief and tribulation of my heart are well known to thy clemency. Thou knowest also, O Lord, that I am innocent of that which causes my sorrow, and Thou likewise art aware of the infamy and danger consequent upon the condition of my Spouse. I do not believe Her an adulteress, because I see in Her great virtue and perfection; yet I certainly see Her pregnant. I do not know by whom or how it was caused; and therefore I find no way to restore my peace. In order to choose the least evil I will withdraw from Her and seek a place where no one knows me and, resigning myself to thy Providence, I will pass my life in a desert. Do not forsake me, my Lord and eternal God, since I desire solely thy honor and service.

Saint Joseph prostrated himself on the ground and made a vow to go to the temple of Jerusalem and offer up a part of the small sum of money which he had provided for his journey, in order that God might help and protect Mary his Spouse from the calamities of men and free Her from all misfortune; for great was the uprightness of that man of God, and the esteem in which he held the heavenly Lady. After this prayer he composed himself for a short sleep with the intention of departing in secret and at midnight from his Spouse.

During this sleep, the great Princess of heaven observed from her retirement all that Saint Joseph was preparing to do. And hearing the vow, which he made for her welfare, and seeing the small bundle and the poor provision he prepared for his journey, She was filled with tender compassion and prayed anew for him, giving praise and thanks to the Lord for his Providence in guiding the actions of men beyond all human power of comprehension. His Majesty so ordained events, that both most holy Mary and Saint Joseph should be brought to the utmost reach of interior sorrow.

Therefore it was befitting, that the angel deliver this message to him at a time, when the senses, which had been scandalized, were inactive and suspended in their operations. Thus the holy man might afterwards, regaining their full use, purify and dispose himself by many acts of virtue for entertaining the operation of the Holy Spirit which had been entirely interrupted by his troubles.

Saint Joseph awoke with the full consciousness, that his Spouse was the true Mother of God. Full of joy on account of his good fortune and of his inconceivable happiness, and at the same time deeply moved by sudden sorrow for what he had done, he prostrated himself to the earth and with many other humble, reverential and joyful tokens of his feelings he performed heroic acts of humiliation and of thanksgiving.

He gave thanks to the Lord for having revealed to him this mystery and for having made him the husband of her, whom God had chosen for his Mother, notwithstanding that he was not worthy to be even her slave. Amid these recognitions and these acts of virtue, the spirit of Saint Joseph remained tranquil and apt for the reception of new influences of the Holy Spirit.

His doubts and anxieties of the past few months had laid in him those deep foundations of humility, which were necessary for one who should be entrusted with the highest mysteries of the Lord; and the remembrance of his experiences was to him a lesson which lasted all his life.

The holy man began to blame himself alone for all that had happened and broke forth in the following prayer: "O my heavenly Spouse and meekest Dove, chosen by the Most High for his dwelling–place and for his Mother: how could thy unworthy slave have dared to doubt thy fidelity? How could dust and ashes ever permit itself to be served by Her, who is the Queen of heaven and earth and the Mistress of the universe? How is it, that I have not kissed the ground which was touched by thy feet? Why have I not made it my most solicitous care to serve Thee on my knees? How will I ever raise my eyes in thy presence and dare to remain in thy company or open my lips to speak to Thee? O my Lord and God, give me grace and strength to ask her forgiveness and move her heart to mercy, that She do not despise her sorrowful servant according to his guilt."

B4C1

The holy spouse now left his little room, finding himself so happily changed in sentiments since the time he had composed himself for sleep. As the Queen of heaven always had kept herself in retirement, he did not wish to disturb her sweet contemplation, until She herself desired. In the meantime the man of God unwrapped the small bundle, which he had prepared, shedding many tears with feelings quite different from those with which he had made it up. Weeping, he began to show his reverence for his heavenly Spouse, by setting the rooms in order, scrubbing the floors, which were to be touched by the sacred feet of most holy Mary. He also performed other chores which he had been accustomed to leave to the heavenly Lady before he knew her dignity. He resolved to change entirely his relation toward Her, assume for himself the position of servant and leave to Her the dignity of Mistress.

From that day on arose a wonderful contention between the two, which of them should be allowed to show most eagerness to serve and most humility. All that happened with Saint Joseph the Queen of heaven saw, and not a thought or movement escaped her attention. When the time arrived, the saint approached the oratory of her Highness, and She awaited him with sweetest kindness and mildness.

The husband of Mary, Saint Joseph, now better informed, waited until his most holy Spouse had finished her contemplation, and at the hour known to him he opened the door of the humble apartment which the Mother of the heavenly king occupied. Immediately upon entering the holy man threw himself on his knees, saying with the deepest reverence and veneration: "My Mistress and Spouse, here am I thy servant prostrate at the feet of thy clemency. For the sake of thy God and Lord, whom Thou bearest in thy virginal womb, I beseech Thee to pardon my audacity. I am certain, O Lady, that none of my thoughts are hidden to thy wisdom and to thy heavenly insight. Great was my presumption in resolving to leave Thee and not less great was my rudeness in treating Thee until now as my inferior, instead of serving Thee as the Mother of my Lord and God. But Thou also

B4C1

knowest that I have done all in ignorance, because I knew not the sacrament of the heavenly King and the greatness of thy dignity, although I revered in Thee other gifts of the Most High. Do not reflect, my Mistress, upon the ignorance of such a lowly creature, who, now better instructed, consecrates his heart and his whole life to thy service and attendance. I will not rise from my knees, before being assured of thy favor, nor until I have obtained thy pardon, thy good will and thy blessing."

The most holy Mary, hearing the humble words of Saint Joseph, experienced diverse feelings. For with tender joy in the Lord She saw how apt he was to be entrusted with the sacraments of the Lord, since he acknowledged and venerated them with such deep faith and humility.

But She was somewhat troubled by his resolve of treating Her henceforth with the respect and self abasement alluded to in his words; for the humble Lady feared by this innovation to lose the occasions of obeying and humiliating Herself as a servant of her spouse. Like one, who suddenly finds herself in danger of being deprived of some jewel or treasure highly valued, most holy Mary was saddened by the thought that saint Joseph would no longer treat Her as an inferior and as subject to him in all things, having now recognized in Her the Mother of the Lord.

She raised her holy spouse from his knees and threw Herself at his feet (although he tried to hinder it), and said: "I myself, my master and spouse, should ask thee to forgive me and thou art the one who must pardon me the sorrows and the bitterness, which I have caused thee; and therefore I ask this forgiveness of thee on my knees, and that thou forget thy anxieties, since the Most High has looked upon my desires and afflictions in divine pleasure."

It seemed good to the heavenly Lady to console her spouse, and therefore, not in order to excuse Herself, She added: "As much as I desired, I could not on my own account give thee any information regarding the sacrament hidden within me by the power of the

Almighty; since, as his slave, it was my duty to await the manifestation of his holy and perfect will. Not because I failed to esteem thee as my lord and spouse did I remain silent: for I was and always will be thy faithful servant, eager to correspond to thy holy wishes and affection. From my inmost heart and in the name of the Lord, whom I bear within me, I beseech thee not to change the manner of thy conversation and interaction with me. The Lord has not made me his Mother in order to be served and to command in this life, but in order to be the servant of all and thy slave, obeying thy will in all things." With these words and others most sweet and persuasive most holy Mary consoled and quieted Saint Joseph, and he raised Her from her knees in order to confer with Her upon all that would be necessary for this purpose. Since on this occasion the heavenly Lady was full of the Holy Ghost and moreover bore within her, as his Mother, the divine Word, who proceeds from the Father and the Holy Ghost, Saint Joseph received special enlightenment and the plenitude of divine graces.

The Lord looked upon him in benevolence and kindness as upon no other man, for He accepted him as his foster–father and conferred upon him that title. In accordance with this dignity, He gifted him with that plenitude of science and heavenly gifts which Christian piety can and must acknowledge.

The Amiable Humility of Mary Toward Her Spouse

The most faithful Joseph, after being informed of the mystery and sacrament of the Incarnation, was filled with such high and befitting sentiments concerning his Spouse, that, although he had always been holy and perfect, he was changed into a new man. He resolved to act toward the heavenly Lady according to a new rule and with much greater reverence. This was conformable to the wisdom of the saint and due to the excellence of his Spouse; for Saint Joseph by heavenly enlightenment saw well that he was the servant and She the Mistress of heaven and earth.

In order to satisfy his desire for honoring and reverencing Her as the Mother of God, whenever he passed Her or spoke to Her alone, he did it with great external veneration and on bended knees. He would not allow Her to serve him, or wait upon him, or perform any other humble services, such as cleaning the house or washing the dishes and the like. All these things the most happy spouse wished to do himself, in order not to derogate from the dignity of the Queen.

But the heavenly Lady, who among the humble was the most humble and whom no one could surpass in humility, so managed all these things, that the palm of victory in all these virtues always remained with Her. She besought Saint Joseph not to bend the knees to her, for though this worship was due to the Lord whom She carried in her womb, yet as long as He was within unseen by any one no distinction was externally manifest between his and her own person.

The Saint therefore allowed himself to be persuaded and conformed to the wishes of the Queen of heaven; only at times, when She was not looking, he continued to give this worship to the

Lord whom She bore in her womb, and also to Her as his Mother, intending thereby to honor Both according to the excellence of Each.

In regard to the other works and services, a humble contention arose between them. For Saint Joseph could not overcome his conviction as to the impropriety of allowing the great Queen and Lady to perform them, and therefore he sought to be beforehand with such household duties. His heavenly Spouse was filled with the same eagerness to seize upon occasions in advance of Saint Joseph. As however he busied himself in these duties during the time which she spent in contemplation, he frustrated her continual desire of serving him and of performing all the duties of the household, which She considered as belonging to Her as a servant.

In her affliction on this account, the heavenly Lady turned to the Lord with humble complaints, and besought Him to oblige Saint Joseph not to hinder Her in the exercise of humility, as She desired. As this virtue is so powerful before the divine tribunal and has free access, no prayers accompanied by it are small. Humility makes all prayers effective and inclines the immutable Being of God to clemency.

He heard Her petition and He ordered the angel guardian of the blessed husband to instruct him as follows: "Do not frustrate the humble desires of Her who is supreme over all the creatures of heaven and earth. Exteriorly allow Her to serve thee and interiorly treat Her with highest reverence, and at all times and in all places worship the incarnate Word. It is his will, equally with that of the heavenly Mother, to serve and not to be served, in order to teach the world the knowledge of life and the excellence of humility. In some of the work thou canst assist Her, but always reverence in Her the Lord of all creation."

Instructed by this command of the Most High, saint Joseph permitted the heavenly Princess to exercise her humility and so both of them were enabled to make an offering of their will to God: most holy Mary, by exercising the deepest humility and obedience toward her spouse in all her acts of virtue which She performed without failing in the least point of perfection; and saint Joseph by obeying the Almighty with a holy and prudent embarrassment, which was occasioned by seeing himself waited upon and served by Her, whom he had recognized as his Mistress and that of the world, and as the Mother of his God and Creator.

The humble but blessed house of Joseph contained three rooms, which occupied nearly all its space and formed the exclusive dwelling place of the two Spouses; for they kept neither a man— nor a maid—servant. In one of the rooms Saint Joseph slept, in another he worked and kept the tools of his trade of carpentering; the third was ordinarily occupied by the Queen of heaven and was also her sleeping room. It contained a couch made by the hands of Saint Joseph. This arrangement they had observed since their espousal and from the day on which they had come to this, their dwelling.

Before knowing the dignity of his Spouse and Lady, Saint Joseph rarely went to see Her; for while She kept her retirement he was engaged in his work, unless some affair made it absolutely necessary to consult Her. But after he was informed of his good fortune, the holy man was more solicitous for her welfare, and in order to renew the joy of his heart he began to come often to the retreat of the sovereign Lady, visiting Her and receiving her commands.

But he always approached Her with extreme humility and reverential fear, and before he spoke to Her, he was careful to note in what She was engaged. Many times he saw Her in ecstasy raised from the earth and resplendent with most brilliant light; at other times in the company of her angels in celestial interaction with them; and at other times, he found Her prostrate upon the earth in the form of a cross, speaking to the Lord. Her most fortunate spouse was a participator in these favors.

But whenever he found the great Lady in these occupations and postures, he would presume no farther than to look upon Her with profound reverence; and thereby he merited sometimes to hear the sweetest harmony of the celestial music, with which the angels regaled their Queen, and perceived a wonderful fragrance which comforted him and filled him entirely with jubilation and joy of spirit.

The two holy spouses lived alone in their house; they had no servants of any kind, not only on account of their humility, but in order more fittingly to bide from any witnesses the wonders, which passed between them and which were not to be communicated to outsiders. Likewise the Princess of heaven did not leave her dwelling, except for very urgent causes in the service of God or her fellow—men.

Whenever anything was necessary She asked that fortunate neighbor, who had served Saint Joseph during the absence of Mary in the house of Zacharias. This woman received such a good return from Mary, that not only she herself became most holy and perfect, but her whole household and family was blessed by the help of the Queen and Mistress of the world. She was visited by most holy Mary in some of her sicknesses and with her family was copiously enriched by the blessings of heaven.

Never did Saint Joseph see his heavenly Spouse asleep, nor did he of his own experience know whether She ever slept, although he besought Her to take some rest, especially during the time of her sacred pregnancy. The resting—place of the Princess was the low couch, which I said had been constructed by Saint Joseph; and on it were the coverings which served her during her brief and holy sleep. Her undergarment was a sort of tunic made of cotton, but softer than the ordinary or common cloth.

This tunic She never changed from the time since She left the temple, nor did it wear out or grow old or soiled, and no person ever saw it, nor did saint Joseph know that She wore that kind of a garment; for he never saw any other part of her clothing except the outside garments, which were open to the view of other persons. Those were of a gray color, and these only and her head–coverings were the garments which the Queen changed now and then; not because they were soiled, but because, being visible to all, She wished to avoid notice by such strange sameness of outward appearance. Nothing that She wore upon her most pure and virginal body became soiled or worn; for She neither perspired, nor was She subject to the punishments, which are laid upon the bodies of the children of Adam. She was in all respects most pure and the works of her hands were like crystal ornaments; and with the same purity She cared for the clothes and other necessities of saint Joseph. The food of which She partook, was most limited in kind and quantity; but She partook of some every day and in company of her spouse; she never ate meat, although he did, and She prepared it for him.

Her sustenance was fruit, fishes, and ordinarily bread and cooked vegetables; but of all these She partook in exact measure and weight, only so much as was necessary for the nourishment of the body and the maintaining of the natural warmth without any superfluities that could pass over into excess of harmful corruption; the same rule She observed in regard to drink, although Her fervent acts of love often caused a superabundance of preternatural ardor. This rule, as to the quantity of her nourishment, She followed during her whole life, although as to the kind of food She adapted Herself to the various circumstances demanding a change.

THE JOURNEY TO BETHLEHEM

It had been decreed by the immutable will of Providence that the Onlybegotten of the Father should be born in the town of Bethlehem, and accordingly it had been foretold by the Saints and Prophets of foregone ages: for the decrees of the absolute will of God are infallible, and since nothing can resist them, sooner would heaven and earth pass away than that they fail of accomplishment.

The fulfillment of this immutable decree the Lord secured by means of an edict of Caesar Augustus for the whole Roman Empire, ordering the registration or enumeration of all the world, as Saint Luke says. The Roman Empire at that time embraced the greater part of what was then known of the earth and therefore they called themselves masters of the world, ignoring all the other nations. The object of this census was to make all the inhabitants acknowledge themselves as vassals of the emperor, and to pay a certain tax to their temporal lord; for this registration every one was to go to his native city in order to be inscribed.

This edict was also proclaimed in Nazareth and came to the hearing of Saint Joseph while he was on some errand. He returned to his house in sorrowful consternation and informed his heavenly Spouse of the news which had spread about concerning the edict. The most prudent Virgin answered: "Let not this edict of our temporal ruler cause thee any concern, my master and spouse, for all that happens to us is ordained by the Lord and King of heaven and earth; and in all events his Providence will assist and direct us. Let us resign ourselves into his hands and we shall not be disappointed."

Most holy Mary was capable of being entrusted with all the mysteries of her most holy Son and She knew of the prophecies and their fulfillment; hence, also, that the Onlybegotten of the

Father and her own was to be born in Bethlehem, a Stranger and an Unknown. But She said nothing of this to Saint Joseph; for without being commissioned by the Lord She would reveal none of his secrets. All that She was not commanded to reveal She concealed with admirable prudence, notwithstanding her desire of consoling her most faithful and holy spouse. She wished to entrust Herself to his direction and arrangement without acting the part of those who are wise in their own conceit, as Wisdom warns us. They therefore conferred with each other about the course to be pursued; for already the pregnancy of the heavenly Lady was far advanced and her parturition was approaching.

Saint Joseph said: "Queen of heaven and earth and my Mistress, if Thou hast no order to the contrary from the Almighty, it seems to me necessary that I go alone. Yet, although this order refers only to the heads of families, I dare not leave Thee without assistance, nor could I live without Thee, nor would I have a moment's peace away from Thee; for my heart could not come to any rest without seeing Thee.

They at the same time resolved upon the day of their departure, and Joseph diligently searched in the town of Nazareth for some beast of burden to bear the Mistress of the world. He could not easily find one because so many people were going to different towns in order to fulfill the requirements of the edict of the emperor. But after much anxious inquiry saint Joseph found an unpretentious little beast which, if we can call such creatures fortunate, was the most fortunate of all the irrational animals; since it was privileged not only to bear the Queen of all creation and the blessed fruit of her womb, the King of kings and the Lord of lords, but afterwards to be present at his Birth; and since it gave to its Creator the homage denied to Him by men.

They provided the articles for the journey, which would last five days. The outfit of the heavenly travellers was the same as that which they had provided for their previous journey to the house of Zacharias on their visit to Elisabeth. They carried with them bread, fruit and some fishes, which ordinarily composed their nourishment. As the most prudent Virgin was enlightened regarding their protracted absence, She made use of prudent concealment in taking along the linens and clothes necessary for her heavenly delivery, for She wished to dispose all things according to the exalted intents of the Lord and in preparation for the events which She expected. Their house they left in charge of some neighbor until they should return.

The most pure Mary and the glorious Saint Joseph departed from Nazareth for Bethlehem alone, poor and humble in the eyes of the world. None of the mortals thought more of them than what was warranted by their poverty and humility. But O the wonderful sacraments of the Most High, hidden to the proud, and unpenetrated by the wisdom of the flesh! They did not walk alone, poor or despised, but prosperous, rich and in magnificence. They were most worthy of the immense love of the eternal Father and most estimable in his eyes. They carried with them the Treasure of heaven, the Deity itself.

The whole court of the celestial ministers venerated them. All the inanimate beings recognized the living and true Ark of the Testament, more readily than the waters of the Jordan recognized its type and shadow, when they courteously laid open and free the path for its passage and for those that followed it.

They were accompanied by the ten thousand angels, appointed by God himself as the servants of her Majesty during that whole journey. These heavenly squadrons marched along as their retinue in human forms visible to the heavenly Lady, more refulgent than so many suns. She herself walked in their midst better guarded and defended than the bed of Solomon, surrounded by the sixty valiant ones of Israel, girded with their swords.

Besides these ten thousand angels there were many others, who descended from heaven as messengers of the eternal Father to his Onlybegotten made man in his most holy Mother, and who ascended from earth as their ambassadors with messages and treaties from them to the heavenly Father.

With these wonderful favors and delights, however, the Lord joined some hardships and inconveniences which the divine Mother encountered on the way. For the concourse of people in the taverns, occasioned by the imperial edict, was very disagreeable and annoying to the modest and retiring Virgin–Mother and her spouse. On account of their poverty and timid retirement they were treated with less hospitality and consideration than others, especially the well–to–do; for the world judges and usually confers its favors according to outward appearance and according to personal influence.

Our holy pilgrims were obliged repeatedly to listen to sharp reprimands in the taverns, at which they arrived tired out by their journey, and in some of them they were refused admittance as worthless and despicable people. Several times they assigned to the Mistress of heaven and earth some corner of the hallway; while at others She did not fare even so well, being obliged to retire with her husband to places still more humble and unbecoming in the estimation of the world. But in whatever places She tarried, how contemptible soever it might be considered, the courtiers of heaven established their court around their supreme King and sovereign Queen.

Immediately they surrounded and enclosed them like an impenetrable wall, securing the bridal chamber of Solomon against the terrors of the night. Her most faithful spouse Joseph, seeing the Mistress of heaven so well guarded by the angelic hosts, betook himself to rest and sleep; for to this She urged him on account of the hardships of travel. She, however, continued her celestial colloquies with the ten thousand angels of her retinue.

Thus variously and wonderfully assisted, our travelers arrived at the town of Bethlehem at four o'clock of the fifth day, a Saturday. As it was at the time of the winter solstice, the sun was already sinking and the night was falling. They entered the town, and wandered through many streets in search of a lodging–house or inn for staying over night. They knocked at the doors of their acquaintances and nearer family relations; but they were admitted nowhere and in many places they met with harsh words and insults.

The most modest Queen followed her spouse through the crowds of people, while he went from house to house and from door to door. Although She knew that the hearts and the houses of men were to be closed to them, and although to expose her state at her age to the public gaze was more painful to her modesty than to their failure to procure a night–lodging, She nevertheless wished to obey Saint Joseph and suffer this indignity and unmerited shame.

While wandering through the streets they passed the office of the public registry and they inscribed their names and paid the fiscal tribute in order to comply with the edict and not be obliged to return. They continued their search, betaking themselves to other houses. But having already applied at more than fifty different places, they found themselves rejected and sent away from them all.

The heavenly spirits were filled with astonishment at these exalted mysteries of the Most High, which manifested the patience and meekness of his Virgin Mother and the unfeeling hardness of men. At the same time they blessed the Almighty in his works and hidden sacraments, since from that day on He began to exalt and honor poverty and humility among men.

It was nine o'clock at night when the most faithful Joseph, full of bitter and heartrending sorrow, returned to his most prudent Spouse and said: "My sweetest Lady, my heart is broken with sorrow at the thought of not only not being able to shelter Thee as Thou deservest and as I desire, but in not being able to offer Thee even any kind of protection from the weather, or a place of rest, a thing rarely or never denied to the most poor and despised in the world. No doubt heaven, in thus allowing the hearts of men to be so unmoved as to refuse us a night–lodging conceals some mystery. I now remember, Lady, that outside the city walls there is a cave, which serves as a shelter for shepherds and their flocks. Let us seek it out; perhaps it is unoccupied, and we may there expect some assistance from heaven, since we receive none from men on earth."

The most prudent Virgin answered: "My spouse and my master, let not thy kindest heart be afflicted because the ardent wishes which the love of thy Lord excites in thee cannot be fulfilled. Since I bear Him in my womb, let us, I beseech thee, give thanks for having disposed events in this way. The place of which thou speakest shall be most satisfactory to me. Let thy tears of sorrow be turned into tears of joy, and let us lovingly embrace poverty, which is the inestimable and precious treasure of my most holy Son. He came from heaven in order to seek it, let us then afford Him an occasion to practice it in the joy of our souls; certainly I cannot be better delighted than to see thee procure it for me. Let us go gladly wherever the Lord shall guide us."

The holy angels accompanied the heavenly pair, brilliantly lighting up the way, and when they arrived at the city gate they saw that the cave was forsaken and unoccupied. Full of heavenly consolation, they thanked the Lord for this favor.

CHRIST OUR SAVIOR IS BORN OF THE VIRGIN MARY

The palace which the supreme King of kings and the Lord of lords had chosen for entering his eternal and incarnate Son in this world was a most poor and insignificant cave, to which most holy Mary and Joseph betook themselves after they had been denied all hospitality and the most ordinary kindness by their fellow–men.

This place was held in such contempt that though the town of Bethlehem was full of strangers in want of night–shelter, none would demean or degrade himself so as to make use of it for a lodging; for there was none who deemed it suitable or desirable for such a purpose, except the Teachers of humility and poverty, Christ our Savior and his purest Mother.

On this account the wisdom of the eternal Father had reserved it for Them consecrating it in all its bareness, loneliness and poverty as the first temple of light and as the house of the true Sun of justice, which was to arise for the upright of heart from the resplendent Aurora Mary, turning the night of sin into the daylight of grace.

Most holy Mary and Saint Joseph entered the lodging thus provided for them and by the effulgence of the ten thousand angels of their guard they could easily ascertain its poverty and loneliness, which they esteemed as favors and welcomed with tears of consolation and joy. Without delay the two holy travellers fell on their knees and praised the Lord, giving Him thanks for his benefit, which they knew had been provided by his wisdom for his own hidden designs.

Of this mystery the heavenly Princess Mary had a better insight; for as soon as She sanctified the interior of the cave by her sacred footsteps She felt a fullness of joy which entirely elevated and vivified Her. She besought the Lord to bless with a liberal hand all the inhabitants of the neighboring city, because by rejecting Her they had given occasion to the vast favors, which She awaited in this neglected cavern. It was formed entirely of the bare and coarse rocks, without any natural beauty or artificial adornment; a place intended merely for the shelter of animals; yet the eternal Father had selected it for the shelter and dwelling–place of his own Son.

The angelic spirits, who like a celestial militia guarded their Queen and Mistress, formed themselves into cohorts in the manner of court guards in a royal palace. They showed themselves in their visible forms also to saint Joseph; for on this occasion it was befitting that he should enjoy such a favor, on the one hand in order to assuage his sorrow by allowing him to behold this poor lodging thus beautified and adorned by their celestial presence, and on the other, in order to enliven and encourage him for the events which the Lord intended to bring about during that night, and in this forsaken place.

The great Queen and Empress, who was already informed of the mystery to be transacted here, set about cleaning with her own hands the cave, which was so soon to serve as a royal throne and sacred mercy–seat; for neither did She want to miss this occasion for exercising her humility, nor would She deprive her onlybegotten Son of the worship and reverence implied by this preparation and cleansing of his temple.

Saint Joseph, mindful of the majesty of his heavenly Spouse (which, it seemed to him, She was forgetting in her ardent longing for humiliation), besought Her not to deprive Him of this work, which he considered as his alone; and he hastened to set about cleaning the floor and the corners of the cave, although the humble Queen continued to assist him therein.

As the angels were then present in visible forms, they were (according to our mode of speaking) abashed at such eagerness for humiliation, and they speedily emulated with each other to join in this work; or rather, in order to say it more succinctly, in the shortest time possible they had cleansed and set in order that cave, filling it with holy fragrance.

Saint Joseph started a fire with the material which he had brought for that purpose. As it was very cold, they sat at the fire in order to get warm. They partook of the food which they had brought, and they ate this, their frugal supper, with incomparable joy of their souls. The Queen of heaven was so absorbed and taken up with the thought of the impending mystery of her divine delivery, that She would not have partaken of food if She had not been urged thereto by obedience to her spouse.

After their supper they gave thanks to the Lord as was their custom. Having spent a short time in this prayer and conferring about the mysteries of the incarnate Word, the most prudent Virgin felt the approach of the most blessed Birth. She requested her spouse Saint Joseph to betake himself to rest and sleep as the night was already far advanced. The man of God yielded to the request of his Spouse and urged Her to do the same; and for this purpose he arranged and prepared a sort of couch with the articles of wear in their possession, making use of a crib or manger, that had been left by the shepherds for their animals.

Leaving most holy Mary in the portion of the cave thus furnished, Saint Joseph retired to a corner of the entrance, where he began to pray. He was immediately visited by the divine Spirit and felt a most sweet and extraordinary influence, by which he was wrapt and elevated into an ecstasy. In it was shown him all that passed during that night in this blessed cave; for he did not return to consciousness until his heavenly Spouse called him. Such was the sleep which Saint Joseph enjoyed in that night, more exalted and blessed than that of Adam in paradise.

The Queen of all creatures was called from her resting–place by a loud voice of the Most High, which strongly and sweetly raised Her above all created things and caused Her to feel new effects of divine power; for this was one of the most singular and admirable ecstasies of her most holy life. Immediately also She was filled with new enlightenment and divine influences, such as I have described in other places, until She reached the clear vision of the Divinity. The veil fell and She saw intuitively the Godhead itself in such glory and plenitude of insight, as all the capacity of men and angels could not describe or fully understand.

All the knowledge of the Divinity and humanity of her most holy Son, which She had ever received in former visions, was renewed and, moreover, other secrets of the inexhaustible archives of the bosom of God were revealed to Her. I have not ideas or words sufficient and adequate for expressing what I have been allowed to see of these sacraments by the divine light; and their abundance and multiplicity convince me of the poverty and want of proper expression in created language.

The Most High announced to his Virgin Mother, that the time of his coming into the world had arrived and what would be the manner in which this was now to be fulfilled and executed. The most prudent Lady perceived in this vision the purpose and exalted scope of these wonderful mysteries and sacraments, as well in so far as related to the Lord himself as also in so far as they concerned creatures, for whose benefit they had been primarily decreed.

She prostrated Herself before the throne of his Divinity and gave Him glory, magnificence, thanks and praise for Herself and for all creatures, such as was befitting the ineffable mercy and condescension of his divine love. At the same time She asked of the divine Majesty new light and grace in order to be able worthily to undertake the service and worship and the rearing up of the Word made flesh, whom She was to bear in Her arms and nourish with her virginal milk. This petition the heavenly Mother brought forward with the profoundest humility, as one who understood the greatness of this new sacrament.

She held Herself unworthy of the office of rearing up and conversing as a Mother with a God incarnate of which even the highest seraphim are incapable. Prudently and humbly did the Mother of wisdom ponder and weigh this matter. And because She humbled Herself to the dust and acknowledged her nothingness in the presence of the Almighty, therefore his Majesty raised Her up and confirmed anew upon Her the title of *Mother of God*.

He commanded Her to exercise this office and ministry of a legitimate and true Mother of Himself; that She should treat Him as the Son of the eternal Father and at the same time the Son of her womb. All this could be easily entrusted to such a Mother, in whom was contained an excellence that words cannot express.

The most holy Mary remained in this ecstasy and beatific vision for over an hour immediately preceding her divine delivery. At the moment when She issued from it and regained the use of her senses She felt and saw that the body of the infant God began to move in her virginal womb; how, releasing and freeing Himself from the place which in the course of nature He had occupied for nine months, He now prepared to issue forth from that sacred bridal chamber.

This movement not only did not cause any pain or hardship, as happens with the other daughters of Adam and Eve in their childbirths; but filled Her with incomparable joy and delight, causing in her soul and in her virginal body such exalted and divine effects that they exceed all thoughts of men. Her body became so spiritualized with the beauty of heaven that She seemed no more a human and earthly creature. Her countenance emitted rays of light, like a sun incarnadined, and shone in indescribable earnestness and majesty, all inflamed with fervent love.

She was kneeling in the manger, her eyes raised to heaven, her hands joined and folded at her breast, her soul wrapped in the Divinity and She herself was entirely deified. In this position, and at the end of the heavenly rapture, the most exalted Lady gave to the world the Onlybegotten of the Father and her own, our Savior Jesus, true God and man, at the hour of midnight, on a Sunday, in the year of the creation of the world five thousand one hundred and ninety–nine (5199), which is the date given in the Roman Church, and which date has been manifested to me as the true and certain one.

At the end of the beatific rapture and vision of the Mother ever Virgin, was born the Sun of Justice, the Onlybegotten of the eternal Father and of Mary most pure, beautiful, refulgent and immaculate, leaving Her untouched in her virginal integrity and purity and making Her more godlike and forever sacred; for He did not divide, but penetrated the virginal chamber as the rays of the sun penetrate the crystal shrine, lighting it up in prismatic beauty.

The infant God therefore was brought forth from the virginal chamber unencumbered by any corporeal material substance foreign to Himself. But He came forth glorious and transfigured for the divine infinite wisdom decreed and ordained that the glory of his most holy soul should in his Birth overflow and communicate itself to his body, participating in the gifts of glory in the same way as happened afterwards in his Transfiguration on mount Tabor in the presence of the Apostles.

This miracle was not necessary in order to penetrate the virginal enclosure and to leave unimpaired the virginal integrity; for without this Transfiguration God could have brought this about by other miracles. Thus say the holy doctors, who see no other miracle in this Birth other than that the Child was born without impairing the virginity of the Mother.

It was the will of God that the most blessed Virgin should look upon the body of her Son, the God–man, for this first time in a glorified state for two reasons. The one was in order that by this divine vision the most prudent Mother should conceive the highest reverence for the Majesty of Him whom She was to treat as her Son, the true God–man.

Although She was already informed of his two–fold nature, the Lord nevertheless ordained that by ocular demonstration She be filled with new graces, corresponding to the greatness of her most holy Son, which was thus manifested to Her in a visible manner.

The second reason was to reward by this wonder the fidelity and holiness of the divine Mother; for her most pure and chaste eyes, that had turned away from all earthly things for love of her most holy Son, were to see Him at his very Birth in this glory and thus be rejoiced and rewarded for her loyalty and beautiful love.

The two sovereign princes, Saint Michael and Saint Gabriel, were the assistants of the Virgin on this occasion. They stood by at proper distance in human corporeal forms at the moment when the incarnate Word, penetrating the virginal chamber by divine power, issued forth to the light, and they received Him in their hands with ineffable reverence.

In the same manner as a priest exhibits the sacred host to the people for adoration, so these two celestial ministers presented to the divine Mother her glorious and refulgent Son. All this happened in a short space of time. In the same moment in which the holy angels thus presented the divine Child to his Mother, both Son and Mother looked upon each other, and in this look, She wounded with love the sweet Infant and was at the same time exalted and transformed in Him.

From the arms of the holy Princess the Prince of all the heavens spoke to his holy Mother: "Mother, become like unto Me, since on this day, for the human existence, which thou hast today given Me, I will give thee another more exalted existence in grace, assimilating thy existence as a mere creature to the likeness of Me, who am God and Man."

The most prudent Mother answered: "Trahe me post Te, curremus in odorem unguentorum tuorum" (Raise me, elevate me, Lord, and I will run after Thee in the odor of thy ointments). In the same way many of the hidden mysteries of the Canticles were fulfilled; and other sayings which passed between the infant God and the Virgin Mother had been recorded in that book of songs, as for instance: "My Beloved to me, and I to Him, and his desire is toward me", "Behold thou art beautiful, my friend, and thy eyes are dove's eyes. Behold, my beloved, for thou art beautiful"; and many other sacramental words.

The words, which most holy Mary heard from the mouth of her most holy Son, served to make Her understand at the same time the interior acts of his holiest soul united with the Divinity; in order that by imitating them She might become like unto Him. This was one of the greatest blessings, which the most faithful and fortunate Mother received at the hands of her Son, the true God and man, not only because it was continued from that day on through all her life, but because it furnished Her the means of copying his own divine life as faithfully as was possible to a mere creature.

At the same time the heavenly Lady perceived and felt the presence of the most holy Trinity, and She heard the voice of the eternal Father saying: "This is my beloved Son, in whom I am greatly pleased and delighted". The most prudent Mother made entirely god–like in the overflow of so many sacraments, answered: "Eternal Father and exalted God, Lord and Creator of the universe, give me anew thy permission and benediction to receive in my arms the Desired of nations; and teach me to fulfill as thy unworthy Mother and lowly slave, thy holy will."

Immediately She heard a voice, which said: "Receive thy Onlybegotten Son, imitate Him and rear Him; and remember, that thou must sacrifice Him when I shall demand it of thee." The divine Mother answered: "Behold the creature of thy hands, adorn me with thy grace so that thy Son and my God receive me for his slave; and if Thou wilt come to my aid with thy Omnipotence, I shall be faithful in his service; and do Thou count it no presumption in thy insignificant creature, that she bear in her arms and nourish at her breast her own Lord and Creator."

B4C4

After this interchange of Words, so full of mysteries, the divine Child suspended the miracle of his transfiguration, or rather He inaugurated the other miracle, that of suspending the effects of glory in his most holy body, confining them solely to his soul; and He now assumed the appearance of one capable of suffering.

In this form the most pure Mother now saw Him and, still remaining in a kneeling position and adoring Him with profound humility and reverence, She received him in her arms from the hands of the holy angels. And when She saw Him in her arms, She spoke to Him and said: "My sweetest Love and light of my eyes and being of my soul, Thou hast arrived in good hour into this world as the Sun of justice, in order to disperse the darkness of sin and death! True God of the true God, save thy servants and let all flesh see him, who shall draw upon it salvation. Receive me thy servant as thy slave and supply my deficiency, in order that I may properly serve Thee. Make me, my Son, such as Thou desirest me to be in thy service."

Then the most prudent Mother turned toward the eternal Father to offer up to Him his Onlybegotten, saying: "Exalted Creator of all the Universe, here is the altar and the sacrifice acceptable in thy eyes. From this hour on, O Lord, look upon the human race with mercy and inasmuch as we have deserved thy anger, it is now time that Thou be appeased in thy Son and mine. Let thy justice now come to rest, and let thy mercy be exalted; for on this account the Word has clothed itself in the semblance of sinful flesh, and became a Brother of mortals and sinners. In this title I recognize them as brothers and I intercede for them from my inmost soul. Thou, Lord, hast made me the Mother of thy Onlybegotten without my merit, since this dignity is above all merit of a creature; but I partly owe to men the occasion of this incomparable good fortune since it is on their account that I am the Mother of the Word made man and Redeemer of them all. I will not deny them my love, or remit my care and watchfulness for their salvation. Receive, eternal God, my wishes and petitions for that which is according to thy pleasure and good will."

B4C4

The Mother of mercy turned also toward all mortals and addressed them, saying: "Be consoled ye afflicted and rejoice ye disconsolate, be raised up ye fallen, come to rest ye uneasy. Let the just be gladdened and the saints be rejoiced; let the heavenly spirits break out in new jubilee, let the Prophets and Patriarchs of limbo draw new hope, and let all the generations praise and magnify the Lord, who renews his wonders. Come, come ye poor; approach ye little ones, without fear, for in my arms I bear the Lion made a lamb, the Almighty, become weak, the Invincible subdued. Come to draw life, hasten to obtain salvation, approach to gain eternal rest, since I have all this for all, and it will be given to you freely and communicated to you without envy. Do not be slow and heavy of heart, ye sons of men; and Thou, O sweetest joy of my soul, give me permission to receive from Thee that kiss desired by all creatures". Therewith the most blessed Mother applied her most chaste and heavenly lips in order to receive the loving caresses of the divine Child, who on his part, as her true Son, had desired them from Her.

Holding Him in Her arms She thus served as the altar and the sanctuary, where the ten thousand angels adored in visible human forms their Creator incarnate. And as the most blessed Trinity assisted in an especial manner at the birth of the Word, heaven was as it were emptied of its inhabitants, for the whole heavenly court had betaken itself to that blessed cave of Bethlehem and was adoring the Creator in his garb and habit of a pilgrim.

And in their concert of praise the holy angels intoned the new canticle: "Gloria in excelsis Deo, et in terra pax hominibus bonae voluntatis" (Glory to God in the highest, and on earth peace to men of goodwill). In sweetest and sonorous harmony they repeated it, transfixed in wonder at the new miracles then being fulfilled and at the unspeakable prudence, grace, humility and beauty of that tender Maiden of fifteen years, who had become the worthy Trustee and Minister of such vast and magnificent sacraments.

It was now time to call Saint Joseph, the faithful spouse of the most discreet and attentive Lady. It was becoming that he should see, and, before all other mortals, should in his corporeal faculties and senses be present and experience, adore and reverence the Word made flesh; for he of all others had been chosen to act as the faithful warden of this great sacrament.

At the desire of his heavenly Spouse he issued from his ecstasy and, on being restored to consciousness, the first sight of his eyes was the divine Child in the arms of the Virgin Mother reclining against her sacred countenance and breast. There he adored Him in profoundest humility and in tears of joy. He kissed his feet in great joy and admiration, which no doubt would have taken away and destroyed life in him, if divine power had not preserved it; and he certainly would have lost all the use of his senses, if the occasion had permitted.

When Saint Joseph had begun to adore the Child, the most prudent Mother asked leave of her Son to arise (for until then She had remained on her knees) and, while Saint Joseph handed Her the wrappings and swaddling–clothes, which She had brought, She clothed Him with incomparable reverence, devotion and tenderness. Having thus swathed and clothed Him, his Mother, with heavenly wisdom, laid Him in the crib, as related by Saint Luke.

For this purpose She had arranged some straw and hay upon a stone in order to prepare for the God–Man his first resting–place upon earth next to that which He had found in her arms. According to divine ordainment an ox from the neighboring fields ran up in great haste and, entering the cave, joined the beast of burden brought by the Queen. The blessed Mother commanded them, with what show of reverence was possible to them to acknowledge and adore their Creator.

The humble animals obeyed their Mistress and prostrated themselves before the Child, warming Him with their breath and rendering Him the service refused by men. And thus the God made man was placed between two animals, wrapped in swaddling–clothes and wonderfully fulfilling the prophecy, that "the ox knoweth his owner, and the ass his master's crib; but Israel hath not known me, and my people hath not understood."

THE ADORATION OF THE SHEPHERDS—THE CIRCUMCISION

After the courtiers of heaven had thus celebrated the birth of God made man near the portals of Bethlehem, some of them were immediately dispatched to different places, in order to announce the happy news to those, who according to the divine will were properly disposed to hear it. The holy prince Michael betook himself to the holy Patriarchs in limbo and announced to them, how the Only be gotten of the eternal Father was already born into the world and was resting, humble and meek, as they had prophesied, in a manger between two beasts.

He addressed also in a special manner holy Joachim and Anne in the name of the blessed Mother, who had enjoined this upon him; he congratulated them, that their Daughter now held in her arms the Desired of nations and Him, who had been foretold by all the Patriarchs and Prophets. It was the most consoling and joyful day, which this great gathering of the just and the saints had yet had during their long banishment. All of them acknowledged this new Godman as the true Author of eternal salvation, and they composed and sang new songs of adoration and worship in his praise.

Another of the holy angels that attended and guarded the heavenly Mother was sent to saint Elisabeth and her son John. On hearing this news of the birth of the Redeemer, the prudent matron and her son, although he was yet of so tender an age, prostrated themselves upon the earth and adored their God made man in spirit and in truth.

The child which had been consecrated as his Precursor, was renewed interiorly with a spirit more inflamed than that of Elias, causing new admiration and jubilation in the angels themselves.

B4C5

Saint John and his mother requested our Queen through the angels, that She in the name of them both, adore her most holy Son and offer Him their services; all of which the heavenly Queen immediately fulfilled.

Amongst all these, the shepherds of that region. who were watching their flocks at the time of the birth of Christ, were especially blessed (Luke 2, 8); not only because they accepted the labor and inconvenience of their calling with resignation from the hand of God; but also because, being poor and humble, and despised by the world, they belonged in sincerity and uprightness of heart to those Israelites, who fervently hoped and longed for the coming of the Messias, speaking and discoursing of Him among themselves many times.

They resembled the Author of life, as they were removed from the riches, vanity and ostentation of the world and far from its diabolical cunning. They exhibited in the circumstances of their calling the office, which the good Shepherd had come to fulfill in knowing his Sheep and being known to them. Hence they merited to be called and invited, as the first fruits of the saints by the Savior himself, to be the very first ones, to whom the eternal and incarnate Word manifested Himself and by whom He wished to be praised, served and adored. Hence the archangel Gabriel was sent to them as they watched on the field, appearing to them in human form and with great splendor.

The shepherds found themselves suddenly enveloped and bathed in the celestial radiance of the angel, and at his sight, being little versed in such visions, they were filled with great fear. The holy prince reassured them and said: "Ye upright men, be not afraid: for I announce to you tidings of great joy, which is, that for you is born today the Redeemer Christ, our Lord, in the city of David. And as a sign of this truth, I announce to you, that you shall find the Infant wrapped in swaddling–clothes and placed in a manger."

At these words of the angel, suddenly appeared a great multitude of the celestial army, who in voices of sweet harmony sang to the

Most High these words: "Glory to God in the highest and on earth peace to men of good will." Rehearsing this divine canticle, so new to the world, the holy angels disappeared. All this happened in the fourth watch of the night. By this angelic vision the humble and fortunate shepherds were filled with divine enlightenment and were unanimously impelled by a fervent longing to make certain of this blessing and to witness with their own eyes the most high mystery of which they had been informed.

The signs which the holy angels had indicated to them did not seem appropriate or proportioned for attesting the greatness of the Newborn to eyes of the flesh. For to lie in a manger and to be wrapped in swaddling—clothes, would not have been convincing proof of the majesty of a king, if these shepherds had not been illumined by divine light and been enabled to penetrate the mystery. As they were free from the arrogant wisdom of the world, they were easily made proficient in the divine wisdom. Conferring among themselves the thoughts excited by this message, they resolved to hasten in all speed to Bethlehem and see the wonder made known to them by the Lord.

They departed without delay and entering the cave or portal, they found Mary and Joseph, and the Infant lying in a manger. Seeing all this they recognized the truth of what they had heard of the Child. Upon this followed an interior enlightenment consequent upon seeing the Word made flesh; for when the shepherds looked upon Him.

He also glanced at them, emitting from his countenance a great effulgence, which wounded with love the sincere heart of each of these poor yet fortunate men; with divine efficiency it changed them and renewed them, constituting them in a new state of grace and holiness and filling them with an exalted knowledge of the divine mysteries of the Incarnation and the Redemption of the human race.

Prostrating themselves on the earth they adored the Word made flesh. Not any more as ignorant rustics, but as wise and prudent men they adored Him, acknowledged and magnified him as true God and man, as Restorer and Redeemer of the human race. The heavenly Lady and Mother of the Child took notice of all that they did interiorly and exteriorly; for She saw into their inmost hearts. In highest wisdom and prudence She preserved the memory of all these happenings and pondered them in her soul, comparing them with the other mysteries therein contained and with the holy prophecies and sayings of the Scriptures.

As She was then the organ of the holy Spirit and the representative of the Infant, She spoke to the shepherds, instructing and exhorting them to persevere in divine love and in the service of the Most High. They also conversed with Her on their part and showed by their answers that they understood many of the mysteries. They remained in the cave from the beginning of dawn until mid–day, when, having given them something to eat, our great Queen sent them off full of heavenly grace and consolation.

When for the first time She placed the infant God in his arms, the most holy Mary said to him: "My husband and my helper, receive in thy arms the Creator of heaven and earth and enjoy his amiable and sweet company, in order that my Lord and my God may be delighted and recompensed by thy faithful services. Take to thyself the Treasure of the eternal Father and participate in this blessing of the human race." And speaking interiorly to the divine Infant, She said: "Sweetest Love of my soul and Light of my eyes, rest in the arms of Joseph, my friend and spouse: do thou hold sweet companionship with him and pardon me my shortcomings. Much do I feel the loss of Thee even for one instant, but I wish to communicate without envy the good I have received, to all that are worthy."

Her most faithful husband, acknowledging this new blessing, humbled himself to the earth and answered: "Lady and Sovereign of the world, my Spouse, how can I, being so unworthy, presume to hold in my arms God himself, in whose presence tremble the pillars of heaven? (Job 26, 11). How can this vile wormlet have courage to accept such an exalted favor? I am but dust and ashes, but do Thou, Lady, assist me in my lowliness and ask his Majesty to look upon me with clemency and make me worthy through his grace."

His desire of holding the infant God and his reverential fear of Him caused in saint Joseph heroic acts of love, of faith, of humility and profoundest reverence. Trembling with discreet fear He fell on his knees to receive Him from the hands of his most holy Mother, while sweetest tears of joy and delight copiously flowed from his eyes at a happiness so extraordinary. The divine Infant looked at him caressingly and at the same time renewed his inmost soul with such divine efficacy as no words will suffice to explain.

He broke out in new canticles of praise at seeing himself thus enriched with such magnificent blessings and favors. After having for some time enjoyed in spirit the sweetest effects of holding in his arms the Lord who contains heaven and earth, he replaced him into the arms of his fortunate Mother, both of them being on their knees in receiving and giving Him.

Similar reverence the most prudent Mother observed every time She took Him up or relinquished Him, in which also Joseph imitated Her, as often as it was his happy lot to hold the incarnate Word. When they approached his Majesty, they also made three genuflections, kissing the earth and exciting heroic acts of humility, worship and reverence. Thus both the great Queen and the blessed Joseph observed all propriety in receiving or giving the Child from and to one another.

From the moment the most prudent Virgin found Herself chosen as the Mother of the divine Word, She began to ponder upon the labors and sufferings in store for her sweetest Son. As her knowledge of Scripture was profound, She understood all the mysteries contained therein and She began to foresee and prepare with incomparable compassion for all that He was to suffer for the

Redemption of Man. This sorrow, foreseen and expected with such a full knowledge of details, was a prolonged martyrdom for the most meek Mother of the sacrificial Lamb of God.

But in regard to the Circumcision, which was to take place after the birth of the Child, the heavenly Lady had received no command or intimation of the will of the eternal Father. This uncertainty excited the loving solicitude and sweet plaints of the tender and affectionate Mother. Her prudent foresight enabled Her to conjecture, that, as her most holy Son had come to honor and confirm his law by fulfilling it and as He had moreover come in order to suffer for men, He would be constrained by his burning love and by other motives to undergo the pains of circumcision.

On the other hand her maternal love and compassion longed to exempt her sweet Child if possible, from this suffering; moreover She knew, that circumcision was a rite instituted for cleansing the newborn children from original sin, whereas the divine Infant was entirely free from this guilt, not having contracted it in Adam.

In this hesitation between love of her divine Son and obedience to the eternal Father, the most prudent Virgin practiced many heroic acts of virtue, unspeakably pleasing to his Majesty. Although She could have easily escaped this uncertainty by directly asking the Lord what was to be done; yet, being as humble as She was prudent, She refrained. Neither would She ask her angels; for with admirable wisdom,

She awaited the opportune time and occasion, assigned by divine Providence for all things, and She would not presume curiously to search or pry into his decrees by consulting supernatural sources of information, especially in order to rid Herself of any suffering. When any grave and doubtful affair arose, in which there was danger of offending God, or some urgent undertaking for the good of creatures, in which it would be necessary to know the divine will, She first asked permission to submit her petition for enlightenment regarding the divine pleasure.

Most holy Mary issued from her prayer and requested saint Joseph to take the necessary steps for the Circumcision of the divine Infant. With rarest prudence She avoided telling Him anything of what She had been told in answer to her prayer. She spoke as if She wished to consult Him or ask his opinion in regard to the Circumcision, saying that the time appointed by law for the Circumcision of the Child had arrived and since they had not received any orders to the contrary, it seemed necessary to comply with it.

They themselves, She said, were more bound to please the Most High, to obey more punctually his precepts, and to be more zealous in the love and care of his most holy Son than all the rest of creatures, seeking to fulfill in all things the divine pleasure in return for his incomparable favors. To these words saint Joseph answered with the greatest modesty and discretion, saying, that, as no command to the contrary had been given concerning the Child, he wished in all things to conform himself to the divine will manifested in the common law; that, although as God the incarnate Word was not subject to the law, yet He was now clothed with our humanity, and, no doubt wished to conform with other men in its fulfillment. Then he asked his heavenly Spouse how the Circumcision was to take place.

The most holy Mary answered, that the Circumcision should be performed substantially in the same way as it was performed on other children but that She need not hand him over or consign Him to any other person, but that She would herself hold Him in her arms. And the delicacy and tenderness of the Infant would make this ceremony more painful to him than to other children, they should have at hand the soothing medicine, which was ordinarily applied at circumcision. Moreover, She requested saint Joseph to procure a crystal or glass vessel for preserving the sacred relic of the Circumcision of the divine Infant.

In the meanwhile the cautious Mother prepared some linen cloths to catch the sacred blood, which was now for the first time to be shed for our rescue, so that not one drop of it might be lost or fall upon the ground. After these preparations the heavenly Lady asked saint Joseph to inform the priest and request him to come to the cave where, without the necessity of bringing the Child to any other place, he might, as a fit and worthy minister of so hidden and great a sacrament, with his priestly hands perform the rite of the Circumcision.

Then most holy Mary and Joseph took counsel concerning the name to be given to the divine Infant in the Circumcision, and the holy spouse said: "My Lady, when the holy angel of the Most High informed me of this great sacrament, he also told me that thy most sacred Son should be called JESUS." The Virgin Mother answered: "This same name was revealed to me when He assumed flesh in my womb; and thus receiving this name from the Most High through the mouth of his holy angels, his ministers, it is befitting that we conform in humble reverence with the hidden and inscrutable judgments of his infinite wisdom in conferring it on my Son and Lord, and that we call Him JESUS. This name we will propose to the priest, for inscription in the register of the other circumcised children."

While the great Mistress of heaven and saint Joseph thus conversed with each other, innumerable angels descended in human forms from on high, clothed in shining white garments, on which were woven red embroideries of wonderful beauty. They had palms in their hands and crowns upon their heads and emitted a greater splendor than many suns. In comparison with the beauty of these holy princes all the loveliness seen in this world appeared repulsive. But pre—eminent in splendor were the devices or escutcheons on their breasts, at each of which the sweet name of Jesus was engraved or embossed.

The effulgence which each of these escutcheons exceeded that of all the angels together, and the variety of the beauty thus exhibited in this great multitude was so rare and exquisite as neither human tongue can express nor human imagination ever compass. The holy angels divided into two choirs in the cave, keeping their gaze fixed upon the King and Lord in the arms of his virginal Mother. The chiefs of these heavenly cohorts were the two princes, saint Michael and saint Gabriel, shining in greater splendor than the rest and bearing in their hands, as a special distinction, the most holy name of JESUS, written in larger letters on something like cards of incomparable beauty and splendor.

The two princes presented themselves apart from the rest before their Queen and said: "Lady, this is the name of thy Son, which was written in the mind of God from all eternity and which the blessed Trinity has given to thy Onlybegotten Son and our Lord as the signal of salvation for the whole human race; establishing Him at the same time on the throne David. He shall reign upon it, chastise his enemies and triumph over them, making them his footstool and passing judgment upon them; He shall raise his friends to the glory of his right hand. But all this is to happen at the cost of suffering and blood; and even now He is to shed it in receiving this name, since it is that of the Savior and Redeemer; it shall be the beginning of his sufferings in obedience to the will of his eternal Father.

We all are come as ministering spirits of the Most High, appointed and sent by the holy Trinity in order to serve the Onlybegotten of the Father and thy own in all the mysteries and sacraments of the law of grace. We are to accompany Him and minister to Him until He shall ascend triumphantly to the celestial Jerusalem and open the portals of heaven; afterwards we shall enjoy an especial accidental glory beyond that of the other blessed, to whom no such commission has been given."

All this was witnessed by the most fortunate spouse Joseph conjointly with the Queen of heaven; but his understanding of these happenings was not so deep as hers, for the Mother of wisdom understood and comprehended the highest mysteries of the Redemption. Although saint Joseph understood many more mysteries than other mortals, yet he did not penetrate them in the same way as his heavenly Spouse. Both of them, however, were full of heavenly joy and admiration, and extolled the Lord in new canticles of glory. All that they experienced in these various and wonderful events surpasses human language, and certainly my own powers, and I cannot find adequate words for expressing my conceptions.

The priest came to the gates or cave of the Nativity, where the incarnate Word, resting in the arms of his Virgin Mother, awaited him. With the priest came also two other officials, who were to render such assistance as was customary at the performance of the rite. The rudeness of the dwelling at first astonished and somewhat disconcerted the priest. But the most prudent Queen spoke to him and welcomed him with such modesty and grace that his constraint soon changed into devotion and into admiration at the composure and noblest majesty of the Mother; and without knowing the cause he was moved to reverence and esteem for such an unusual personage.

When the priest looked upon the face of Mary and of the Child in her arms he was filled with great devotion and tenderness, wondering at the contrast exhibited amid such poverty and in a place so lowly and despised. The priest thereupon proceeded to his duty and circumcised the Child, the true God and man. At the same time the Son of God, with immeasurable love, offered up to the eternal Father three sacrifices of so great value that each one would have been sufficient for the Redemption of a thousand worlds. The first was that He, being innocent and the Son of the true God, assumed the condition of a sinner by subjecting Himself to a rite instituted as a remedy for original sin, and to a law not binding on Him. The second was his willingness to suffer the pains of circumcision, which He felt as a true and perfect man. The third was the most ardent love with which He began shed his blood for the human race, giving thanks to eternal Father for having given Him a human nature capable of suffering for his exaltation and glory.

This prayerful sacrifice of JESUS our Savior the Father accepted, and He began to declare Himself satisfied and paid for the indebtedness of humanity. The incarnate Word offered these first fruits of his blood as pledges that He would give it all in order to consummate the Redemption and extinguish the debt of the sons of Adam.

All these interior acts and movements of the Onlybegotten his most holy Mother perceived, and in her heavenly wisdom She penetrated the mystery of this sacrament, acting as his Mother and in concert with Her Son and Lord in all He was doing and suffering. True to his human nature, the divine Infant shed tears as other children. Although the pains caused by the wounding were most severe, as well on account of the delicacy of his body as on account of the coarseness of the knife, which was made of flint, yet his tears were caused not so much by the sensible pain as by the supernatural sorrow caused by his knowledge of the hard–heartedness of mortals.

For this was more rude and unyielding than the flint, resisting his sweetest love and the divine fire He had come to enkindle in the world and in the hearts of the faithful. Also the tender and affectionate Mother wept, like the guileless sheep, which raises its voice in unison with the innocent lamb. In reciprocal love and compassion the Child clung to his Mother, while She sweetly caressed Him at her virginal breast and caught the sacred relics and the falling blood in the towel.

In the meanwhile the priest asked the parents what name they wished to give to the Child in Circumcision; the great Lady, always attentive to honor her spouse, asked saint Joseph to mention the name. Saint Joseph turned toward Her in like reverence and gave Her to understand that He thought it proper this sweet name should first flow from her mouth. Therefore, by divine interference, both Mary and Joseph said at the same time; "JESUS is his name." The priest answered: "The parents are unanimously agreed, and great is the name which they give to the Child"; and thereupon he inscribed it in the tablet or register of names of the rest of the children.

B4C5

While writing it the priest felt great interior movements, so that he shed copious tears; and wondering at what he felt yet not being able to account for, he said: "I am convinced that this Child is to be a great Prophet of the Lord. Have great care in raising Him, and tell me in what I can relieve your needs." Most holy Mary and Joseph answered the priest with humble gratitude and dismissed him after offering him the gift of some candles and other articles.

Being again left alone with the Child, most holy Mary and Joseph celebrated anew the mystery of the Circumcision, commenting on the holy name of JESUS amid sweet canticles and tears of joy, the fuller knowledge of which (as also of other mysteries which I have mentioned) is reserved as an additional accidental glory to the saints in heaven. The most prudent Mother applied to the wound caused by the knife such medicines as were wont to be used on such occasions for other children, and during the time while the pain and the healing lasted She would not for a moment part with holding Him in her arms day and night.

The tender love of the heavenly Mother is beyond all comprehension or understanding of man; for her natural love was greater than any other mother was capable of, and her supernatural love exceeded that of all the angels and saints together. Her reverence and worship cannot be compared with that of any other created being. These were the delights of the incarnate Word , which He desired and longed for among the children of men; and this was the recompense, which his loving heart drew from the exceeding sanctity of the Virgin Mother for the sorrows occasioned Him by their behavior.

THE ADORATION OF THE MAGI

The three Magi Kings, who came to find the divine Infant after his birth, were natives of Persia, Arabia and Sabba, countries to the east of Palestine. Their coming was prophesied especially by David, and before him, by Balaam, who, having been hired by Balaac, king of the Moabites, to curse the Israelites, blessed them instead. In this blessing Balaam said, that he would see the King Christ, although not at once, and that he would behold Him, although not present; for he did not see Him with his own eyes, but through the Magi, his descendants many centuries after. He said, also, that a star would arise unto Jacob, which was Christ, who arose to reign forever in the house of Jacob.

At the same time the holy angel, who had brought the news from Bethlehem to the kings, formed of the material air a most resplendent star, although not so large as those of the firmament; for it was not to ascend higher than was necessary for the purpose of its formation. It took its course through the atmospheric regions in order to guide and direct the holy Kings to the cave, where the Child awaited them.

Its splendor was of a different kind from that of the sun and the other stars; with its most beautiful light it illumined the night like a brilliant torch, and it mingled its own most active brilliancy with that of the sun by day.

On coming out of their palaces each one of the kings saw this new star, although each from a different standpoint, because it was only one star and it was placed in such distance and height that it could be seen by each one at the same time. As the three of them followed the guidance of this miraculous star, they soon met.

Thereupon it immediately approached them much more closely, descending through many shifts of the aerial space and rejoicing them by shedding its refulgence over them at closer range. They began to confer among themselves about the revelation they had received and about their plans, finding that they were identical.

They were more and more inflamed with devotion and with the pious desire of adoring the newborn God, and broke out in praise and admiration at the inscrutable works and mysteries of the Almighty.

The heavenly Mother awaited the pious and devout kings, standing with the Child in her arms. Amid the humble and poor surroundings of the cave, in incomparable modesty and beauty, She exhibited at same time a majesty more than human, the light of heaven shining in her countenance. Still more visible was this light in the Child, shedding through the cavern effulgent splendor, which made it like a heaven.

The three kings of the East entered and at the first sight of the Son and Mother they were for a considerable space of time overwhelmed with wonder. They prostrated themselves upon the earth, and in this position they worshiped and adored the Infant, acknowledging Him as the true God and man, and as the Savior of the human race.

By the divine power, which the sight of Him and his presence exerted in their souls, they were filled with new enlightenment. They perceived the multitude of angelic spirits, who as servants and ministers of the King of kings and Lord of lords attended upon him in reverential fear.

Arising, they congratulated their and our Queen as Mother of the Son of the eternal Father; and they approached to reverence Her on their knees. They sought her hand in order to kiss it, as they were accustomed to do to their queens in their countries. But the most prudent Lady withdrew her hand, and offered instead that of the Redeemer of the world, saying: "My spirit rejoices in the Lord and my soul blesses and extols Him; because among all the nations He has called and selected you to look upon and behold that which many kings and prophets have in vain desired to see, namely, Him who is the eternal Word incarnate. Let us extol and praise his name on account of the sacraments and mysteries wrought among his people; let us kiss the earth which He sanctifies by his real presence."

At these words of most holy Mary the three kings humiliated themselves anew, adoring the infant Jesus; they acknowledged the great blessings of living in the time when the Sun of justice was arising in order to illumine the darkness. Thereupon they spoke to saint Joseph, congratulating him and extolling his good fortune in being chosen as the spouse of the Mother of God; and they expressed wonder and compassion at the great poverty, beneath which were hidden the greatest mysteries of heaven and earth.

Thereupon the three kings consumed three hours, and then the kings asked permission of most holy Mary to go to the city in order to seek a lodging, as they could find no room for themselves in the cave. Some people had accompanied them; but the Magi alone participated in the light and the grace of this visit. The others took notice merely of what passed exteriorly, and witnessed only the destitute and neglected condition of the Mother and her husband. Though wondering at the strange event, they perceived nothing of its mystery.

The Magi took leave and departed, while most holy Mary and Joseph, being again alone with their Child, glorified his Majesty with new songs of praise, because his name was beginning to be known and adored among the Gentiles. What else the three wise men did will be related in the following chapter.

From the grotto of the Nativity, into which the three Kings had entered directly on their way to Jerusalem, they betook themselves to a lodging inside of the town of Bethlehem. They retired to a room where, in an abundance of affectionate tears and aspirations, they spent the greater part of the night, speaking of what they had

B4C6

seen, of the feelings and affections aroused in each, and of what each had noticed for himself in the divine Child and his Mother.

During this conference they were more and more inflamed with divine love, amazed at the majesty and divine effulgence of the Infant Jesus at the prudence, modesty and reserve of his Mother; at the holiness of her spouse Joseph, and the poverty of all three; at the humbleness of the place, where the Lord of heaven and earth had wished to be born.

The devout kings felt a divine fire, which flamed up in their hearts, and, not being able to restrain themselves, they broke out into exclamations of sweet affection and acts of great reverence and love. "What is this that we feel?" they said. "What influence of this great King is it that moves us to such desires and affections? After this, how shall we converse with men? What can we do, who have been instructed in such new, hidden and supernatural mysteries?"

During these divine colloquies the Magi remembered the dire destitution of Jesus, Mary and Joseph in their cave, and they resolved immediately to send them some gifts in order to show their affection and to satisfy their desire of serving them, since they could not do anything else for them. They sent through their servants many of the presents, which they had already set aside for them, and others which they could procure. Most holy Mary and Joseph received these gifts with humble acknowledgment and they made a return not of emptyworded thanks, but with many efficacious blessings for the spiritual consolation of the three Kings.

These gifts enabled our great Queen to prepare for her ordinary guests, the poor, an abundant repast; for the needy ones were accustomed to receive alms from Her, and, attracted still more by her sweet words, were wont to come and visit Her. The Kings went to rest full of incomparable joy in the Lord; and in their sleep the angels advised them as to their journey homeward.

On the following day at dawn they returned to the cave of the Nativity in order to offer to the heavenly King the special gifts which they had provided. Arriving they prostrated themselves anew in profound humility; and opening their treasures, as Scripture relates, they offered Him gold, incense and myrrh. They consulted the heavenly Mother in regard to many mysteries and practices of faith, and concerning matters pertaining to their consciences and to the government of their countries; for they wished to return well instructed and capable of directing themselves to holiness and perfection in their daily life.

The great Lady heard them with exceeding pleasure and She conferred interiorly with the divine Infant concerning all that they had asked, in order to answer and properly to instruct these sons of the new Law. As a Teacher and an instrument of divine wisdom She answered all their questions, giving them such high precepts of sanctity that they could scarcely part from her on account of the sweetness and attraction of her words.

However, an angel of the Lord appeared to them, reminding them of the necessity and of the will of the Lord that they should return to their country. No wonder that her words should so deeply affect these Kings; for all her words were inspired by the holy Spirit and full of infused science regarding all that they had inquired and many other matters.

The heavenly Mother received the gifts of the Kings and in their name offered them to the Infant Jesus. His Majesty showed by signs of highest pleasure, that He accepted their gifts: they themselves became aware of the exalted and heavenly blessings with which He repaid them more than a hundredfold.

According to the custom of their country they also offered to the heavenly Princess some gems of great value; but because these gifts had no mysterious signification and referred not to Jesus, She returned them to the Kings, reserving only the gifts of gold, incense and myrrh. In order to send them away more rejoiced, She gave them some of the clothes in which She had wrapped the infant God; for She neither had nor could have had any greater visible pledges of esteem with which to enrich them at their departure.

The three Kings received these relics with such reverence and esteem that they encased them in gold and precious stones in order to keep them ever after. As a proof of their value these relics spread about such a copious fragrance that they revealed their presence a league in circumference. However, only those who believed in the coming of God into the world were able to perceive it; while the incredulous perceived none of the fragrance emitted by the relics. In their own countries the Magi performed great miracles with these relics.

The holy Kings also offered their property and possession to the Mother of the sweetest Jesus, or, if She did not wish to accept of them and preferred to live in this place, where her most holy Son had been born, they would build Her a house, wherein She could live more comfortably. The most prudent Mother thanked them for their offers without accepting them.

On taking leave of Her, the three Kings besought Her from their inmost hearts not to forget them, which She promised and fulfilled in the same way they asked of Saint Joseph. With the blessing of Jesus, Mary and Joseph, they departed, so moved by tenderest affection that it seemed to them they had left their hearts all melted into sighs and tears in that place.

They chose another way for their return journey, in order not to meet Herod in Jerusalem; for thus they had been instructed by the angel on the preceding night. On their departure from Bethlehem the same or a similar star appeared in order to guide them home, conducting them on their new route to the place where they had first met, whence each one separated to reach his own country.

PRESENTATION OF THE INFANT JESUS IN THE TEMPLE

The sacred humanity of Christ belonged to the eternal Father, not only because it was created like other beings, but it was his special property by virtue of the hypostatic union with the person of the Word; for this person of the Word, being his Onlybegotten Son, was engendered of his substance, true God of true God.

Nevertheless the eternal Father had decreed, that his Son should be presented to Him in the temple in mysterious compliance with the law, of which Christ our Lord was the end. It was established for no other purpose than that the just men of the old Testament should perpetually sanctify and offer to the Lord their first–born sons, in the hope that one thus presented might prove to be the Son of God and a Child of the Mother of the expected Messiah.

On the next morning, the Sun of heaven being now ready to issue from its purest dawning, the Virgin Mary, on whose arms He reclined, and being about to rise up in full view of the world, the heavenly Lady, having provided the turtle–dove and two candles, wrapped Him in swaddling–clothes and betook Herself with saint Joseph from their lodging to the temple.

The holy angels, who had come with them from Bethlehem, again formed in procession in corporeal and most beautiful forms, just as has been said concerning the journey of the preceding day. On this occasion however the holy spirits added many other hymns of the sweetest and most entrancing harmony in honor of the infant God, which were heard only by the most pure Mary.

Besides the ten thousand, who had formed the procession on the previous day, innumerable others descended from heaven, which, accompanied by those that bore the shields of the holy name Jesus, formed the guard of honor of the incarnate Word on the occasion of his presentation. These however were not in corporeal shapes and only the heavenly Princess perceived their presence.

Having arrived at the temple–gate, the most blessed Mother was filled with new exalted sentiments of devotion. Joining the other women, she bowed and knelt to adore the Lord in spirit and in truth in his holy temple and She presented Herself before the exalted Majesty of God with his Son upon her arms.

Immediately She was immersed in an intellectual vision of the most holy Trinity and She heard a voice issuing from the eternal Father, saying: "This is my beloved Son, in whom I well pleased". Saint Joseph, the most fortunate of men, felt at the same time a new sweetness of the Holy Ghost, which filled him with joy and divine light.

The holy high–priest Simeon also entered temple at that time. Approaching the place where the Queen stood with the infant Jesus in her arms, he saw both Mother and Child enveloped in splendor and glory.

The prophetess Anne, who had come at the same hour, also saw Mary and her Infant surrounded by this wonderful light. In the joy of their spirit both of them approached the Queen of heaven, and the priest received the Infant Jesus from her arms upon his hands.

Raising up his eyes to heaven he offered Him up to the eternal Father, pronouncing at the same time these words so full of mysteries: "Now dost thou dismiss thy servant, O Lord, according to thy Word in peace. Because my eyes have seen thy salvation, which thou hast prepared before the face of all peoples: a light for the revelation of the gentiles, and the glory of thy people Israel".

It was as if He had said: "Now, Lord, thou wilt release me from the bondage of this mortal body and let me go free and in peace; for until now have I been detained in it by the hope of seeing thy promises fulfilled and by the desire of seeing thy Onlybegotten made man."

Most holy Mary and Saint Joseph heard this canticle of Simeon, wondering at the exalted revelation it contained. The Evangelist calls them in this place the parents of the divine Infant, for such they were in the estimation of the people who were present at this event. Simeon, addressing himself to the most holy Mother of the Infant Jesus, then added: "Behold this Child is set for the fall and for the resurrection of many in Israel, and for a sign which shall be contradicted. And thy own soul a sword shall pierce, that out of many hearts thoughts may be revealed." Thus saint Simeon; and being a priest he gave his blessing to the happy parents of the Child.

Then also the prophetess Anne acknowledged the incarnate Word, and full of the Holy Ghost, she spoke of the mysteries of the Messiah to many, who were expecting the redemption of Israel. By these two holy old people public testimony of the coming of the Redeemer was given to the world.

At the moment when the priest Simeon mentioned the sword and the sign of contradiction, which were prophetical of the passion and death of the Lord, the Child bowed its head. Thereby, and by many interior acts of obedience, Jesus ratified the prophecy of the priest and accepted it as the sentence of the eternal Father pronounced by his minister.

All this the loving Mother noticed and understood; She presently began to feel the sorrow predicted by Simeon and thus in advance was She wounded by the sword, of which She had thus been warned.

As in a mirror her spirit was made to see all the mysteries included in this prophecy; how her most holy Son was to be the stone of stumbling, the perdition of the unbelievers, and the salvation of the faithful; the fall of the synagogue and the establishment the Church among the heathens; She foresaw the triumph to be gained over the devils and over death, but also that a great price was to be paid for it, namely the frightful agony and death of the Cross. She

B4C8

foresaw the boundless opposition and contradiction, which the Lord Jesus was to sustain both personally and in his Church.

At the same time She also saw the glory and excellence of the predestined souls. Most holy Mary knew it all and in the joy and sorrow of her most pure soul, excited by the prophecies of Simeon and these hidden mysteries, She performed heroic acts of virtue. All these sayings and happenings were indelibly impressed upon her memory, and, of all that She understood and experienced, She forgot not the least iota.

At all times She looked upon her most holy Son with such a living sorrow, as we shall never be able to feel. The holy spouse Saint Joseph was by these prophecies also made to see many of the mysteries of the Redemption and of the labors and sufferings of Jesus.

But the Lord did not reveal them to him so copiously and openly as they were perceived and understood by his heavenly spouse; for in him these revelations were to serve a different purpose, and besides, Saint Joseph was not to be an eyewitness of them during his mortal life.

The ceremony of the presentation thus being over, the great Lady kissed the hand of the priest and again asked his blessing. The same She did also to Anne, her former teacher; for her dignity as Mother of God, the highest possible to angels or men, did not prevent Her from these acts of deepest humility. Then, in the company of Saint Joseph, her spouse, and of the fourteen thousand angels in procession, She returned with the divine Infant to her lodging. They remained for some days in Jerusalem, in order to satisfy their devotion and during that time She spoke a few times with the priest about the mysteries of the Redemption and of the prophecies above mentioned.

When the most holy Mary and glorious saint Joseph returned from the presentation of the Infant Jesus in the temple, they concluded to stay in Jerusalem for nine days in order to be able each day to visit the temple and repeat the offering of the sacred Victim, their divine Son, thus rendering fitting thanks for the immense blessing for which they had been singled out from among all men.

The heavenly Lady had a special veneration for this number in memory of the nine days, during which She had been prepared and adorned by God for the incarnation of the Word, and also in memory of the nine months, during which She had borne Jesus in her virginal womb. In honor of these events She wished make this novena with her divine Child, presenting Him that many times to the eternal Father as an acceptable offering for her lofty purposes. They began the devotions of the novena every day before the third hour, praying in the temple until nightfall.

As an answer to her petitions, He conceded to Her new and great privileges, among which was also this one, that, as long as the world should last, She should obtain all that She would ever ask for her clients; that the greatest sinners, if they availed themselves of her intercession, should find salvation; that in the new Church and law of the Gospel She should be the Cooperatrix and Teacher of salvation with Christ her most holy Son.

This was to be her privilege especially after his Ascension into heaven, when She should remain, as Queen of the universe, as the representative and instrument of the divine power on earth. Many other favors and mysteries the Most High confirmed upon the heavenly Mother in answer to her prayers.

In the course of these manifestations, on the fifth day of the novena after the presentation and purification, while the heavenly Lady was in the temple with the Infant on her arms, the Deity revealed Itself to Her, although not intuitively, and She was wholly raised and filled by the Spirit. It is true, that this had been done to Her before; but as God's power and treasures are infinite, He never gives so much as not to be able to give still more to the creatures.

In this abstractive vision the Most High visited anew his only Spouse, wishing to prepare Her for the labors, that were awaiting Her. Speaking to Her, He comforted Her saying: "My Spouse and my Dove, thy wishes and intentions are pleasing in my eyes and I delight in them always. But Thou canst not finish the nine days' devotion, which Thou hast begun, for I have in store for Thee other exercises of Thy love.

In order to save the life of thy Son and raise Him up, Thou must leave thy home and thy country; fly with Him and thy spouse Joseph into Egypt, where Thou art to remain until I shall ordain otherwise: for Herod is seeking the life of the Child. The journey is long, most laborious and most fatiguing; do thou suffer it all for my sake; for I am, and always will be, with Thee."

Any other faith and virtue might have been disturbed to see the powerful God flying from a miserable earthly being, and that He should do so in order to save his life, as if He, being both God and man, could be affected by the fear of death.

But the most prudent and obedient Mother advanced no objection or doubt: She was not in the least disturbed or moved by this unlooked for order. Answering, She said: "My Lord and Master, ...This only do I ask of thy immense goodness, that, overlooking my want of merit and gratitude, Thou permit not my Son and Lord to suffer, and that Thou turn all pains and labor upon me, who am obliged to suffer them."

The Lord referred Her to Saint Joseph, bidding Her to follow his directions in all things concerning the journey. Therewith She issued from her vision, which She had enjoyed without losing the use of her exterior senses and while holding in her arms the Infant Jesus.

On account of the incomparable love, which the Queen bore toward her most holy Son, her maternal and compassionate heart was somewhat harrowed at the thought of the labors which She foresaw in the vision impending upon the infant God. Shedding

B4C7

many tears, She left the temple to go to her lodging–place, without manifesting to her spouse the cause of her sorrow.

Saint Joseph therefore thought that She grieved on account of the prophecy of Simeon. As the most faithful Joseph loved Her so much, and as he was of a kind and solicitous disposition, he was troubled to see his Spouse so tearful and afflicted, and that She should not manifest to him the cause of this new affliction.

\This disturbance of his soul was one of the reasons why the holy angels spoke to him in sleep... For in the same night, while saint Joseph was asleep, the angel of the Lord appeared to him, and spoke to him as recorded by saint Matthew: "Arise, take the Child and its Mother and fly into Egypt; there shalt thou remain until I shall return to give thee other advice; for Herod is seeking after the Child in order to take away its life."

Immediately the holy spouse arose full of solicitude and sorrow, foreseeing also that of his most loving Spouse. Entering upon her retirement, he said: "My Lady, God wills that we should be afflicted; for his holy angel has announced to me the pleasure and the decree of the Almighty, that we arise and fly with the Child into Egypt, because Herod is seeking to take away its life. Encourage thyself, my Lady, to bear the labors of this journey and tell me what I can do for thy comfort, since I hold my life and being at the service of thy Child and of Thee."

"My husband and my master," answered the Queen, "if we have received from the hands of the Most High such great blessings of grace, it is meet that we joyfully accept temporal affliction. We bear with us the Creator of heaven and earth; if He has placed us so near to Him, what arms shall be able to harm us, even if it be the arm of Herod?

Wherever we carry with us all our Good, the highest treasure of heaven, our Lord, our guide and true light, there can be no desert;

B4C8

but He is our rest, our portion, and our country. All these goods we possess in having his company; let us proceed to fulfill his will."

Then most holy Mary and Joseph approached the crib where the Infant Jesus lay; and where He, not by chance, slept at that time. The heavenly Mother uncovered Him without awakening Him; then the heavenly Mother, falling upon her knees, awakened the sweetest Infant, and took Him in her arms. Jesus, in order to move Her to greater tenderness and in order to show Himself as true man, wept a little.

Yet He was soon again quieted; and when the most holy Mother and Saint Joseph asked his blessing He gave it them in visible manner. Gathering their poor clothing into the casket and loading it on the beast of burden which they had brought from Nazareth, departed shortly after midnight, and hastened without delay on their journey to Egypt.

THE FLIGHT TO EGYPT

Our heavenly Pilgrims left Jerusalem and entered upon their banishment while yet the silence and obscurity of night held sway. They were full of solicitude for the Pledge of heaven, which they carried with them into a strange and unknown land. Although faith and hope strengthened them, nevertheless the Lord afforded them occasion for anxiety.

Their love for the Infant Jesus would naturally excite in them anxiety and suffering on an occasion like this. They knew not what would happen during such a long journey, nor when it should end, nor how they would fare in Egypt, where they would be entire strangers, nor what comfort or convenience they would find there for raising the Child, nor even how they would be able to ward off great sufferings from Him on the way to Egypt.

Therefore the hearts of these holy Parents were filled with many misgivings and anxious thoughts when they parted with so much haste from their lodging–place; but their sorrow was much relieved when the ten thousand heavenly courtiers again appeared to them in human forms and in their former splendor and beauty, and when they again changed the night into the brightest day for the holy Pilgrims.

As they set forth from the portals of the city the holy angels humiliated themselves and adored the incarnate Word in the arms of the Virgin Mother. They also encouraged Her by again offering their homage and service, stating that it was the will of the Lord that they guide and accompany Her on the journey.

In this town of Gaza they remained two days, for Saint Joseph and the beast of burden which carried the Queen were worn out by the fatigue of the journey. From that place they sent back the servant of Saint Elisabeth, taking care to caution him not to tell any one of their whereabouts.

But God provided still more effectually against this danger; for He took away from this man all remembrance of what Saint Joseph had charged him to conceal, so that he retained only his message to saint Elisabeth. Most holy Mary expended the presents sent by Elisabeth in entertaining the poor; for She, who was Mother of the poor, could not bear to pass them by unassisted. Of the clothes sent to Her She made a cloak for the divine Infant, and one for Saint Joseph, to shelter Them from the discomforts of the season and of the journey. She also used other things in their possession for the comfort of her Child and of Saint Joseph.

The most prudent Virgin would not rely on miraculous assistance whenever She could provide for the daily needs by her own diligence and labor; for in these matters She desired to subject Herself to the natural order and depend upon her own efforts.

During the two days which they spent in that city the most pure Mary, in order to enrich it with great blessings, performed some wonderful deeds. She freed two sick persons from the danger of death and cured their ailments. She restored to another person, a crippled woman, the use of her limbs. In the souls of many, who met Her and conversed with Her, She caused divine effects of the knowledge of God and of a change of life.

All of them felt themselves moved to praise their Creator. But neither Mary nor Joseph spoke a word about their native country, nor of the destination or object of their journey; for if this information had been added to the public notice caused by their wonderful actions, the attention of Herod's agents might have been drawn toward them, and they might have found sufficient inducement to follow them after their departure.

On the third day after our Pilgrims had touched Gaza, they departed from that city for Egypt. Soon leaving the inhabited parts of Palestine, they entered the sandy deserts of Bersabe, which they were obliged to traverse for sixty leagues in order to arrive and take their abode in Heliopolis, the present Cairo in Egypt.

This journey through the desert consumed a number of days, for the distance they could travel each day was but short, not only on account of the laborious progress over the deep sand, but also on account of the hardships occasioned by the want of shelter. There were many incidents on their way through this solitude.

In order to understand how much Mary and Joseph and also the Infant Jesus suffered on their pilgrimage, it must be remembered that the Almighty permitted his Onlybegotten, with his most holy Mother and Saint Joseph, to suffer the inconveniences and hardships naturally connected with travel through this desert.

And although the heavenly Lady made no complaints, yet She was much afflicted, which was also true of her most faithful husband. For both of them suffered many personal inconveniences and discomforts, while the Mother, in addition thereto, was afflicted still more on account of the sufferings of her Son and of Saint Joseph; and the latter was deeply grieved not to be able by his diligence and care to ease the hardships of the Child and his Spouse.

During all this journey of sixty leagues through desert they had no other night–shelter than the sky and open air; moreover, it was in the time of winter, for journey took place in the month of February, only six days after the Purification.

In the first night on these sandy plains they rested at the foot of a small hill, this being the only protection they could find. The Queen of heaven with the Child in her arms seated herself on the earth, and with her husband She ate of the victuals brought with them from Gaza. The Empress of heaven also nursed the Infant Jesus at her breast and He on his part rejoiced his Mother and her husband by his contentment.

In order to furnish them with some kind of shelter against the open air; however narrow and humble it might be, Saint Joseph formed a sort of tent for the divine Word and most holy Mary by means of his cloak and some sticks. During that night the ten thousand angels who, full of marvel, assisted these earthly Pilgrims in visible human shapes, formed a guard around their King and Queen.

The great Lady perceived that her divine Son offered up to the eternal Father the hardships and labors both of Himself and of Mary and Joseph. In these prayers and in the other acts of his deified Soul, the Queen joined him for the greater part of the night. The divine Infant slept for a short time in her arms, while She continued wakeful and engaged in heavenly colloquies with the Most High and his angels. Saint Joseph slept upon the ground, resting his head upon the chest, which contained the clothing and other articles of their baggage.

On the next day they pursued their journey and their little store of fruit and bread was soon exhausted, that they began to suffer great want and to feel the hunger. Although Joseph was more deeply concerned, yet both of them felt this privation very much.

On one of the first days of their journey they partook of no sustenance until nine o'clock at night, not having any more even of the coarse and poor food which until then had sustained them in their hardships and labor.

As nature demanded some refreshment after the exertion and weariness of travel, and as there was no way of supplying their want by natural means, the heavenly Lady addressed Herself to the Most High in these words: "Eternal, great and powerful God, I give Thee thanks and bless Thee for thy magnificent bounty; and also that, without my merits, only on account of thy merciful condescension, Thou gavest me life and being and preservest me in it, though I am but dust and a useless creature. I have not made a proper return for all these benefits; therefore how can I ask for myself what I cannot repay? But, my Lord and Father; look upon thy Onlybegotten and grant me what is necessary to sustain my natural life and also that of my spouse, so that I may serve thy Majesty and thy Word made flesh for the salvation of men."

In order that the clamors of the sweetest Mother might proceed from yet greater tribulation, the Most High permitted the elements to afflict them more than at other times and in addition to the sufferings caused by their fatigue, destitution and hunger. For there arose a storm of wind and rain, which harassed and blinded them by its fury. This hardship grieved still more the tender–hearted and loving Mother on account of the delicate Child, which was not yet fifty days old.

Although She tried to cover and protect Him as much as possible, yet She could not prevent Him from feeling the inclemency of the weather, so that He shed tears and shivered from the cold in the same manner as other children are wont to do. Then the anxious Mother, making use of her power as Queen and Mistress of creatures, commanded the elements not to afflict their Creator, but to afford Him shelter and refreshment, and wreak their vengeance upon Her alone. And the wind immediately moderated and the storm abated, not daring to approach Mother and Child.

In return for this loving forethought, the Infant Jesus commanded his angels to assist his kindest Mother and to serve Her as a shield against the inclemency of the weather. They immediately complied and constructed a resplendent and beautiful globe round about and over their incarnate God, his Mother and her spouse. In this they were protected and defended more effectually than all the wealthy and powerful of the world in their palaces and rich garments. The same they did several times during the journey through the desert.

Nevertheless, they were in want of food, and they were destitute of other things unprovidable by their own mere human effort. But the Lord allowed them to fall into this need in order that, listening

B4C8

to the acceptable prayers of his Spouse, He might make provision also for this by the hands of the angels.

They brought them delicious bread and well–seasoned fruits, and moreover a most delicious drink; all of which they administered and served with their own hands. Then all of them together sang hymns of praise and thanksgiving to the Lord, who gives food to all creatures at opportune times, in order that the poor may eat and be filled whose eyes and hopes are fixed upon his kingly Providence and bounty. Of such a kind was the delicate feast, with which the Lord regaled his three exiled Wanderers in the desert of Bersabe.

So then the Infant Jesus, with his Mother and Saint Joseph, reached the inhabited country of Egypt. On entering the towns the divine Infant, in the arms of his Mother, raised his eyes and his hands to the Father asking for the salvation of these inhabitants held captive by Satan. And immediately He made use of his sovereign and divine power and drove the demons from the idols and hurled them to the infernal abyss. Like lightning flashed from the clouds they darted forth and descended to the lowermost caverns of hell and darkness.

At the same instant the idols crashed to the ground, the altars fell to pieces, and the temples crumbled to ruins. The cause of these marvelous effects were known to the heavenly Lady, for She united her prayers with those of her most holy Son as Co–operatrix of his salvation. Saint Joseph also knew this to be the work of the incarnate Word; and He praised and extolled Him in holy admiration. But the demons, although they felt the divine power, knew not whence this power proceeded.

The Egyptian people were astounded at these inexplicable happenings; although among the more learned, ever since the sojourn of Jeremias in Egypt, an ancient tradition was current that a King of the Jews would come and that the temples of the idols would be destroyed.

Yet of this prophecy the common people had no knowledge, nor did the learned know how it was to be fulfilled: and therefore the terror and confusion was spread among all of them, as was prophesied by Isaias. In this disturbance and fear, some, reflecting on these events, came to our great Lady and saint Joseph; and, in their curiosity at seeing these strangers in their midst, they also spoke to them about the ruin of their temples and their idols.

Making use of this occasion the Mother of wisdom began to undeceive these people, speaking to them of the true God and teaching them that He is the one and only Creator of heaven and earth, who is alone to be adored, and acknowledged as God; that all others are but false and deceitful gods, nothing more than the wood, or clay, or metal of which they are made, having neither eyes, nor ears, nor any power; that the same artisans that made them, and any other man, could destroy them at pleasure; since any man is more noble and powerful than they; that the oracles which they gave forth were answers of the lying and deceitful demons within them; and that the latter had no power, since there is but one true God.

The heavenly Lady was so sweet and kind in her words, and at the same time so full of life and force; her appearance was so charming, and all her interaction was accompanied by such salutary effects, that the rumor of the arrival of these strange Pilgrims quickly spread about in the different towns, and many people gathered to see and hear Them.

Moreover, the powerful prayers of the incarnate Word wrought a change of hearts, and the crumbling of the idols caused an incredible commotion among these people, instilling into their minds knowledge of the true God and sorrow for their sins without their knowing whence or through whom these blessings came to them. Jesus, Mary and Joseph pursued their way through many towns of Egypt, performing these and many other miracles driving out the demons not only from the idols, but out of many bodies possessed by them, curing many that were grievously and dangerously ill, enlightening the hearts by the doctrines of truth and eternal life.

By these temporal benefits and others, so effectual in moving the ignorant, earthly–minded people, many were drawn to listen to the instructions of Mary and Joseph concerning a good and salutary life.

They reached Heliopolis, where they took up their abode. Their holy guardian angels instructed the heavenly Queen and Saint Joseph, that They were to settle in this city. For, besides the ruin of the temples and idols, which, just as in other places, took place at their arrival here, the Lord had resolved to perform still other miracles for his glory and for the rescue of souls; and the inhabitants of this city were to see the Sun of justice and grace arise over them and shine upon them.

Following these orders, Saint Joseph sought to purchase for a suitable price some dwelling in the neighborhood; and the Lord ordained that he should find a poor and humble, yet serviceable house, at small distance from the city, just such as the Queen of heaven desired.

The most prudent Lady and her spouse, forsaken and destitute of all temporal help, accommodated themselves joyfully to the poverty of their little dwelling. Of the three rooms, which it contained, they assigned one to be the sanctuary or temple of the Infant Jesus under the tender care of the most pure Mother; there they placed the cradle and her bare couch, until, after some days, by the labor of the holy spouse, and through the kindness of some pious women, they could obtain wherewith to cover it. Another room was set aside for the sleeping place and oratory of Saint Joseph. The third served as a workshop for plying his trade.

In view of their great poverty, and of the great difficulty of sufficient employment as a carpenter, the great Lady resolved to assist him by the work of her hands to earn a livelihood. She immediately executed her resolve by seeking to obtain needlework through the intervention of the pious women, who, attracted by her modesty and sweetness, were beginning to have interactions with Her. As all that She attended to or busied Herself with was so perfect, the reputation of her skill soon spread about, so that She never was in want of employment whereby to eke out the slender means of livelihood for her Son, the true God and man.

In order to obtain the indispensable victuals and clothing, furnish the house ever so moderately, and pay the necessary expenses, it seemed to our Queen that She must employ all day in work and consume the night in attending to her spiritual exercises.

This She resolved upon, not for any motives of gain, or because She did not continue in her contemplations during the day; for this was her incessant occupation in the presence of the infant God. But some of the hours, which She was wont to spend in special exercises.

She wished to transfer to the night–time in order to be able to extend the hours of manual labor, not being minded to ask or expect God's miraculous assistance for anything which She could attain by greater diligence and additional labor on her own part.

The most prudent Queen asked the eternal Father to provide sustenance for her divine Son; but at the same time She continued to labor. Like one who does not trust in herself, or in her own efforts, She united prayer with her labors, in order to obtain the necessities of life like other men.

On account of the excessive heat prevailing in Egypt, and on account of many disorders rampant among the people, the distempers of the Egyptians were wide–spread and grievous. During the years of the stay of the Infant Jesus and his most holy Mother, pestilence devastated Heliopolis and other places. On this account, and on account of the report of their wonderful deeds, multitudes of people came to them from all parts of the country and returned home cured in body and soul.

B4C8

In order that the grace of the Lord might flow more abundantly, and in order that his kindest Mother might have assistance in her works of mercy, God, at the instance of the heavenly Mistress, ordained Saint Joseph as her helper in the teaching and healing of the infirm. For this purpose He was endowed with new light and power of healing.

The holy Mary began to make use of his assistance in the third year of their stay in Egypt; so that now he ordinarily taught and cured the men, while the blessed Lady attended to the women. Incredible was the fruit resulting from their labors in the souls of men for her uninterrupted beneficence and the gracious efficacy of her words drew all toward our Queen, and her modesty and holiness filled them with devoted love.

They offered her many presents and large possessions, anxious to see Her make use of them: but never did She receive anything for Herself, or reserve it for her own use; for they continued to provide for their wants by the labor of her hands and the earnings of Saint Joseph.

When at time the blessed Lady was offered some gift that seemed serviceable and proper for helping the needy and the poor, She would accept it for that purpose. Only with this understanding would She ever yield to the pious and affectionate importunities of devout persons; and even then She often made them a present in return of things made by her own hands.

From what I have related we can form some idea how great and how numerous were the miracles wrought by the holy Family during their seven years' stay in Egypt and Heliopolis; for it would be impossible to enumerate and describe all of them.

Their Return from Egypt

During one of the conversations of Mary with Joseph concerning the mysteries of the Lord, the Infant Jesus, having reached the age of one year, resolved to break the silence and speak in plain words to Joseph, who so faithfully fulfilled the duties of a foster–father. He had thus conversed with his heavenly Mother from the time of his Birth.

The two holy Spouses were speaking of the infinite being of God, of his goodness and excessive love, which induced Him to send his Onlybegotten Son as the Teacher and Savior of men, clothing Him in human form in order that He might converse with them and suffer the punishments of their depraved natures.

Saint Joseph was lost in wonder at the works of the Lord and inflamed by affectionate gratitude and exaltation of the Lord. Seizing upon this occasion the infant God, resting upon the arms of his Mother as upon the seat of wisdom, began to speak to saint Joseph in an intelligible voice, saying: "My father, I came from heaven upon this earth in order to be the light of the world, and in order to rescue it from darkness of sin; in order to seek and know my sheep as a good Shepherd, to give them nourishment of eternal life, teach them the way of heaven, open its gates, which had been closed by their sins. I desire that you both be children of the Light, which you have so close at hand."

These words of the Infant Jesus, being full of divine life, filled the heart of the patriarch Saint Joseph with new love, reverence and joy. He fell on his knees before the infant God with the profoundest humility and thanked Him for having called Him "father" by the very first word spoken to him.

He besought the Lord with many tears to enlighten him and enable him to fulfill entirely his most holy will, to teach him to be thankful for the incomparable benefits flowing from his generous hands. Although saint Joseph was not the natural, but the foster–father of Jesus, his love for Him exceeded by far all the love of parents for their children, since in him grace, or even natural love, was more powerful than others, yea than in all the parents together.

Hence the joy of his soul is to be measured by this love and appreciation of Saint Joseph as being the foster–father of the Infant Jesus. For he at the same time heard himself called the father of the Son of the eternal Father, and saw Him so beautiful in grace, while listening to such exalted wisdom and knowledge in the Child.

During the whole of this first year his sweetest Mother had wrapped the infant God in clothes and coverings usual with other children; for He did not wish to be distinguished in this from others, and He wished to bear witness to his true humanity and to his love for mortals, enduring this inconvenience otherwise not required of Him. His boundless love for mortals inflamed Her with loving gratitude toward the Lord and produced in her heroic acts of many virtues.

Seeing that the Child Jesus desired no footgear and only one garment, She said to Him: "My Son and my Lord, thy Mother has not the heart to allow Thee to go barefoot upon the ground at thy tender age; permit me, my Love, to provide some kind of covering to protect them. I also fear that the rough garment, which Thou askest of me, will wound thy tender body, if thou permit no linen to be worn beneath." "My Mother, I will permit a slight and ordinary covering for my feet until the time of my public preaching shall come, for this I must do barefooted. But I do not wish to wear linen, because it foments carnal pleasures, and is the causes of many vices in men. I wish to teach many by my example to renounce it for love and imitation of Me."

Immediately the great Queen set diligently about fulfilling the will of her most holy Son. Procuring some wool in its natural and uncolored state, She spun it very finely with her own hands and of it She wove a garment of one piece and without any seam, similar to knitted stuff, or rather like twilled cloth; for it was woven of twisted cords, not like smooth—woven goods. She wove it upon a small loom, by meshes, crocheting it of one seamless piece in a mysterious manner.

Two things were wonderful about it: that it was entirely even and uniform, without any folds, and that, at her request, the natural color was changed to a more suitable one, which was a mixture of brown and a most exquisite silver—gray, so that it could not be called either, appearing to be neither altogether brown, nor silvery, nor gray, but having a mixture of them all.

She also wove a pair of sandals of strong thread, like hempen shoes, with which She covered the feet of the infant God. Besides these She made a half tunic of linen, which was to serve as an undergarment.

From the time the Child Jesus was on his feet He commenced to retire and spent certain hours of the day in the oratory of his Mother. As the most prudent Mother was anxious to know his wishes in regard to her interactions with Him, the Lord responded to her mute appeal, saying: "My Mother, enter and remain with Me always in order that thou mayest imitate Me in my works for I wish that in thee be modeled and exhibited the high perfection which I desire to see accomplished in the souls. For if they had not resisted my first intentions, they would have been endowed with my most abundant and copious gifts; but since the human race has hindered this, I have chosen thee as the vessel of all perfection and of the treasures of my right hand, which the rest of the creatures have abused and lost. Observe me therefore in all my actions for the purpose of imitating Me."

Thus the heavenly Lady was installed anew as the Disciple of her most holy Son. Thenceforward passed such great and hidden mysteries between these Two, that not until the day of eternity will they be known. Many times the divine Child prostrated Himself on the ground, at others He was raised from the ground in the form of a cross, earnestly praying to the eternal Father for the salvation of mortals.

In all this his most loving Mother imitated Him. For to Her were manifest the interior operations of his most holy soul, just as well as the exterior movements of his body.

The great Lady did not always enjoy visions of the Divinity; but always the sight of the most holy humanity and soul of her Son with all their activities. In a special manner She was witness of the effects of the hypostatic and beatific union of the humanity with the Divinity.

Although She did not always see this glory and this union substantially; yet She perceived the interior acts by which his humanity reverenced, loved and magnified the Divinity to which it was united; and this privilege was reserved solely to most holy Mary.

On these occasions it often happened that the Child Jesus in the presence of his most holy Mother wept and perspired blood, for this happened many times before his agony in the garden. Then the blessed Lady would wipe his face interiorly perceiving and knowing the cause of this agony, namely the loss of the foreknown and of those who would be ungrateful for the benefits of their Creator and Redeemer and in whom the works of the infinite power and goodness of the Lord would be wasted. At other times the blessed Mother would find Him refulgent with heavenly light and surrounded by angels that sang sweet hymns of praise; and She was made aware, that the heavenly Father was pleased in his beloved and Onlybegotten Son.

All these wonders commenced from the time when at the age of one year He began to walk, witnessed only by his most holy Mother, whose heart was to be the treasure–house of his wonders. The works of love, praise and worshipful gratitude, his petitions for the human race, all exceed my ability to describe. I must refer the understanding of it to the faith and piety of the Christians.

Many of the children of Heliopolis gathered around the Child Jesus, as it is natural with children of similar age and condition. Since they were free from great malice and were not given to inquire, whether He was more than man, but freely admitted the heavenly light, the Master of truth welcomed them as far as was befitting. He instilled into them the knowledge of God and of the virtues; He taught and catechised them in the way of eternal life, even more abundantly than the adults.

As his words were full of life and strength. He won their hearts and impressed his truths so deeply upon them, that all those, who had this good fortune, afterwards became great and saintly men; for in the course of time they ripened in themselves the fruit of this heavenly seed sown so early into their souls.

The Child Jesus reached the end of his seventh year while in Egypt, which was also the term set by the eternal Wisdom for his mysterious sojourn in that land. In order that the prophecies might he fulfilled, it was necessary that He return to Nazareth. This decree the eternal Father intimated to his most holy Son on a certain day in the presence of his holy Mother and while She was with Him in prayer. She saw it mirrored in his deified soul and She saw how He submitted to it in obedience to the Father.

Therein the great Lady joined Him, although they had already become better acquainted and habituated to their present abode than to their own native city of Nazareth. Neither the Mother nor the Son made known to Saint Joseph this new decree of heaven. But in that very night the angel of the Lord spoke to him in his sleep, as Matthew relates, and bade him take the Child and its Mother and return to the land of Israel for Herod and those who with him had sought the life of the Child, were dead.

So much value does the Almighty set on the proper order in created things, that, though Jesus was the true God and his Mother so highly exalted above saint Joseph in sanctity, He did not permit the arrangements of this journey to proceed from his Son nor from his Mother, but from saint Joseph, who was the head of this Family.

God intended to teach all mortals, that He wishes all things to be governed by the natural order set up by his Providence; and that the inferiors and subjects of the mystical body of the Church, even though they may excel in virtue and in certain other respects, must obey and submit to their superiors and prelates in the visible order.

They departed for Palestine in the company of angels as on their way thence. The great Queen sat on the ass with the divine Child on her lap and Saint Joseph walked afoot, closely following the Son and Mother. On account of the loss of such great Benefactors their acquaintances and friends were very sorrowful at the news of their departure; with incredible weeping and sighing they saw Them leave, knowing and loudly complaining that they were now losing all their consolation and refuge in their necessities. If the divine power had not interfered, the holy Family would have found great difficulty in leaving Heliopolis; for its inhabitants began to feel the night of their miseries secretly setting upon their hearts at the parting of the Sun, which had dispersed and brightened its darkness.

In traversing the inhabited country they passed through some towns of Egypt, where They scattered their graces and blessings. The news of their passage spreading about, all the sick, the afflicted and disconsolate gathered to seek Them out, and they found themselves relieved in body and soul. Many of the sick were cured, many demons were expelled without their knowing who it was that thus hurled them back to hell. Yet they felt the divine power, which compelled them and wrought such blessings among men.

They reached Nazareth, their home, for the Child was to be called a Nazarene. They found their former humble house in charge of the devout cousin of saint Joseph, who had offered to serve him while our Queen was absent in the house of Elisabeth.

Before They had left Judea for Egypt, Saint Joseph had written to this woman, asking her to take care of the house and what it contained. They found it all in good condition and his cousin received Them with great joy on account of her love for the great Queen, though at the same time she did not know of her dignity.

The heavenly Lady entered with her Son and Saint Joseph, and immediately she prostrated herself in adoration of the Lord and in thanksgiving for having led them, safe from the cruelty of Herod, to this retreat, and preserved them in the dangers of their banishment and their long and arduous journeys. Above all did she render thanks for having returned in company with her Son, now grown both in years and in grace and virtue.

Taking counsel with her divine Child She proceeded to set up a rule of life and regulate her pious practices; not that She had failed to observe a rule of life on her journey; for the most prudent Lady, in imitation of her Son, had always observed the most perfect order according to circumstances. But being now peacefully settled in her home She wished to include many exercises, which on the journey were impossible.

Her greatest solicitude was always to cooperate with her most holy Son for the salvation of souls which was the work most urgently enjoined upon her by the eternal Father. Toward this most high end our Queen directed all her practices in union with the Redeemer, and this was their constant occupation.

The holy Joseph also ordered his occupations and his work so as most worthily to earn sustenance for the divine Child and his Mother as well as for himself. That which in other sons of Adam is considered a punishment and a hardship was to this holy Patriarch a great happiness. For while others were condemned to sustain their natural life by the labor of their hands in the sweat of their brows, saint Joseph was blessed and consoled beyond measure to know, that he had been chosen by his labor and sweat to support God himself and his Mother, to whom belonged heaven and earth and all that they contain.

Chapter 5

JESUS IN THE TEMPLE

Jesus, Mary and Joseph settled in Nazareth and changed their poor and humble dwelling into a heaven. In order to describe the mysteries and sacraments which passed between the divine Child and his purest Mother before his twelfth year and later on, until his public preaching, many chapters and many books would be required; and in them all, I would be able to relate but the smallest part in view of the vastness of the subject. Even with the light given me by this great Lady I can speak of only a few incidents and must leave the greater part unsaid.

Upon the request of the loving Mother Saint Joseph had made a couch, which she covered with a single blanket and upon which the Child Jesus rested and took his sleep; for from the time in which He had left the cradle, when they were yet in Egypt, He would not accept of any other bed or of more covering.

Although He did not stretch Himself out on this couch, nor even always made use of it, He sometimes reclined in a sitting posture upon it, resting upon a poor pillow made of wool by the same Lady. When She spoke of preparing for him a better resting–place, her most holy Son answered, that the only couch upon which He was to be stretched out, was that of his Cross, in order to teach men by his example, that no one can enter eternal rest by things beloved of Babylon and that to suffer is our true relief in mortal life. Thenceforward the heavenly Lady imitated him in this manner of taking rest with new earnestness and attention.

Some days after our Queen and Lady with her most holy Son and Saint Joseph had settled in Nazareth, the time of the year in which the Jews were obliged to present themselves before the Lord in the temple of Jerusalem, was at hand. This commandment obliged the Jews to this duty three times each year, as can be seen in Exodus and Deuteronomy. But it obliged only the men, not the women; therefore the women could go or not, according to their devotion; for it was neither commanded nor prohibited to them.

The heavenly Lady and her spouse conferred with each other as to what they should do in this regard. The holy husband much desired the company of the great Queen, his wife, and of her most holy Son; for he wished to offer Him anew to the eternal Father in the temple. The most pure Mother also was drawn by her piety to worship the Lord in the temple; but as in things of that kind She did not permit Herself to decide without the counsel and direction of the incarnate Word, her Teacher, She asked his advice upon this matter.

They finally arranged that two times a year Saint Joseph was to go to Jerusalem by himself, while on the third occasion they would go together. The Israelites visited the temple on the feast of the Tabernacles, the feast of the Weeks, or Pentecost, and the feast of the unleavened Breads or the Pasch of the preparation. To this latter the sweetest Jesus, most pure Mary, and Joseph went up together. It lasted seven days. For the other solemnities Saint Joseph went alone, leaving the Child and the Mother at home.

Mary and Joseph repeated their visit to the temple at the feast of the unleavened Bread every year. When the divine Child was twelve years old and when it was time to allow the splendors his inaccessible and divine light to shine forth, they went to the temple for this feast.

This festival of the unleavened Bread lasted seven days, according to the command of the divine law; and the more solemn days were the first and the last. On this account heavenly Pilgrims remained in Jerusalem during the whole week, spending their time in acts of worship and devotion as the rest of the Jews, although on account the sacraments connected with each of Them their worship and devotion was entirely different and greatly above that of the others. The blessed Mother and holy Joseph received during these days favors and blessings beyond the conception of the human mind.

Having thus spent all the seven days of the feast. They betook themselves on their way home to Nazareth. When his parents departed from Jerusalem and were pursuing their way homeward, the Child Jesus withdrew from them without their knowledge. For this purpose the Lord availed Himself of the separation of the men and women, which had become customary among the pilgrims for reasons of decency, as well as for greater recollection during their return homeward.

The children which accompanied their parents were taken in charge promiscuously either by the men or the women, since their company with either was a matter of indifference. Thus it happened that Saint Joseph could easily suppose that the Child Jesus had remained with his most holy Mother, with whom He generally remained. The thought that She would go without Him was far from his mind, since the heavenly Queen loved and delighted in Him more than any other creature human or angelic.

The great Lady did not have so many reasons for supposing that her most holy Son was in the company of Saint Joseph: but the Lord himself so diverted her thoughts by holy and divine contemplations, that She did not notice his absence at first. When afterwards She became aware of her not being accompanied by her sweetest and beloved Son, She supposed that the blessed Joseph had taken Him along and that the Lord accompanied his foster–father for his consolation.

Thus assured, holy Mary and Joseph pursued their home journey for an entire day, as saint Luke tells us. As the pilgrims proceeded onwards they gradually thinned out, each taking his own direction and joining again with his wife or family. The most holy Mary and Saint Joseph found themselves at length in the place where they had agreed to meet on the first evening after leaving Jerusalem.

When the great Lady saw that the Child was not with Saint Joseph and when the holy Patriarch found that He was not with his Mother, the two were struck dumb with amazement and surprise for quite a while. Both, governed in their judgment by their most profound humility, felt overwhelmed with self—reproach at their remissness in watching over their most holy Son and thus blamed themselves for his absence; for neither of them had any suspicion of the mysterious manner in which He had been able to elude their vigilance.

After a time they recovered somewhat from their astonishment and with deepest sorrow took counsel with each other as to what was to be done. The loving Mother said to Saint Joseph: "My Spouse and my master, my heart cannot rest, unless we return with all haste to Jerusalem in order to seek my most holy Son." This they proceeded to do, beginning their search among their relations and friends, of whom, however, none could give them any information or any comfort in their sorrow; on the contrary their answers only increased their anxiety, since none of them had so much as seen their Son since their departure from Jerusalem.

Thus this sincerest Dove persevered in her tears and groans without cessation or rest, without sleeping or eating anything for three whole days. Although the thousand angels accompanied Her in corporeal forms and witnessed her affliction and sorrow, yet they gave Her no clue to find her lost Child.

On the third day the great Queen resolved to seek Him in the desert where Saint John was. She began to believe more firmly, that her most holy Son was with Saint John. When She was about to execute her resolve and was on the point of departing for the desert, the holy angels detained Her, urging Her not to undertake the journey, since the divine Word was not there.

She wanted also to go to Bethlehem, in the hope of finding Him in the cave of the Nativity; but this the holy angels likewise prevented, telling Her that He was not so far off. Although the blessed Mother heard these answers and well perceived that the holy angels knew the whereabouts of the Child Jesus, She was so considerate and reserved in her humility and prudence, that She gave no response, nor asked where She could find Him; for She understood that they withheld this information by command of the Lord. With such magnanimous reverence did the Queen of the angels treat the sacraments of the Most High and of his ministers and ambassadors. This was one of the occasions in which the greatness of her queenly and magnanimous heart was made manifest.

Not all the sorrows suffered by all the martyrs ever reached the height of the sorrows of most holy Mary in this trial; nor will the patience, resignation and tolerance of this Lady ever be equalled, nor can they; for the loss of Jesus was greater to Her than the loss of anything created, while her love and appreciation of Him exceeded all that can be conceived by any other creature.

Since She did not know the cause of the loss, her anxiety was beyond all measure. Moreover, during these three days the Lord left Her to her natural resources of nature and of grace, deprived of special privileges and favors; for, with the exception of the company and companionship of the angels, He suspended all the other consolations and blessings so constantly vouchsafed to her most holy soul. From all this we can surmise what sorrow filled the loving heart of the heavenly Mother.

With this heavenly wisdom and with greatest diligence She sought Him for three successive days, roaming through the streets of the city, asking different persons and describing to the daughters of Jerusalem the marks of her Beloved, searching the byways and the open squares of the city. Some of the women asked Her what were the distinctive marks of her lost and only Son; and She answered in the words of the Spouse: "My Beloved is white and ruddy, chosen out of thousands."

One of the women, hearing Her thus describing Him, said: "This Child, with those same marks, came yesterday to my door to ask

B5C1

for alms, and I gave some to Him; and his grace and beauty have ravished my heart. And when I gave Him alms, I felt myself overcome by compassion to see a Child so gracious in poverty and want." These were the first news the sorrowful Mother heard of her Onlybegotten in Jerusalem. A little respited in her sorrow, She pursued her quest and met other persons, who spoke of Him in like manner.

Guided by this information She directed her steps to the hospital of the city, thinking that among the afflicted She would find the Spouse and the Originator of patient poverty among his own legitimate brethren and friends. Inquiring at that place, She was informed that a Child of that description had paid his visits to the inmates, leaving some alms and speaking words of much consolation to the afflicted.

The report of these doings of her Beloved caused sentiments of sweetest and most tender affection in the heart of the heavenly Lady, which She sent forth from her inmost heart as messengers to her lost and absent Son. Then the thought struck Her, that, since He was not with the poor, He no doubt tarried in the temple, as in the house of God and of prayer.

The holy angels encouraged Her and said: "Our Queen and Lady, the hour of thy consolation is at hand: soon wilt Thou see the Light of thy eyes; hasten thy footsteps and go to the temple." The glorious patriarch Saint Joseph at this moment again met his Spouse, for, in order to increase their chance of finding the divine Child, they had separated in different directions. By another angel he had now been likewise ordered to proceed to the temple.

During all these three days he had suffered unspeakable sorrow and affliction, hastening from one place to another, sometimes without his heavenly Spouse, sometimes with Her. He was in serious danger of losing his life during this time, if the hand of the Lord had not strengthened Him and if the most prudent Lady had not consoled him and forced him to take some food and rest. His sincere and exquisite love for the divine Child made him so anxious and solicitous to find Him, that he would have allowed himself no time or care to take nourishment for the support of nature.

It was very near to the gate of the city, that the divine Child turned and hastened back through the streets. Foreseeing in his divine fore–knowledge all that was to happen, He offered it up to his eternal Father for the benefit of souls. He asked for alms during these three days in order to ennoble from that time on humble mendacity as the first–born of holy poverty.

He visited the hospitals of the poor, consoling them and giving them the alms which He had received; secretly He restored bodily health to some and spiritual health to many, enlightening them interiorly and leading them back to the way of salvation. On some of the benefactors, who gave Him alms, He performed these wonders with greater abundance of grace and light; thus fulfilling from that time on the promise, which He was afterwards to make to his Church; that he who gives to the just and to the prophet in the name of a prophet, shall receive the reward of the just.

Having thus busied Himself with these and other works of his Father, He betook Himself to the temple. On the day which the Evangelist mentions it happened that also the rabbis, who were the learned and the teachers of the temple, met in a certain part of the buildings in order to confer among themselves concerning some doubtful points of Holy Scriptures.

On this occasion the coming of the Messiah was discussed; for on account of the report of the wonderful events, which had spread about since the birth of the Baptist and the visit of the Kings of the east, the rumour of the coming of the Redeemer and of his being already in the world, though yet unknown, had gained ground among the Jews. They were all seated in their places filled with the sense of authority customary to those who are teachers and considered as learned.

B5C1

The Child Jesus came to the meeting of these distinguished men; and He that was the King of kings, and Lord of lords, the infinite Wisdom itself, and who corrects the wise, presented Himself before the teachers of this world as an humble disciple, giving them to understand that He had come to hear the discussion and inform Himself on the question treated of, namely: whether the Messiah was already come, or, if not, concerning the time in which He should come into the world.

Therefore the divine Child presented Himself to the disputants, manifesting the grace poured out over his lips. He stepped into their midst with exceeding majesty and grace, as one who would propose some doubt or solution. By his pleasing appearance He awakened in the hearts of these learned men a desire to hear Him attentively.

The scribes and learned men who heard Him were all dumbfounded. Convinced by his arguments they looked at each other and in great astonishment asked: "What miracle is this? And what prodigy of a boy! Whence has He come and who is the Child?" But though thus astonished, they did not recognize or suspect who it was, that thus taught and enlightened them concerning such an important truth.

During this time and before Jesus had finished his argument, his most holy Mother and Saint Joseph her most chaste spouse arrived, just in time to hear him advance his last arguments. When He had finished, all the teachers of the law arose with stupendous amazement. The heavenly Lady, absorbed in joy, approached her most loving Son and in the presence of the whole assembly, spoke to Him the words recorded by saint Luke: "Son, why hast Thou done so to us? Behold thy father and I have sought Thee sorrowing". This loving complaint the heavenly Mother uttered with equal reverence and affection, adoring Him as God and manifesting her maternal affliction. The Lord answered: "Why is it that you sought me? Did you not know that I must be about my Father's business?"

The Evangelist says that they did not understand the mystery of these words; for it was hidden at the time to most holy Mary and Saint Joseph. And for two reasons; on the one hand, the interior joy now reaping what they had sown in so much sorrow, and the visible presence of their precious Treasure, entirely filled the faculties of their souls; and on the other hand, the time for the full comprehension of what had just been treated of in this discussion had not yet arrived for them.

Moreover, for the most solicitous Queen there was another hindrance just at that time, and it was, that the veil, concealing the interior of her most holy Son had again intervened and was not removed until some time later. The learned men departed, commenting in their amazement upon the wonderful event, by which they had been privileged to hear the teaching of eternal Wisdom though they did not recognize it.

Being thus left almost alone, the blessed Mother, embracing Him with maternal affection, said to Him: "Permit my longing heart, my son, to give expression to its sorrow and pain; so that it may not die of grief as long as it can be of use to Thee. Do not cast me off from thy sight; but accept me as thy slave. If it was my negligence, which deprived me of thy presence, pardons me and makes me worthy of thy company, and do not punish me with thy absence." The divine Child received Her with signs of pleasure and offered Himself as her Teacher and Companion until the proper time should arrive. Thus was the dove–like and affectionate heart of the great Lady appeased, and they departed for Nazareth.

They arrived at Nazareth, where they occupied themselves. The evangelist Luke compendiously mentions all the mysteries in few words, saying the Child Jesus was subject to his parents, namely most holy Mary and Saint Joseph, and that his heavenly Mother noted and preserved within her heart all these events; and that Jesus advanced in wisdom, and age, and grace with God and men.

B5C1

Just now I wish only to mention, that the humility and obedience of our God and Master toward his parents were the admiration of the angels. But so was also the dignity and excellence of his most blessed Mother, who thus merited that the incarnate God should subject himself and resign Himself to her care; so much so, that She, with the assistance of saint Joseph, governed Him and disposed of Him as her own.

JESUS INSTRUCTS HIS MOTHER IN THE LAW OF GRACE

I have already said in former chapters, that our Lady was the first and specially privileged Disciple of her most holy Son, chosen among all creatures as the model of the new evangelical law and its Author, according to which He was to mould all the saints of the new evangelical law and judge of all the results of the Redemption.

In regard to Her the incarnate Word proceeded like a most skillful artist, who understands the art of painting and that pertains to it most thoroughly; who, throwing all powers into one chosen work, seeks to gain from it alone renown and fame as from the full exposition of his art. It is certain that all the holiness and glory of the saints was the result of the love and merits of Christ: but in comparison with the excellence of Mary they seem insignificant and as it were only rough sketches; for in all the saints are found defects.

But this living image of the Onlybegotten was free from all imperfections; and the first strokes of his pencil in Her were of greater beauty than the last touches in the highest angels and saints. She is the model for all the perfection of holiness and virtues of all his elect, and the utmost limit to which the love of Christ can proceed in mere creatures. No one received any grace or glory that most holy Mary could not receive, and She received all that others were incapable of receiving; and her most blessed Son gave to Her all that She could receive and that He could communicate.

The multitude and variety of the saints silently enhance the Artificer of their great sanctity, and the greatness of the highest is made more conspicuous by the beauty of the lowest: but all of them together are a glorification of most holy Mary. For by her incomparable holiness they are all surpassed and they all partake of so much the greater felicity as they imitate Her, whose holiness redounds over all. If the most pure Mary has reached the highest pinnacle in the ranks of the just, She may also on this very account be considered as the instrument or the motive power through which the saints themselves have reached their station.

As we must judge of her excellence (even if only from afar), by the labor which Christ the Lord applied for her formation, let us consider what labor He spent upon Her and how much upon the whole Church. To establish and to enrich his Church He deemed it sufficient to spend only three years in preaching, selecting the Apostles, teaching the people, and inculcating the evangelical law by his public life; and this was amply sufficient to accomplish the work enjoined upon Him by the eternal Father and to justify and sanctify all the true believers.

 But in order to stamp upon his most holy Mother the image of his holiness, He consumed not three years, but ten times three years, engaging in this work with all the power of his divine love, without ever ceasing hour after hour to add grace to grace, gifts to gifts, blessings to blessings, and holiness to holiness. And at the end of all this He still left Her in a state, in which He could continue to add excellence after his Ascension to his eternal Father as I will describe in the third part. Our reason is unbalanced, our words fail at the greatness of this incomparable Lady; for She is elect as the sun; and her effulgence cannot be borne by terrestrial eyes, nor comprehended by any earthly creatures.

Christ our Redeemer began to manifest his designs in regard to his heavenly Mother after they had come back from Egypt to Nazareth, as I have already mentioned; from that time on He continued to follow up his purpose in his quality as Teacher and as the divine Enlightener in all the mysteries of the Incarnation and Redemption.

After they returned from Jerusalem in his twelfth year, the great Queen had a vision of the Divinity, not an intuitive vision, but one consisting of intellectual images; one very exalted and full of the new influences of the Divinity and of the secrets of the Most High. She was especially enlightened in regard to the decrees of the divine Will concerning the law of grace, which was now established by the incarnate Word, and concerning the power, which was given to Him in the consistory of the most blessed Trinity.

At the same time She saw for this purpose the eternal Father consigned to His Son the seven—sealed book, of which Saint John speaks, and how none could be found either in heaven or on earth, who could unseal and open it, until the Lamb broke its seals by his Passion and Death and by his doctrines and merits. For in this figure God wished to intimate, that the secret of this book was nothing else than the new law of the Gospel and the Church founded upon it in this world.

Then the heavenly Queen saw in spirit that, by decree of the most blessed Trinity, She was to be the first one to read and understand this book; that her Onlybegotten was to open it for Her and manifest it all to Her, while She was to put it perfectly into practice; that She was the first one, who was to accompany the Word, and who was to occupy the first place next to Him on the way to heaven, which He had opened up for mortals and traced out in this book. In Her, as his true Mother, was to be deposited this New Testament. She saw how the Son of the eternal Father and of Herself accepted this decree with great pleasure; and how his sacred humanity obeyed it with ineffable joy on her account.

She issued from this ecstatic vision and betook Herself to her most holy Son, prostrating Herself at his feet and saying: "My Lord, my Light and my Teacher, behold thy unworthy Mother prepared for the fulfillment of thy wishes admit me anew as thy disciple and servant and make use of me as the instrument of thy wisdom and power. Execute in me thy pleasure and that of thy eternal Father."

Her most holy Son received Her with the majesty and authority of a divine Teacher and instructed Her in most exalted mysteries. In most persuasive and powerful words He explained to Her the profoundest meanings of the works enjoined upon Him by the eternal Father in regard to the Redemption of man, the founding of the Church and the establishment of the new evangelical law.

He declared and reaffirmed, that in the execution of these high and hidden mysteries She was to be his Companion and Coadjutrix, receiving and enjoying the first–fruits of grace; and that therefore She, the most pure Lady, was to follow Him in his labors until his death on the Cross with a magnanimous and well prepared heart in invincible and unhesitating constancy. He added heavenly instruction such as enabled Her to prepare for the reception of the whole evangelical Law, the understanding and practice of all its precepts and counsels in their highest perfection.

Other sacramental secrets concerning his works in this world the Child Jesus manifested to his most blessed Mother on this occasion. And the heavenly Lady met all his words and intentions with profound humility, obedience, reverence, thanksgiving and most ardent love.

THE CONTINUED PRAYERS OF JESUS AND MARY FOR MANKIND

The more our limited discourse seeks to make clear and extol the mysterious works of Christ, our Redeemer, and of his most holy Mother, the more evident it becomes, that mere human words are far from being able to compass the greatness of these sacraments; for, as Ecclesiastic says, they surpass all our words of praise.

Nor can we ever fathom or compass them, and there will always remain many greater secrets than those we have sought to explain. For those which we do explain are very insignificant, and we do not deserve to comprehend, nor to speak about the few, which we attempt to fathom.

Inadequate is the intellect of the highest seraphim to weigh and pierce the secrets that passed between Jesus and Mary during the years in which They lived together. Especially is this true of the years, of which I am now speaking, during which the Teacher of life instructed Her in everything that was to happen in the law of grace; namely, how much this new law was to accomplish in this the sixth age of the world, which includes these sixteen hundred and fifty–seven years and all the unknown future until the end of the World.

In all this the most blessed Lady was instructed in the school of her divine Son; for He foretold Her all by word of mouth, pointing out the time and place of each event, the kingdoms and provinces of their history during the existence of the Church.

All these hidden sacraments ordinarily transpired in that humble oratory of the Queen, where the greatest of all mysteries, the Incarnation of the divine Word in her virginal womb, had taken place. Though it was such a narrow and poorly furnished room, consisting merely of the bare and rude walls, yet it enclosed the grandeur of Him who is immense and shed forth all the majesty and sacredness, which since then is attached to the rich temples and innumerable sanctuaries of the world. In this holy of holies the Highpriest of the new Law ordinarily performed his prayers, which always concluded with fervent intercessions for men.

At these times also He spoke to his Virgin Mother about all the works of Redemption and communicated to Her the rich gifts and treasures of grace, which He had come to shower upon the children of light in the new Testament and in his holy Church. Many times did He beseech his eternal Father not to allow the sins and the ingratitude of men to hinder their Redemption. As Christ in his foreknowledge was always conscious of the sins of the human race and of the damnation of so many thankless souls, the thought of dying for them caused Him to sweat blood many times on these occasions.

Although the Evangelists, because they never intended to relate all the events of his life, mention this sweating of blood but once before his Passion, it is certain that this happened many times and in the presence of his most holy Mother; and has been intimated to me several times.

During prayer our blessed Master sometimes assumed a kneeling posture, sometimes He was prostrate in the form of a cross or at other times raised in the air in this same position which He loved so much. In the presence of his Mother He was wont to pray: "O most blessed Cross! When shall thy arms receive mine, when shall I rest on thee and when shall my arms, nailed to thine, be spread to welcome all sinners?" But as I came from heaven for no other purpose than to invite them to imitate Me and associate with Me, they are even now and forever open to embrace and enrich all men.

Come then, all ye that are blind, to the light. Come ye poor, to the treasures of my grace. Come, ye little ones, to the caresses and delights of your true Father. Come, ye afflicted and worn out ones, for I will relieve and refresh you. Come, ye just, since you are my possession and inheritance. Come all ye children of Adam, for I call upon you all. I am the way, the truth and the life, and I will deny nothing that you desire to receive.

My eternal Father, they are the works of thy hands, do not despise them; for I will offer Myself as a sacrifice on the Cross, in order to restore them to justice and freedom. If they be but willing I will lead them back to the bosom of thy elect and to their heavenly kingdom, where thy name shall be glorified."

At all these prayers the beloved Mother was present, and in her purest soul, as in the purest crystal, the light of the Onlybegotten was reflected. His interior and exterior prayers re–echoed in Her, causing Her to imitate his petitions and prayers in the same postures. When the great Lady for the first time saw Him sweat blood, her maternal heart was transfixed with sorrow and filled with astonishment at the effects caused in Christ, our Lord, by the sins and ingratitudes committed by men, foreseen by the Lord and known to Her.

In the anguish of her heart She turned to her fellow mortals and exclaimed: "O children of men! Little do ye understand how highly the Lord esteems his image and likeness in you! For, as the price of your salvation, He offers his own blood and deems it little to shed all of it for you. O could I but unite your wills with mine, in order that I might bring you to love and obey Him! Blessed by his right hand be the grateful and the just among men, who will be faithful children of their Father! Let those be filled with light and with the treasures of grace, who will respond to the ardent desires of my Lord in regard to their salvation."

" Would that I could be the insignificant slave of the children of Adam and thereby induce and assist them to put an end to their sins and their own damnation! Lord and Master! Life and light of my soul! Who can be so hard of heart and hostile to himself, that he should not feel himself urged on by thy blessings? Who can be so ungrateful and so unheedful, as to ignore thy most burning love? How can my heart bear with men, who, being so favored by thy bounty, are so coarse and rebellious?"

" O children of Adam! Turn your inhuman cruelty upon me. Afflict me and insult me as much as you will, only pay my beloved Lord the reverence and love which you owe to his endearments. Thou, my Son and Lord, art Light of light, Son of the eternal Father, as everlasting, as immense, as infinite as He, equal to Him in essence and attributes, being with Him one God and one supreme Majesty. Thou art chosen among thousands, beautiful above all the sons of men, holy, innocent and without defect of any kind. How then, eternal God, can mortals ignore the object of their most noble love? The Principle, which gives them existence? The End wherein consists their eternal true happiness? O that I could give my life in order that all might escape their error!"

Many other sentiments of burning love, far beyond the powers of my heart and tongue, this heavenly Lady uttered in her dove–like sincerity; and in this love, and in profoundest reverence, She wiped the sweat from the face of her sweetest Son. At other times She found Him in quite a different condition, shining with glory and transfigured as afterwards on mount Tabor, in the midst of a great multitude of angels, who adored Him and in the sweet harmony of their voices gave praise and thanksgiving to the Onlybegotten of the Father made man.

These celestial voices our blessed Lady heard and She joined hers with them. At other times this happened while He was not transfigured; for the divine will ordained that the sensitive part of the divine humanity of the Word should sometimes have this solace, while at other times it should enjoy also the transfiguring overflow of the glory of the soul into the body; yet this only at great intervals. But whenever the heavenly Mother found Him in this state and beheld his glorified body, or when She heard the hymns of the angels, She participated in these delights to such an extent, that, if her spirit had not been so strong, and if her Lord and Son had not fortified Her, She would have lost all her natural powers;

and even as it was, the holy angels had to support the failing strength of her body on those occasions.

Many times, when her divine Son was in one of these states of suffering or joy, and was praying to the eternal Father or, as it were, conferring with Him concerning the highest mysteries of the Redemption, the Person of the Father approved or conceded his petitions for the relief of men, or showed to the most holy humanity of Christ the secret decrees of predestination, reprobation or condemnation of some souls.

All this our blessed Lady heard, humbling Herself to the dust. With unequaled reverence and fear She adored the Omnipotent, and accompanied her Son in his prayers, petitions and thanksgivings, offered up to the eternal Father for mankind in praise of all his inscrutable judgments. Such secrets and mysteries the most prudent Virgin conferred in her heart, and stored them up in her memory, converting them into the material and nourishment of her fiery love.

None of these blessings and secret favors were in her unprofitable or fruitless. To all of them She corresponded according to the inmost desires of her Lord. In all of them She fulfilled the highest intentions of the Almighty, and all his works found due response from Her as far as was possible from a mere creature.

The Happy Death of Saint Joseph

Already eight years saint Joseph had been exercised by his infirmities and sufferings, and his noble soul been purified more and more each day in the crucible of affliction and of divine love. As the time passed his bodily strength gradually diminished and he approached the unavoidable end, in which the stipend of death is paid by all of us children of Adam.

In like manner it also increased the care and solicitude of his heavenly Spouse, our Queen, assisting and serving him with unbroken punctuality. Perceiving, in her exalted wisdom, that the day and hour for his departure from this cumbrous earth was very near, the loving Lady betook Herself to her blessed Son and said to Him:

"Lord God Most High, by thy divine light I see the hour approaching which thou hast decreed for the death of thy servant Joseph. I beseech Thee, by thy ancient mercies and by thy infinite bounty, to assist him in that hour by thy almighty power. Let his death be as precious in thy eyes, as the uprightness of his life was pleasing to Thee, so that he may depart in peace and in the hope of the eternal reward to be given to him on the day in which Thou shalt open the gates of heaven for all the faithful. Be mindful, my Son, of the humility and love of thy servant; of his exceeding great merits and virtues; of the fidelity and solicitude by which this just man has supported Thee and me, thy humble handmaid, in the sweat of his brow."

Our Savior answered: "My Mother, thy request is pleasing to me, and the merits of Joseph are acceptable in my eyes. I will now assist him and will assign him a place among the princes of my people, so high that he will be the admiration of the angels and will cause them and all men to break forth in highest praise. With none of the human born shall I do as with thy spouse."

The great Lady gave thanks to her sweetest Son for this promise; and, for nine days and nights before the death of Saint Joseph he uninterruptedly enjoyed the company and attendance of Mary or her divine Son. By command of the Lord the holy angels, three times on each of the nine days, furnished celestial music, mixing their hymns of praise with the benedictions of the sick man. Moreover, their humble but most precious dwelling was filled with the sweetest fragrance and odors so wonderful that they comforted not only Saint Joseph, but invigorated all the numerous persons who happened to come near the house.

One day before he died, being wholly inflamed with divine love on account of these blessings, he was wrapped in an ecstasy which lasted twenty–four hours. The Lord himself supplied Joseph the strength he needed for this miracle. In this ecstasy he saw clearly the divine Essence, and, manifested therein, all that he had believed by faith the incomprehensible Divinity, the mystery of the Incarnation and Redemption, the militant Church with all its Sacraments and mysteries.

The blessed Trinity commissioned and assigned him as the messenger of our Savior to the holy Patriarchs and Prophets of limbo; and commanded him to prepare them for their issuing forth from this bosom of Abraham to eternal rest and happiness. All this most holy Mary saw reflected in the soul of her divine Son together with all the other mysteries, just as they had been made known to her beloved spouse and She offered her sincerest thanks for all this to her Lord.

When Saint Joseph issued from this ecstasy his face shone with wonderful splendor and his soul was transformed by his vision of the essence of God. He asked his blessed Spouse to give him her benediction; but She requested her divine Son to bless him in her stead, which He did. Then the great Queen of humility, falling on her knees, besought Saint Joseph to bless Her, as being her husband and head.

Not without divine impulse the man of God fulfilled this request for the consolation of his most prudent Spouse. She kissed the hand with which he blessed Her and asked him to salute the just ones of limbo in her name. The most humble Joseph, sealing his life with an act of self–abasement, asked pardon of his heavenly Spouse for all his deficiencies in her service and love, and begged Her to grant him her assistance and intercession in this hour of passing away.

The holy man also rendered humblest thanks to her Son for all the blessings of his life and especially for those received during this sickness. The last words which Saint Joseph spoke to his Spouse were: "Blessed art Thou among all women and elect of all the creatures. Let angels and men praise Thee; let all the generations know, praise and exalt thy dignity; and may in Thee be known, adored and exalted the name of the Most High through all the coming ages; may He be eternally praised for having created Thee so pleasing in his eyes and in the sight of all the blessed spirits. I hope to enjoy thy sight in the heavenly fatherland."

Then this man of God, turning toward Christ, our Lord, in profoundest reverence, wished to kneel before Him. But the sweetest Jesus, coming near, received him in his arms, where, reclining his head upon them, Joseph said: "My highest Lord and God, Son of the eternal Father, Creator and Redeemer of the World, give thy blessing to thy servant and the works of thy hand; pardon, O most merciful King, the faults which I have committed in thy service and interactions. I extol and magnify Thee and render eternal and heartfelt thanks to Thee for having, in thy ineffable condescension, chosen me to be the spouse of thy true Mother; let thy greatness and glory be my thanksgiving for all eternity."

B5C4

The Redeemer of the world gave him his benediction, saying: "My father, rest in peace and in the grace of my eternal Father and mine; and to the Prophets and Saints, who await thee in limbo, bring the joyful news of the approach of their redemption." At these words of Jesus, and reclining in his arms, the most fortunate Saint Joseph expired and the Lord himself closed his eyes.

At the same time the multitude of the angels, who attended upon their King and Queen, intoned hymns of praise in loud and harmonious voices. By command of the Lord they carried his most holy soul to the gathering–place of the Patriarchs and Prophets, where it was immediately recognized by all as clothed in the splendors of incomparable grace, as the putative father and the intimate friend of the Redeemer, worthy of highest veneration. Conformably to the will and mandate of the Lord, his arrival spread inutterable joy in this countless gathering of the saints by the announcement of their speedy rescue.

It is necessary to mention that the long sickness and sufferings which preceded the death of Saint Joseph was not the sole cause and occasion of his passing away; for with all his infirmities he could have extended the term of his life, if to them he had not joined the fire of the intense love within his bosom. In order that his death might be more the triumph of his love than of the effects of original sin, the Lord suspended the special and miraculous assistance by which his natural forces were enabled to withstand the violence of his love during his lifetime.

As soon as this divine assistance was withdrawn, nature was overcome by his love and the bonds and chains, by which this most holy soul was detained in its mortal body, were at once dissolved and the separation of the soul from the body in which death consists took place. Love was then the real cause of the death of Saint Joseph. This was at the same time the greatest and most glorious of all his infirmities for in it death is but a sleep of the body and the beginning of real life.

The most fortunate of men, Saint Joseph reached an age of sixty years and a few days. For at the age of thirty–three he espoused the blessed Virgin lived with Her a little longer than twenty–seven years as her husband. When Saint Joseph died, She had completed the half of her forty–second year; for She was espoused to Saint Joseph at the age of fourteen. The twenty–seven years of her married life completed her forty–first year, to which must be added the time from the eighth of September until the death of her blessed spouse.

The Queen of heaven still remained in the same disposition of natural perfection as in her thirty–third year; for She showed no signs of decline, or of more advanced age, or of weakness, but always in that same most perfect state of womanhood. She felt the natural sorrow due to the death of Saint Joseph; for She loved him as her spouse, as a man pre–eminent in perfection and holiness, as her protector and benefactor.

MARY OFFERS HER SON AS VICTIM TO THE ETERNAL FATHER

The love of our great Queen for her divine Son must always remain the standard by which we must measure as well her actions as all her emotions either of joy or sorrow during her earthly life. But we cannot measure the greatness of her love itself, nor can the holy angels measure it, except by the love which they see in God by the intuitive vision. All that can ever be expressed by our inadequate words, similes and analogies, is but the least portion of what this heavenly furnace of love really contained. For She loved Jesus as the Son of the eternal Father, equal to Him in essence and in all the divine attributes and perfections.

She loved Him as her own natural Son, Son to Her in as far as He was man, formed of her own flesh and blood; She loved Him because as man He was the Saint of saints and the meritorious cause of all other holiness. He was the most beautiful among the sons of men.

He was the most dutiful Son of his Mother, her most magnificent Benefactor; since it was He, that by his sonship, had raised Her to the highest dignity possible among creatures. He had exalted Her among all and above all by the treasures of his Divinity and by conferring upon Her the dominion over all creation together with favors, blessings and graces, such as were never to be conferred upon any other being.

These motives and foundations of her love were established and as it were, all comprehended in the wisdom of the heavenly Lady, together with many others, which only her exalted knowledge could appreciate. In her heart there was no hindrance of love, since it was the most innocent and pure; She was not ungrateful, because her profoundest humility urged Her to a most faithful correspondence; She was not remiss, because in Her the most abundant grace wrought with all its efficacy; She was not slow or careless since She was filled with most zealous and diligent fervor ; not forgetful, since her most faithful memory was constantly fixed upon the blessings received and upon the reasons and the precepts of deepest love.

She moved in the sphere of the divine love itself, since She remained in his visible presence and attended the school of divine love of her Son, copying his works and his doings in his very company. Nothing was wanting to this peerless One among lovers for entertaining love without limitations of measure or manner.

This most beautiful Moon then being at its fullness, and looking into this Sun of justice just as it had risen like a divine aurora from height to height and reached the noontide splendor of the most clear light of grace; this Moon, Mary, detached from all material creatures and entirely transformed by the light of this Sun, having experienced on her part all the effects of his reciprocal love, favors and gifts, in the height of her blessedness, at a time when the loss of all these blessings in her Son made it most arduous, heard the voice of the eternal Father, calling Her as once He called upon her prototype, Abraham, and demanding the deposit of all her love and hope, her beloved Isaac.

The most prudent Mother was not unaware, the time of her sacrifice was approaching; for her sweetest Son had already entered the thirtieth year of his life and the time and place for satisfying the debt He had assumed was at hand. But in the full possession of the Treasure, which represented all her happiness, Mary was still considering its loss as far off, not having as yet had its experience.

The hour therefore drawing near, She was wrapt in a most exalted vision and felt that She was being called and placed in the presence of the throne of the most blessed Trinity. From it issued a voice of wonderful power saying to Her: "Mary, my Daughter and Spouse, offer to Me thy onlybegotten Son in sacrifice."

By the living power of these words came to Her the light and intelligence of the Almighty's will, and in it the most blessed Mother understood the decree of the Redemption of man through the Passion and Death of her most holy Son, together with all that from now on would happen in the preaching and public life of the Savior. As this knowledge was renewed and perfected in Her, She felt her soul overpowered by sentiments of subjection, humility, love of God and man, compassion and tenderest Sorrow for all that her Son was to suffer.

But with an undismayed and magnanimous heart She gave answer to the Most High: "Eternal King, all that has being outside of Thee exists solely for thy mercy and greatness, and Thou art undiminished Lord of all. How then dost Thou command me to sacrifice and deliver over to thy will the Son, whom thy condescension has given me? He is thine, eternal Father, since from all eternity before the morning star Thou hast engendered Him, and Thou begettest Him and shalt beget Him through all the eternities and if I have clothed Him in the form of servant in my womb and from my own blood, and if I have nourished his humanity at my breast and ministered to it as a Mother: this most holy humanity is also thy property, and so am I, since I have received from Thee all that I am and that I could give Him."

" What then can I offer to Thee, that is not more thine than mine? I confess, most high King, that thy magnificence and beneficence are so liberal in heaping upon thy creatures thy infinite treasures, that in order to bind Thyself to them Thou wishest to receive from them as a free gift, even thy own onlybegotten Son, Him whom Thou begettest from thy own substance and from the light of thy Divinity"

"With Him came to me all blessings together and from his hands I received immense gifts and graces; He is the Virtue of my virtue, the Substance of my spirit, Life of my soul and Soul of my life, the Sustenance of all my joy of living. It would be a sweet sacrifice, indeed, to yield Him up to Thee who alone knowest his value; but to yield Him for the satisfaction of thy justice into the hands of his cruel enemies the cost of his life, more precious than all the works of creation; this indeed, most high Lord, is a great sacrifice which Thou askest of his Mother."

"However let not my will but thine be done. Let the freedom of the human race be thus bought; let thy justice and equity be satisfied; let thy infinite love become manifest; let thy name be known and magnified before all creatures. I deliver Him over into thy hands before all creatures. I deliver over into thy hands my beloved Isaac, that He may be truly sacrificed; I offer my Son, the Fruit of my womb, in order that, according to the unchangeable decree of thy Will, He may pay the debt contracted not by his fault, but by the children of Adam, and in order that in his Death He may fulfill all that thy holy Prophets, inspired by Thee, have written and foretold."

This sacrifice with all that pertained to it, was the greatest and the most acceptable that ever had been made to the eternal Father since the creation of the world, or ever will be made to the end, outside of that made by his own Son, the Redeemer; and hers was most intimately connected with and like to that, which He offered.

If the greatest charity consists in offering one's life for the beloved, without a doubt most holy Mary far surpassed this highest degree of love toward men, as She loved Her Son much more than her own life. For in order to preserve the life of her Son, She would have given the lives of all men, if She had possessed them, yea and countless more.

Among men there is no measure by which to estimate the love of that heavenly Lady, and it can be estimated only by the love of the eternal Father for his Son. As Christ says to Nikodemus: so God loved the world, that He gave his only Son in order that none of those who believed in him might perish; so this might also be said in its degree of the love of the Mother of mercy and in the same way do we owe to Her proportionately our salvation.

For She also loved us so much, that She gave her only Son for our salvation; and if She had not given it in this manner, when it was asked of Her by the eternal Father on this occasion, the salvation of men could not have been executed by this same decree, since this decree was to be fulfilled on condition, that the Mother's will should coincide with that of the eternal Father. Such is the obligation which the children of Adam owe to most holy Mary.

Having accepted the offering of the great Lady, it was fitting that the most Blessed Trinity should reward and immediately pay Her by some favor, which would comfort Her in her sorrow and manifest more clearly the will of the eternal Father and the reasons for his command.

Therefore the heavenly Lady, still in the same vision and raised to a more exalted ecstasy, in which She was prepared and enlightened in the manner elsewhere described; the Divinity manifested Itself to Her by an intuitive and direct vision. In this vision, by the clear light of the essence of God, She comprehended the inclination of the infinite Good to communicate his fathomless treasures to the rational creatures by means of the works of the incarnate Word, and She saw the glory, that would result from these wonders to the name of he Most High.

Filled with jubilation of her soul at the prospect of all these sacramental mysteries, the heavenly Mother renewed the offering of her divine Son to the Father; and God comforted Her with the life–giving bread of heavenly understanding, in order that She might with invincible fortitude assist the incarnate Word in the work of Redemption as Coadjutrix and Helper, according to the disposition of infinite Wisdom and according as it really happened afterwards in the rest of her life.

Then most holy Mary issued forth from this exalted rapture. But by its effects and the strength imparted through it, She was now prepared to separate from her divine Son, who had already resolved to enter upon his fast in the desert in view of receiving his Baptism.

He therefore called his Mother and, speaking to Her with the tokens of sweetest love and compassion, He said: "My Mother, my existence as man I derive entirely from thy substance and blood, of which I have taken the form of a servant in thy virginal womb. Thou also hast nursed Me at thy breast and taken care of Me by thy labors and sweat. For this reason I account Me more thine own and as thy Son, than any other ever acknowledged, or more than any ever will acknowledge himself as the son of his mother."

"Give Me thy permission and consent toward accomplishing the will of my eternal Father. Already the time has arrived, in which I must leave thy sweet interaction and company and begin the work of the Redemption of man. The time of rest has come to an end and the hour of suffering for the rescue of the sons of Adam has arrived. But I wish to perform this work of my Father with thy assistance, and Thou art to be my companion and helper in preparing for my Passion and Death of the Cross. Although I must now leave Thee alone, my blessing shall remain with Thee, and my loving and powerful protection. I shall afterwards return to claim thy assistance and company in my labors; for I am to undergo them in the form of man, which Thou hast given Me."

With these words, while both Mother and Son were overflowing with abundant tears, the Lord placed his arms around the neck of the most tender Mother, yet Both maintaining a majestic composure such as befitted these Masters in the art of suffering.

The heavenly Lady fell at the feet of her divine Son and, with ineffable sorrow and reverence, answered: "My Lord and eternal God: Thou art indeed my Son and in Thee is fulfilled all the force of love, which I have received of Thee: my inmost soul is laid open to the eyes of thy divine wisdom. My life I would account but little, if I could thereby save thy own, or if I could die for Thee many times. But the will of the eternal Father and thy own must be fulfilled and I offer my own will as a sacrifice for this fulfillment."

B5C5

"Receive it, my Son and as Master of all my being; let it be an acceptable offering, and let thy divine protection never be wanting to me. It would be a much greater for me, not to be allowed to accompany Thee in thy labors and in thy Cross. May I merit this favor, my Son, and I ask it of Thee as thy true Mother in return for the human form, which Thou hast received of me."

The most loving Mother also besought Him to take along some food from the house, or that He allow it to be sent to where He was to go. But the Savior would not consent to anything of the sort, at the same enlightening his Mother of what was befitting for the occasion. They went together to the door of their house, where She again fell at his feet to ask his blessing and kiss his feet. The divine Master gave Her his benediction and then began his journey to the Jordan, issuing forth as the good Shepherd to seek his lost sheep and bring them back on his shoulders to the way of eternal life, from which they had been decayed by deceit.

When our Redeemer sought Saint John in order to be baptized, He had already entered his thirtieth year, although not much of it had yet passed; for He betook Himself directly to the banks of the Jordan, where Saint John was baptizing, and He received Baptism at his hands about thirty days after He had finished the twenty–ninth year of his life on the same day as is set aside for its celebration by the Church. I cannot worthily describe the sorrow of most holy Mary at his departure, nor the compassion of the Savior for Her.

All words and description are far too inadequate to manifest what passed in the heart of the Son and Mother. As this was to be part of their meritorious sufferings, it was not befitting that the natural effects of their mutual loves should be diminished. God permitted these effects to work in Them to their full extent, and as far as was compatible with the holiness of both Mother and Son.

Our divine Teacher found no relief in hastening his steps toward the goal of our Redemption, to which He was drawn by the force of his immense charity; nor was the thought of what He intended a lessening of the sense of loss, which She sustained at his departure; for all this only made more certain and more conspicuous the torments which He was to undergo.

O my dearest Love! Why does not our ingratitude and hardness of heart allow us to meet Thee with a responsive love? Why does not the perfect uselessness of man, and still more, his ingratitude, influence Thee to desist? Without us, O my eternal Goodness and Life, Thou wilt be just as happy without us as with us, just as infinite in perfections, holiness and glory; we can add nothing to that which Thou hast in Thyself, since Thou art entirely independent of creatures.

Why then, O my Love, dost Thou so anxiously seek us out and care for us? Why dost Thou, at the cost of thy Passion and the Cross, purchase our happiness? Without doubt, because thy incomprehensible love and goodness esteems it as thy own, and we alone insist in treating our own happiness as alien to Thee and to ourselves.

BAPTISM OF CHRIST—HIS FAST

Leaving his beloved Mother in the poor dwelling at Nazareth, our Redeemer, without accompaniment of any human creature, but altogether taken up with the exercise of his most ardent charity, pursued his journey to the Jordan, where, in the neighborhood of a town called Bethany, otherwise called Betharaba, on the farther side of the river, his Precursor was preaching and baptizing.

At the first steps from the house, our Redeemer, raising his eyes to the eternal Father, offered up to Him anew with an infinite love, whatever He was now about to begin for the salvation of mankind: his labors, sorrows, passion and death of the Cross, assumed for them in obedience to the eternal Will, the natural grief at parting as a true and loving Son from his Mother and at leaving her sweet company, which for twenty–nine years He had now enjoyed.

The Lord of all creation walked alone, without show and ostentation of human retinue. The supreme King of kings and Lord of lords was unknown and despised by his own vassals, vassals so much his own, that they owed their life and preservation entirely to Him. His royal outfit was nothing but the utmost poverty and destitution.

While proceeding on his way to the Jordan our Savior dispensed his ancient mercies by relieving the necessities of body and soul in many of those whom He encountered at different places. Yet this was always done in secret; for before his Baptism He gave no public token of his divine power and his exalted office.

Before appearing at the Jordan, He filled the heart of Saint John with new light and joy, which changed and elevated his soul. Perceiving these new workings of grace within himself, he reflected upon them full of wonder, saying: "What mystery is this? What presentiments of happiness? From the moment when I recognized the presence of my Lord in the womb of my mother, I have not felt such stirring of my soul as now! Is it possible that He is now happily come, or that the Savior of the world is now near me?"

Upon this enlightenment of the Baptist followed an intellectual vision, wherein he perceived with greater clearness the mystery of the hypostatic union of the person of the Word with the humanity and other mysteries of the Redemption. In the fullness of this intellectual light he gave the testimonies, which are recorded by Saint John in his Gospel and which occurred while the Lord was in the desert and afterwards, when He returned to the banks of the Jordan.

The Evangelist mentions one of these public testimonies as happening at the interpellation of the Jews, and the other when the Precursor exclaimed: "Behold the lamb of God," Although the Baptist had been instructed in great mysteries, when he was commanded to go forth to preach and baptize; yet all of them were manifested to him anew and with greater clearness and abundance on this occasion, and he was then notified that the Savior of the world was coming to be baptized.

The Lord then joined the multitude and asked Baptism of Saint John as one of the rest. The Baptist knew Him and, falling at his feet, hesitated, saying: "I have need of being baptized, and Thou, Lord, askest Baptism of me?" as is recorded by Saint Matthew. But the Savior answered: "Suffer it to be so now. For so it becometh us to fulfill all justice."

When Saint John had finished baptizing our Lord, the heavens opened and the Holy Ghost descended visibly in the form of a dove upon his head and the voice of his Father was heard: "This is my beloved Son, in whom I am well pleased". Many of the bystanders heard this voice, namely, those who were not worthy of such a wonderful favor; they also saw the Holy Ghost descending upon the Savior.

This was the most convincing proof which could ever be given of the Divinity of the Savior, as well on the part of the Father, who acknowledged Him his Son, as also in to the nature of the testimony given; for without any reserve was Christ manifested as the true God, equal to his eternal Father in substance and in perfection.

The Father himself wished to be the first to testify to the Divinity of Christ in order that by virtue of his testimony all the other witnesses might be ratified. There was also another mystery in this voice of the eternal Father: it was as it were a restoration of the honor or Son before the world and a recompense for his having thus humiliated Himself by receiving the Baptism of the remission of sins, though He was entirely free from fault and never could have upon Him the guilt of one who is holy, blameless, pure, set apart from sinners, exalted above the heavens.

Let us return now to the main subject of this history, namely, to the occupations of our great Queen and Lady. As soon as her most holy Son was baptized, although She knew by the divine light of his movements, the holy angels who had attended upon their Lord brought Her intelligence of all that had happened at the Jordan; they were those that carried the ensigns or shields of the passion of the Savior, as described in the first part.

To celebrate all these mysteries of Christ's Baptism and the public proclamation of his Divinity, the most prudent Mother composed new hymns and canticle of praise and of incomparable thanksgiving to the Most High and to the incarnate Word. All his actions of humility and prayers She imitated, exerting Herself by many acts of her own to accompany and follow Him in all of them.

With ardent charity She interceded for men, that they might profit by the sacrament of Baptism and that it might be administered all over the world. In addition to these prayers and hymns of thanksgiving, She asked the heavenly courtiers to help Her in magnifying her most holy Son for having thus humiliated Himself in receiving Baptism at the hands of one of his creatures.

Without delay Christ our Lord pursued his journey from the Jordan to the desert after his Baptism. Only his holy angels attended and accompanied Him, serving and worshipping Him, singing the divine praises on account of what He was now about to undertake for the salvation of mankind.

He came to the place chosen by Him for his fast: a desert spot among bare and beetling rocks, where there was also a cavern much concealed. Here He halted, choosing it for his habitation during the days of his fast. In deepest humility He prostrated Himself upon the ground which was always the prelude of his prayer and that of his most blessed Mother.

He praised the eternal Father and gave Him thanks for the works of his divine right hand and for having according to his pleasure afforded Him this retirement. In a suitable manner He thanked even this desert for accepting his presence and keeping Him hidden from the world during the time He was to spend there. He continued his prayers prostrate in the form of a cross, this was his most frequent occupation in the desert; for in this manner He often prayed to the eternal Father for the salvation of men.

After the Savior had begun his fast He persevered therein without eating anything for forty days, offering his fast to the eternal Father as a satisfaction for the disorder and sins to which men are drawn by the so vile and debasing, yet so common and even esteemed vice of gluttony. Just as our Lord overcame this vice so He also vanquished all the rest, and He made recompense to the eternal Judge and supreme Legislator for the injuries perpetrated through these vices by men.

According to the enlightenment vouchsafed to me, our Savior, in order to assume the office of Preacher and Teacher and to become our Mediator and Redeemer before the Father, thus vanquished all the vices of mortals and He satisfied the offenses committed through them by the exercises of the virtues contrary to them, just as He did in regard to gluttony. Although He continued this exercise during all his life with the most ardent charity, yet during his fast He directed in a special manner all his efforts toward this purpose.

A loving Father, whose sons have committed great crimes for which they are to endure the most horrible punishment, sacrifices all his possessions in order ward off their impending fate: so our most loving Father and Brother, Jesus Christ, wished to pay our debts.

In satisfaction for our pride He offered his profound humility; for our avarice, his voluntary poverty and total privation of all that was his; for our base and lustful inclinations, his penance and austerity; for our hastiness and vengeful anger, his meekness and charity toward his enemies; for our negligence and laziness, his ceaseless labors; for our deceitfulness and our envy, his candid and upright sincerity and truthfulness and the sweetness of his loving interactions.

In this manner He continued to appease the just Judge and solicited pardon for us disobedient and bastard children; and He not only obtained this pardon for them, but He merited for them new graces and favors, so that they might make themselves worthy of his company and of the vision of his Father and his own inheritance for all eternity. Though He could have obtained all this for us by the most insignificant of his works; yet He acted not like we. He demonstrated his love so abundantly, that our ingratitude and hardness of heart will have no excuse.

In order to keep informed of the doings of our Savior the most blessed Mary needed no other assistance than her continual visions and revelations; but in addition to all these, She made use of the service of her holy angels, whom She sent to her divine Son.

The Lord himself thus ordered it, in order that, by means of these faithful messengers, both He and She might rejoice in the sentiments and thoughts of their inmost hearts faithfully rehearsed by these celestial messengers; and thus They each heard the very same words as uttered by Each, although both Son and Mother already knew them in another way.

As soon as the great Lady understood that our Redeemer was on the way to the desert to fulfill his intention, She locked the doors of her dwelling, without letting any one know of her presence; and her retirement during the time of our Lord's fast was so complete, that her neighbors thought that She had left with her divine Son.

She entered into her oratory and remained there for forty days and nights without ever leaving it and without eating anything, just as She knew was done by her most holy Son. Both of them observed the same course of rigorous fasting. In all his prayers and exercises, his prostrations and genuflections She followed our Savior, not omitting any of them; moreover She performed them just at the same time; for, leaving aside all other occupations, She thus profited by the information obtained from the angels and by that other knowledge. Whether He was present or not, She knew the interior operations of the soul of Christ. All his bodily movements, which She had been wont to perceive with her own senses, She now knew by intellectual vision or through her holy angels.

While the Savior was in the desert He made every day three hundred genuflections, which also was done by our Queen Mary in her oratory; the other portion of her time She spent in composing hymns with the angels. Thus imitating Christ the Lord, the Holy Queen co-operated with Him in all his prayers and petitions, gaining the same victories over the vices, and on her part proportionately satisfying for them by her virtues and her exertions.

Thus it happened, that, while Christ as our Redeemer gained for us so many blessings and abundantly paid all our debts, most holy

Mary, as his Helper and our Mother, lent us her merciful intercession and became our Mediatrix to the fullest extent possible to a mere creature.

Christ the Savior permitted Lucifer to remain under the false impression, that He was a mere human creature though very holy and just; He wished to raise his courage and malice for the contest, for such is the effect of any advantages espied by the devil in his attacks upon the victims of his temptations.

Rousing his courage by his own arrogance, he began this battle in the wilderness with greater prowess and fierceness than the demons ever exhibited in their battles with men. Lucifer and his satellites strained all their power and malice, lashing themselves into fury against the superior strength which they soon found in Christ our Lord.

Yet our Savior tempered all his actions with divine wisdom and goodness, and in justice and equity concealed the secret source of his infinite power, exhibiting just so much as would suffice to prove Him to be a man so far advanced in holiness as to be able to gain these victories against the infernal foes.

In order to begin the battle as man, He directed a prayer to the eternal Father from his inmost soul, to which the intelligence of the demon could not penetrate, saying: "My Father and eternal God, I now enter into battle with the enemy in order to crush his power and humble his pride and his malice against my beloved souls. For thy glory, and for the benefit of souls I submit to the daring presumption of Lucifer. I wish thereby to crush his head in order that when mortals are attacked by his temptations without their fault, they may find his arrogance already broken. I beseech Thee, my Father, to remember my battle and victory in favor of mortals assailed by the common enemy. Strengthen their weakness through my triumph, let them obtain victory; let them be encouraged by my example, and let them learn from Me how to resist and overcome their enemies."

B5C6

During this battle the holy angels that attended upon Christ were hidden from the sight of Lucifer, in order that he might not begin to understand and suspect the divine power of our Savior. The holy spirits gave glory and praise to the Father and the Holy Ghost, who rejoiced in the works of the incarnate Word. The most blessed Virgin also from her oratory witnessed the battle.

The temptation of Christ began on the thirty–fifth day of his fast in the desert, and lasted to the end of the fast. Lucifer assumed the shape of a man and presented himself before the Lord as a stranger, who had never seen or known Him before. He clothed himself in refulgent light, like that of an angel, and conjecturing that the Lord after his long fast must be suffering great hunger, he said to Him: "If Thou be the Son of God, command that these stones be made bread.

By thus cunningly resting his advice on the supposition of his being the Son of God, the demon sought some information on what was giving him the greatest concern. But the Savior of the world answered only in these few words: "Not in bread alone doth man live, but in every word that proceedeth from mouth of God."

Lucifer found himself repulsed by the force or answer and by the hidden power which accompanied it; but he wished to show no weakness, nor desist from the contest. The Lord allowed the demon to continue in his temptation and for this purpose permitted Himself carried by the devil bodily to Jerusalem and to be placed on the pinnacle of the temple.

Here the Lord could see multitudes of people, though He himself was not seen by anybody. Lucifer tried to arouse in the Lord, the vain desire of casting Himself down from this high place, so that the crowds of men, seeing Him unhurt, might proclaim Him as a great and wonderful man of God.

Again using the words of the Holy Scriptures, he said to Him: "If Thou be the Son of God, cast Thyself down, for it is written that He hath given his angels charge over Thee, and in their hands they shall bear Thee up, lest perhaps Thou dash thy foot against a stone".

The heavenly spirits who accompanied their King, were full of wonder that He should permit Lucifer to carry Him bodily in his hands, solely for the benefit of mortal man. With the prince of darkness were gathered innumerable demons; for on that occasion hell was almost emptied of its inhabitants in order to furnish assistance for this enterprise.

The Author of wisdom answered: "It is also written: Thou shalt not tempt the Lord thy God". While giving these answers the Redeemer of the world exhibited a matchless meekness, profoundest humility, and a majesty so superior to all the attempts of Satan, as was of itself alone sufficient to crush Lucifer's arrogance and to cause him torments and confusion never felt before.

Being thus foiled, he attacked our Lord in still another way, seeking to rouse his ambition by offering Him some share in his dominion. For this purpose he took the Lord upon a high mount, from whence could be seen many lands, and said to Him with perfidious daring: "All these will I give to Thee, if falling down, Thou wilt adore me."

Exorbitant boldness, and more than insane madness and perfidy! Offering to the Lord what he did not possess, nor ever could give, since the earth, the stars, the kingdoms, principalities, riches and treasures, all belong to the Lord, and He alone can give or withhold them when it serves and pleases Him! Never can Lucifer give anything, even not of the things of the earth, and therefore all his promises are false.

The King and Lord answered with imperial majesty: "Begone, Satan, for it is written: The Lord thy God thou shalt adore, and Him only shalt thou serve." By this command, "Begone Satan," Christ the Redeemer took away from Lucifer permission further to tempt Him, and hurled him and all his legions into the deepest abysses of hell. There they found themselves entirely crushed and buried in its deepest caverns, unable to move for three days.

When they were permitted again to rise, seeing themselves thus vanquished and annihilated, they began to doubt whether He, who had so overwhelmed them, might not be the incarnate Son of God. In this doubt and uncertainty they remained, without ever being able to come to certain conviction until the death of the Savior. Lucifer was overcome by hellish wrath at his defeat and was almost consumed in his fury.

Our divine Conqueror Christ then sang hymns of praise and thanks to the eternal Father for having given Him this triumph over the common enemy of God and man; and amid the triumphal songs of a multitude of angels, He was borne back to the desert.

They carried Him in their hands, although He had not need of their help, since He could make use of his own divine power; but this service of the angels was due to Him in recompense for enduring the audacity of Lucifer in carrying to the pinnacle of the temple and to the mountaintop the sacred humanity of Christ, in which dwelt substantially and truly the Divinity itself. It would never have entered into the thoughts of man, that the Lord should give such a permission to Satan, if it had been made known to us in the Gospels.

Let us return to Nazareth, where, in her oratory, the Princess of the angels had witnessed the battles of her most holy Son. She had seen them all by the divine light and by the uninterrupted messages of her angels, who brought them back and forth between the Savior and the blessed Queen.

She repeated the same prayers as the Lord and at the same time! She entered likewise into the conflict with the dragon, though invisibly and spiritually. From her retreat She anathemized and crushed Lucifer and his followers co—operating in all the doings of Christ in our favor.

B5C6

When She perceived that the demon carried the Lord from place to place, She wept bitterly, because the malice of sin reduced the King of kings to such misusage. In honor of all the victories, which He gained over the devil, She composed hymns of praise to the Divinity and the most holy humanity of Christ, while the angels set them to music and were sent with them to congratulate Him for the blessings won for the human race. Christ on his part sent back the angels with words of sweet consolation and rejoicing on account of his triumphs over Lucifer.

The Master directed his most faithful steps toward the Jordan, where his great Precursor Saint John was still preaching and baptizing. By his presence and appearance there He wished to secure new testimony of his mission and Divinity through the mouth of Saint John.

Moreover He was drawn by his own love to see and speak with him, for during his Baptism the heart of the Precursor had become inflamed and wounded by the divine love of the Savior, which so resistlessly attracted all creatures. In the hearts which were well disposed, as was that of Saint John, the fire of love burned with so much the greater ardor and violence.

When the Baptist saw the Savior coming to him the second time, his first words were those recorded by the Evangelist: "Behold the Lamb of God, behold Him who taketh away the sin of the world." Saint John gave this testimony while pointing out the Lord with his finger to those who were listening to his instructions and were receiving Baptism at his hands. He added: "This is He of whom I said: after me there cometh a Man, who is preferred before me; because He was before me. And I knew Him not; but that He may be made manifest in Israel, therefore I am come baptizing with water."

The two first disciples of Christ who were with saint John at the time, heard this testimony and, moved by it and by the light and grace interiorly imparted to them began to follow the Lord.

B5C6

Benignantly turning to them the Lord asked them, what they sought. They answered that they wished to know where He lived; and the Lord bade them follow. They were with him that day as Saint John tells us. One of them, he says, was Saint Andrew, the brother of Saint Peter; the other he does not mention. But I was made to understand that it was Saint John himself, who in his great modesty, did not wish to give his name.

These two, then, Saint John and Saint Andrew, were the first of the Baptist's apostolate, being the first of the disciples of the Baptist who followed the Savior in consequence of his express testimony and without being outwardly called by the Lord. Saint Andrew immediately sought his brother Simon and took him along, saying that he had found the Messiah, who called Himself Christ.

Looking upon Peter He said: "Thou art the son of Jonah: thou shalt be called Cephas, which is interpreted Peter." All this happened within the confines of Judea and on the next day the Lord entered Galilee. There He found Saint Philip and called him to his following.

Philip immediately sought Nathanael and brought him to Jesus, telling him what had happened and that they had found the Messiah in the Person of Jesus of Nazareth. Nathanael, having spoken with the Lord as recorded in the first chapter of Saint John's Gospel, joined as the fifth of the disciples of Christ.

With these five disciples, the first stones in the foundation of the new Church, Christ, the Savior, entered Galilee for the purpose of beginning his public preaching and baptizing. In the Apostles thus called He enkindled, from the moment of their joining the Master, a new light and fire of divine love and showered upon them the sweetness of his blessings.

It is not possible worthily to describe the labors undergone by the divine Teacher in the vocation and education of these and of the other disciples, in order to found upon them the Church. He sought them out with great diligence and solicitude; He urged them on frequently by the powerful and efficacious help of his grace; He enlightened their hearts and enriched them with incomparable gifts and blessings; He received them with admirable kindness; He nourished them with the sweetest milk of his doctrines; He bore with them with invincible patience; He caressed them as a most loving Father caresses his tender and darling sons.

As our nature is base and uncouth material for the exalted and exquisite aspirations of the Spirit, and as they were to not only perfect disciples, but consummate masters of perfection in the world and in the Church, the work of transforming and raising them from their rough natural state into such a heavenly and divine position by his instructions and example, necessarily was a vast enterprise.

In the performance of this work the Lord has left a most exalted example of patience, and charity for all the prelates, princes and whoever is charged with the guidance of subjects. Not less significant for us sinners are the proofs of his fatherly kindness: for He was not satisfied with simply bearing with their faults and defects, their natural inclinations and passions but He allowed his tender kindness to overflow thus wonderfully toward them, in order that we might be cheered on to trust Him and not permit ourselves to be dismayed amidst the countless imperfections and weaknesses natural to our earthly existence.

The Queen of heaven was informed of all the wonderful doings of our Savior in the vocation of the Apostles and disciples and in his public preaching. She gave thanks to the eternal Father for these the first disciples, acknowledging and admitting them in imitation of her Son as her spiritual children, and offering them to the divine Majesty with new songs of praise and joy.

On this occasion of the choice of the first disciples She was favored by a new revelation of the Most High in which She was informed again of his holy and eternal decree concerning the Redemption of man and of the manner in which it was to be executed in the preaching of his most holy Son.

The five disciples of the Lord begged Him to grant them the consolation of seeing and reverencing his mother. In accordance with their petition, He journeyed directly to Nazareth through Galilee, continuing to preach and teach publicly on the way and proclaiming Himself as the Master of truth and eternal life.

Many, carried away by the force of his doctrines and by the light and grace overflowing into their hearts, began to listen to Him and to follow Him; though He did not, for the present, call any more to be his disciples. It is worthy of notice that though the five disciples had conceived such an ardent devotion to the heavenly Lady and though they saw with their own eyes how worthy She was of her eminent position among creatures, yet they all maintained strict silence about their thoughts.

The Savior then pursued his way to Nazareth instructing his new children and disciples not only the mysteries of faith, but in all virtues by word and example, as He continued to do during the whole period of his evangelical preaching. With this in view He searched out the poor and afflicted, consoled the sick and sorrowful, visited the infirmaries and prisons, performing miracles of mercy as well for body as for soul.

Yet He did not profess Himself as the Author of miracles until he attended the marriage feast at Cana. While the Savior proceeded on his journey his most holy Mother prepared to receive him and his disciples at Nazareth; for She was aware of all that happened, and therefore hospitably set her poor dwelling in order and solicitously procured the necessary victuals beforehand for their entertainment.

Thus, just as the Son had in absence instilled into their minds the reverence for the dignity of his Mother, so the most prudent and faithful Mother, in the presence of her Son, wished to instruct them in regard to the worship due to their divine Master, as to their God and Redeemer. The profound humility and worship with which the great Lady received Christ the Savior filled the disciples with new devotion and reverential fear for their divine Master; henceforth She served them as an example and model of true devotion, entering at once into her office as Instructress and spiritual Mother of the disciples of Christ by showing then how to converse with their God and Redeemer.

They were immediately drawn toward their Queen and cast themselves on their knees before Her, asking to be received as her sons and servants. The first to do this was Saint John, who from that time on distinguished himself in exalting and reverencing Mary before all the apostles, while She on her part received him with an especial love; for, besides his excelling in virginal chastity, he was of a meek and humble disposition.

The great Lady received them all as her guests, serving them their meals and combining the solicitude of a Mother with the modesty and majesty of a Queen, so that She caused admiration even in the holy angels. She served her divine Son on her knees in deepest reverence. At the same time She spoke of the Majesty of their Teacher and Redeemer to the Apostles instructing them in the great doctrines of the Christian faith.

During that night, when the Apostles had retired, the Savior betook himself to the oratory of his purest Mother as He had been wont to do, and She, the most Humble among the humble, placed Herself at his feet as in the years gone by. In regard to the practice of humility, all that She could do seemed little to the great Queen, and much less than She ought to in view of his infinite love and the immense gifts received at his hands.

The Lord lifted Her from the ground and spoke to Her words of life and eternal salvation, yet quietly and serenely. For at this period He began to treat Her with greater reserve in order to afford Her a chance of merit.

B5C6

Chapter Six

MARY ACCOMPANIES JESUS ON HIS JOURNEY

It would not be foreign to the purpose of this history to describe the miracles and the heroic works of Christ, our Redeemer and Master; for in almost all of them his most blessed and holy Mother concurred and took a part. But I cannot presume to undertake a work so arduous and so far above human strength and capacity.

For the Evangelist Saint John, after having described many miracles of Christ, says at the end of his Gospel, that Jesus did many other things, which, if they were all described, could not be contained in all the books of the world.

All that is necessary and proper, and abundantly sufficient for founding and preserving the Church has been written by the four Evangelists; it is not necessary to repeat it in this history. Yet in order to compose this history and in order not to pass over in silence so many great works of the exalted Queen, which have not been mentioned, it is necessary to touch on a few particulars.

Moreover, I think that to write of them and thus fasten them in my memory will be both consoling and useful for my advancement. The others, which the Evangelists recorded in their Gospels and of which I have not been commanded to write, are better preserved for the beatific vision, where the saints shall see them manifested to them by the Lord and where they will eternally praise Him for such magnificent works.

From Cana in Galilee Christ, the Redeemer, walked to Capernaum, a large and populous city near the sea of Tiberias. Here, according to Saint John. He remained some days, for as the time of the Pasch was approaching, He gradually drew nigh to Jerusalem in order to celebrate this feast on the fourteenth of the moon of March.

His most blessed Mother, having rid Herself of her house in Nazareth, accompanied Him thenceforth in his tours of preaching and of teaching to the very foot of the Cross. She was absent from Him only a few times, as when the Lord absented Himself on Mount Tabor, or on some particular conversions, as for instance that of the Samaritan woman, or when the heavenly Lady herself remained behind with certain persons in order to instruct and catechize them.

But always after a short time, She returned to her Lord and Master, following the Sun of justice until it sank into the abyss of Death. During these journeys the Queen of heaven proceeded on foot, just as her divine Son.

If even the Lord was fatigued on the way, as Saint John says, how much more fatigued was this purest Lady? What hardships did She not endure on such arduous journeys in all sorts of weather? Such is the rigorous treatment accorded by the Mother of mercy to her most delicate body! What She endured in labors alone is so great that not all the mortals together can ever satisfy their obligations to Her in this regard.

Sometimes by permission of the Lord, She suffered such great weakness and pains that He was constrained to relieve Her miraculously. At other times He commanded Her to rest Herself at some stopping–place for a few days; while again on certain occasions, He gave such lightness to her body, that She could move about without difficulty as if on wings.

The heavenly Lady had the whole doctrine of the evangelical law written in her heart. Nevertheless She was as solicitous and attentive as a new disciple to the preaching and doctrine of her divine Son, and She had instructed her angels to report to Her, if necessary, the sermons of the Master whenever She was absent.

To the sermons of her Son She always listened on her knees, thus according to the utmost of her powers showing the reverence and worship due to his Person and doctrine. As She was aware each moment, of the interior operations of the Soul of Christ, and of his continual prayers to the eternal Father for the proper disposition of the hearts of his hearers and for the growth of the seed of his doctrine into eternal life, the most loving Mother joined the divine Master in his petitions and prayers and in securing for them the blessings of her most ardent and tearful charity.

By her attention and reverence She taught and moved others to appreciate duly the teaching and instructions of the Savior of the world. She also knew the interior of those that listened to the preaching of the Lord, their state of grace or sin, their vices and virtues.

This various and hidden knowledge, so far above the capacity of men, caused in the heavenly Mother many wonderful effects of highest charity and other virtues; it inflamed Her with zeal for the Honor of the Lord and with ardent desires, that the fruits of the Redemption be not lost to the souls, while at the same time, the danger of their loss to the souls through sin moved Her to exert Herself in the most fervent prayer for their welfare.

She felt in her heart a piercing and cruel sorrow, that God should not be known, adored and served by all his creatures: and this sorrow was in proportion to the unequaled knowledge and understanding She had of all these mysteries.

For the souls, that would not give entrance to divine grace and virtue, She sorrowed with ineffable grief, and was wont to shed tears of blood at the thought of their misfortune.

What the great Queen suffered in this her solicitude and in her labors exceeds beyond all measure the pains endured by all the martyrs of the world.

All the followers of the Savior, and whomever He received into his ministry, She treated with incomparable prudence and wisdom, especially those whom She held in such high veneration and esteem as the Apostles of Christ.

B6C1

As a Mother She took care of all, and as a powerful Queen She procured necessaries for their bodily nourishment and comforts. Sometimes when She had no other resources, She commanded the holy angels to bring provisions for them and for the women in their company.

 In order to assist them toward advancing in the spiritual life, the great Queen labored beyond possibility of human understanding; not only by her continual and fervent prayers for them but by her precious example and by her counsels, with which She nourished and strengthened them as a most prudent Mother and Teacher.

When the Apostles or disciples were assailed by any doubts, which frequently happened in the beginning, or when they were attacked by some secret temptation, the great Lady immediately hastened to their assistance in order to enlighten and encourage them by the peerless light and charity shining forth in her; and by the sweetness of her words they were exquisitely consoled and rejoiced.

They were enlightened by her wisdom, chastened by her humility, quieted by her modesty, enriched by all the blessings that flowed from this storehouse of all the gifts of the Holy Ghost. For all these benefits, for the calling of the disciples, for the conversion and perseverance of the just, and for all the works of grace and virtue, She made a proper return to God, celebrating these events in festive hymns.

As the Evangelists tell us, some of the women of Galilee followed Christ the Redeemer on his journeys. Saint Matthew, saint Mark and saint Luke tell us that some of those whom He had cured of demoniacal possession and of other infirmities, accompanied and served Him; for the Master of eternal life excluded no sex from his following, imitation and doctrine.

Hence some of the women attended upon Him and served him from the very beginning of his preaching. The divine wisdom so ordered it for certain purposes, among which was also the desire to provide proper companions for his blessed Mother during these travels.

Our Queen interested Herself in a special manner in these pious and holy women, gathering them around Her, teaching and catechising them and bringing them as listeners to the sermons of her divine Son.

Although She herself was fully enlightened and instructed in the evangelical doctrine and abundantly able to teach them the way of eternal life, nevertheless, partly in order to conceal this secret of her heart, She always availed Herself of the sayings of Christ in his public preaching as a text for her instructions and exhortations, whenever She taught these and many other women who came to Her either before or after hearing the Savior of the world.

One of the great miracles of divine omnipotence and a wonder of wonders was the conduct of the most holy Mary toward the Apostles and disciples of her Son and Savior Christ, A full account of her wisdom is impossible to human tongue, and if I would wish to describe no more than what I have been made to understand concerning this matter, I would be obliged to write a large volume. I will touch upon it in this chapter and as occasion requires in the rest of this history. All that I can say is very little, yet from it the faithful can infer enough for their instruction.

All those whom the Savior received into his divine school, were to see and treat familiarly his most blessed Mother. Hence He infused into their hearts an especial reverence and devotion toward that blessed Lady. But though this infused reverence was common to all, it was not equal in all the disciples; for the Lord distributed his gifts according to his free will in reference to their dispositions and in accordance with the duties and offices for which each one was destined.

By conversation and regular interaction with their great Queen and Lady their reverential love and devotion was to grow and increase; for the blessed Lady spoke to all, loved them, consoled them, instructed and assisted them in their necessities, without ever permitting them to leave Her conversation and presence unreplenished by interior joy and consolation greater than they had asked for.

Yet the measure of good fruit derived from them was dependent upon the disposition of the heart of those that received these favors. They were all enabled to begin their interaction with the Mother of God in high admiration of her prudence, wisdom, purity, holiness and great majesty, and made sensible of a sweetness in Her inexpressibly humble and pleasing.

This was so ordained by the Most High, because it was not yet time to reveal this mystic Ark of the New Testament to the world. Thus, just as the Lord, however much He wished to break forth in her praise, could not manifest it in words and concentrated it within his heart; so the holy Apostles, sweetly constrained into silence, found a vent for their fervent feelings in a so much the more intense love of most holy Mary and praise of her Maker.

As the great Lady, on account of her peerless insight knew the natural disposition of each of the disciples, his measure of grace, his present condition and future office, She proceeded according to this knowledge in her petitions and prayers, in her instructions and conversings with them, and in the favors She obtained for each in support of his vocation.

Such a loving zeal in the conduct of a mere Creature so entirely pleasing to the wishes of his Lord, excited a new and boundless admiration in the holy angels. Of no less admiration was the hidden providence of the Almighty by which the Apostles were made to correspond to the blessings and favors received by them at the intercession of the most holy Mother. All this caused a divine harmony of action, hidden to men and manifest only to the heavenly spirits.

Especially signalized for the reception of these sacramental favors were saint Peter and saint John; the former because he was destined to be the vicar of Christ and head of the militant Church and because he therefore deserved the special reverence and love of the holy Mother; the latter because he was to take the place of the Lord after his Passion in attending upon and conversing with the heavenly Lady upon earth.

As therefore the government and custody of the mystic Church namely of Mary immaculate and of the visible militant Church, namely the faithful on earth, was to be divided between these two Apostles, it was no wonder, that they should be singularly favored by the great Queen of the world.

But as Saint John was chosen to serve Mary and attain the dignity of an adopted son of the Mistress of heaven, he at once began to experience special urgings of grace and signalize himself in the service of the most holy Mary.

Although all the Apostles excelled in devotion to the Queen beyond our power of understanding or conception the evangelist Saint John penetrated deeper into the mysteries of this City of God and received through Her such divine enlightenment as to excel all the other Apostles.

This is also evident from his Gospel; all the divine insight therein manifested he received through the Queen of heaven, and the distinction of being called the beloved disciple of Jesus, he gained by his love toward the most blessed Mother. As this love was reciprocated by the heavenly Lady, he became the most beloved disciple both of Jesus and Mary.

The Evangelist, besides chastity and virginal purity, possessed some other virtues which were especially pleasing to the Queen; among then, were a dovelike simplicity, as is manifest from his writings, and a great gentleness and humility, which made him most meek and tractable.

B6C1

The heavenly Mother always looked upon the peaceful and the humble as the most faithful imitators of her divine Son. On this account the blessed Queen favored Saint John above all the other Apostles and he himself became more and more anxious to serve Her with ever increasing reverential love and affection.

From the very first moment of his vocation saint John commenced to excel all the rest in piety toward the Mother and to fulfill the least of her wishes as her most humble slave. He attended upon Her more assiduously than the rest; and whenever it was possible he sought to be in her company and take upon himself some of the bodily labors connected with her present life.

Sometimes it happened that the fortunate Apostle competed with the angels in his zeal for thus assisting the great Queen; while She still more eagerly sought to perform these works of humility Herself; for in this virtue She triumphed over all other creatures and none of them could ever hope in the least to surpass or equal Her in acts of humility.

The beloved disciple was very diligent in reporting to the heavenly Lady the works and miracles wrought by the Savior, whenever She herself could not be present, and in informing Her of the new disciples converted by his teaching. He was constantly alert and studious to serve Her in the least of her wishes, fulfilling each one of them with a loving eagerness.

I will, however, say something of that which has been made known to me concerning the wicked Apostle Judas; for it belongs to this history and less is known of him. It will at the same time be a warning to the obstinate and an admonition for those little devoted to the most blessed Mary; for it is a sad truth that there should be any mortals who entertain little love toward a Creature so lovable, and One whom the infinite God himself loves without bound or measure; whom angels love with all their heavenly powers, the Apostles and saints from their inmost souls, whom all creatures should eagerly strive to love, and who never can be loved according to her merits.

Yet this unhappy Apostle strayed from the royal road of divine love and its blessings. The understanding, which has been given me concerning this defection for the purpose of making it known in this history, is contained in the following paragraphs.

Judas was attracted to the school of Christ our Teacher by his forceful doctrines, and was filled with the same good intentions which moved the others. Powerfully drawn by these motives, he asked the Savior to admit him among his disciples, and the Savior receive him with the bowels of a loving Father, who rejects none that come to Him in search of truth.

In the beginning Judas merited special favors and forged ahead of some of the other disciples, deserving to be numbered among the twelve Apostles; for the Savior loved his soul according to its present state of grace and his good works, just as He did the others.

The Mother of grace and mercy observed the same course with him, although by her infused knowledge She immediately became aware of the perfidious treachery with which he was to end his apostolate.

She did not, on this account, deny him her intercession and maternal love; but she applied Herself even more zealously to justify as far as possible the cause of her divine Son against this perfidious and unfortunate man, in order that his wickedness, as soon as it should be put into action, might not have the shadow of an excuse before men.

Well knowing that such a character as his could not be overcome by rigor, but would only be driven by it to so much the greater obstinacy, the most prudent Lady took care, that none of the wants or the comforts of Judas should be ignored and She began to treat him, speak and listen to him more gently and lovingly than to all the rest.

This She carried so far, that Judas, when the disciples once disputed among themselves concerning their standing with the Queen, never experienced the jealousy or doubt in this matter; for the blessed Lady in the beginning always distinguished him by tokens of special love and he, at that time, also showed himself thankful for these favors.

But as Judas found little support in his natural disposition, and as the disciples, not being as yet confirmed in virtue and not as yet even in grace, were guilty of some human failings, the imprudent man began to compliment himself on his perfection and to take notice more of the faults of his brethren than of his own.

He permitted himself thus to be deceived, making no effort to amend or repent, he allowed the beam in his own eyes to grow while watching the splinters in the eyes of others. Complaining of their little faults and seeking, with more presumption than zeal, to the weaknesses of his brethren, he committed greater sins himself.

Among the other Apostles he singled out Saint John, looking upon him as an intermeddler and accusing him in his heart of ingratiating himself with the Master and his blessed Mother. The fact that he received so many special favors from them was of no avail to deter him from this false assumption.

Yet so far Judas had committed only venial sins and had not lost sanctifying grace. But they argued a very bad disposition, in which he wilfully persevered. He had freely entertained a certain vain complacency in himself; this at once called into existence a certain amount of envy, which brought on a calumnious spirit and harshness in judging of the faults of his brethren.

These sins opened the way for greater sins; for immediately the fervor of his devotion decreased, his charity toward God and men grew cold, and his interior light was lost and extinguished; he began to look upon the Apostles and upon the most holy Mother with a certain disgust and find little pleasure in their interactions and their heavenly activity.

B6C1

The most prudent Lady perceived the growth of this defection in Judas. Eagerly seeking his recovery and salvation before he should cast himself entirely into the death of sin, She spoke to him and exhorted him as her beloved child and with extreme sweetness and force of reasoning.

Although at times this storm of tormenting thoughts, which had begun to rise in the breast of Judas, was allayed; yet it was only for a short time, and soon it arose and disturbed him anew. Giving entrance to the devil into his heart, he permitted a furious rage against the most meek Dove to take possession of him. With insidious hypocrisy he sought to deny his sins or palliate them by alleging other reasons for his conduct: as if he could ever deceive Jesus and Mary and hide from Them the secrets of his heart.

Thereby he lost his interior reverence for the Mother of mercy, despising exhortations and openly reproaching Her for her gentle words and reasonings. This ungrateful presumption threw him from the state of grace; the Lord was highly incensed and deservedly left him to his own evil counsels.

By thus designedly rejecting the kindness and the intercession of most holy Mary, he closed against himself the gates of mercy and of his only salvation. His disgust with the sweetest Mother soon engendered in him an abhorrence of his Master; he grew dissatisfied with his doctrines and began to look upon the life of an Apostle and intercourse with the disciples as too burdensome.

Nevertheless divine Providence did not abandon him immediately, but continued to send him interior assistance, although in comparison with former helps they were of a kind more common and ordinary. They were, however, in themselves sufficient for his salvation, if he would have made use of them.

To these graces were added the gentle exhortations of the kindest Mistress, urging him to restrain himself and to humble himself and ask pardon of his divine Master. She offered him mercy in his name and her own kind assistance in obtaining it, promising to do penance for him, if he would consent to be sorry for his sins and amend his life.

All these advances did the Mother of grace make in order to prevent the fall of Judas. She was well aware, that not seeking to arise from a fall and to persevere in sin was a much greater evil than to have fallen.

The conscience of this proud disciple could not but reproach him with his wickedness; but becoming hardened in his heart, he began to dread the humiliation, which would have been to his credit, and he fell into still greater sins.

In his pride he rejected the salutary counsels of the Mother of Christ and chose rather to deny his guilt, protesting with a lying tongue, that he loved his Master and all the rest, that there was no occasion for amending his conscience in this regard.

Another cause that contributed to the ruin of Judas; when the number of the Apostles and disciples increased, the Lord resolved to appoint one of them to take charge of the alms received; thus to supply the common needs and pay the imperial tribute. Jesus made known his wishes to all indiscriminately without addressing Himself to any one in particular.

While all of them feared such an office and sought to evade it, Judas immediately strove obtain it. In order to secure his appointment he humbled himself so far as to ask Saint John to speak to the holy Queen and induce Her to arrange this matter for him with her Son. Saint John yielded to the request of Judas and spoke to the most prudent Mother; but She, knowing that this request of Judas was not proper or just, but proceeded from ambition and avarice, did not wish to propose it to the divine Master.

The same kind of influence Judas sought to bring into play through Saint Peter and the other Apostles, without success; for the Lord in his goodness wished to stay his ruin, and justify his cause before men, if He should grant the request.

At this resistance, the heart of Judas already corrupted by avarice, instead of quietly yielding, was consumed with unhappy desires for the office, and the devil stirred up thoughts of vilest ambition, such as would have been most improper and wicked in any one, and hence were much more culpable in Judas, who had been a disciple in the school of highest perfection and who had lived in the light of the Sun of justice and its beautiful Moon Mary!

Neither in the day of abundant graces, when the Sun Jesus lighted his paths, nor in the night of temptations, when the Moon Mary disclosed to him the wiles of the poisonous serpent, could he have failed to become aware of the wickedness of such suggestions.

But, as he flew from the light and cast himself willfully into darkness, he presumed to ask most holy Mary in a direct manner for her influence in obtaining his object. He had lost all fear and hid his avarice in the cloak of virtue.

Approaching Her, he said that he had made his request through saint Peter and saint John, with the sole desire of diligently serving Her and his divine Master, since not all would attend to the duties of this office with proper solicitude; and that, therefore, he now asked to obtain the position of purser for him from the Master.

The great Lady answered him with extreme gentleness: "Consider well, my dearest, what thou askest, and examine whether thy intentions are upright. Ponder well, whether it is good for thee to seek that which all thy brethren fear and refuse to accept, unless they shall be compelled thereto by the command of their Lord and Master. He loves thee more than thou lovest thyself and without doubt knows what will benefit thee; resign thyself to his most holy will, change thy purpose, and seek to grow rich in humility and poverty. Rise from thy fall, for I will extend thee a helpful hand and my Son will show thee his loving mercy."

Who would not have yielded to these sweetest words and such urgent advice, spoken by such an amiable and heavenly Creature as was most holy Mary? But this fierce and adamantine heart was not softened or moved. On the contrary, the soul of Judas was offended and enraged against the heavenly Lady for thus offering him a means of escaping from his dreadful danger.

Boundless ambition and avarice roused his fury against Her who seemed to hinder him in his projects and he considered her well–meant advice as an insult. But the meek and loving Dove pretended not to notice his obstinacy and said nothing more to him at that time.

After his interview with most holy Mary, the avarice of Judas would not allow him to rest; casting of all modesty and natural shame (and the least spark of faith), Judas now resolved to apply to his divine Master and Savior.

Clothing himself like a consummate hypocrite in the garb of a sheep, he went to his Master and said: "Master, I wish to fulfill thy wishes and serve Thee as thy purser and as the dispenser of alms which we receive; I will look to the interests of the poor, fulfilling thy doctrine that we should do unto others as we wish them to do unto us, and I will see to it that alms are distributed according to thy wishes, more profitably and orderly than hitherto."

Such reasoning the specious hypocrite boldly used, committing many enormous sins in one and the same act. For, first of all he lied, concealing his real intention. Then, being ambitious of an honor which he did not merit, he neither wished to appear in his true light nor did he wish to be in truth what he merely pretended to be.

He also blamed his brethren, discrediting them and praising himself: the ordinary course of those who are ambitious. What is especially to be noticed in this conduct of Judas is that he showed his loss of infused faith; for he attempted to deceive Christ, his divine Master, by wearing the cloak of hypocrisy.

For, if he had firmly believe that Christ was true God and man who penetrated into the secrets of the heart, he could not have hoped to able to deceive Him; nor would he have attempted such double dealing, not only because he would have known Christ as the omniscient God, but because he would not have hoped to impose upon the infused and beatific science of Christ as man. Hence Judas had lost belief in all these prerogatives, and to his other sins, added the sin of heresy.

The answer given to Judas by the Master, whom he asked to make him purser. We shall see how hidden and terrible are the judgments of the Most High.

The Redeemer wished to ward off from him the danger which lay behind this request and which threatened the avaricious Apostle with final perdition. In order that Judas might not excuse himself under plea of ignorance, the Lord answered him: "Dost thou know, Judas, what thou seekest and what thou askest? Be not so cruel toward thy own self as to solicit and seek to obtain the poison and the arms which may cause thy death."

Judas replied: "Master I desire to serve Thee by employing my strength in the service of thy faithful followers and in this way I can do it better than in any other; for I offer to fulfill all the duties of this office without fail."

This daring presumption of Judas in seeking and coveting danger, justified the cause of God in allowing him to enter and perish in the danger thus sought and coveted. He resisted the light, and hardened himself against it, water and fire was shown him, life and death: he stretched forth his hand and chose perdition.

B6C1

The Transfiguration of Our Lord— His Triumphal Entry into Jerusalem

Our Redeemer and Master Jesus had already consumed more than two years and a half in preaching and performing wonders, and He was approaching the time predestined by the eternal wisdom for satisfying divine justice for redeeming the human race through his Passion and Death and thus to return to his eternal Father.

Since all his works were ordered with the highest wisdom for our instruction and salvation, the Lord resolved to prepare and strengthen some of his Apostles for the scandal of his Passion by manifesting to them beforehand in its glory that same body, which was so soon to exhibit in the disfigurement of the Cross.

Thus would they be reassured by the thought, they had seen it transfigured in glory before they looked upon it disfigured by his sufferings. This he had promised a short time before in the presence of all, although not to all, but only to some of his disciples, as is recorded by Saint Matthew.

For his Transfiguration He selected a high mountain in the center of Galilee, two leagues east of Nazareth and called Mount Tabor. Ascending to its highest summit with the three Apostles, Peter and the two brothers James and John, He was transfigured before them.

The three Evangelists tell us that besides these Apostles, were present also the prophets, Moses and Elias, discoursing with Jesus about his Passion, and that, while He was thus transfigured, a voice resounded from heaven in the name of the eternal Father, saying "This is my beloved Son in whom I am well pleased: hear ye Him."

For the purpose of recording this event here, I was given to understand that at the same time in which some of the holy angels were commissioned to bring the soul of Moses and Elias from their abode, others of her own guard carried the heavenly Lady to Mount Tabor, in order to witness the Transfiguration of her divine Son,

But no human ingenuity can suffice fully to describe the effects of this glorious vision of her Son on her most holy soul. With inmost gratitude and deepest penetration She began to ponder upon what She had seen and heard; exalted praise of the omnipotent welled forth from her lips, when She considered how her eyes had seen refulgent in glory that same bodily substance, which had been formed of her blood, carried in her womb and nursed at her breast; how She had with her own ears heard the voice of the eternal Father acknowledge her Son as his own and appoint Him as the Teacher of all the human race.

With her holy angels She composed new canticles to celebrate an event so full of festive joy for her soul and for the most sacred humanity of her Son. I will not expatiate upon this mystery, nor discuss in what the Transfiguration of the body of Jesus really consisted. It is enough to know that his countenance began to shine like the sun and his garments became whiter than the snow.

After the Transfiguration the most blessed Mother was brought back to her house in Nazareth; her divine Son descended the mountain and immediately came to visit her in order to take final leave of his parental province and set out for Jerusalem.

There, on the following Pasch, which was to be for Him the last upon earth, He was to enter upon his Passion. Having spent only a few days at Nazareth, He departed with his Mother, his disciples and Apostles and some of the holy women, traveling about through Galilee and Samaria before entering Judea and Jerusalem.

The Evangelist Saint Luke writes of this journey where he says, that He set his face toward Jerusalem; for He journeyed to Jerusalem with a joyous countenance and full of desire to enter upon his sufferings, in order thereby, according to his own most ardent and generous desire, to sacrifice Himself for the human race.

He was not to return to Galilee, where He had wrought so many miracles. Knowing this at his departure from Nazareth, He glorified his eternal Father and, in the name of his sacred humanity, gave thanks for having, in that house and neighborhood, received the human form and existence which He was now to deliver over to suffering and death.

Of the prayers spoken by Christ our Lord on this occasion, I will record as I can the following one: "My eternal Father, in compliance with thy will, I gladly haste to satisfy thy justice by suffering even unto death. Thus shall I reconcile to Thee all the children of Adam, paying their debts and opening to them the gates of heaven which have been closed against them. I shall seek those who have turned away and lost themselves, so that they may be restored by the force of my love. I shall find and gather together the lost of the house of Jacob, raise up the fallen, enrich the poor, refresh the thirsty, cast down the haughty and exalt the humble. I wish to vanquish hell and enhance the glories of the triumph over Lucifer, and over the vices which he has sown into the world."

"I wish to raise up the standard of the Cross, beneath which virtue, and all those that put themselves under its protection, are to fight their battles. I wish to satiate my heart with insults and affronts, which are so estimable in thy eyes. I wish to humiliate Myself even to death at the hands of my enemies, in order that our chosen friends may be consoled in their tribulations and that they may be honored by high rewards, whenever they choose to humiliate themselves in suffering the same persecutions."

"O beloved Cross! When shalt thou receive Me in thy arms? O sweet ignominies and affronts! When shalt thou bear Me on to overcome death through the sufferings of my entirely guiltless flesh? Ye pains, affronts, ignominies, scourges, thorns, torments, death, come to Me, who wish to embrace you, yield yourselves to my welcome, since I well understand your value. If the world abhors you, I long for you. If the world in its ignorance, despises you, I, who am truth and wisdom, love and embrace you. Come then to Me, for in welcoming you as man, I exalt you as the true God and am ready to efface the touch of sin from you and from all that will embrace you."

"Come to Me, ye pains, and disappoint Me not; heed not my Omnipotence, for I shall permit you to exert your full force upon my humanity. You shall not be rejected and abhorred by Me as you are by mortals. The deceitful fascination of the children of Adam in vainly judging the poor and the afflicted of this world as unhappy, shall now disappear; for if they see their true God, their Creator, Master and Father, suffering horrible insults, scourgings, the ignominious torment and destitution of the Cross, they will understand their error and esteem it as an honor to follow their crucified God."

I cannot worthily express all the thoughts and affections of Mary as to her departure from Nazareth, her prayers and petitions to the eternal Father, her most sweet and sorrowful conversations with her divine Son, the greatness of her grief and the vastness of her merits. For, on account of the conflict between the love of a true Mother, by which She naturally desired to preserve Him from the terrible torments, and the conformity of her will with that of Jesus and of his eternal Father, her heart was pierced by the sword of sorrow, prophesied by Simeon.

In her affliction She complained to her divine Son in words of deepest prudence and wisdom, yet also of sweetest sorrow, that She should be unable to prevent his sufferings, or at least die with Him.

These sorrows of the Mother of God exceeded the sufferings of martyrs who have died or will die for love of God to the end of the world. In such a state of mind and affection the Sovereigns of the world pursued their way from Nazareth toward Jerusalem through Galilee, which the Savior was not to revisit in this life.

As the end of his labors for the salvation of men drew to a close, his miraculous works increased in number, and, as the sacred writers of the Gospels relate, they became especially numerous in the last months intervening between his departure from Galilee and the day of entrance into Jerusalem.

Until that day, after having celebrated the feast or the Pasch of the Tabernacles, the Savior traveled about and labored in Judea, awaiting the appointed time, when, according to his will, He was to offer Himself in sacrifice.

Our Savior continued to perform his miracles in Judea. Among them was also the resurrection of Lazarus in Bethany, whither He had been called by the two sisters, Martha and Mary. As this miracle took place so near to Jerusalem, the report of it was soon spread throughout the city.

The priests and Pharisees, irritated by this miracle, held a council, in which they resolved the death of the Redeemer and commanded all those that had any knowledge of his whereabouts, to make it known; for after the resurrection of Lazarus, Jesus retired to the town of Ephrem, until the proximate feast of the Pasch should arrive.

As the time of celebrating his own Death drew nigh, He showed Himself more openly with his twelve disciples, the Apostles; and He told them privately that they should now get themselves ready to go Jerusalem, where the Son of man, He himself, should be delivered over to the chiefs of the Pharisees, bound as a prisoner, scourged, and ill–treated unto the death of the Cross. In the meanwhile the priests kept a sharp watch to find Him among those who came to celebrate the Pasch.

Six days previous He again visited Bethania, where He had called Lazarus to life, and where He was entertained by the two sisters. They arranged a banquet for the Lord and his Mother, and for all of his company. Among those that were at table with Them, was also Lazarus, whom He had brought back to life a few days before.

Thursday, the eve of the Passion and Death of the Savior, had arrived; at earliest dawn the Lord called his most beloved Mother and She, hastening to prostrate Herself at his feet, responded; "Speak, my Lord and Master, for thy servant heareth." Raising Her up from the ground, He spoke to Her in words of soothing and tenderest love: "My Mother, the hour decreed by the eternal wisdom of my Father for accomplishing the salvation and restoration of the human race and imposed upon Me by his most holy and acceptable will, has now arrived; it is proper that now We subject to Him our own will, as We have so often offered to do."

"Give Me thy permission to enter upon my suffering and death, and, as my true Mother, consent that I deliver Myself over to my enemies in obedience to my Father. In this manner do Thou also willingly co–operate with Me in this work of eternal salvation, since I have received from Thee in thy virginal womb the form of a suffering and mortal man in which I am to redeem the world and satisfy the divine justice."

"Just as thou, of thy own free will, didst consent to my Incarnation, so I now desire thee to give consent also to my passion and death of the Cross. To sacrifice Me now of thy own free will to the decree of my eternal Father, this shall be the return which I ask of thee for having made thee my Mother; for He has sent Me in order that by the sufferings of my flesh I might recover the lost sheep of his house, the children of Adam".

These and other words of the Savior, spoken on that occasion, pierced the most loving heart of Mary and cast Her into the throes of a sorrow greater than She had ever endured before. For now had arrived that dreadful hour, whence there was no issue for her pains, neither in an appeal to the swift–fleeting time nor to any other tribunal against the inevitable decree of the eternal Father, that had fixed the term of her beloved Son's life.

When now the most prudent Mother looked upon Him as her God, infinite in his attributes and perfections, and as the true Godman in hypostatical union with the person of the Word, and beheld Him sanctified and ineffably exalted by this union with the Godhead:

She remembered the obedience He had shown Her as his Mother during so many years and the blessings He had conferred upon Her during his long companionship with Her; She realized that soon She was to be deprived of this blessed companionship and of the beauty of his countenance, of the vivifying sweetness of his words; that She was not only to lose all this at once, but moreover that She was to deliver Him over into the hands of wicked enemies, to ignominies and torments and to the bloody sacrifice of a death on the Cross.

How deeply must all these considerations and circumstances, now so clearly before Her mind, have penetrated into her tender and loving heart and filled it with a sorrow unmeasurable! But with the magnanimity of a Queen, vanquishing this invincible pain, She prostrated Herself at the feet of Her divine Son and Master, and, in deepest reverence, kissing his feet, answered:

"Lord and highest God, Author of all that has being, though Thou art the Son of my womb, I am thy handmaid; the condescension of thy ineffable love alone has raised me from the dust to the dignity of being thy Mother."

"It is altogether becoming that I, vile wormlet, acknowledge and thank thy most liberal clemency by obeying the will of the eternal Father and thy own. I offer myself and resign myself to his divine pleasure in order that in Me, just as in Thee, my Son and Lord his eternal and adorable will be fulfilled. The greatest sacrifice which I can make, is that I shall not be able to die with Thee, and that our lot should not be inverted; for to suffer in imitation of Thee and in thy company would be a great relief for my pains, and all torments would be sweet, if undergone in union with thine."

"That Thou shouldst endure all these torments for the salvation of mankind shall be my only relief in my pains. Receive, O my God, this sacrifice of my desire to die with Thee, and of my still continuing to live, while thou, the most innocent Lamb and figure of the substance of thy eternal Father undergoest Death. Receive also the agonies of my sorrow to see the inhuman cruelty of thy enemies executed on thy exalted Person because of the wickedness of the human kind."

"O ye heavens and elements and all creatures within them, ye sovereign spirits, ye Patriarchs and Prophets, assist me to deplore the death of my Beloved, who gave you being, and bewail with me the misery of men, who are the cause of this Death, and who, failing to profit of such great blessings, shall lose that eternal life so dearly bought!"

"O unhappy you, that are foreknown as doomed! and O ye happy predestined, who shall wash your stoles in the blood of the Lamb, you who knew how to profit by this blessed sacrifice, praise ye the Lord Almighty!

"O my Son and infinite delight of my soul, give fortitude and strength to thy afflicted Mother; admit Her as thy disciple and companion, in order that she may participate in thy Passion and Cross, in order that the eternal Father may receive the sacrifice of thy Mother in union with thine."

With these and other expressions of her sentiments the Queen of heaven answered her most holy Son, and offered Herself as a companion and a coadjutrix in his Passion

Thereupon, thoroughly instructed and prepared by divine light for all the mysteries to be wrought by the Master of life towards accomplishing all his great ends, the most pure Mother, having the Lord's permission, added another request in the following words: "Beloved of my soul and light of my eyes, my Son, I am not worthy to ask Thee what I desire from my inmost soul; but Thou, O Lord, art the life of my hope, and this my trust I beseech Thee, if such be thy pleasure, make me a participant in the ineffable Sacrament of thy body and blood."

"Thou hast resolved to institute it as a pledge of thy glory and I desire in receiving Thee sacramentally in my heart to share the effects of this new and admirable Sacrament. Well do I know, O Lord, that no creature can ever merit such an exquisite blessing, which Thou hast resolved to set above all the works of thy magnificence; and in order to induce Thee to confer upon me, I have nothing else to offer except thy own and all thy infinite merits."

"If by perpetuating merits through the same humanity which thou hast received from my womb, creates for me a certain right, let this right consist not so much in giving Thyself to me in this Sacrament, as in making me thine by this new possession, which restores to me thy sweetest companionship."

"All my desires and exertions I have devoted to the worthy reception of this Holy Communion from the moment in which Thou gavest me knowledge of it and ever since it was thy fixed decree to remain in the holy Church under the species of consecrated bread and wine."

"Thou then, my Lord and God, return to thy first habitation which Thou didst find in thy beloved Mother and thy slave, whom Thou hast prepared for thy reception by exempting Her from the common touch of sin."

"Then shall I receive within me the humanity, which I have communicated to Thee from my own blood, and thus we shall be united in a renewed and close embrace. This prospect enkindles my heart with most ardent love, and may I never be separated from Thee, who art the infinite Good and the Love of my soul."

Our Savior, having thus parted with his most beloved Mother and sorrowful Spouse, and taking along with Him all his Apostles, a little before midday of the Thursday of the last Supper, departed on his last journey from Bethany to Jerusalem.

At the very outset He raised his eyes to the eternal Father, and, confessing Him in words of thankfulness and praise, again professed his most ardent love and most lovingly and obediently offered to suffer and die for the Redemption of the human race.

This prayer and sacrifice of our Savior and Master sprang from such ineffable love and ardor of his spirit, that it cannot be described; "Eternal Father and my God," said Christ our Lord, "in compliance with thy will I now go to suffer and die for the liberation of men, my brethren and the creatures of thy hands. I deliver Myself up for their salvation and to gather those who have been scattered and divided by the sin of Adam.

The Last Supper

Christ had partaken of the prescribed supper with his disciples reclining on the floor around a table, which was elevated from it little more than the distance of six or seven fingers; for such was the custom of the Jews.

But after the washing of the feet He ordered another, higher table to be prepared, such as we now use for our meals. By this arrangement He wished to put an end to the legal suppers and to the lower and figurative law and establish the new Supper of the Law of Grace.

From that time on He wished the sacred mysteries to be performed on the tables or altars, which are in use in the Catholic Church. The table was covered with a very rich cloth and upon it was placed a plate or salver and a large cup in the form of a chalice, capacious enough to hold the wine.

All this was done in pursuance of the will of Christ our Savior, who by his divine power and wisdom directed all these particulars. The master of the house was inspired to offer these rich vessels, which were made of what seemed a precious stone like emerald.

The Apostles often used it afterwards in consecrating, whenever the occasion permitted it. The Lord seated himself at this table with the Apostles and some of the other disciples, and then ordered some unleavened bread to be placed on the table and some wine to be brought, of which He took sufficient to prepare the chalice.

Then the Master of life spoke words of most endearing love to his Apostles, and, though his sayings were wont to penetrate to the inmost heart at all times, yet on this occasion they were like the flames of a great fire of charity, which consumed the souls of his hearers.

He manifested to them anew the most exalted mysteries of his Divinity, humanity and of the works of the Redemption. He enjoined upon them peace and charity, of which He was now to leave a pledge in the mysteries about to be celebrated. He reminded them, that in loving one another, they would be loved by the eternal Father with the same love in which He was beloved.

He gave them an understanding of the fulfillment of this promise having chosen them to found the new Church and the law of grace. He renewed in them the light concerning the supreme dignity, excellence and prerogatives of his most pure Virgin Mother.

Thereupon Christ our Lord took into his venerable hands the bread, which lay upon the plate, and interiorly asked the permission and co–operation of the eternal Father, that now and ever afterwards in virtue of the words about to be uttered by Him, and later to be repeated in his holy Church, He should really and truly become present in the host, Himself to yield obedience to these sacred words.

While making this petition He raised his eyes toward heaven with an expression of such sublime majesty, that He inspired the Apostles, the angels and his Virgin Mother with new and deepest reverence. Then He pronounced the words of consecration over the bread, changing its substance into the substance of his true body and immediately thereupon He uttered the words of consecration also over the wine, changing it into his true blood.

As an answer to these words of consecration was heard the voice of the eternal Father, saying: "This is my beloved Son, in whom I delight, and shall take my delight to the end of the world; and He shall be with men during all the time of their banishment." In like manner was this confirmed by the Holy Ghost.

The most sacred humanity of Christ, in the Person of the Word, gave tokens of profoundest veneration to the Divinity contained in the Sacrament of his body and blood.

The Virgin Mother, in her retreat prostrated Herself on the ground and adored her Son in the Blessed Sacrament with incomparable reverence. Then also the angels of her guard, all the angels of heaven, and among them likewise the souls of Enoch and Elias, in their own name and in the name of the Patriarchs and Prophets of the old law, fell down in adoration of their Lord in the holy Sacrament.

All the Apostles and disciples, who, with the exception of the traitor, believed in this holy Sacrament, adored it with great humility and reverence according to each one's disposition. The great high priest Christ raised up his own consecrated body and blood in order that all who were present at this first Mass might adore it in a special manner, as they also did.

During this elevation his most pure Mother, Saint John, Enoch and Elias, were favored with an especial insight into the mystery of his presence in the sacred species. They understood more profoundly, how, in the species of the bread, was contained his body and in those of the wine, his blood; how in both, on account of the inseparable union of his soul with his body and blood, was present the living and true Christ; how with the Person of the Word, was also therein united the Person of the Father and of the Holy Ghost; and how therefore, on account of the inseparable existence and union of the Father, Son and Holy Ghost, the holy Eucharist contained the perfect humanity of the Lord with the three divine Persons of the Godhead.

All this was understood most profoundly by the heavenly Lady and by the others according to their degree. They understood also the efficacy of the words of the consecration, now endowed with such divine virtue, that as soon as they are pronounced with the intention of doing what Christ did at that time, by any priest since that time over the proper material, they would change the bread into his body and the wine into his blood, leaving the accidents to subsist in a new way and without their proper subject.

They saw, that this change would take place so certainly and infallibly that heaven and earth would sooner fall to pieces, than that the effect of these words of consecration, when pronounced in the proper manner by the sacerdotal minister of Christ, should ever fail.

The heavenly Queen understood also by a special vision how the most sacred body of Christ is hidden beneath the accidents of bread and wine without change in them or alteration of the sacred humanity; for neither can the Body be the subject of the accidents, nor can the accidents be the form of the body.

The accidents retain the same extension and qualities as before, and each of their parts retain the same position after the host has been consecrated; and the sacred body is present in an invisible form, also retaining the same size without intermingling of parts.

It remains in the whole host, and all of it in every particle of the host, without being strained by the host, or the host by the body. For neither is the extension of his body correlative with the accidental species, nor do they depend upon the sacred body for their existence. They therefore have a totally different mode of existence and the body interpenetrates the accidents without hindrance.

Still greater was my admiration when Jesus our God, having raised the most holy Sacrament for their adoration, divided it by his own sacred hands, first partook of it himself as being the First and chief of all the priests.

Recognizing himself, as man, inferior to the Divinity, which He was now to receive in this his own consecrated body and blood. He humiliated and, as it were, with a trembling of the inferior part of his being, shrank within Himself before that Divinity, thereby not only teaching us the reverence with which holy Communion is to be received; but also showing us what was his sorrow at the temerity and presumption of many men during the reception and handling of this exalted and sublime Sacrament.

The effects of holy Communion in the body of Christ were altogether miraculous and divine; for during a short space of time the gifts of glory flowed over in his body just as on mount Tabor, though the effects of this transfiguration were manifest only to his blessed Mother, and partly also to John, Enoch and Elias.

This was the last consolation He permitted his humanity to enjoy as to its inferior part during his earthly life, and from that moment until his Death He rejected all such alleviation.

The Virgin Mother, by a special vision, also understood how Christ her divine Son received Himself in the Blessed Sacrament and what was the manner of its presence in his divine Heart. All this caused inestimable affection in our Queen and Lady.

While receiving his own body and blood Christ our Lord composed a canticle of praise to the eternal Father and offered Himself in the Blessed Sacrament as a sacrifice for the salvation of man. He took another particle of the consecrated bread and handed it to the archangel Gabriel who brought and communicated it to the most holy Mary.

By having such a privilege conferred on one of their number, the holy angels considered themselves sufficiently recompensed for being excluded from the sacerdotal dignity and for yielding it to man. The privilege of merely having even one of their number hold the sacramental body of their Lord and true God filled them with a new and immense joy. In abundant tears of consolation the great Queen awaited Holy Communion.

When saint Gabriel with innumerable other angels approached, She received it, the first after her Son, imitating His self–abasement, reverence and holy fear. The most Blessed Sacrament

B6C4

was deposited in the breast and above the heart of the most holy Virgin Mother, as in the most legitimate shrine and tabernacle of the Most High. There the ineffable sacrament of the holy Eucharist remained deposited from that hour until after the Resurrection, when Saint Peter said the first Mass and consecrated anew.

After having thus favored the heavenly Princess, our Savior distributed the sacramental bread to the Apostles, commanding them to divide it among themselves and partake of it. By this commandment He conferred upon them the sacerdotal dignity and they began to exercise it by giving Communion each to Himself.

This they did with the greatest reverence, shedding copious tears and adoring the body and blood of our Lord, whom they were receiving. They were established in the power of the priesthood, as being founders of the holy Church and enjoying the distinction of priority over all others

Then Saint Peter, at the command of Christ the Lord, administered two of the particles of Holy Communion to the two patriarchs, Enoch and Elias. This holy Communion so rejoiced these two holy men, that they were encouraged anew in their hope of the beatific vision, which for them was to be deferred for so many ages, and they were strengthened to live on in this hope until the end of the world.

Having given most fervent and humble thanks to the Almighty for this blessing, they were brought back to their abiding–place by the hands of the holy angels. The Lord desired to work this miracle in order to pledge Himself to include the ancient natural and written laws in the benefits of the Incarnation, Redemption and general resurrection; since all these mysteries were contained in the most holy Eucharist.

By thus communicating Himself to the two men, Enoch and Elias, who were still in their mortal flesh, these blessings were extended over the human race such as it existed under the natural and the written laws, while all the succeeding generations were to be included in the new law of grace, the Apostles at the head. This was all well understood by Enoch and Elias, and, returning to the midst of their contemporaries, they gave thanks to their and our Redeemer for this mysterious blessing.

THE PRAYER IN GETHSEMANI—HOW MARY JOINED THEREIN

By the wonderful mysteries, which our Savior Jesus had celebrated in the Cenacle, the reign which according to his inscrutable decree, his eternal Father had consigned to Him, was well established; and the Thursday night of his last Supper having already advanced some hours, He chose to go forth to that dreadful battle of his suffering and death by which the Redemption was to be accomplished.

The Lord then rose to depart from the hall of the miraculous feast and also most holy Mary left her retreat in order to meet Him on the way. At this face to face meeting of the Prince of eternity and of the Queen, a sword of sorrow pierced the heart of Son and Mother, inflicting a pang of grief beyond all human and angelic thought.

The sorrowful Mother threw Herself at the feet of Jesus, adoring Him as her true God and Redeemer. The Lord, looking upon Her with a majesty divine and at the same time with the overflowing love of a Son, spoke to Her only these words: "My Mother, I shall be with thee in tribulation; let Us accomplish the will of the eternal Father and the salvation of men."

The great Queen offered herself as a sacrifice with her whole heart and asked his blessing. Having received this She returned to her retirement, where, by a special favor of the Lord, she was enabled to see all that passed in connection with her divine Son. Thus She was enabled to accompany Him and co−operate with Him in his activity as far as devolved upon Her.

The owner of the house, who was present at this meeting, moved by a divine impulse, offered his house and all that it contained to the Mistress of heaven, asking her to make use of all that was his during Her stay in Jerusalem; and the Queen accepted his offer with humble thanks. The thousand angels of her guard, in forms visible to Her, together with some of the pious women of her company, remained with the Lady.

Our Redeemer and Master left the house of the Cenacle with all the men, who had been present at the ration of the mysterious Supper; and soon many of them dispersed in the different streets in order to attend to their own affairs. Followed by his twelve Apostles, the Lord directed his steps toward mount Olivet outside and close to the eastern walls of Jerusalem.

Judas, alert in his treacherous solicitude for the betrayal of his divine Master, conjectured that Jesus intended to pass the night in prayer as was his custom. This appeared to him a most opportune occasion for delivering his Master into the hands of his confederates, the scribes and the Pharisees. Having taken this dire resolve, he lagged behind and permitted the Master and his Apostles to proceed.

Unnoticed by the latter he lost them from view and departed in all haste to his own ruin and destruction. Within him was the turmoil of sudden fear and anxiety, interior witnesses of the wicked deed he was about to commit. Driven on in the stormy hurricane of thoughts raised by his bad conscience, he arrived breathless at the house of the high priests.

On the way it happened, that Lucifer, perceiving the haste of Judas in procuring the death of Jesus Christ, and fearing that after all Jesus might be the true Messiah, came toward him in the shape of a very wicked man, a friend of Judas acquainted with the intended betrayal.

In this shape Lucifer could speak to Judas without being recognized. He tried to persuade him that this project of selling his Master did at first seem advisable on account of the wicked deeds attributed to Jesus; but that, having more naturally considered the matter, he did not now deem it advisable to deliver Him over to the priests and Pharisees; for Jesus was not so bad as Judas might imagine; nor did He deserve death; and besides He might free Himself by some miracles and involve his betrayer into great difficulties.

In the meanwhile our divine Lord with the eleven Apostles was engaged in the work of our salvation and the salvation of those who were scheming his death. Unheard of and wonderful contest between the deepest malice of man and the unmeasurable goodness and charity of God! If this stupendous struggle between good and evil began with the first man, it certainly reached its highest point in the death of the Repairer; for then good and evil stood face to face and exerted their highest powers: human malice in taking away the life and honor of the Creator and Redeemer, and his immense charity freely sacrificing both for men.

According to our way of reasoning, it was as it were necessary that the most holy soul of Christ, yea that even his Divinity, should revert to his blessed Mother, in order that He might find some object in creation, in which his love should be recompensed and some excuse for disregarding the dictates of his justice.

For in this Creature alone could He expect to see his Passion and Death bring forth full fruit; in her immeasurable holiness did his justice find some compensation for human malice; and in the humility and constant charity of this great Lady could be deposited the treasures of his merits, so that afterwards, as the New Phoenix from the rekindled ashes, his Church might arise from his sacrifice.

The consolation which the humanity of Christ drew from the certainty of his blessed Mother's holiness gave Him strength and, as it were, new courage to conquer the malice of mortals; and He counted Himself well recompensed for suffering such atrocious pains by the fact that to mankind belonged also his most beloved Mother.

Our Savior pursued his way across the torrent of Cedron to mount Olivet and entered the garden of Gethsemane. Then He said to all the Apostles: "Wait for Me, and seat yourselves here while I go a short distance from here to pray; do you also pray, in order that you may not enter into temptation."

The divine Master gave them advice, in order that they might be firm in the temptations, of which He had spoken to them at the Supper: that all of them should be scandalized on account of what they should see Him suffer that night, that Satan would assail them to sift and stir them up by his false suggestions; for the Pastor (as prophesied) was to be illtreated and wounded and the sheep were to be dispersed.

Then the Master of life, leaving the band of eight Apostles at that place and taking with Him saint Peter, saint John, and saint James, retired to another place, where they could neither be seen nor heard by the rest. Being with the three Apostles He raised his eyes up to the eternal Father confessing and praising Him as was his custom; while interiorly He prayed in fulfillment of the prophecy of Zacharias, permitting death to approach the most innocent of men and commanding the sword of divine justice to be unsheathed over the Shepherd and descend upon the Godman with all its deathly force.

In this prayer Christ our Lord offered Himself anew to the eternal Father in satisfaction of his justice for the rescue of the human race; and He gave consent, that all the torments of his Passion and Death be let loose over that part of his human being, which was capable of suffering.

From that moment He suspended and strained whatever consolation or relief would otherwise overflow from the impassable to the passable part of his being, so that in this dereliction his passion and sufferings might reach the highest degree possible. The eternal Father granted these petitions and approved this total sacrifice of the sacred humanity.

B6C4

This prayer was as if it were the floodgate through which the rivers of his suffering were to find entrance like the resistless onslaught of the ocean, as was foretold by David. And immediately He began to be sorrowful and feel the anguish of his soul and therefore said to the Apostles: "My soul is sorrowful unto death"

He threw himself with his divine face upon the ground and prayed to the eternal Father: "Father, if it is possible, let this chalice pass from Me". This prayer Christ our Lord uttered, though He had come down from heaven with the express purpose of really suffering and dying for men; though He had counted as naught the shame of his Passion, had willingly embraced it and rejected all human consolation; though He was hastening with most ardent love into the jaws of death, to affronts, sorrows and afflictions; though He had set such a high price upon men, that He determined to redeem them at the shedding of his life–blood.

Since by virtue of his divine and human wisdom and his inextinguishable love He had shown Himself so superior to the natural fear of death, that it seems this petition did not arise from any motive solely coming from Himself. That this was so in fact, was made known to me in the light which was vouchsafed me concerning the mysteries contained in this prayer of the Savior.

This agony of Christ our Savior grew in proportion to the greatness of his charity and the certainty of his knowledge, that men would persist in neglecting to profit by his Passion and Death.

His agony increased to such an extent, that great drops of bloody sweat were pressed from Him, which flowed to the very earth. Although this prayer was uttered subject to a condition and failed in regard to the reprobate who fell under this condition; yet He gained thereby a greater abundance and secured a greater frequency of favors for mortals.

Through it the blessings were multiplied for those who placed no obstacles, the fruits of the Redemption were applied to the saints and to the just more abundantly, and many gifts and graces, of which the reprobates made themselves unworthy, were diverted to the elect.

The human will of Christ, conforming itself to that of the Divinity, then accepted suffering for each respectively: for the reprobate, as sufficient to procure them the necessary help, if they would make use of its merits, and for the predestined, as an efficacious means, of which they would avail themselves to secure their salvation by co–operating with grace. Thus was set in order, and as it were realized, the salvation of the mystical body of his holy Church, of which Christ the Lord was the Creator and Head.

As a ratification of this divine decree, while yet our Master was in his agony, the eternal Father for the third time sent the archangel Michael to the earth in order to comfort Him by a sensible message and confirmation of what He already knew by the infused science of his most holy soul; for the angel could not tell our Lord anything He did not know, nor could he produce any additional effect on his interior consciousness for this purpose.

Let us now return to the Cenacle, where the Queen of heaven had retired with the holy women of her company. From her retreat, by divine enlightenment, She saw most clearly all the mysteries and doings of her most holy Son in the garden. At the moment when the Savior separated Himself with the three Apostles Peter, John and James, the heavenly Queen separated Herself from the other women and went into another room.

Upon leaving them She exhorted them pray and watch lest they enter into temptation, but She took with Her the three Marys, treating Mary Magdalene as the superior of the rest. Secluding Herself with these three as her more intimate companions, She begged the eternal Father to suspend in Her all human alleviation and comfort, both in the sensitive and in the spiritual part of her being, so that nothing might hinder Her from suffering to the highest degree in union with her divine Son.

She prayed that She might be permitted to feel and participate in her virginal body all the pains of the wounds and tortures about to be undergone by Jesus. This petition was granted by the blessed Trinity and the Mother in consequence suffered all the torments of her most holy Son in exact duplication.

Although they were such, that, if the right hand of the Almighty had not preserved Her, they would have caused her death many times over; yet, on the other hand, these sufferings, inflicted by God himself were like a pledge and a new lease of life. For in her most ardent love She would have considered it incomparably more painful to see her divine Son suffer and die without being allowed to share in his torments.

The three Marys were instructed by the Queen to accompany and assist Her in her affliction, and for this purpose they were endowed with greater light and grace than the other women. In retiring with them the most pure Mother began to feel unwonted sorrow and anguish and She said to them: "My soul is sorrowful, because my beloved Son is about to suffer and die, and it is not permitted me to suffer and die of his torments. Pray my friends, in order that you may not be overcome by temptation."

Having said this She went apart a short distance from them, and following the Lord in his supplications. She, as far as was possible to Her and as far as She knew it to be conformable to the human will of her Son, continued her prayers and petitions, feeling the same agony as that of the Savior in the garden.

She also returned at the same intervals to her companions to exhort them, because She knew of the wrath of the demon against them. She wept at the perdition of the foreknown; for She was highly enlightened in the mysteries of eternal predestination and reprobation.

In order to imitate and co-operate in all things with the Redeemer of the world, the great Lady also suffered a bloody sweat, similar to that of Jesus in the garden, and by divine intervention She was visited by the archangel saint Gabriel, as Christ her Son was visited by the archangel Michael.

The holy prince expounded to Her the will of the Most High in the same manner as Saint Michael had expounded it to Christ the Lord. In both of them the prayer offered and the cause of sorrow was the same; and therefore They were also proportionally alike to one another in their actions and in their knowledge.

While they were approaching, the Lord returned the third time to his Apostles and finding them asleep spoke to them: "Sleep ye now, and take your rest. It is enough: the hour is come; behold the Son of man shall be betrayed into the hands of sinners. Rise up, let us go. Behold he that will betray Me is at hand. Such were the words of the Master of holiness to the three most privileged Apostles; He was unwilling to reprehend them more severely than in this most meek and loving manner.

Being oppressed, they did not know what to answer their Lord, as Scripture says. They arose and Jesus went with them to join the other eight disciples. He found them likewise overcome and oppressed by their great sorrow and fallen asleep.

The Master then gave orders, that all of them together, mystically forming one body with Him their Head, should advance toward the enemies, thereby teaching them the power of mutual and perfect unity for overcoming the demons and their followers and for avoiding defeat by them.

The Lord again exhorted all the Apostles and forewarned them of what was to happen. Already the confused noise of the advancing band of soldiers and their helpmates began to be heard. Our Savior then proceeded to meet them on the way, and, with incomparable love, magnanimous courage and tender piety prayed:"O sufferings longingly desired from my inmost soul, ye pains, wounds, affronts, labors, afflictions and ignominious death, come, come, come quickly, for the fire of love, which burns for the salvation of men, is anxious to see you meet the Innocent one of all creatures. Well do I know your value, I have sought, desired, and solicited you and I meet you joyously of my own free will; I have purchased you by my anxiety in searching for you and I esteem you for your merits. I desire to remedy and enhance your value and raise you to highest dignity. Let death come, in order that by my accepting it without having deserved it I may triumph over it and gain life for those who have been punished by death for their sins. I give permission to my friends to forsake Me; for I alone desire and am able to enter into this battle and gain for them triumph and victory".

During these words and prayers of the Author of life Judas advanced in order to give the signal upon which he had agreed with his companions, namely the customary, but now feigned kiss of peace, by which they were to distinguish Jesus as the One whom they should single out from the rest and immediately seize. These precautions the unhappy disciple had taken, not only out of avarice for the money and hatred against his Master, but also, on account of the fear with which he was filled. For he dreaded the inevitable necessity of meeting Him and encountering Him in the future, if Christ was not put to death on this occasion.

Such a confusion he feared more than the death of his soul, or the death of his divine Master, and, in order to forestall it, he hastened to complete his treachery and desired to see the Author of life die at the hands of his enemies. The traitor then ran up to the meekest Lord, and, as a consummate hypocrite hiding his hatred, he imprinted on his countenance the kiss of peace, saying: "God save Thee, Master."

By this so treacherous act the perdition of Judas was matured and God was justified in withholding his grace and help. On the part of the unfaithful disciple, malice and temerity reached their highest degree; for, interiorly denying or disbelieving the uncreated and created wisdom by which Christ must know of his treason, and ignoring his power to destroy him, he sought to hide his malice under the cloak of the friendship of a true disciple; and all this for the purpose of delivering over to such a frightful and cruel death his Creator and Master, to whom he was bound by so many obligations.

In this one act of treason he committed so many and such formidable sins, that it is impossible to fathom their immensity; for he was treacherous, murderous, sacrilegious, ungrateful, inhuman, disobedient, false, lying, impious and unequalled in hypocrisy; and all this was included in one and the same crime perpetrated against the person of God made man.

The most pure Mother of Christ our Lord was most attentive to all that passed in his capture, and by means of her clear visions saw it more clearly than if She had been present in person; for by means of supernatural visions She penetrated into all the mysteries of his words and actions.

When She beheld the band of soldiers and servants issuing from the house of the high priest, the prudent Lady foresaw the irreverence and insults with which they would treat their Creator and Redeemer; and in order to do what was within her power, She invited the holy angels and many others in union with Her to render adoration and praise to the Lord of creation as an offset to the injuries and affronts He would sustain at the hands of those ministers of darkness.

The same request She made to the holy women who were praying with Her. She told them, that her most holy Son had now given permission to his enemies to take him prisoner and illtreat him, and that they were about to make use of this permission in a most impious and cruel manner. Assisted by the holy angels and the pious women the faithful Queen engaged in interior and exterior acts of devoted faith and love, confessing, adoring, praising and magnifying the infinite Deity and the most holy humanity of her Creator and Lord.

The holy women imitated Her in the genuflections and prostrations, and the angelic princes responded to the canticles with which She magnified, celebrated and glorified the Divinity and humanity of Christ. In the measure in which the children of malice increased their irreverence and injuries, She sought to compensate them by her praise and veneration. Thus She continued to placate the divine justice, lest it be roused against his persecutors and destroy them; for only most holy Mary was capable of staying the punishment of such great offenses.

And the great Lady not only placated the just Judge, but even obtained favors and blessings from the divine clemency for the very persons who irritated Him and thus secured a return of good for those who were heaping wrongs upon Christ the Lord for his doctrine and benefits.

This mercy attained its highest point in the disloyal and obstinate Judas; for the tender Mother, seeing him deliver Jesus by the kiss of feigned friendship and considering how shortly before his mouth had contained the sacramental body of the Lord, with whose sacred countenance so soon after those same foul lips were permitted to come in contact, was transfixed with sorrow and entranced by charity.

She asked the Lord to grant new graces, whereby this man, who had enjoyed the privilege of touching the face whereon angels desire to look, might, if he chose to use them, save himself from perdition. In response to this prayer of most holy Mary, her Son and Lord granted Judas powerful graces in the very consummation of his treacherous delivery.

If the unfortunate man had given heed and had commenced to respond to them, the Mother of mercy would have obtained for him many others and at last also pardon for his sin. She has done so with many other great sinners, who were willing to give that glory to Her and thus obtain eternal glory for themselves. But

Judas failed to realize this and thus lost all chance of salvation, as I shall relate in the next chapter.

When the servants of the high priest laid hands on and bound the Savior, the most blessed Mother felt on her own hands the pains caused by the ropes and chains, as if She Herself was being bound and fettered; in the same manner She felt in her body the blows and torments further inflicted upon the Lord, got this favor was granted to his Mother. Thus her sensible participation in his sufferings was some kind of relief of the pain, which She would have suffered in her loving soul at the thought of not being with Him in his torments.

JESUS BROUGHT BEFORE ANNAS AND CAIPHAS

Having been taken prisoner and firmly bound, the most meek Lamb Jesus was dragged from the garden to the house of the highpriests, first to the house of Annas. The turbulent band of soldiers and servants, having been advised by the traitorous disciple that his Master was a sorcerer and could easily escape their hands, if they did not carefully bind and chain Him securely before starting on their way, took all precautions inspired by such a mistrust.

Lucifer (Satan) and his compeers of darkness secretly irritated and provoked them to increase their impious and sacrilegious ill-treatment of the Lord beyond all bounds of humanity and decency. As they were willing accomplices of Lucifer's malice, they omitted no outrage against the person of their Creator within the limits set them by the Almighty.

They bound Him with a heavy iron chain with such ingenuity, that it encircled as well the waist as the neck. The two ends of the chain which remained free, were attached to large rings or handcuffs, with which they manacled the hands of the Lord, who created the heavens, the angels and the whole universe.

The hands thus secured and bound, they fastened not in front, but behind. This chain they had brought from the house of Annias the Highpriest, where it had served to raise the portcullis of a dungeon. They had wrenched it from its place and provided it with padlock handcuffs.

But they were not satisfied with this unheard–of way of securing a prisoner; for in their distrust they added two pieces of strong rope: the one they wound around the throat of Jesus and, crossing it at the breast, bound it in heavy knots all about the body, leaving two long ends free in front, in order that the servants and soldiers might jerk Him in different directions along the way. The second rope served to tie his arms, being bound likewise around his waist. The two ends of this rope were left hanging free to be used by two other executioners for jerking Him from behind.

The Author of our salvation, hiding his power of annihilating his enemies in order that our Redemption might be the more abundant, submitted to all the consequences of the impious fury which Lucifer and his hellish squadron fomented in the Jews.

They dragged Him bound and chained under continued ill–treatment to the house of Annas, before whom they presented Him as a malefactor worthy of death. It was the custom of the Jews to present thus bound, those criminals who merited capital punishment; and they now made use of this custom in regard to Jesus, in order to intimate his sentence even before the trial.

The sacrilegious priest Annas seated himself in proud and arrogant state on the platform or tribunal of a great hall. Immediately Lucifer placed himself at his side with a multitude of evil spirits. Imperiously and haughtily the Highpriest asked Him about his disciples, and what doctrine He was preaching and teaching. This question was put merely for the purpose of misinterpreting his answer, if Jesus should utter any word that afforded such a chance.

But the Master of holiness, who is the Guide and the Corrector of the most wise, offered to the eternal Father the humiliation of being presented as a criminal before the Highpriest and of being questioned by him as a prevaricator and author of a false doctrine.

Our Redeemer with a humble and cheerful countenance answered the question as to his doctrines: "I have spoken openly to the world: I have always taught in the synagogue and in the temple, whither all the Jews resort: and in secret I have spoken nothing. Why askest thou Me? Ask these, who have heard what I have spoken unto them: behold they know what I have said,"

B6C5

As the doctrine of Christ our Lord came from his eternal Father, He spoke for it and defended its honor. He referred them to his hearers, both because those by whom He was now surrounded, would not believe Him and wished to distort all He should say, and because the truth and force of his teachings recommended and forced themselves upon the minds of his greatest enemies by their own excellence.

Concerning the Apostles He said nothing, because it was not necessary on this occasion and because they were not reflecting much credit upon their Master by their present conduct. Though his answer was so full of wisdom and so well suited to the question, yet one of the servants of the Highpriest rushed up with raised hand and audaciously struck the venerable and sacred face of Jesus, saying: "Answerest Thou the high priest so?"

The Lord accepted this boundless injury, praying for the one who had inflicted it; and holding Himself ready, if necessary, to turn and offer the other cheek for a second stroke, according to the doctrine He had himself inculcated.

But in order that the atrocious and daring offender might not shamelessly boast of his wickedness, the Lord replied with great tranquility and meekness: "If I have spoken evil, give testimony of the evil; if well, why strikest thou Me?" O sight most astounding to the supernal spirits! Since this is He, at the mere sound of whose voice the foundations of the heavens tremble and ought to tremble and the whole firmament is shaken!

While this ill–treatment of the Lord was going on, Saint Peter and the other disciple, who was none other than Saint John, arrived at the house of Annas. Saint John, as being well known there, readily obtained entrance, while Saint Peter remained outside. Afterwards the servant maid, who was an acquaintance of Saint John, allowed also him to enter and see what would happen to the Lord.

The two disciples remained in the portico adjoining the court–hall of the priest, and Saint Peter approached the fire, which the soldiers, on account of the coldness of the night, had built in the enclosure near the portico. The servant maid, on closer inspection, noticed the depressed bearing of Saint Peter. Coming up to him she recognized him as a disciple of Jesus, and said: "Art thou not perhaps one of the disciples of this Man?"

This question was asked by the maid with an air of contempt and reproach. Peter in his great weakness and hesitancy yielded to a sense of shame. Overcome also by his fear he answered: "I am not his disciple." Having given this answer, he slipped away to avoid further conversation, and left the premises. But he soon afterwards followed his Master to the house of Caliphs, where he denied Him again at two different times.

The denial of Peter caused greater pain to the Lord than the buffet which He had received; for this sin was directly opposed and abhorrent to his immense charity, while pains and sufferings were sweet and welcome to Him, since He could thereby atone for our sins. After this first denial of Peter, Christ prayed for him to his eternal Father and ordained that through the intercession of the blessed Mary he should obtain pardon even after the third denial.

The great Lady witnessed all that passed from her oratory. As She contained in her own breast the propitiatory and sacrifice of her Son and Lord in sacramental form, She directed her petitions and loving aspirations to Him, eliciting most heroic acts of compassion, thanksgiving adoration and worship. She bitterly wept over the denial of Saint Peter, and ceased not, until She perceived that the Lord would not refuse him the necessary helps for effectually rising from his fall.

The whole rabble of infernal spirits and merciless foes of Christ left the house of Annas and dragged our Lord Savior through the streets to the house of Caiphas, exercising upon Him all the cruelty of their ignominious fury. The Highpriest and his attendants broke out in loud derision and laughter, when they saw Jesus brought amid tumultuous noise into their presence beheld Him now subject to their power and jurisdiction without hope of escape.

The Highpriest Caiphas, filled with a deadly envy and hatred against the Master of life, was seated in his chair of state or throne. With him were Lucifer and all his demons, who had come from the house of Annas. The scribes and Pharisees, like bloodthirsty wolves, surrounded the gentle Lamb; all of them were full of the exultation of the envious, who see the object of their envy confounded and brought down.

By common consent they sought for witnesses, whom they could bribe to bring false testimonies against Jesus our Savior. Those that had been procured, advanced to proffer their accusations and testimony; but their accusations neither agreed with each other, nor could any of their slander be made to apply to Him, who of his very nature was innocence and holiness.

Our Savior Jesus answered not a word to all calumnies and lies brought forward against his innocence. Caiphas, provoked by the patient silence of the Lord, rose up in his seat and said to Him: "Why dost Thou not answer to what so many witnesses testify against Thee?"

But even to this the Lord made no response. For Caiphas and the rest were not only indisposed to believe Him; but they treacherously wished to make use of his answer in order to calumniate Him and satisfy the people in their proceedings against the Galileean, so that they might not be thought to have condemned Him to death without cause.

This humble silence, which should have appeased the wicked priest only infuriated him so much the more because it frustrated his evil purpose. Lucifer, who incited the high priest and all the rest, intently watched the conduct of the Savior. But the intention of the dragon was different from that of the high priest. He merely wanted to irritate the Lord, or to hear some word, by which could ascertain whether he was true God.

With this purpose Satan stirred up Caiphas to the highest pitch of rage and to ask in great wrath and haughtiness: "I adjure Thee by the living God, that Thou tell us, if Thou be the Christ, the Son of God."

This question of the Highpriest certainly convicted him at once of the deepest folly and of dreadful blasphemy for if it was sincere, he had permitted Christ to be brought before his tribunal in doubt whether He was the true God or not, which would make him guilty of the most formidable and audacious crime.

The doubt in such a matter should have been solved in quite another way, conformable to the demands of right reason and justice. Christ our Savior, hearing Himself conjured by the living God, inwardly adored and reverenced the Divinity, though appealed to by such sacrilegious lips.

Out of reverence for the name of God He therefore answered: "Thou hast said: I am He. Nevertheless I say to you, hereafter you shall see the Son of man (who I am) sitting on the right hand of the power of God, and coming in the clouds of heaven"

But the Highpriest, furious at the answer of the Lord, instead of looking upon it as a solution of his doubt rose once more in his seat, and rending his garments as an outward manifestation of his zeal for the honor of God, loudly cried out: "He hath blasphemed; what further need have we of witnesses? Behold, now you have heard the blasphemy: what think you?"

The real blasphemy however consisted rather in these words of Caiphas, since he denied the certain fact that Christ was the Son of God by his very nature, and since he attributed to the divine Personality sinfulness, which was directly repugnant to his very nature.

Such was the folly of the wicked priest, who by his office should have recognized and proclaimed the universal truth. He made of himself an execrable blasphemer in maintaining that He, who is holiness itself, had blasphemed.

Having previously, with satanical instinct, abused his high office in prophesying that the death of one man is better than the ruin of all the people, he now was hindered by his sins from understanding his own prophecy.

As the example and the opinions of princes and prelates powerfully stirs up the flattery and subserviency of inferiors, that whole gathering of wickedness was incensed at the Savior Jesus: all exclaimed in a loud voice: "He is guilty of death, let Him die, let Him die!" Roused by satanic fury they all fell upon their most meek Master and discharged upon Him their wrath.

Some of them struck Him in the face, others kicked Him, others tore out his hair, others spat upon his venerable countenance others slapped or struck Him in the neck, which was a treatment reserved among the Jews only for the most abject and vile of criminals.

All these affronts, reproaches and insults were seen and felt by the most holy Mary causing in Her the same pains and wounds in the same parts of her body and at the same time as inflicted upon the Lord. The only difference was that in our Lord the blows and torments were inflicted by the Jews themselves, while in his most pure Mother they were caused by the Almighty in a miraculous manner and upon request of the Lady.

According to natural laws, the vehemence of her interior sorrow and anxiety would have put an end to her life; but She was strengthened by divine power, so as to be able to continue to suffer with her beloved Son and Lord.

The interior acts performed by the Savior under these barbarous and unheard of persecutions, cannot be fathomed by human reason or faculties. Mary alone understood them fully, so as to be able to imitate them with the highest perfection.

But as the divine Master now experienced in his own Person, how necessary his sympathy would be for those who were to follow him and practice his doctrine, He exerted Himself so much the more in procuring for them grace and blessings on this occasion, in which He was teaching them by his own example the narrow way of perfection. In the midst of these injuries and torments, and those which followed thereafter, the Lord established for his perfect and chosen souls the beatitudes, which He had promised and proposed to them some time before.

He looked upon the poor in spirit, who were to imitate Him in this virtue and said: "Blessed are you in being stripped of the earthly goods; for by my Passion and Death I am to entail upon you the heavenly kingdom as a secure and certain possession of voluntary poverty.

Blessed are those who meekly suffer and bear adversities and tribulations; for, besides the joy of having imitated Me, they shall possess the land of the hearts and the good will of men through the peacefulness of their interactions and the sweetness of their virtues.

Blessed are they that weep while they sow in tears; for in them, they receive the bread of understanding and life, and they shall afterwards harvest the fruits of everlasting joy and bliss."

"Blessed are also those who hunger and thirst for justice and truth; for I shall earn for them satiation far beyond all their desires, as well in the reign of grace as in the reign of glory.

Blessed are they, who, imitating Me in my offers of pardon and friendship, mercifully pity those that offend and persecute them; for I promise them the fullness of mercy from my Father. Blessed be the pure of heart, who imitate Me in crucifying their flesh in order to preserve the purity of their souls. I promise them the vision of peace and of my Divinity, by becoming like unto Me and by partaking of Me.

Blessed are the peaceful, who, yielding their rights, do not resist the evil—minded and deal with them with a sincere and tranquil heart without vengeance; they shall be called my children, because they imitate my eternal Father and I shall write them in my memory and in my mind as my adopted sons.

Those that suffer persecution for justice's sake shall be the blessed heirs of my celestial kingdom, since they suffer with Me; and where I am, there also they shall be in eternity.

Rejoice, ye poor; be consoled all ye that are and shall be afflicted; glory in your lot, ye little ones and despised ones of this world, you who suffer in humility and longanimity, suffer with an interior rejoicing; since all of you are following Me in the path of truth.

Renounce vanity, despise the pomp and haughtiness of the false and deceitful Babylon; pass ye through the fires and the waters of tribulation until you reach Me, who am the light, the truth and your guide to the eternal rest and refreshment."

By the ill—treatment, which the Lord received in the presence of Caiphas, the wrath of this Hughpriest and of all his supporters and ministers was much gratified though not at all satiated. But as it was already past midnight, the whole council of these wicked men resolved to take good care, that the Savior be securely watched and confined until the morning, lest He should escape while they were asleep.

For this purpose they ordered Him to be locked, bound as He was, in one of the subterranean dungeons, a prison cell set apart for the most audacious robbers and criminals of the state. Scarcely any light penetrated into this prison to dispel its darkness.

It was filled with such uncleanness and stench, that it would have infected the whole house, if it had not been so remote and so well enclosed; for it had not been cleaned for many years, both because it was so deep down and because of the degradation of the criminals that were confined in it; for none thought it worthwhile making it habitable than for mere wild beasts, unworthy of all human kindness.

Jesus Before Pilate—Scourging/Crowning with Thorns

At the dawn of Friday morning, the ancients, the chief priests and scribes, who according to the law were looked upon with greatest respect by the people, gathered together in order to come to a common decision concerning the death of Christ. This they all desired; however they were anxious to preserve the semblance of justice before the people.

This council was held in the house of Caiphas, where the Lord was imprisoned. Once more they commanded Him to be brought from the dungeon to the hall of the council in order to be examined. The satellites of justice rushed below to drag Him forth bound and fettered as He was.

They again asked Him to tell them whether He was the Christ, that is, the Anointed. Just as in all their previous questions, this was put with the malicious determination not to listen or to admit the truth, but to calumniate and fabricate a charge against Him.

But the Lord, being perfectly willing to die for the truth, denied it not; at the same time He did not wish to confess it in such a manner that they could despise it, or borrow out of it some color for their calumny; for this was not becoming his innocence and wisdom.

Therefore He veiled his answer in such a way, that if the Pharisees chose to yield to even the least kindly feeling, they would be able to trace up the mystery hidden in his words; but if they had no such feeling, then should it become clear through their answer, that the evil which they imputed to Him was the result of their wicked intentions and lay not in his answer.

He therefore said to them: "If I tell you that I am He of whom you ask, you will not believe what I say; and if I shall ask you, you will not answer, nor release Me. But I tell you, that the Son of man, after this, shall seat Himself at the right hand of the power of God".

The priests answered: "Then thou art the Son of God?" and the Lord replied: "You say that I am." This was as if He had said: You have made a very correct inference, that I am the Son of God: for my works, my doctrines, and your own Scripture, as well as what you are now doing with Me, testify to the fact that I am the Christ, the One promised in the law.

But this council of the wicked was not disposed to assent to divine truth, although they themselves inferred it very correctly from the antecedents and could easily have believed it. They would neither give assent nor belief, but preferred to call it a blasphemy deserving death.

Since the Lord had now reaffirmed what He had said before, they all cried out: "What need have we of further witnesses, since He himself asserts it by his own lips?" And they immediately came to the unanimous conclusion that He should, as one worthy of death, be brought before Pontius Pilate, who governed Judea in the name of the Roman emperor and was the temporal Lord of Palestine.

The sun had already arisen while these things happened and the most holy Mother, who saw it all from afar, now resolved to leave her retreat and follow her divine Son to the house of Pilate and to his death on the Cross. When the great Queen and Lady was about to set forth from the Cenacle, saint John arrived in order to give an account of all that was happening; for the beloved disciple at that time did not know the visions, by which all the doings and sufferings of her most holy Son were manifest to the blessed Mother.

After the denial of Saint Peter, Saint John had retired and had observed, more from afar what was going on. Recognizing also the wickedness of his flight in the garden, he confessed it to the Mother of God and asked her pardon as soon as he came into her presence; and then he gave an account of all that passed in his heart and of what he had done and what he had seen in following his Master.

Saint John thought it well to prepare the afflicted Mother for her meeting with her most holy Son, in order that She might not be overcome by the fearful spectacle of his present condition. Therefore He sought to impress Her beforehand with some image of his sufferings by saying: "O my Lady, in what a state of suffering is our divine Master! The sight of Him cannot but break one's heart; for by the buffets and the blows and by the spittle, his most beautiful countenance is so disfigured and defiled, that Thou wilt scarcely recognize Him with thy own eyes."

The most prudent Lady listened to his description, as if She knew nothing of the events; but She broke out in bitterest tears of heart-rending sorrow. The holy women, who had came forth with the Lady, also listened to Saint John, and all of them were filled with grief and terror at his words.

The Queen of heaven asked the Apostle to accompany Her and the devout women, and, exhorting them all, She said: "Let us hasten our steps, in order that my eyes may see the Son of the eternal Father, who took human form in my womb; and you shall see, my dearest friends, to what the love of mankind has driven Him, my Lord and God, and what it costs Him to redeem men from sin and death, and to open for them the gates of heaven."

The Queen of heaven set forth through the streets of Jerusalem accompanied by Saint John and by some holy women. Of these not all, but only the three Marys and other very pious women, followed Her to the end. With Her were also the angels of her guard, whom She asked to open a way for Her to her divine Son. The holy angels obeyed and acted as her guard.

On the streets She heard the people expressing their various opinions and sentiments concerning the sorrowful events now transpiring in reference to Jesus of Nazareth. The more kindly hearted lamented over his fate, and they were fewest in number.

Others spake about the intention of his enemies to crucify Him; others related where He now was and how He was conducted through the streets, bound as a criminal; others spoke of the illtreatment He was undergoing; others asked, what evil He had done, that He should be so misused; others again in their astonishment and in their doubts, exclaimed: To this then have his miracles brought Him! Without a doubt they were all impostures, since He cannot defend or free himself!

Through the swarming and confused crowds the angels conducted the Empress of heaven to a sharp turn of the street, where She met her most holy Son. With the profoundest reverence She prostrated Herself before his sovereign Person and adored it more fervently and with a reverence more deep and more ardent than ever was given or ever shall be given to it by all the creatures.

She arose and then the Mother and Son looked upon each other with ineffable tenderness, interiorly conversing with each other in transports of an unspeakable sorrow. The most prudent Lady stepped aside and then followed Christ our Lord, continuing at a distance her interior communication with Him and with the eternal Father. The words of her soul are not for the mortal and corruptible tongue.

The image of her divine Son, thus wounded, defiled and bound, remained so firmly fixed and imprinted in the soul of our Queen, that during her life it never effaced, and remained in her mind as distinctly as if She were continually beholding Him with her own eyes.

Christ our God arrived at the house of Pilate, followed by many of the council and a countless multitude of the people. The Jews, wishing to preserve themselves as clean before the law as possible for the celebration of the Pasch and the unleavened bread, excused themselves before Pilate for their refusing to enter the pretorium or court of Pilate in presenting Jesus. As most absurd hypocrites they paid no attention to the sacrilegious uncleanness, with which their souls were affected in becoming the murderers of the innocent Godman.

Pilate, although a heathen, yielded to their ceremonic scruples, and seeing that they hesitated to enter his pretorium, he went out to meet them. According to formality customary among the Romans, he asked them: "What accusation have you against this Man?" They answered: "If He were not a criminal, we would not have brought Him to thee thus bound and fettered." This was as much as to say: We have convinced ourselves of the misdeeds and we are so attached to justice and to our obligations, that we would not begin any proceedings against Him, if He were not a great malefactor.

But Pilate pressed his inquiry and said: "What then are the misdeeds, of which has made Himself guilty?" They answered: "He is convicted of disturbing the commonwealth, He wishes to make Himself our king and forbids paying tribute to Caesar; He claims to be the son of God, and has preached a new doctrine, commencing in Galilee, through all Judea and Jerusalem."

"Take Him then yourselves," said Pilate, "and judge Him according to your laws; I do not find a just cause for proceeding against Him." But the Jews replied: "It is not permitted us to sentence any one to death, nor to execute such a sentence."

The most holy Mary, with Saint John and the women who followed Her, was present at this interview; for the holy angels made room for them where they could hear and see all that was passing. Shielded by her mantle She wept tears of blood, pressed forth by the sorrow which pierced her virginal heart. In her interior acts of virtue She faithfully reproduced those practiced by her most holy Son, while in her pains and endurance She copied those of his body. She asked the eternal Father to grant Her the favor of not losing sight of her divine Son, as far as was naturally possible, until his Death; and this was conceded to Her, excepting during the time in which He was in prison.

One of the accusations of the Jews and the priests before Pilate was, that Jesus our Savior had begun to stir up the people by his preaching in the province of Galilee. This caused Pilate to inquire, whether He was a Galilean; and as they told him, that Jesus was born and raised in that country, he thought this circumstance useful for the solution of his difficulties in regard to Jesus and for escaping the molestations of the Jews, who so urgently demanded his death.

Herod was at that time in Jerusalem, celebrating the Pasch of the Jews. He was the son of the first Herod, who had murdered the Innocents to procure the death of Jesus soon after his birth. This murderer had become a proselyte of the Jews at the time of his marriage with a Jewish woman. On this account his son Herod likewise observed the law of Moses, and he had come to Jerusalem from Galilee, of which he was governor.

Pilate was at enmity with Herod, for the two governed the two principal provinces of Palestine namely, Judea and Galilee, and a short time before it had happened that Pilate, in his zeal for the supremacy of the Roman empire, had murdered some Galileeans during a public function in the temple, mixing the blood of the insurgents with that of the holy sacrifices.

Herod was highly incensed at this sacrilege, and Pilate, in order to afford him some satisfaction without much trouble to himself, resolved to send to him Christ the Lord to be examined and judged as one of the subjects of Herod's sway. Pilate also expected that Herod would set Jesus free as being innocent and a Victim of the malice and envy of the priests and scribes.

When Herod was informed that Pilate would send Jesus of Nazareth to him, he was highly pleased. He knew that Jesus was a great friend of John the Baptist whom he had ordered to be put to death, and had heard many reports of his preaching. In vain and foolish curiosity he harbored the desire of seeing Jesus do something new and extraordinary for his entertainment and wonder. The Author of life therefore came into the presence of the murderer Herod, against whom the blood of the Baptist was calling more loudly to this same Lord for vengeance, than in its time the blood of Abel.

But the unhappy adulterer, ignorant of the terrible judgment of the Almighty, received Him with loud laughter as an enchanter and conjurer. In this dreadful misconception he commenced to examine and question Him, persuaded that he could thereby induce Him to work some miracle to satisfy his curiosity.

But the Master of wisdom and prudence, standing with a humble reserve before his most unworthy judge, answered him not a word. For on account of his evil–doing he well merited the punishment of not hearing the words of life, which he would certainly have heard if he had been disposed to listen to them with reverence.

The princes and priests of the Jews stood around, continually rehearsing the same accusations and charge they had advanced in the presence of Pilate. But the Lord maintained silence also in regard to these calumnies, much to the disappointment of Herod. In his presence the Lord would not open his lips, neither in order to answer his questions, nor in order to refute the accusations.

Herod was altogether unworthy of hearing the truth, this being his greatest punishment and the punishment most to be dreaded by all the princes and the powerful of this earth. Herod was much put out by the silence and meekness of our Savior and was much disappointed in his vain curiosity. But the unjust judge tried to hide his confusion by mocking and ridiculing the innocent Master with his whole cohort of soldiers and ordering him to be sent back to Pilate.

Pilate was again confronted with Jesus in his palace and was bestormed anew by the Jews to condemn Him to death of the cross. Convinced of the innocence of Christ and of the mortal envy of the Jews, he was much put out at Herod's again referring the disagreeable decision to his own tribunal. Feeling himself obliged in his quality of judge to give this decision, he sought to placate the Jews in different ways.

One of these was a private interview with some of the servants and friends of the highpriests and priests. He urged them to prevail upon their masters and friends, not any more to ask for the release of the malefactor Barabbas, but instead demand the release of our Redeemer; and to be satisfied with some punishment he was willing to administer before setting Him free.

This measure Pilate had taken before they arrived a second time to press their demand for a sentence upon Jesus. The proposal to choose between freeing either Barabbas or Jesus was made to the Jews, not only once, but two or three times; the first time before sending Him to Herod and the second time after his return.

Pilate spoke to the Jews and said: "You have brought this Man before me, accusing Him of perverting the people by his doctrines; and having examined Him in your presence, I was not convinced of the truth of your accusations. And Herod, to whom I have sent Him and before whom you repeated your accusations, refused to condemn Him to death.

It will be sufficient to correct and chastise Him for the present, in order that He may amend. As I am to release some malefactor for the feast of the Pasch, I will release Christ, if you will have Him freed, and punish Barabbas." But the multitude of the Jews, thus informed how much Pilate desired to set Jesus free, shouted with one voice: "Enough, enough, not Christ, but Barabbas deliver unto us."

While Pilate was thus disputing with the Jews in the pretorium, his wife, Procula, happened to hear of his doings and she sent him a message telling him: "What hast thou to do with this Man? Let him go free: for I warn thee that I have had this very day some visions in regard to Him!"

This warning of Procula originated through the activity of Lucifer and his demons. For they, observing all that was happening in regard to the person of Christ and the unchangeable patience with which He bore all injuries, were more and more confused and staggered in their rabid fury. Despairing of success the demons betook themselves to the wife of Pilate and spoke to her in dreams, representing to her that this Man was just and without guilt, that if her husband should sentence Him he would be deprived of his rank and she herself would meet with great adversity. They urged her to advise Pilate to release Jesus and punish Barabbas, if she did not wish to draw misfortune upon their house and their persons.

Procula was filled with great fear and terror at these visions, and as soon as she heard what was passing between the Jews and her husband, she sent him the message to not meddle with this Man nor condemn one to death, whom she told to be just. The demon also injected similar misgivings into the mind of Pilate and these warnings of his wife only increased them. Yet, as all his considerations rested upon worldly policy, and as he had not co-operated with the true helps given him by the Savior, all these fears retarded his unjust proceedings only so long as no other more powerful consideration arose, as will be seen in effect. But just now he began for the third time to argue (as saint Luke tells us), insisting upon the innocence of Christ our Lord and that he found no crime in Him nor any guilt worthy of death, and therefore he would punish and then dismiss Him.

But the Jews, on the contrary, demanded that Christ be crucified. Thereupon Pilate asked for water and released Barabbas. Then he washed his hands in the presence of all the people, saying: "I have no share in the death of this just Man, whom you condemn. Look to yourselves in what you are doing, for I wash my hands in order that you may understand they are not sullied in the blood of the Innocent."

Pilate thought that by this ceremony he could excuse himself entirely and that he thereby could put its blame upon the princes of the Jews and upon the people who demanded it. The wrath of the Jews was so blind and foolish that for the satisfaction of seeing Jesus crucified, they entered upon this agreement with Pilate and took upon themselves and upon their children the responsibility for this crime. Loudly proclaiming this terrible sentence and curse, they exclaimed: "His blood come upon us and upon our children"

In the house of Pilate, through the ministry of the holy angels, our Queen was placed in such a position that She could hear the disputes of the iniquitous judge with the scribes and priests concerning the innocence of Christ our Savior, and concerning the release of Barabbas in preference to Him. All the clamors of these human tigers She heard in silence and admirable meekness, as the living counterpart of her most holy Son.

Although She preserved the unchanging propriety modesty of her exterior, all the malicious words of the Jews pierced her sorrowful heart like a two–edged sword. But the voices of her unspoken sorrows resounded in the ears of the eternal Father more pleasantly and sweetly than the lamentation of the beautiful Rachel who, as Jeremias says, was beweeping her children because they cannot be restored.

Our most beautiful Rachel, the purest Mary, sought not revenge, but pardon for her enemies, who were depriving Her of the Onlybegotten of the Father and her only Son. She imitated all the actions of the most holy Soul of Christ and accompanied Him in the works of most exalted holiness and perfection; for neither could her torments hinder her charity, nor her affliction diminish her fervor, nor could the tumult distract her attention, nor the outrageous injuries of the multitudes prevent her interior recollection: under all circumstances She practiced the most exalted virtues in the most eminent degree.

B6C6

Such was the implacable fury of the priests and confederates, the Pharisees, against the Author of life. For Lucifer, despairing of being able to hinder his murder by the Jews, inspired them with his own dreadful malice and outrageous cruelty. Pilate, placed between the known truth and his human and terrestrial considerations, chose to follow the erroneous leading of the latter, and ordered Jesus to be severely scourged, though he had himself declared Him free from guilt.

Thereupon those ministers of Satan, with many others, brought Jesus our Savior to the place of punishment, which was a courtyard or enclosure attached to the house and set apart for the torture of criminals in order to force them to confess their crimes. It was surrounded by a low, open building, surrounded by columns, some of which supported the roof, while others were lower and stood free. To one of these columns, which were of marble, they bound Jesus very securely; for they still thought Him a magician and feared his escape.

They first took off the white garment with not less ignominy than when they clothed Him therein in the house of the adulterous homicide Herod. In loosening the ropes and chains, which He had borne since his capture in the garden, they cruelly widened the wounds which his bonds had made in his arms and wrists. Having freed his hands, they commanded Him with infamous blasphemies to despoil Himself of the seamless tunic which He wore. This was the identical garment with which his most blessed Mother had clothed Him in Egypt when He first began to walk.

Thus the Lord stood uncovered in the presence of a great multitude and the six torturers bound Him brutally to one of the columns in order to chastise Him so much the more at their ease. Then, two and two at a time, they began to scourge Him with such inhuman cruelty, as was possible only in men possessed by Lucifer as were these executioners.

B6C6

The first two scourged the innocent Savior with hard and thick cords, full of rough knots, and in their sacrilegious fury strained all the powers of their body to inflict the blows. This first scourging raised in the deified body of the Lord great welts and livid tumors, so that the sacred blood gathered beneath the skin and disfigured his entire body. Already it began to ooze through the wounds.

The first two having at length desisted, the second pair continued the scourging in still greater emulation; with hardened leather thongs they leveled their strokes upon the places already sore and caused the discolored tumors to break open and shed forth the sacred blood until it bespattered and drenched the garments of the sacrilegious torturers, running down also in streams to the pavement.

Those two gave way to the third pair of scourgers, who commenced to beat the Lord with extremely tough rawhides, dried hard like osier twigs. They scourged Him still more cruelly, because they were wounding, not so much his virginal body, as cutting into the wounds already produced by the previous scourging. Besides they had been secretly incited to greater fury by the demons, who were filled with new rage at the patience of Christ.

As the veins of the sacred body had now been opened and his whole Person seemed but one continued wound, the third pair found no more room for new wounds. Their ceaseless blows inhumanly tore the immaculate and virginal flesh of Christ our Redeemer and scattered many pieces of it about the pavement; so much so that a large portion of the shoulder–bones were exposed and showed red through the flowing blood: in other places also the bones were laid bare larger than the palm of the hand.

In order to wipe out entirely that beauty, which exceeded that of all other men, they beat Him in the face and in the feet and hands, thus leaving unwounded not a single spot in which they could exert their fury and wrath against the most innocent Lamb. The divine blood flowed to the ground, gathering here and there in great abundance. The scourging in the face, and in the hands and feet, was unspeakably painful, because these parts are so full of sensitive and delicate nerves. His venerable countenance became so swollen and wounded that the blood and the swellings blinded Him.

In addition to their blows the executioners spat upon his Person their disgusting spittle and loaded Him with insulting epithets. The exact number of blows dealt out to the Savior from head to foot was 5,115. The great Lord and Author of all creation who, by his divine nature was incapable of suffering, was, in his human flesh and for our sake, reduced to a man of sorrows as prophesied, and was made to experience our infirmities, becoming the last of men, a man of sorrows and the outcast of the people.

The multitudes who had followed the Lord, filled up the courtyard of Pilate's house and the surrounding streets; for all of them waited for the issue of this event, discussing and arguing about it according to each one's views. Amid all this confusion the Virgin Mother endured unheard of insults, and She was deeply afflicted by the injuries and blasphemies heaped upon her divine Son by the Jews and gentiles.

When they brought Jesus to the scourging place She retired in the company of the Marys and Saint John to a corner of the courtyard. Assisted by her divine visions, She there witnessed the scourging and the torments of our Savior. Although She did not see it with the eyes of her body nothing was hidden to Her, no more than if She had been standing quite near.

Human thoughts cannot comprehend how great and how diverse were the afflictions and sorrows of the great Queen and Mistress of the angels: together with many other mysteries of the Divinity they shall become manifest in the next life, for the glory of the Son and Mother.

The blessed Mother felt in her own body the torments of her Son. This was true also of the scourging, which She felt in all the parts of her virginal body, in the same intensity as they were felt by Christ in his body. Although She shed no blood except what flowed from her eyes with her tears, nor was lacerated in her flesh; yet the bodily pains so changed and disfigured Her, that Saint John and the holy women failed to find in Her any resemblance of Herself.

Besides the tortures of the body She suffered ineffable sorrows of the soul; there sorrow was augmented in proportion to the immensity of her insight. For her sorrow flowed not only from the natural love of a mother and a supreme love of Christ as her God, but it was proportioned to her power of judging more accurately than all creatures of the innocence of Christ, the dignity of his divine Person, the atrocity of the insults coming from the perfidious Jews and the children of Adam, whom He was freeing from eternal death.

Thereupon they took Jesus to the pretorium, where, with the same cruelty and contempt, they again despoiled him of his garments and in order to deride Him before all the people as a counterfeit king, clothed in a much torn and soiled mantle of purple color. They placed also upon his sacred head a cap made of woven thorns, to serve Him as a crown. This cap was woven of thorn branches and in such a manner that many of the hard and sharp thorns would penetrate into the skull, some of them to the ears and others to the eyes. Hence one of the greatest tortures suffered by the Lord was that of the crown of thorns.

Instead of a sceptre they placed into his hands a contemptible reed. They also threw over His shoulders a violet colored mantle, something of the style of capes worn in churches; for such a garment belonged to the vestiture of a king. In this array of a mock–king the perfidious Jews decked out Him, who by his nature and by every right was the King of kings and the Lord of lords.

Then all the soldiers, in the presence of the priests and Pharisees, gathered around Him and heaped upon Him their blasphemous mockery and derision. Some of them bent their knees and mockingly said to Him: God save Thee, King of the Jews. Others buffeted Him; others snatched the cane from his hands and struck Him on his crowned head; others ejected their disgusting spittle upon Him; all of them, instigated by furious demons, insulted and affronted Him in different manners.

It seemed to Pilate that the spectacle of a man so illtreated as Jesus of Nazareth would move and fill shame the hearts of that ungrateful people. He therefore commanded Jesus to be brought from the pretorium to an open window, where all could see Him crowned with thorns, disfigured by the scourging and the ignominious vestiture of a mock–king.

Pilate himself spoke to the people, calling out to them: "Ecce Homo," "Behold, what a man!". See this Man, whom you hold as your enemy! What can I do with Him than to have punished Him in this severe manner? You certainly have nothing more to fear from Him."

When the Blessed among women, most holy Mary, saw her divine Son as Pilate showed Him to the people and heard him say: "Ecce homo!" She fell upon her knees and openly adored Him as the true Godman. The same was also done by saint John and the women, together with all the holy angels of the Queen and Lady; for they saw that not only Mary, as the Mother of the Savior, but that God himself desired them thus to act

THE WAY OF THE CROSS

The sentence of Pilate against our Savior having been published in a loud voice before all the people, the executioners loaded the heavy Cross, on which He was to be crucified, upon his tender and wounded shoulders. In order that He might carry it they loosened the bonds holding his hands, but not the others, since they wish to drag Him along by the loose ends of the ropes bound his body. In order to torment Him the more they drew two loops around his throat.

The Cross was fifteen feet long, of thick and heavy timbers. The herald began to proclaim the sentence and the whole confused and turbulent multitude of the people, the executioners and soldiers, with great noise, uproar and disorder began to move from the house of Pilate to mount Calvary through the streets of Jerusalem.

The Master and Redeemer of the world, Jesus, before receiving the Cross looked upon it with a countenance full of extreme joy and exultation such as would be shown by a bridegroom looking at the rich adornments of his bride, and on receiving it, He addressed it as follows:

"O Cross, beloved of my soul, now prepared and ready to still my longings, come to Me, that I may be received in thy arms, and that, attached to them as on an altar, I may be accepted by the eternal Father as the sacrifice of his everlasting reconciliation with the human race. In order to die upon thee, I have descended from heaven and assumed mortal and passable flesh; for thou art to be the scepter with which I shall triumph over all my enemies, the key with which I shall open the gates of heaven for all the predestined, the sanctuary in which the guilty sons of Adam shall find mercy and the treasure house for the enrichment of their poverty."

"Upon thee I desire to exalt and recommend dishonor and reproach among men, in order that my friends embrace them with joy, seek them with anxious longings, and follow Me on the path which I through thee shall open up before them. My Father and eternal God, I confess Thee as the Lord of heaven and earth, subjecting Myself to thy power and to thy divine wishes, I take upon my shoulders the wood for the sacrifice of my innocent and passable humanity and I accept it willingly for the salvation of men. Receive Thou, eternal Father, this sacrifice as acceptable to thy justice, in order that from today on they may not any more be servants, but sons and heirs of thy kingdom together with Me"

None of these sacred mysteries and happenings were hidden from the great Lady of the world, Mary; for she had a most intimate knowledge and understanding of them, far beyond that of all the angels. The events, which She could not see with the eyes of her body, She perceived by her intelligence and revealed science, which manifested to Her the interior operation of her most holy Son. By this divine light She recognized the infinite value of the wood of the Cross after it had come in contact with the deified humanity of Jesus our Redeemer.

Immediately She venerated and adored it in a manner befitting it. The same was also done by the heavenly spirits attending upon the Queen. She imitated her divine Son in the tokens of affections, with which He received the Cross, addressing it in the words suited to her office as Coadjutrix of the Redeemer. By her prayers to the eternal Father She followed Him in his exalted sentiments as the living original and exemplar, without failing in the least point.

When She heard the voice of the herald publishing and rehearsing the sentence through the streets, the heavenly Mother in protest against the accusations contained in the sentence and in the form of comments on the glory and honor of the Lord, composed a canticle of praise worship of the innocence and sinlessness of her all—holy Son and God.

The most loving Mother was so admirably faithful in her sufferings and in imitating the example of Christ our God, that She never permitted Herself any easement either of her bodily pains, such as rest, nourishment, or sleep; nor any relaxation of the spirit, such as any consoling thoughts or considerations, except when She was visited from on high by divine influence.

Then only would She humbly and thankfully accept relief, in order that She might recover strength to attend still more fervently to the object of her sorrows and to the cause of his sufferings. The same wise consideration She applied to the malicious behavior of the Jews and their servants, to the needs of the human race, to their threatening ruin, and to the ingratitude of men, for whom He suffered. Thus She perfectly and intimately knew of all these things and felt it more deeply than all the creatures.

Another hidden and astonishing miracle was wrought by the right hand of God through the instrumentality of the blessed Mary against Lucifer and his infernal spirits. It took place in the following manner: The dragon and his associates, though they could not understand the humiliation of the Lord, were most attentive to all that happened in the Passion of the Lord. Now, when He took upon Himself the Cross, all these enemies felt a new and mysterious tremor and weakness, which caused in them great consternation and confused distress.

Conscious of these unwonted and invincible feelings the prince of darkness feared, that in the Passion and Death of Christ our Lord some dire and irreparable destruction of his reign was imminent. In order not to be overtaken by it in the presence of Christ our God, the dragon resolved to retire and fly with all his followers to the caverns of hell. But when he sought to execute this resolve, he was prevented by the great Queen and Mistress of all creation; for the Most High, enlightening Her and intimating to Her what She was to do, at the same time invested Her with his power.

The heavenly Mother, turning toward Lucifer and his squadrons, by her imperial command hindered them from flying; ordering them to await and witness the Passion to the end on mount Calvary. The demons could not resist the command of the mighty Queen; for they recognized and felt the divine power operating in Her. Subject to her sway they followed Christ as so many prisoners dragged along in chains to Calvary, where the eternal wisdom had decreed to triumph over from the throne of the Cross, as we shall see later on.

There is nothing which can exemplify the discouragement and dismay, which from that moment began to oppress Lucifer and his demons. According to our way of speaking, they walked along to Calvary like criminals condemned to a terrible death, and seized by the dismay and consternation of an inevitable punishment.

The executioners, bare of all human compassion and kindness, dragged our Savior Jesus along with incredible cruelty and insults. Some of them jerked Him forward by the ropes in order to accelerate his passage, while others pulled from behind in order to retard it.

On account of this jerking and the weight of the Cross they caused Him to sway to and fro and often to fall to the ground. By the hard knocks He thus received on the rough stones great wounds were opened, especially on the two knees and they were widened at each repeated fall.

The heavy Cross also inflicted a wound on the shoulder on which it was carried. The unsteadiness caused the Cross sometimes to knock against his sacred head, and sometimes the head against the Cross; thus the thorns of his crown penetrated deeper and wounded the parts, which they had not yet reached.

To these torments of the body the ministers of evil added many insulting words and execrable affronts, ejecting their impure spittle and throwing the dirt of the pavement into his face so mercilessly, that they blinded the eyes that looked upon them with such divine mercy.

Thus they of their own account condemned themselves to the loss of the graces, with which his very looks were fraught. By the haste with which they dragged Him along in their eagerness to see Him die, they did not allow Him to catch his breath; for his most innocent body, having been in so few hours overwhelmed with such a storm of torments, was so weakened and bruised that to all appearances He was ready to yield up life under his pains and sorrows.

From the house of Pilate the sorrowful and stricken Mother followed with the multitudes on the way of her divine Son, accompanied by Saint John and the pious women. As the surging crowds hindered Her from getting very near to the Lord, She asked the eternal Father to be permitted to stand at the foot of the Cross of her blessed Son and see Him die with her own eyes.

With the divine consent She ordered her angels to manage things in such a way as to make it possible for her to execute her wishes. The holy angels obeyed Her with great reverence; and they speedily led the Queen through some bystreet, in order that She might meet her Son.

Thus it came that both of Them met face to face in sweetest recognition of each Other and in mutual renewal of each other's interior sorrows. Yet They did not speak to one another, nor would the fierce cruelty of the executioners have permitted such interaction. But the most prudent Mother adored her divine Son and true God, laden with the Cross; and interiorly besought Him, that, since She could not relieve him of the weight of the Cross since She was not permitted to command her holy angels to lighten it, He would inspire these ministers of cruelty to procure some one for his assistance. This prayer was heard by the Lord Christ; and so it happened, that Simon of Cyrene was afterwards impressed to carry the Cross with the Lord.

B6C7

The Pharisees and the executioners were moved to this measure, some of them out of natural compassion, others for fear lest Christ, the Author of life, should lose his life by exhaustion before it could be taken from Him on the Cross.

Beyond all human thought and estimation was the sorrow of the most sincere Dove and Virgin Mother while She thus witnessed with her own eyes her Son carrying the Cross to Mount Calvary; for She alone could fittingly know and love Him according to his true worth. It would have been impossible for Her to live through this ordeal, if the divine power had not strengthened Her and preserved Her life.

With bitterest sorrow She addressed the Lord and spoke to Him in her heart: "My Son and eternal God, light of my eyes and life of my soul, receive, O Lord, the sacrifice of my not being able to relieve Thee of the burden of the Cross and carry it myself, who am a daughter of Adam; for it is I who should die upon it in love of Thee, as Thou now wishest to die in most ardent love of the human race. O most loving Mediator between guilt and justice!"

"How dost Thou cherish mercy in the midst of so great injuries and such heinous offenses! O charity without measure or bounds, which permits such torments and affronts in order to afford it a wider scope for its ardor and efficacy! O infinite and sweetest love, would that hearts and the wills of men were all mine, so that they could give no such thankless return for all that Thou endurest! O who will speak to the hearts of the mortals to teach them what they owe to Thee, since Thou hast paid so dearly for their salvation from ruin!"

THE CRUCIFIXION

Our Savior then reached the mountain of sacrifice. Mount Calvary was held to be a place of defilement and ignominy, as being reserved for the chastisement of condemned criminals, whose cadavers spread around it their stench and attached to it a still more evil fame. Our most loving Jesus arrived at its summit so worn out, wounded, torn and disfigured, that He seemed altogether transformed into an object of pain and sorrows.

When the most prudent Mother perceived that now the mysteries of the Redemption were to be fulfilled and that the executioners were about to strip Jesus of his clothes for crucifixion, She turned in spirit to the eternal Father and prayed as follows:

"My Lord and eternal God, Thou art the Father of thy onlybegotten Son. He was born of my womb and received from me this human nature, in which He now suffers. I have nursed and sustained Him at my own breast; and as the best sons that ever can be born of any creature, I love Him with maternal love."

"Now as a Mother, I yield to Thee and once more place in thy hands thy and my Son as a sacrifice for the Redemption of man. Accept, my Lord, this pleasing offering, since this is more than I can ever offer by submitting my own self as a victim or to suffering. This sacrifice is greater, not only because my Son is the true God and of thy own substance, but because this sacrifice costs me a much greater sorrow and pain. For if the lots were changed and I should be permitted to die in order to preserve his most life, I would consider it a great relief and the fulfillment of my dearest wishes."

It was already the sixth hour, which corresponds to our noontime, and the executioners, intending to crucify the Savior naked, despoiled Him of the seamless tunic and of his garments. As the tunic was large and without opening in front, they pulled it over the head of Jesus without taking off the crown of thorns; but on account of the rudeness with which they proceeded, they inhumanly tore off the crown with the tunic.

Thus they opened anew all the wounds of his head, and in some of them remained the thorns, which, in spite of their being so hard and sharp, were wrenched off by the violence with which the executioners despoiled Him of his tunic and, with it, of the crown. With heartless cruelty they again forced it down upon his sacred head, opening up wounds upon wounds. By the rude tearing off of the tunic were renewed also the wounds of his whole body, since the tunic had dried into the open places and its removal was adding new pains to his wound. Four times during the Passion did they despoil Jesus of his garments and again vest Him.

The first time in order to scourge him at the pillar; the second time in order to clothe Him in the mock purple; the third when they took this off in order to clothe Him in his tunic; the fourth, when they finally took away his clothes. This last was the most painful, because his wounds were more numerous, his holy humanity was much weakened, and there was less shelter against the sharp wind on mount Calvary; for also this element was permitted to increase the sufferings of his death—struggle by sending its cold blasts across the mount.

The holy Cross was lying on the ground and the executioners were busy making the necessary preparations for crucifying Him and the two thieves. In the meanwhile our Redeemer and Master prayed to the Father in the following terms: "Eternal Father, I offer my entire humanity and all that according to thy will it has accomplished in descending from thy bosom to assume passable and mortal flesh for the Redemption of men, my brethren."

"I offer Thee, Lord, with Myself, also my most loving Mother, her love, her most perfect works, her sorrows, her sufferings, and her anxious and prudent solicitude in serving Me, imitating Me and accompanying Me unto death. I offer Thee the little flock of my

Apostles, the holy Church and congregation of the faithful, such as it is now and as it shall be to the end of the world; and with it I offer to Thee all the mortal children of Adam.

"All this I place in thy hands as the true and almighty Lord and God. As far as my wishes are concerned, I suffer and die for all, and I desire that all shall be saved, under the condition that all follow Me and profit of my Redemption. Thus may they pass from the slavery of the devil to be thy children, my brethren and co-heirs of the grace merited by Me."

"Especially, O my Lord, do I offer to Thee the poor, despised and afflicted, who are my friends and who follow Me on the way to the Cross. I desire that the just and the predestined be written in thy eternal memory. I beseech Thee, my Father, to withhold thy chastisement and not to raise the scourge of thy justice over men; let them not be punished as they merit for their sins. Be Thou from now on their Father as Thou art mine. I beseech Thee also, that they may be helped to ponder upon my Death in pious affection and be enlightened from above; and I pray for those who are persecuting Me, in order that they may be converted to the truth. Above all do I ask Thee for the exaltation of thy ineffable and most holy name."

This prayer and supplication of our Savior were known to the most blessed Mother, and She imitated Him and made the same petitions to the Father in as far as She was concerned. The most prudent Virgin never forgot or disregarded the first word which She had heard from the mouth of her divine Son as an infant: "Become like unto Me, my Beloved." His promise, that in return for the new human existence which She had given Him in her virginal womb, He would, by his almighty power, give Her a new existence of divine and eminent grace above all other creatures, was continually fulfilled.

In order to find the places for the auger-holes on the Cross, the executioners haughtily commanded the Creator of the universe to stretch Himself out upon it. The Teacher of humility obeyed without hesitation. But they, following their inhuman instinct of cruelty, marked the places for the holes, not according to the size of his body, but larger, having in mind a new torture for their Victim.

This inhuman intent was known to the Mother of light, and the knowledge of it was one of the greatest afflictions of her chastest heart during the whole Passion. She saw through the intentions of these ministers of sin and She anticipated the torments to be endured by her beloved Son when his limbs should be wrenched from their sockets in being nailed to the Cross. But She could not do anything to prevent it, as it was the will of the Lord to suffer these pains for men.

When He rose from the Cross and they set about boring the holes, the great Lady approached and took hold of one of his hands, adoring Him and kissing it with greatest reverence. The executioners allowed this because they thought that the sight of his Mother would cause so much the greater affliction to the Lord; for they wished to spare Him no sorrow they could cause Him.

But they were ignorant of the hidden mysteries; for the Lord during his Passion had no greater source of consolation and interior joy than to see in the soul of his most blessed Mother, the beautiful likeness of Himself and the full fruits of his Passion and Death. This joy, to a certain extent, comforted Christ our Lord also in that hour.

Presently one of the executioners seized the hand of Jesus our Savior and placed it upon the auger–hole while another hammered a large and rough nail through the palm. The veins and sinews were torn, and the bones of the sacred hand, which made the heavens and all that exists, were forced apart.

When they stretched out the other hand, they found that it did not reach up to the auger–hole; for the sinews of the other arm had been shortened and the executioners had maliciously set the holes too far apart. In order to overcome the difficulty, they took the chain with which the Savior had been bound in the garden, and looping one end through a ring around his wrist, they, with unheard of cruelty, pulled the hand over the hole and fastened it with another nail.

Thereupon they seized his feet, and placing them one above the other, they tied the same chain around both and stretched them with barbarous ferocity down to the third hole. Then they drove through both feet a large nail into the Cross. Thus the sacred body, in which dwelled the Divinity, was nailed motionless to the holy Cross, and the handiwork of his deified members was so stretched and torn asunder, that the bones of his body, dislocated and forced from their natural position, could all be counted. The bones of his breast, of his shoulders and arms, and of his whole body yielded to the cruel violence and were torn from their sinews.

Then they dragged the lower end of the Cross with the crucified God near to the hole, wherein it was to be planted. Some of them getting under the upper part of the Cross with their shoulders, others pushing upward with their halberds and lances, they raised the Savior on his Cross and fastened its foot in the hole they had drilled into the ground. Thus our true life and salvation now hung in the air upon the sacred wood in full view of the innumerable multitudes of different nations and countries.

I must not omit mentioning another barbarity inflicted upon the Lord as they raised Him: for some of them placed the sharp points of their lances and halberds to his body and fearfully lacerating Him under the armpits in helping to push the Cross into position. At this spectacle new cries of protest arose with still more vehemence and confusion from the multitude of people.

The Jews blasphemed, the kind–hearted lamented, the strangers were astounded, some of them called the attention of the bystanders to the proceedings, others turned away their heads in horror and pity; others took to themselves a warning from this spectacle of suffering, and still others proclaimed Him a just Man.

All these different sentiments were like arrows piercing the heart of the afflicted Mother. The sacred body now shed much blood from the nail wounds, which, by its weight and the shock of the Cross falling into the hole, had widened. They were the fountains, now opened up, to which Isaiah invites us to hasten with joy to quench our thirst and wash off the stains of our sins. No one shall be excused who does not quickly approach to drink of them.

Then they crucified also the two thieves and planted their crosses to the right and the left of the Savior; for thereby they wished to indicate that He deserved the most conspicuous place as being the greatest malefactor. The Pharisees and priests, forgetting the two thieves, turned all the venom of their fury against the sinless and holy One by nature.

Wagging their heads in scorn and mockery they threw stones and dirt at the Cross of the Lord and his royal Person, saying: "Ah Thou, who destroyest the temple and in three days rebuildest it, save now Thyself; others He has made whole, Himself He cannot save; if this be the Son of God let him descend from the Cross, and we will believe in Him."

The two thieves in the beginning also mocked the Lord and said: "If Thou art the Son of God, save Thyself and us." These blasphemies of the two thieves caused special sorrow to our Lord, since they were so near to death and losing the fruit of their death—pains, by which they could have satisfied in part for their justly punished crimes. Soon after, however, one of them availed himself of the greatest opportunity that a sinner ever had in this world, and was converted from his sins.

As the wood of the Cross was the throne of majesty and the chair of the doctrine of life, and as He was now raised upon it, confirming his doctrine by his example, Christ now uttered those words of highest charity and perfection: "Father, forgive them, for they know not what they do!" This principle of charity and fraternal love the divine Teacher had appropriated to himself and proclaimed by his own lips. He now confirmed and executed it upon the Cross, not only pardoning and loving his enemies, but excusing those under the plea of ignorance whose malice had reached the highest point possible to men in persecuting, blaspheming and crucifying their God and Redeemer.

Such was the difference between the behavior of ungrateful men favored with so great enlightenment, instruction and blessing; and the behavior of Jesus in his most burning charity while suffering the crown of thorns, the nails, and the Cross and unheard of blasphemy at the hands of men.

One of the two thieves, called Dismas, became aware of some of the mysteries. Being assisted at the same time by the prayers and intercession of most holy Mary, he was interiorly enlightened concerning his Rescuer and Master by the first word on the Cross. Moved by true sorrow and contrition for his sins, he turned to his companion and said: "Neither dost thou fear God, seeing that thou art under the same condemnation? And we indeed justly, for we receive the due reward of our deeds; but this Man hath done no evil." And thereupon speaking to Jesus, he said: "Lord, remember me when Thou shalt come into thy kingdom!"

In this happiest of thieves, in the centurion and in the others who confessed Jesus Christ on the Cross, began to appear the results of the Redemption. But the one most favored was this Dismas, who merited to hear the second word of the Savior on the Cross: "Amen, I say to thee, this day shalt thou be with Me in Paradise." Having thus justified the good thief, Jesus turned his loving gaze upon his afflicted Mother, who with Saint John was standing at the foot of the Cross.

Speaking to both, he first addressed his Mother, saying: "Woman, behold thy son!" and then to the Apostle: "Behoid thy Mother!" The Lord called Her Woman and not Mother, because this name of

Mother had in it something of sweetness and consolation, the very pronouncing of which would have been a sensible relief.

During his Passion He would admit of no exterior consolation, having renounced for that time all exterior alleviation and easement, as I have mentioned above. By this word "woman" he tacitly and by implication wished to say: Woman blessed among all women, the most prudent among all the daughters of Adam, Woman, strong and constant, unconquered by any fault of thy own, unfailing in my service and most faithful in thy love toward Me, which even the mighty waters of my Passion could not extinguish or resist.

I am going to my Father and cannot accompany Thee further; my beloved disciple will attend upon Thee and serve Thee as his Mother, and he will be thy son. All this the heavenly Queen understood. The holy Apostle on his part received Her as his own from that hour on; for he was enlightened anew in order to understand and appreciate the greatest treasure of the Divinity in the whole creation next to the humanity of Christ our Savior. In this light He reverenced and served Her for the rest of her life, as I will relate farther on. Our Lady also accepted him as her son in humble subjection and obedience.

Already the ninth hour of the day was approaching, although the darkness and confusion of nature made it appear to be rather a chaotic night. Our Savior spoke the fourth word from the Cross in a loud and strong voice, so that all the bystanders could hear it: "My God, my God, why hast thou forsaken Me?"

Although the Lord had uttered these words in his Hebrew language, they were not understood by all. Since they began with: "Eli, eli," some of them thought He was calling upon Elias, and a number of them mocked Him saying: "Let us see whether Elias shall come to free Him from our hands?"

He grieved that his copious and superabundant Redemption, offered for the whole human race, should not be efficacious in the reprobate and that He should find Himself deprived of them in the eternal happiness, for which He had created and redeemed them. As this was to happen in consequence of the decree of his Father's eternal will, He lovingly and sorrowfully complained of it in the words: "My God, my God why hast Thou forsaken Me?" that is, in so God deprived Him of the salvation of the reprobate.

In confirmation of this sorrow the Lord added: "I thirst!" The sufferings of the Lord and his anguish could easily cause a natural thirst. But for Him this was not a time to complain of this thirst or to quench it; and therefore Jesus would not have spoken of it so near to its expiration, unless in order to give expression to a most exalted mystery.

He was thirsting to see the captive children of Adam make use of the liberty, which He merited for them and offered to them, and which so many were abusing. He was athirst with the anxious desire that all should correspond with Him in the faith and love due to Him, that they profit by his merits and sufferings, accept his friendship and grace now acquired for them, and that they should not lose the eternal happiness which He was to leave as an inheritance to those that wished to merit and accept it.

This was the thirst of our Savior and Master; and the most blessed Mary alone understood it perfectly and began, with ardent ion and charity, to invite and interiorly to call upon all the poor, the afflicted, the humble, the despised and downtrodden to approach their Savior and thus quench, at least in part, his thirst which they could not quench entirely.

But the perfidious Jews and the executioners, evidencing their unhappy hard–heartedness, fastened a sponge soaked in gall and vinegar to a reed and mockingly raised it to his mouth, in order that He might drink of it. Thus was fulfilled the prophecy of David: "In my thirst they gave me vinegar to drink".

B6C8

In connection with this same mystery the Savior then pronounced the sixth word: "Consummatum est," It is consummated". Now is consummated this work of my coming from heaven and I have obeyed the command of my eternal Father, who sent Me to suffer and die for the salvation of mankind. Now are fulfilled the holy Scriptures, the prophecies figures of the old Testament, and the course of my earthly and mortal life assumed in the womb of my Mother. Now are established on earth my example, my doctrines, my Sacraments and my remedies for the sickness of sin.

Now is appeased the justice of my eternal Father in regard to the debt of the children of Adam. Now is my holy Church enriched with the remedies for the sins committed by men; the whole work of my coming into the world is perfected in so far as it concerns Me, its Restorer; the secure foundation of the triumphant Church is now laid in the Church militant, so that nothing can overthrow or change it. These are the mysteries contained in the few words "Consummatum est."

Having finished and established the work of Redemption in all its perfection, it was becoming that the incarnate Word, just as He came forth from the Father to enter mortal life, should enter into immortal life of the Father through death. Therefore Christ our Savior added the last words uttered by Him: "Father, into thy hands I commend my spirit."

The Lord spoke these words in a loud and strong voice, so that the bystanders heard them. In pronouncing them He raised his eyes to heaven, as one speaking with the eternal Father, and with the last accent He gave up his spirit and inclined his head.

By the divine force of these words Lucifer with all his demons were hurled into the deepest caverns of hell, there they lay motionless. The invincible Queen and Mistress of all virtues understood these mysteries beyond the understanding of all creatures, as She was the Mother of the Savior and the Coadjutrix of his Passion.

In order that She might participate in it to the end, just as She had felt in her own body the other torments of her Son, She now, though remaining alive, felt and suffered the pangs and agony of his death. She did not die in reality; but this was because God miraculously preserved her life, when according to the natural course death should have followed.

This miraculous aid was more wonderful than all the other favors She received during the Passion. For this last pain was more intense and penetrating; and all that the martyrs and the men sentenced to death have suffered from the beginning of the world cannot equal what the blessed Mary suffered during the Passion. The great Lady remained at the foot of the Cross until evening, when the sacred body was interred. But in return for this last anguish of death, all that was still of this mortal life in the virginal body of the purest Mother, was more than ever exalted and spiritualized.

The Resurrection

The fullness of wisdom in the soul of our great Queen and Lady amid all her sorrows permitted no defect or remissness in noticing and attending to all the duties of each occasion and at all times. By this heavenly foresight She met her obligations and practiced the highest and most eminent of all the virtues. The Queen retired, after the burial of Christ, to the house of the Cenacle.

Remaining in the hall of the last Supper in the company of saint John, the Marys, and the other women who had followed Christ from Galilee, She spoke to them and the Apostle, thanking them in profound humility and abundant tears for persevering with Her up to this time throughout the Passion of her beloved Son and promising them in his name the reward of having followed Him with so much constancy and devotion.

At the same time She offered Herself as a servant and as a friend to those holy women. All of them with Saint John acknowledged this great favor, kissed her hands and asked for her blessing. They also begged her to take some rest and some bodily refreshment. But the Queen answered: "My rest and my consolation shall be to see my Son and Lord arisen from the dead. Do you, my dearest friends, satisfy our wants according to your necessities, while I retire alone with my Son."

In her retirement during this evening the great Lady contemplated the doings of the most holy soul of her Son after it left the sacred body. For from the first the blessed Mother knew that the soul of Christ, united to the Divinity, descended to limbo in order to release the holy Fathers from the subterranean prison, where they had been detained since the death of the first just man that had died in expectation of the advent of the Redeemer of the whole human race.

By the presence of the most holy Soul this obscure cavern was converted into a heaven and was filled with a wonderful splendor; and to the souls therein contained was imparted the clear vision of the Divinity. In one instant they passed from the state of long–deferred hope to the possession of glory, and from darkness to the inaccessible light, which they now began to enjoy.

All of them recognized their true God and Redeemer, and gave him thanks and glory, breaking forth in canticles of praise saying: "The Lamb that was slain is worthy to receive power and Divinity, and wisdom, and strength, and honor, and glory and benediction. Thou hast redeemed us, Lord, in thy blood, out of every tribe, and tongue, and people, and nation; and hast made us to our God a kingdom and priests, and we shall reign on the earth. Thine is, O Lord, the power, thine the reign, and thine is the glory of thy works."

Then the Lord commanded the angels to bring all the souls in purgatory, and this was immediately done. As if in earnest of the human Redemption they were absolved then and there by the Redeemer from the punishments still due to them, and they were glorified with the other souls of the just by the beatific vision. Thus on that day of the presence of the King were depopulated the prisonhouses of both limbo and purgatory.

The divine soul of Christ our Redeemer remained in limbo from half past three of Friday afternoon, until after three of the Sunday morning following. During this hour He returned to the Sepulchre as the victorious Prince of the angels and of the saints, whom had delivered from those nether prisons as Spoils of His victory and as an earnest of His glorious triumph over the chastised and prostrate rebels of hell.

In the sepulchre were many angels as its guard, venerating the sacred body united to the Divinity. Some of them, obeying the command of their Queen and Mistress, had gathered the relics of the sacred blood shed by her divine Son, the particles of flesh scattered about, the hair torn from his divine face and head, and all else that belonged to the perfection and integrity of his most sacred humanity.

On these the Mother of prudence lavished her solicitous care. The angels took charge of these relics, each one filled with joy at being privileged to hold the particles, which he was able to secure. Before any change was made, the body of the Redeemer was shown to the holy Fathers, in the same wounded, lacerated and disfigured state in which it was left by the cruelty of the Jews.

Beholding Him thus disfigured in death, the Patriarchs and Prophets and other saints adored Him and again confessed Him as the incarnate Word, who had truly taken upon Himself our infirmities and sorrows and paid abundantly our debts, satisfying in his innocence and guiltlessness for what we ourselves owed to the justice of the eternal Father.

There did our first parents Adam and Eve see the havoc wrought by their disobedience, the priceless remedy it necessitated, the immense goodness and mercy of the Redeemer. As they felt the effects of his copious Redemption in the glory of their souls, they praised anew the Omnipotent and Saints of saints, who had with such marvelous wisdom wrought such a salvation.

Then, in the presence of all those saints, through the ministry of those angels, were united to the sacred body all the relics, which they had gathered, restoring it to its natural perfection and integrity. In the same moment the most holy soul reunited with the body, giving it immortal life and glory.

Instead of the winding–sheets and the ointments, in which it had been buried, it was clothed with the four gifts of glory, namely: with clearness, impassibility, agility and subtility. These gifts overflowed from the immense glory of the soul of Christ into the sacred body.

Although these gifts were due to it as a natural inheritance and participation from the instant of its conception, because from that

B6C11

very moment his soul was glorified and his whole humanity was united to the Divinity; yet they had been suspended in their effects upon the purest body, in order to permit it to remain passable and capable of meriting for us our own glory.

In the Resurrection these gifts were justly called into activity in the proper degree corresponding to the glory of his soul and to his union with the Divinity. As the glory of the most holy soul of Christ our Savior is incomprehensible and ineffable to man, it is also impossible entirely to describe in our words or by our examples the glorious gifts of his deified body; for in comparison to its purity, crystal would be obscure.

The light inherent and shining forth from his body so far exceeds that of the others, as the day does the night, or as many suns the light of one star; and all the beauty of creatures, if it were joined, would appear ugliness in comparison with his, nothing else being comparable to It in all creation.

The excellence of these gifts in the Resurrection were far beyond the glory of his Transfiguration or that manifested on other occasions of the kind men mentioned in this history. For on these occasions He received it transitorily and for special purposes, while now He received it in plenitude and forever.

Through impassibility his body became invincible to all created power, since no power can ever move or change Him. By subtility the gross and earthly matter was so purified, that it could now penetrate other matter like a pure spirit.

Accordingly He penetrated through the rocks of the sepulchre without removing or displacing them, as He had issued forth from the womb of his most blessed Mother.

Agility so freed Him from the weight and slowness of matter, that it exceeded the agility of the immaterial angels, while He himself could move about more quickly than they, as shown in his apparitions to the Apostles and on other occasions.

B6C11

The sacred wounds, which had disfigured his body, now shone forth from his hands and feet and side so refulgent and brilliant, that they added a most entrancing beauty and charm.

In all this glory and heavenly adornment the Savior now arose from the grave; and in the presence of the saints and Patriarchs He promised universal resurrection in their own flesh and body to all men, and that they moreover, as an effect of his own Resurrection, should be similarly glorified.

As an earnest and as a pledge of the universal resurrection, the Lord commanded the souls of many saints there present to reunite with their bodies and rise up to immortal life. Immediately this divine command was executed, and their bodies arose in anticipation of this mystery.

Among them were saint Anne, saint Joseph and saint Joachim, and others of the ancient Fathers and Patriarchs, who had distinguished themselves in the faith and hope of the Incarnation, and had desired and prayed for it with greater earnestness to the Lord. As a reward for their zeal, the resurrection and glory of their bodies was now anticipated.

Of all these mysteries the great Queen of heaven was aware and She participated in them from her retreat in the Cenacle. In the same instant in which the most holy soul of Christ entered and gave life to his body the joy of her immaculate soul, overflowed into her immaculate body. And this overflow was so exquisite in its effects, that She was transformed from sorrow to joy, from pain to delight from grief to ineffable jubilation and rest.

It happened that just at this time the Evangelist John, as he had done on the previous morning, stepped in to visit and console Her in her bitter solitude, and thus unexpectedly, in the midst of splendor and glory, met Her whom he had before scarcely recognized on account of her overwhelming sorrow. The Apostle now beheld Her with wonder and deepest reverence and concluded that the Lord had risen, since his blessed Mother was thus transfigured with joy.

In this new joy and under the divine influences of her supernatural vision the great Lady began to prepare herself for the visit of the Lord, which was near at hand. While eliciting acts of praise, and in her canticles and prayers, She immediately felt within Her a new kind of jubilation and celestial delight, reaching far beyond the first joy, and corresponding in a wonderful manner to the sorrows and tribulations She had undergone in the Passion; and this new favor was different and much more exalted than the joys overflowing naturally from her soul into her body. Moreover She perceived within Herself another third and still more different effect, implying new divine favors.

The blessed Mary being thus prepared, Christ our Savior, arisen and glorious, in the company of all Saints and Patriarchs, made his appearance. The ever humble Queen prostrated Herself upon the ground and adored her divine Son; and the Lord raised Her and drew Her to Himself.

In this contact, which was more intimate than the contact with the humanity and the wounds of the Savior sought by Magdalen, the Virgin Mother participated in an extraordinary favor, which She alone, as exempt from sin, could merit. Although it was not the greatest of the favors She attained on this occasion, yet She could not have received it without failing of her faculties, if She had not been previously strengthened by the angels and by the Lord himself.

This favor was, that the glorious body of the Son so closely united itself to that of his purest Mother, that He penetrated into it or She into his, as when, for instance, a crystal globe takes up within itself the light of the sun and is saturated with the splendor and beauty of its light. In the same way the body of the most holy Mary entered into that of her divine Son by this heavenly embrace; it was, as it were, the portal of her intimate knowledge concerning the glory of the holy soul and body of her Lord.

As a consequence of these favors, constituting higher and higher degrees of ineffable gifts, the spirit of the Virgin Mother rose to the knowledge of the most hidden sacraments. In the midst of them She heard a voice saying to Her: "My beloved, ascend higher!". By the power of these words She was entirely transformed and saw the Divinity clearly and intuitively, wherein She found complete, though only temporary, rest and reward for all her sorrows and labors.

Silence alone here is proper, since reason and language are entirely inadequate to comprehend or express what passed in the blessed Mary during this beatific vision, the highest She had until then enjoyed. Let us celebrate this day in wonder and praise, with congratulations and loving and humble thanks for what She then merited for us, and for her exaltation and joy.

For some hours the heavenly Princess continued to enjoy the essence of God with her divine Son, participating now in his triumph as She had in his torments. Then by similar degrees She again descended from this vision and found Herself in the end reclining on the right arm of the most sacred humanity and regaled in other ways by the right hand of his Divinity.

She held sweetest converse with her Son concerning the mysteries of his Passion and of his glory. In these conferences She was again inebriated with the wine of love and charity, which now She drank unmeasured from the original fount. All that a mere creature can receive was conferred upon the blessed Mary on this occasion; for, according to our way of conceiving such things, the divine equity wished to compensate the injury which a Creature so pure and immaculate had undergone in suffering the sorrows and torments of the Passion. For, as I have mentioned many times before, She suffered the same pains as her Son, and now in this mystery She was inundated with a proportionate joy and delight.

The Ascension of Christ

A few days before the Ascension of the Lord, the eternal Father and the Holy Ghost appeared in the Cenacle upon a throne of ineffable splendor surrounded by the choirs of angels and saints there present and other heavenly spirits, which had now come with the divine Persons.

Then the incarnate Word ascended the throne and seated Himself with the other Two. The ever humble Mother of the Most High, prostrate in a corner of a room, in deepest reverence adored the most blessed Trinity, and in it her own incarnate Son. The eternal Father commanded two of the highest angels to call Mary, which they did by approaching Her, and in sweetest voices intimating to Her the divine will.

She arose from the dust with the most profound humility, modesty and reverence. Accompanied by the angels She approached the foot of the Throne, humbling herself anew. The eternal Father said to Her: "Beloved, ascend higher!" As these words at the same time effected what they signified, She was raised up and placed on the throne of royal Majesty with the three divine Persons.

New admiration was caused in the saints to see a mere Creature exalted to such dignity. Being made to understand the sanctity and equity of the works of the Most High, they gave new glory and praise proclaiming Him immense, Just, Holy and Admirable in all his counsels.

The Father then spoke to the blessed Mary saying: "My Daughter, to Thee do I entrust the Church founded by my Onlybegotten, the new law of grace He established in the world, and the people, which He redeemed: to Thee do I consign them all."

Thereupon also the Holy Ghost spoke to Her: "My Spouse, chosen from all creatures, I communicate to Thee my wisdom and grace together with which shall be deposited in thy heart the mysteries, the works and teachings and all that the incarnate Word has accomplished in the world."

And the Son also said: "My most beloved Mother, I go to my Father and in my stead I shall leave Thee and I charge Thee with the care of my Church; to Thee do I commend its children and my brethren, as the Father has consigned them to Me."

Then the three Divine Persons, addressing the choir of holy angels and the other saints, said: "This is the Queen of all created things in heaven and earth; She is the Protectress of the Church, the Mistress of creatures, the Mother of piety, the Intercessor of the faithful, the Advocate of sinners, the Mother of beautiful love and holy hope.

She is mighty in drawing our will to mercy and clemency. In Her shall be deposited the treasures of our grace and her most faithful heart shall the tablet whereon shall be written and engraved our holy law. In her are contained the mysteries of our Omnipotence for the salvation of mankind.

She is the perfect work of our hands, through whom the plenitude of our desires shall be communicated and satisfied without hindrance in the currents of our divine perfections. Whoever shall call upon Her from his heart shall not perish; whoever shall obtain her intercession shall secure for himself eternal life. What She asks of Us, shall be granted, and We shall always hear her requests and prayers and fulfill her will; for She has consecrated Herself perfectly to what pleases Us."

The most blessed Mary, hearing Herself thus exalted, humiliated Herself so much the deeper the more highly She was raised by the right hand of the Most High above all the human and angelic creatures. As if She were the least of all, She adored the Lord and offered Herself, in the most prudent terms and in the most ardent love, to work as a faithful servant in the Church and obey promptly all the biddings of the divine will.

From that day on She took upon Herself anew the care of the evangelical Church, as a loving Mother of all children; She renewed all the petitions She had until then made, so that during the whole further course of her life they were most fervent and incessant, as we shall see in the third part, where will appear more clearly what the Church owes to this great Queen and Lady, and what blessings She gained and merited for it.

On that same day, by divine dispensation, while the Lord was at table with the eleven Apostles, other disciples and pious women gathered at the Cenacle to the number of one hundred and twenty; for the divine Master wished them to be present at his Ascension. Moreover, just as He had instructed the Apostles, so He now wanted to instruct these faithful respectively in what each was to know before his leaving them and ascending into heaven.

All of them being thus gathered and united in peace and charity within those walls in the hall of the last Supper, the Author of life manifested Himself to them as a kind and loving Father and said to them:

"My sweetest children, I am about to ascend to my Father, from whose bosom I descended in order to rescue and save men. I leave with you in my stead my own Mother as your Protectress, Consoler and Advocate, and as your Mother, whom you are to hear and obey in all things."

"Just as I have told you, that he who sees Me sees my Father, and he who knows Me, knows also Him; so I now tell you, that He who knows my Mother, knows Me; he who hears Her, hears Me; and who honors Her, honors Me. All of you shall have Her as your Mother, as your Superior and Head, so shall also your successors. She shall answer doubts, solve your difficulties; in Her, those who seek Me shall always find Me; for I shall remain in Her until the end of the world, and I am in Her now, although you do not understand how."

This the Lord said, because He was sacramentally present in the bosom of his Mother; for the sacred species, which She had received at the last Supper, were preserved in Her until consecration of the first Mass. The Lord thus fulfilled that which He promised in saint Matthew: "I am with you to the consummation of the world."

The Lord added and said: "You will have Peter as the supreme head of the Church, for I leave him as my Vicar; and you shall obey him as the chief highpriest. Saint John you shall hold as the son of my Mother; for I have chosen and appointed him for this office on the Cross."

The Lord then looked upon his most beloved Mother, who was there present and intimated his desire of expressly commanding that whole congregation to worship and reverence Her in a manner suited to the dignity of Mother of God, and of leaving this command under form of a precept for the whole Church.

But the most humble Lady besought her Onlybegotten to be pleased not to secure Her more honor than was absolutely necessary for executing all that He had charged Her with; and that the new children of the Church should not be induced to show Her greater honor than they had shown until then.

On contrary, She desired to divert all the sacred worship of the Church immediately upon the Lord himself and to make the propagation of the Gospel redound entirely to the exaltation of his holy name. Christ our Savior yielded to this most prudent petition of his Mother, reserving to Himself the duty of spreading the knowledge of Her at a more convenient and opportune time yet in secret He conferred upon Her new extraordinary favors.

In considering the loving exhortations of their Divine Master, the mysteries which He had revealed them, and the prospect of his leaving them, that whole congregation was moved to their inmost hearts; for He had enkindled in them the divine love by the vivid faith of his Divinity and humanity. Reviving within them the memory of his words and his teachings of eternal life, the delights of his most loving companionship, and sorrowfully realizing, that they were now all at once to be deprived of these blessings, they wept most tenderly and sighed from their inmost souls.

They longed to detain Him, although they could not, because they saw it was not befitting; words of parting rose to their lips, but they could not bring themselves to utter them; each one felt sentiments of sorrow arising amid feelings both of joy and yet also of pious regret. How shall we live without such a Master? they thought. Who can ever speak to us such words of life and consolation as He? Who will receive us so lovingly and kindly? Who shall be our Father and protector? We shall be helpless children and orphans in this world. Some of them broke their silence and exclaimed: "O most loving Lord and Father! O joy and life of our souls! Now that we know Thee as our Redeemer, Thou departest and leavest us! Take us along with Thee, O Lord; banish us not from thy sight. Our blessed Hope, what shall we do without thy presence? Whither shall we turn, if thou goest away? Whither shall we direct our steps, if cannot follow Thee, our Father, our Chief, and our Teacher?"

To these and other pleadings the Lord answered by bidding them not to leave Jerusalem and to persevere in prayer until He should send the Holy Spirit, the Consoler, as promised by the Father and as already foretold to the Apostles at the last Supper.

The most auspicious hour, in which the Onlybegotten of the eternal Father, after descending from heaven in order to assume human flesh, was to ascend by his own power and in a most wonderful manner to the right hand of God, the Inheritor of his eternities, one and equal with Him in nature and infinite glory. He was to ascend, also, because He had previously descended to the lowest regions of the earth, having fulfilled all that had been written and prophesied concerning his coming into the world, his Life, Death and the Redemption of man, and having penetrated, as the Lord of all, to the very centre of the earth.

By this Ascension he sealed all the mysteries and hastened the fulfillment of his promise, according to which He was, with the Father, to send the Paraclete upon his Church after He himself should have ascended into heaven.

In order to celebrate this festive and mysterious day, Christ our Lord selected as witnesses the hundred and twenty persons to whom He had spoken in the Cenacle. They were the most holy Mary, the eleven Apostles, the seventy—two disciples, Mary Magdalen, Lazarus their brother, the other Marys and the faithful men and women making up the above—mentioned number of one hundred and twenty.

With this little flock our divine Shepherd Jesus left the Cenacle, and, with his most blessed Mother at his side, He conducted them all through the streets of Jerusalem. The Apostles and all the rest in order, proceeded in the direction of Bethany, which was less than half a league over the brow of mount Olivet. The company of angels and saints from limbo and purgatory followed the Victor with new songs of praise, although Mary alone was privileged to see them.

The Resurrection of Jesus of Nazareth was already divulged throughout Jerusalem and Palestine. Although the perfidious and malicious princes and priests had spread about the false testimony of his being stolen by disciples, yet many would not accept their testimony nor give it any credit. It was divinely provided, that none of the inhabitants of the city, and none of the unbelievers or doubters, should pay any attention to this holy procession, or hinder it on its way from the Cenacle.

All, except the one hundred and twenty just, who were chosen by the Lord to witness his Ascension into heaven, were justly punished by being prevented from noticing this wonderful mystery, and the Chieftain and Head of this procession remained invisible to them.

The Lord having thus secured them this privacy, they all ascended mount Olivet to its highest point. There they formed three choirs, one of the angels, another of the saints, and a third of the Apostles and faithful, which again divided into two bands, while Christ the Savior presided.

Then the most prudent Mother prostrated Herself at the feet of her Son worshipping Him with admirable humility, She adored Him as the true God and as the Redeemer of the world, asking his last blessing. All the faithful there present imitated Her and did the same. Weeping and sighing, they asked the Lord, whether He was now to restore the kingdom of Israel.

The Lord answered that this was a secret of the eternal Father and not to be made known to them; but, for the present, it was necessary and befitting, that they receive the Holy Ghost and preach, in Jerusalem, in Samaria and in all the world, the mysteries of the Redemption of the world.

Jesus, having taken leave of this holy and fortunate gathering of the faithful, his countenance beaming forth peace and majesty, joined his hands and, by his own power, began to raise himself from the earth, leaving thereon the impression of his sacred feet.

In gentlest motion He was wafted toward the aerial regions, drawing after Him the eyes and the hearts of those first–born children, who amid sighs and tears vented their affection. And as, at the moving of the first Cause of all motion, it is proper that also the nether spheres should be set in motion, so the Savior Jesus drew after Him also the celestial choirs of the angels, the holy Patriarchs and the rest of the glorified saints, some of them with body and soul, others only as to their soul.

All of them in heavenly order were raised up together from the earth, accompanying and following their King, their Chief and

Head. The new and mysterious sacrament, which the right hand of the Most High wrought on this occasion for his most holy Mother, was that He raised Her up with Him in order to put Her in possession of the glory, which He had assigned to Her as his true Mother and which She had by her merits prepared and earned for Herself. Of this favor the great Queen was capable even before it happened; for her divine Son had offered it to Her during the forty days which He spent in her company after his Resurrection.

In order that this sacrament might be kept secret from all other living creatures at that time, and in order that the heavenly Mistress might be present in the gathering of the Apostles and the faithful in their prayerful waiting upon the coming of the Holy Ghost the divine power enabled the blessed Mother miraculously to be in two places at once; remaining with the children of the Church for their comfort during their stay in the Cenacle and at the time ascending with the Redeemer of the world to His heavenly throne, where She remained for three days. There She enjoyed the perfect use of all her powers and faculties, whereas She was more restricted in the use of them during that time in the Cenacle.

Amidst this jubilee and other rejoicings exceeding all our conceptions that new divinely arranged procession approached the empyrean heavens. Between the two choirs of angels and saints, Christ and his most blessed Mother made their entry. All in their order gave supreme honor to each respectively and to Both together, breaking forth in hymns of praise in honor of the Authors of grace and of life.

Then the eternal Father placed upon the throne of his Divinity at His right hand, the incarnate Word, and in such glory and majesty, that He filled with new admiration and reverential fear all the inhabitants of heaven. In clear and intuitive vision they recognized the infinite glory and perfection of the Divinity inseparably and substantially united in one personality to the most holy humanity, beautified and exalted by the pre—eminence and glory due to this union, such as eyes have not seen, nor ears heard, nor ever has entered into the thoughts of creatures.

On this occasion the humility and wisdom of our most prudent Queen reached their highest point; for, overwhelmed by such divine and admirable favors, She hovered at the footstool of the royal throne, annihilated in the consciousness of being a mere earthly creature. Prostrate She adored the Father and broke out in new canticles of praise for the glory communicated to his Son and for elevating in Him the deified humanity to such greatness and splendor.

Again the angels and saints were filled with admiration and joy to see the most prudent humility of their Queen, whose living example of virtue, as exhibited on that occasion, they emulated among themselves in copying. Then the voice of the eternal Father was heard saying: "My Daughter, ascend higher!" Her divine Son also called Her, saying: "My Mother rise up and take possession of the place, which I owe Thee for having followed and imitated Me. The Holy Ghost said: "My Spouse and Beloved, come to my eternal embraces!"

Immediately was proclaimed to all the blessed the decree of the most holy Trinity, by which the most blessed Mother, for having furnished her own life–blood toward the Incarnation and for having nourished, served, imitated and followed Him with all the perfection possible to a creature, was exalted and placed at the right hand of her Son for all eternity.

None other of the human creatures should ever hold that place or position, nor rival Her in the unfailing glory connected with it; but it was to be reserved to the Queen and to be her possession by right after her earthly life, as of one who pre–eminently excelled all the rest of the saints.

In fulfillment of this decree, the most blessed Mary was raised to the throne of the holy Trinity at the right hand of her Son. At the same time She, with all the saints, was informed, that She was given possession of this throne not only for all the ages of eternity, but that it was left to her choice to remain there even now and without returning to the earth.

For it was the conditional will of the divine Persons, that as far as they were concerned, She should now remain in that state. In order that She might make her own choice, She was shown anew the state of the Church upon earth, the orphaned and necessitous condition of the faithful, whom She was left free to assist.

This admirable proceeding of the divine Providence was to afford the Mother of mercy an occasion of going beyond, so to say, even her own Self in doing good and in obliging the human race with an act of love similar to that of her Son in assuming a passable state and in suspending the glory due to his body during and for our Redemption.

The most blessed Mother imitated Him also in this respect, so that She might be in all things like the incarnate Word. The great Lady therefore, having clearly before her eyes all the sacrifices included in this proposition, left the throne and, prostrating Herself at the feet of the Three Persons, said:

"Eternal and almighty God, my Lord, to accept at once this reward, which thy condescending kindness offers me, would be to secure my rest; but to return to the world and continue to labor in mortal life for the good of the children of Adam and the faithful of thy holy Church, would be to the glory and according to the pleasure of thy Majesty and would benefit my sojourning and banished children on earth. I accept this labor and renounce for the present the peace and joy of thy presence. Well do I know, what I possess and receive, but I will sacrifice it to further the love Thou hast for men. Accept, Lord and Master of all my being, this sacrifice and let thy divine strength govern in the undertaking confided to me. Let faith in Thee be spread, let thy holy name be exalted, let thy holy Church be enlarged, for Thou hast acquired it by the blood of thy

Onlybegotten and mine; I offer myself anew to labor for thy glory and for the conquest of the souls, as far as I am able."

Such was the sacrifice made by the most loving Mother and Queen, one greater than ever was conceived by creature, and it was so pleasing to the Lord, that He immediately rewarded it by operating in Her those purifications and enlightenments necessary to the intuitive vision of the Divinity; for so far She had on this occasion seen only by abstractive vision. Thus elevated She partook of the beatific vision and was filled with splendor and celestial gifts, altogether beyond the power of man describe or conceive in mortal life.

In the midst of her glory the most holy Mary did not forget the congregation of the faithful, whom we left so sorrowful on mount Olivet; as they stood weeping and lost in grief and, absorbed in looking into the aerial regions, into which their Redeemer and Master had disappeared.

She turned her eyes upon them from the cloud on which She had ascended, in order to send them her assistance. Moved by their sorrow, She besought Jesus lovingly to console these little children, whom He had left as orphans upon the earth. Moved by the prayers of his Mother, the Redeemer of the human race sent down two angels in white and resplendent garments, who appeared to all the disciples and the faithful and spoke to them: "Ye men of Galilee, do not look up to heaven in so great astonishment, for this Lord Jesus, who departed from you and has ascended into heaven, shall again return with the same glory and majesty in which you have just seen him".

By such words and others which they added they consoled the Apostles and disciples and all the rest, so that they might not grow faint, but in their retirement hope for the coming and the consolation of the Holy Ghost promised by their divine Master.

B6C12

Chapter Seven

Descent of the Holy Ghost—Mary's Intuitive Vision of Him

In the company of the great Queen of heaven, and encouraged by Her, the twelve Apostles and the rest of the disciples and faithful joyfully waited for the fulfillment of the promise of the Savior, that He would send them the Holy Ghost, the Consoler, who should instruct them and administer unto them all that they heard in the teaching of their Lord.

They were so unanimous and united in charity, that during all these days none of them had any thought, affection or inclination contrary to those of the rest. They were of one heart and soul in thought and action.

Although the election of Saint Mathias had occurred, the least movement or sign of discord arose among those first–born children of the Church; yet this was a transaction, which is otherwise apt to arouse differences of opinion in the most excellently disposed; since each is apt to follow his own insight and does not easily yield to the opinion of others.

But into this holy congregation no discord found entrance, because they were united in prayer, in fasting and in the expectation of the Holy Ghost, who does not seek repose in discordant and unyielding hearts. In order that it may be inferred, how powerful was this union in charity, not only for disposing them toward the reception of the Holy Ghost, but for overcoming and dispersing the evil spirits, I will say; that the demons, who since the death of the Savior had lain prostrate in hell, felt in themselves a new kind of oppression and terror, resulting from the virtues of those assembled in the Cenacle.

Although they could not explain it to themselves, they perceived a new terrifying force, emanating from that place, and when they perceived the effects of the doctrine and example of Christ in the behavior of the disciples, they feared the ruin of their dominion. The Queen of the angels, most holy Mary, in the plenitude of her wisdom and grace, knew the time and predestined hour for the sending of the Holy Ghost upon the apostolic college.

When the days of Pentecost were about to be fulfilled, (which happened fifty days after the Resurrection of the Lord our Redeemer), the most blessed Mother saw, how in heaven the humanity of the Word conferred with the eternal Father concerning the promised sending of the divine Paraclete to the Apostles, and that the time predetermined by his infinite wisdom for planting the faith and all his gifts in his Holy Church, was at hand.

The Lord also referred to the merits acquired by Him in the flesh through his most holy Life, Passion and Death, to the mysteries wrought by Him for the salvation of the human race and to the fact, that He was the Mediator, Advocate and Intercessor between the eternal Father and men, and that among them lived his sweetest Mother, in whom the divine Persons were so well pleased.

He besought his Father also, that, besides bringing grace and the invisible gifts the Holy Ghost appear in the world in visible form, that so the evangelical law might be honored before all the world; that the Apostles and faithful, who were to spread the divine truth, might be encouraged, and that the enemies of the Lord, who had in this life persecuted despised and Him unto the death of the Cross, might be filled with terror.

This petition of our Redeemer in heaven was supported on earth by most holy Mary in a manner befitting the merciful Mother of the faithful. Prostrated upon the earth in the form of a cross and in profoundest humility, She saw, how in that consistory of the blessed Trinity, the request of the Savior was favorably accepted, and how, to fulfill and execute it, the persons of the Father and the

Son, as the Principle from which the Holy Ghost proceeded, decreed the active mission of the Holy Spirit; for to these Two is attributed the sending of the third Person, because He proceeds from Both; and the third Person passively took upon Himself this mission and consented to come into the world.

On Pentecost morning the Blessed Virgin Mary exhorted the Apostles, the disciples and the pious women, numbering about one hundred and twenty, to pray more fervently and renew their hopes, since the hour was at hand in which they were to be visited by the divine Spirit from on high.

At the third hour (nine o'clock), when all of them were gathered around their heavenly Mistress and engaged in fervent prayer, the air resounded with a tremendous thunder and the blowing of a violent wind mixed with the brightness of fire or lightning, all centering upon the house of the Cenacle.

The house was enveloped in light and the divine fire was poured out over all of that holy gathering. Over the head of each of the hundred and twenty persons appeared a tongue of that same fire, in which the Holy Ghost had come, filling each one with divine influences and heavenly gifts and causing at one and the same time the most diverse and contrary effects in the Cenacle and in the whole of Jerusalem, according to the diversity of the persons affected.

In the most holy Mary these effects were altogether divine, and most wonderful in the sight of all the heavenly courtiers; for as regard us men, we are incapable of understanding and explaining them. The purest Lady was transformed and exalted in God; for She saw intuitively and clearly the Holy Ghost, and for a short time enjoyed the beatific vision of he Divinity.

Of his gifts and divine influences She by Herself received more than all the rest of the saints. Her glory for that space of time, exceeded that of the angels and of the blessed. She alone gave to the Lord more glory, praise and thanksgiving than all the universe for the benefit of the descent of his Holy Spirit upon his Church and for his having pledged Himself so many times to send Him and through Him to govern it to the end of the world.

The blessed Trinity was so pleased with the conduct of Mary on this occasion, that It considered Itself fully repaid and compensated for having created the world; and not only compensated, but God acted as if He were under a certain obligation for possessing such a peerless Creature, whom the Father could look upon as his Daughter, the Son as his Mother, and the Holy Ghost as his Spouse; and whom (according to our way of thinking) He was now obliged to visit and enrich after having conferred upon Her such high dignity. In this exalted and blessed Spouse were renewed all the gifts and graces of the Holy Spirit, creating new effects and operations altogether beyond our capacity to understand.

The Apostles, as Saint Luke says, were also replenished and filled with the Holy Ghost; for they received a wonderful increase of justifying grace of a most exalted degree. The twelve Apostles were confirmed in this sanctifying grace and were never to lose it. In all of them, according to each one's condition were infused the habits of the seven gifts: Wisdom, Understanding, Science, Piety, Counsel, Fortitude and Fear.

In this magnificent blessing, as new as it was admirable in the world, the twelve Apostles were created fit ministers of the new Testament and founders of the evangelical Church for the whole world: for this new grace and blessing communicated to them a divine strength most efficacious and sweet, which inclined them to practice the most heroic virtue and the highest sanctity.

Thus strengthened they prayed, they labored willingly and accomplished the most difficult and arduous tasks, engaging in their labors not with sorrow or from necessity, but with the greatest joy and alacrity.

B7C2

In all the rest of the disciples and the faithful, who received the Holy Ghost in the Cenacle, the Most High wrought proportionally and respectively the same effects, except that they were not confirmed in grace like the Apostles. According to the disposition of each the gifts of grace were communicated in greater or less abundance in view of the ministry they were to hold in the holy Church.

The same proportion was maintained in regard to the Apostles; yet Saint Peter and Saint John were more singularly favored on account of the high offices assigned to them: the one to govern the Church as its head, and the other to attend upon and serve the Queen and Mistress of heaven and of earth, most holy Mary. The sacred text of Saint Luke says, that the Holy Ghost filled the whole house in which this happy congregation was gathered, not only because all of them were filled with the Holy Ghost and his admirable gifts, but because the house itself was filled with wonderful light and splendor.

This plenitude of wonders and prodigies overflowed and communicated itself also to others outside of the Cenacle; for it caused diverse and various effects of the Holy Spirit among the inhabitants of Jerusalem and its vicinity. All those, who with some piety had compassioned our Savior Jesus in his Passion and Death, deprecating his most bitter torments and reverencing his sacred Person, were interiorly visited with new light and grace, which disposed them afterwards to accept the doctrine of the Apostles.

Those that were converted by the first sermon of Saint Peter were to a great extent of the number of those who, by their compassion and sorrow at the death of the Lord, had merited for themselves such a great blessing. Others of the just who were in Jerusalem outside of the Cenacle, also felt great interior consolations, by which they were moved and predisposed by new effects of grace wrought in each one proportionately by the Holy Ghost.

Not less wonderful, although more hidden, were some contrary effects produced on that day by the Holy Ghost in Jerusalem. By the dreadful thunders and violent commotion of the atmosphere and the lightnings accompanying his advent, He disturbed and terrified the enemies of the Lord in that city, each one according to his own malice and perfidy.

This chastisement was particularly evident in those who had actively concurred in procuring the death of Christ, and who had signalized themselves in their rabid fury against Him. All these fell to the ground on their faces and remained thus for three hours.

Those that had scourged the Lord were suddenly choked in their own blood, which shot forth from their veins in punishment for shedding that of the Master. The audacious servant, who had buffeted the Lord, not only suddenly died, but was hurled into hell body and soul.

Others of the Jews, although they did not die, were chastised with intense pains and abominable sicknesses. These disorders, consequent upon shedding the blood of Christ, descended to their posterity and even to this day continue to afflict their children with most horrible impurities.

This chastisement became notorious in Jerusalem, although the priests and Pharisees diligently sought to cover it up, just as they had tried to conceal the Resurrection of the Savior. As these events, however, were not so important, neither the Apostles nor the Evangelists wrote about them, and in the confusion of the city the multitude soon forgot them.

Sermon of the Apostles—Mary's Care for the Converts

On account of the visible and open signs, by which the Holy Ghost descended upon the Apostles, the whole city of Jerusalem with its inhabitants was stirred to wonder. When the news of the astounding events at the house of the Cenacle spread about, the multitude of the people gathered in crowds to know more of the happenings.

On that day was being celebrated one of the paschs or feasts of the Jews; and as well on this account, as on account of the special dispensation of heaven, the city was crowded with foreigners and strangers from all parts of the world. For to them the Most High wished to manifest the wonders of the first preaching and spreading of the new law of grace, which the incarnate Word, our Redeemer and Master, had ordained for the salvation of men.

The sacred Apostles, who were filled with charity by the plenitude of the gifts of the Holy Ghost and who knew that all Jerusalem was gathering at the doors of the Cenacle, asked permission of their Mistress and Queen to go forth and preach to them; in order that such great graces might not even for a moment fail to redound to the benefit of souls and to new glory of their Author.

They all left the house of the Cenacle and, placing themselves before the multitudes, began to preach the mysteries of the faith and of eternal life. Though until then they had been so shy and seclusive, they now stepped forth with unhesitating boldness and poured forth burning words, that like a flashing fire penetrated to the souls of their hearers.

This miracle, that all the men of so many different tongues then assembled in Jerusalem should hear the Apostles in their own language, joined to the doctrine which they preached, caused great astonishment. Yet I wish to remark, that though all the Apostles, on account of the plenitude of science and of gifts gratuitously received, were able to speak in the languages of all nations, because that was necessary for the preaching of the Gospel, yet on that occasion they all spoke the language of Palestine.

Using only this idiom they were understood by all the different nationalities there present, as if they had spoken in the several idioms. This miracle the Lord wrought at the time in order that they might be understood and believed by those different nations, and in order that Saint Peter might not be obliged to repeat in the different languages of those present, what he preached to them concerning the mysteries of faith. He preached only once and all heard and understood him, each in his own language, and so it happened also with the other Apostles.

For if each one had spoken in the language of those who heard them, and which they knew as their mother tongue, it would have been necessary for them to repeat what they said at least seven or eight times according to the different nationalities mentioned by saint Luke. This would have consumed a longer time than is intimated by the sacred text, and it would have caused great confusion and trouble to repeat the same doctrines over and over again or to speak so many languages on one occasion; nor would the miracle be so intelligible to us as the one mentioned.

The people who heard the Apostles did not understand the miracle, although they wondered at hearing each their own idiom. What Saint Luke says about their speaking different languages, must be understood as meaning, that the Apostles were then and there able to understand them, because on that day, those that came to the Cenacle understood them all speaking in their own language.

But this miracle and wonderment caused in their hearers different effects and opinions, according to the dispositions of each one. Those that listened piously received deep understanding of the

Divinity and of the Redemption of man, now so eloquently and fervently propounded to them. They were moved eagerly to desire the knowledge of the truth; by the divine light they were filled with compunction and sorrow for their sins and with desire of divine mercy and forgiveness.

With tears in their eyes they cried out to the Apostles and asked what they must do to gain eternal life. Others, who hardened their hearts, altogether untouched by the divine truths preached by them, became indignant at the Apostles, and instead of yielding to them, called them innovators and adventurers. Many of the Jews, more impious in their perfidy and envy, inveighed against the Apostles, saying they were drunk and insane. Among these were some of those who had again come to their senses after having fallen to the ground at the thunder caused by the coming of the Holy Ghost;

The three thousand, who were converted by the first sermon of saint Peter, were from all the nations then gathered in Jerusalem, so that forthwith all nations, without excluding any, might partake of the fruits of the Redemption, all might be gathered to the Church, and all might experience the grace of the Holy Spirit; for the holy Church was to be composed of all nations and tribes.

Many were Jews, who had followed Christ our Savior with kindly feelings and witnessed his sufferings and Death with compassion, as I said above. Some also of those, who had concurred in his Passion were converted, though these were few, because many would not alter their disposition; for, if they had done so, all of them would have been admitted to mercy and received pardon for their error.

After their preaching the Apostles retired that evening within the Cenacle, in order to give an account to the Mother of mercy, the purest Mary. With them also entered a great number of the new children of the Church, in order that they might come to know and venerate the Mother of mercy.

B7C3

But the great Queen of the angels was ignorant of nothing that had happened; for from her retreat She had heard the preaching of the Apostles and She knew the secret hearts and thoughts of all the hearers. The tenderest Mother remained prostrate with her face upon the ground during the whole time, tearfully praying for the conversion of all that subjected themselves to the faith of the Savior, and for all the rest, if they should consent to cooperate with the helps and the graces of the Lord.

In order to help the Apostles in their great work of beginning to preach, and the bystanders in properly listening to them, the most Holy Mary sent many of her accompanying angels with holy inspirations, encouraging the sacred Apostles and giving them strength to inquire and to manifest more explicitly the hidden mysteries of the humanity and Divinity of Christ our Redeemer. The angels fulfilled all the commands of their Queen, while She Herself exercised her own power and gifts according to the circumstances of the occasion.

\When the Apostles came to Her with those copious first–fruits of their preaching and of the Holy Ghost, She received them with incredible joy and sweetness and with the most loving kindness of a true Mother.

The Apostle Saint Peter spoke to the recently converted and said to them: "My brethren, and servants of the Most High, this is the Mother of our Redeemer and Master, Jesus Christ, whose faith you have received in acknowledging Him as true God and man. She has given Him the human form, conceiving Him in her womb, and She bore Him, remaining a Virgin before, during and after his birth. Receive Her as your Mother, our Refuge and Intercessor, for through Her you and we shall receive light, direction, and release from our sins and miseries."

At these words of the Apostle and at the sight of most holy Mary these new adherents of the faith were filled with admirable light and consolation; for this privilege of conferring great interior blessings and of giving light to those who looked upon Her with pious veneration, was renewed and extended in Her time when She was at the right hand of her divine Son in heaven.

As all of those faithful partook of these blessings in the presence of their Queen, they prostrated themselves at her feet and with tears besought her assistance and blessing. But the humble and prudent Queen evaded this latter, because of the presence of the Apostles, who were priests, and of Saint Peter, the Vicar of Christ. Then this Apostle said to Her "Lady, do not refuse to these faithful what they piously ask for the consolation their souls." The blessed Mary obeyed the head of the Church and in humble serenity of a Queen She gave her blessing to the newly converted.

The love which filled their hearts made them desire to hear from their heavenly Mother some words of consolation; yet their humility and reverence prevented them from asking for this favor. As they perceived how obediently She had yielded to Saint Peter, they turned to him and begged him to ask Her not to send them away without some word of encouragement.

Saint Peter though he considered this favor very proper for the souls who had been born again to Christ by his preaching and that of the other Apostles, nevertheless, aware that the Mother of Wisdom knew well what was to be done, presumed to say no more than these words; "Lady, listen to the petitions of thy servants and children."

Then the great Lady obeyed and said to the converts: "My dearest brethren in the Lord, give thanks and praise with your whole hearts to the Almighty God, because from among all men He has called and drawn you to the sure path of eternal life in the knowledge of the holy faith you have received. Be firm in your confession of it from all your hearts and in hearing and believing all that the law of grace contains as preached and ordained by its true Teacher Jesus, my Son and your Redeemer.

Be eager to hear and obey his Apostles, who teach and instruct you, so that you may be signed and marked by Baptism in the character of children of the Most High. I offer myself as your handmaid to assist you in all that serves toward your consolation, and I shall ask Him to look upon you as a kind Father and to manifest to you the true joy of his countenance, communicating to you also his grace."

By this sweetest of exhortations those new Children of the Church were filled with consolation, light, veneration and admiration of what they saw of the Mistress of the world; asking again for her blessing, they for that day left her presence, renewed and replete with the wonderful gifts of the Most High.

The Apostles and disciples from that day on continued without intermission their preaching and their miracles, and through the entire octave they instructed not only the three thousand, who had been converted on Pentecost day, but multitudes of others, who day by day accepted the faith. Since they came from all parts of the world, they conversed and spoke with each one in his own language. This grace was given not only to the Apostles, although it was more complete and noticeable in them; also the disciples and all the one hundred and twenty, who were in the Cenacle at the time, and also the holy women, who received the Holy Ghost, were thus favored.

This was really necessary at the time on account of the great multitudes who came to the faith. Although all the men and many of the women came to the Apostles, yet many, after having heard them, went to Magdalen and her companions, who catechized, instructed and converted them and others that came at the report of the miracles they performed. For this gift was also conferred on the women, who, by the imposition of hands, cured all the sicknesses, gave sight to the blind, tongue to the mute, motion to the lame, and life to many of the dead.

These and other wonders were principally wrought by the Apostles, nevertheless both their miracles and those of the women excited the wonder and astonishment of all Jerusalem; so that nothing else was talked about except the prodigies and the preaching of the Apostles of Jesus, of his disciples, and followers of his doctrine.

This was the happy beginning and the golden age of the evangelical Church, where the rushing of the stream rejoiced the City of God and the current of grace and the gifts of the Holy Ghost fertilized this new paradise recently planted by the hands of the Savior Jesus, while in its midst stood the tree of life, most Holy Mary.

Then was faith alive, hope firm, charity ardent, sincerity pure, humility true, justice most equitable, when the faithful neither knew avarice nor followed vanity, when they trod under foot vain pomp, were free from covetousness, pride, ambition, which later prevailed among the professors of the faith, who while confessing themselves followers of Christ, denied Him in their works.

It will be possible in this third part to describe only a minute portion of the wonderful and great works accomplished by the mighty Queen in the primitive Church; but from those which I will describe, and from her life in this world after the Ascension, much can be inferred. For She did not rest or lose one moment or occasion of conferring some singular favor either upon the whole Church or some of its members. For She consumed Herself either in praying and beseeching her divine Son, without ever experiencing a refusal; or in exhorting, instructing, counseling, and, as Treasurer and Dispenser of the divine favors, distributing graces in diverse manners among the children of the Gospel.

Among the hidden mysteries, which were made known to me concerning this power of the blessed Mary, was also this, that in those first ages, during which She lived in the holy Church, the number of the damned was proportionately very small; and that, comparatively, in those few years a greater number were saved than in many succeeding ages.

B7C3

I acknowledge, that, if the lapse of time had decreased the power, the charity and clemency of that highest Sovereign, the good fortune of those living in that happy time might cause a holy envy in those living by the light of faith in our more protracted and less favored times. It is true we have not the happiness of seeing Her, conversing with Her and listening to Her with bodily senses; and in this respect those first children of the Church were more fortunate.

But let us all remember, that in the heavenly knowledge and charity of this most loving Mother we were all present to Her, also during those times; for She saw and knew us all in the order and succession in which we were be born in the Church; and She prayed and interceded for us no less than for those who lived in her times. Nor is She at present less powerful in heaven, than She was then upon earth; nor less our Mother, than of those first children; and She held us as her own, just as well them.

But alas! that our faith and our fervor and devotion should be so very different! Not She has changed, nor is her love less ardent, nor would we experience less of her intercession and protection, if in troubled times we would hasten to her with the same sentiments of humility and fervor, asking for her prayers and trustfully relying upon Her for help, as was the case with those devoted Christians in the first beginning. Without a doubt the whole Catholic Church would then immediately experience the same assistance of the Queen throughout the whole world.

Many of those new faithful, highly impressed with her greatness by their conversation with the heavenly Mistress, returned to present to Her jewels and the richest gifts; especially the women despoiled themselves of fineries to lay them at her feet. But She would receive or permit none of these gifts. When it seemed to her appropriate not to refuse entirely, She secretly inspired the minds of the givers to bring them to the Apostles, in order that they might be equitably and justly distributed in charity among the most poor and needy of the faithful.

But the humble Mother gratefully acknowledged them as if they had been given to Her. The poor and the sick She received with ineffable kindness, and many of them she cured of inveterate and long–standing infirmities. Through the hands of Saint John She supplied many secret wants, never omitting the least point of virtue.

As the Apostles and disciples were engaged all day in preaching the faith and in converting those that came, the great Queen busied Herself in preparing their food and attending to their comfort; and at stated times She served the priests on her knees and with incredible humility and reverence asked to kiss their hands.

This She observed especially with the Apostles, knowing and beholding their souls confirmed in grace, endowed with all that the Holy Ghost had wrought in them and exalted by their dignity of being the highpriests and the founders of the Church. Sometimes She saw them clothed in great splendor, which elicited from Her increased reverence and veneration.

Baptism of the Converts—The First Mass— Perpetual Presence of the Holy Species in Mary

As the Apostles continued their preaching and wonders in Jerusalem the number of the faithful increased and, as Saint Luke says in the fourth chapter of the Acts, after seven days reached five thousand. All of them were busy catechising the newcomers in preparation for Baptism, though that work was done principally by the disciples; for the Apostles were preaching and were conducting some controversies with the Pharisees and Sadducees.

The Queen, with the assistance of her angels and of the other Marys, proceeded to prepare and adorn the hall, in which her divine Son had celebrated the last Supper; and with her own hands She cleansed it and scrubbed it for his return in the consecration to be performed on the next day.

She asked the owner to furnish it in the same way as I have described for the Thursday of the Last Supper and the devout host deferred to her wishes with deepest reverence. She also prepared the unleavened bread and the wine necessary for the consecration, together with the same paten and chalice in which the Savior had consecrated.

For the Baptism She provided pure water and the basins for administering it with ease and reverence. Then the loving Mother retired and passed the night in most fervent aspirations, prostrations, thanksgiving and other exercises of exalted prayer; offering to the eternal Father all that She, in her heavenly wisdom, knew would help worthily to prepare Herself and all the rest for the worthy administration of Baptism.

Early the next day, which was the octave of the coming of the Holy Ghost, all the faithful and catechumens gathered with the Apostles and disciples in the house of the Cenacle. Saint Peter preached to this gathering instructing them in the nature and excellence of Baptism, the need in which they stood of it and its divine effects, how they would, through it, be made members of the mystical body of the Church, receive an interior character; be regenerated to a new existence as children of God and inheritors of his glory through the remission of sins and sanctifying grace.

He exhorted them to the observance of the divine law, to which they subjected themselves by their own free will, and to humble thanksgiving for this benefit and for all the others, which they received from the hands of the Most High. He explained to them also the mysterious and sacred truth of the Holy Eucharist, which was to be celebrated in the consecration of the true body and blood of Jesus Christ, and he admonished all those especially, who were to receive Holy Communion after their Baptism.

Through this sermon all the converts were inspired with additional fervor; for their dispositions were altogether sincere, the words of the Apostles full of life and penetration, and the interior grace very abundant. Then the Apostles themselves began to baptize amid the most devout and orderly attention of the others. The catechumens entered one door of the Cenacle and after being baptized, they passed out through another, while the disciples and other of the faithful acted as ushers.

The most Holy Mary was present at the entire ceremony, although keeping to one side of the hall. She prayed for all of them and broke forth in canticles of praise. She recognized the effects of Baptism in each one, according to the greater or less degree of virtues infused in their souls. She beheld them renewed and washed in the blood of the Lamb, and their souls restored to a divine purity and spotlessness. In witness of these effects, a most clear light visible to all that were present, descended upon each one that was baptized.

By this miracle God wished to authenticate the first beginnings of this Sacrament in his holy Church, and to console both those first children and us, who are made partakers of this blessing without much adverting to it or giving thanks for it.

This administration of Baptism was continued on that day until all were baptized, although there were about five thousand to receive it. While the baptized were making their thanksgiving for this admirable blessing, the Apostles with all the disciples and the faithful spent some time in prayer. All of them prostrated themselves on the ground adoring the infinite and immutable God, and confessing their own unworthiness of receiving Him in the most august sacrament of the Altar.

In this profound humility and adoration they prepared themselves more immediately for Communion. And then they recited the same psalms and prayers which Christ had recited before consecrating, imitating faithfully that sacred function just as they had seen it performed by their divine Master.

Saint Peter took in his hands the unleavened bread, and, after raising up his eyes to heaven with admirable devotion, he pronounced over the bread the words of consecration of the most holy body of Christ, as had been done before the Lord Jesus.

Immediately the Cenacle was filled with the visible splendor of innumerable angels; and this light converged in a most singular manner on the Queen of heaven and earth and was seen by all those present.

Then Saint Peter consecrated the chalice and performed all the ceremonies, which Christ had observed with the consecrated body and blood, raising them up for the adoration of all the faithful. The Apostle partook himself of the Sacrament and communicated it to the eleven Apostles as most Holy Mary had instructed him.

Thereupon, at the hands of Saint Peter, the heavenly Mother partook of it, while the celestial spirits then present attended with ineffable reverence. In approaching the altar the great Lady made three profound prostrations, touching the ground with her face.

She returned to her place, and it is impossible to describe in words the effects of this participation of the holy Eucharist in this most exalted of creatures. She was entirely transformed and elevated, completely absorbed in this divine conflagration of the love of her most holy Son, whom She had now received bodily. She remained in a trance, elevated from the floor; but the holy angels shielded Her somewhat from view according to her own wish, in order that the attention of those present might not be unduly attracted by the divine effects apparent in Her.

The disciples continued to distribute Holy Communion, first to the disciples and then to the others who had been believers before the Ascension. But of the five thousand newly baptized only one thousand received Communion on that day; because not all were entirely prepared or furnished with the insight and attention required for receiving the Lord in this great sacrament and mystery of the Altar.

To explain the rare and prodigious favor, that the sacramental body of Christ in the sacred species should be preserved continually in the bosom of Mary, it is not necessary to seek for another cause than that underlying all the other favors with which God distinguished this great Lady, namely: that it was his holy will and according to his infinite wisdom, by which He performs according to measure and weight all that is befitting.

Christian prudence and piety will be content to know as a reason, that God had singled this mere Creature out to be his natural Mother, and that therefore She alone, of all creatures, deserved this distinction.

As this miracle of her Mothership was unique and without parallel, it would be shameful ignorance to seek proofs of what the Lord did in Her by comparing it with what He did or ever will do in other souls; since Mary alone rises supereminently above the common order of all.

Yet, though all this is true, the Lord nevertheless wishes that by the light of faith and by enlightenment, we seek the reasons of the propriety and equity, according to which the powerful arm of the Almighty wrought these wonders in his most worthy Mother, so that in them we may know and bless Him in Her and through Her; and so that we may understand, how secure our salvation, all our hope, and our lot are in the hands of that powerful Queen, toward whom her Son has directed all the excess of his love. In accordance with these truths I will explain what has been made known to me of this mystery.

The heavenly Mother lived thirty–three years in the company of her Son and true God; and from the time when He was born of her virginal womb She never left Him to the time of his death on the Cross. She nursed Him, served Him, followed Him and imitated Him conducting Herself always as a Mother, Daughter and Spouse, as a most faithful Servant and Friend; She enjoyed the sight of Him, his conversation, his doctrine and the favors, which, by all these meritorious services, She attained in this mortal life.

Christ ascended into heaven, and the force of love and right reason demanded, that He should take to heaven with Him his most loving Mother, in order that He should not be deprived of Her there, nor She in this world of his presence and company. But the most ardent love which both of Them had for men, dissolved in a manner these bonds of union, inducing our kindest Mother to return to the world in order to establish the Church; and moving the Son to give his consent to her absence from Him during that time.

But as the Son of God was powerful enough to recompense Her for this privation to a certain extent, it became for Him an obligation of his love to make such a recompense. And the fulfillment of this obligation would not have been so publicly acknowledged or made so manifest, if He denied his blessed Mother the favor of accompanying Her upon earth, while He remained seated at the glory of the right hand of his Father.

B7C4

Besides, the most ardent love of the blessed Mother, having been accustomed and nourished in the presence of the Lord her Son, would have inflicted upon Her insufferable violence, if for so many years She was to be deprived of that kind of presence of Him, which was possible during her stay in the Church.

From the understanding which has been given me of the mystery of the love of Christ the Lord for his most holy Mother and of the force with which He was drawn toward Her, I would go so far as to say, that if He had not found this way of remaining with Her in the sacramental species, He would have come down from the right hand of the Father to the world in order to render companionship to his Mother while She sojourned with his Church.

And if it had been necessary that the heavenly mansions and the celestial courtiers should be deprived of the presence of the most sacred humanity from that time, He would have considered that of less importance than to be deprived of the company of his Mother. It is no exaggeration to say this, when we all must confess, that in the purest Mary the Lord found a correspondence and a degree of love more conformable to his will than in all the blessed combined; and consequently, his own love for Her exceeded his love for all others.

If the Shepherd of the Gospel leaves the ninety—nine sheep in order to go in search of only one that is lost, and if we nevertheless dare not say of Him that He leaves the greater for the less; it should not cause wonder in us that this divine Shepherd should leave all the rest of the saints in order to be in the company of his most sincere Sheep, who clothed Him with her own nature and raised and nourished Him as a Mother.

Without a doubt the eyes of his beloved Spouse and Mother would attract Him in swiftest flight from those heights to that earth, where He had lived, whither He before this come for the salvation of the children of Adam, toward whom He was less attracted, yea rather repelled by their sins and by the necessity of suffering for them.

B7C4

If now He descended to live with his beloved Mother, it would not
be to suffer and die; but to enjoy the delights of her company.
Fortunately it is not necessary to rob heaven of his presence; since
by descending in sacramental form He could satisfy both his own
love and that of his most blessed Mother, in whose heart, as in his
couch, this true Solomon could take up his rest without leaving the
right hand of his eternal Father.

SOLICITUDE OF MARY FOR THE APOSTLES AND THE FAITHFUL

As the new law of grace continued to spread in Jerusalem so the number of the faithful increased and the new evangelical Church was augmented day by day. In like manner did the solicitude and attention of its great Queen and Teacher, Mary, expand toward the new children engendered by the Apostles through their preaching. As they were the foundation–stones of the Church, on which the security of that building was to depend, the most prudent Lady lavished especial care upon the apostolic college.

Her heavenly solicitude augmented in proportion to the wrath of Lucifer against the followers of Christ and especially against the Apostles, as the ministers of eternal salvation to the other faithful. It will never be possible to describe or to estimate in this life the blessings and favors conferred by Her upon the Church and upon each of its mystical members.

This happened especially in regard to the Apostles and disciples; for as has been revealed to me not a day or hour passed, in which she did not work for them many wonders. I will relate in this chapter some of the events, which are very instructive on account of the secrets of divine Providence therein contained. From them we can form an estimate of the most vigilant charity and zeal of the blessed Mary for souls.

All the Apostles She loved and served with incredible affection and reverence, both on account of their great holiness and on account of their dignity as priests, as ministers, preachers and founders of the Gospel. During all their stay in Jerusalem She attended upon them, counseled them and directed them in the manner noted above.

With the increase of the Church they were obliged to go outside of Jerusalem in order to baptize and admit to faith many of the inhabitants of the neighboring places; but they always returned to the city, because they had purposely delayed separating from each other, or leaving Jerusalem, until they should receive orders to do so.

From the Acts we learn that saint Peter went to Lydda and Jaffa, where he raised Tabitha from the dead and performed other miracles, returning again to Jerusalem. Although Saint Luke relates these excursions after speaking of the death of Saint Stephen, yet during these events, many were converted throughout Palestine, and it was necessary, that the Apostles go forth to preach to them and to confirm them in the faith, always returning in order to give an account of their doings to their heavenly Mistress.

During all their journeys and preachings the common enemy of all sought to hinder the spread of the divine Word, or its fruit, by rousing the unbelievers to many contradictions and altercations with the Apostles and their listeners or converts; for it seemed to the infernal dragon more easy to assault them, when he saw them removed and far from the protection of their Mistress.

So formidable the great Queen of the angels appeared to the hellish hosts, that in spite of the eminent holiness of the Apostles, Lucifer imagined them disarmed and at his mercy, easily approachable to his temptations, as soon as they left the presence of Mary.

The furious pride of this dragon, as is written in Job, esteems the toughest steel as weak straw, and the hardest bronze as a stick of rotten wood. He fears not the dart nor the sling; but he dreaded the protection of the most blessed Mary, and in tempting the Apostles, he waited until they should have left her presence.

But her protection failed them not on that account; for the great Lady, from the watch–tower of her exalted knowledge, reached out in every direction. Like a most vigilant sentinel She discovered the assaults of Lucifer and hastened to the relief of her sons and ministers of her Lord. When in her absence She could not speak to the Apostles in any of their afflictions, She immediately sent her holy angels to their assistance in order to encourage, forewarn and console them; and sometimes also to drive away the assaulting demons.

All these the celestial spirits executed promptly in compliance with the orders of their Queen. At times they would do it secretly by inspirations and interior consolations; at others, and more frequently, they manifested themselves visibly, assuming most beautiful and refulgent bodies and informing the Apostles of what was proper for the occasion, or what had been ordered by their Mistress.

This happened very often on account of their purity and holiness and on account of the necessity of favoring them with such an abundance of consolation and encouragement. In all their difficulties and labors the most loving Mother thus assisted them, besides offering up for them her continual prayers and thanksgiving. She was the strong Woman, whose domestics were sheltered by double garments; the Mother of the family, who supplied all with nourishment and who by the labors of her hands planted the vineyard of the Lord.

With all the other faithful She proportionately exhibited the same care; and although there were many converts in Jerusalem and in Palestine, She remembered them all in their necessities and tribulations. And She thought not only of the needs of their souls, but of those of the body, and many She cured of most grave sicknesses. Others, whom She knew were not to be cured miraculously, She visited and assisted in person. Of the poor She took a still greater care, with her own hand administering to them food on their beds of sickness, and seeing to their being kept clean, as if She were the servant of all, infirm with the infirm.

So great was the humility, the charity and solicitude of the great Queen of the world, that She refused no service or lowliest ministry to the faithful, no matter how humble and insignificant the condition of those applying for her assistance. She filled each one with joy and consolation and lightened all their labors. Those upon whom on account of their absence She could not personally attend, She assisted secretly through her holy angels or by her prayers and petitions.

In an especial manner her maternal kindness exhibited itself to those who were in the agony of death; for she attended many of the dying and would not leave them until they had secured their eternal salvation. For those who went to purgatory She offered up most fervent prayers and performed some works of penance, such as prostrations in the form of a cross, genuflections and other exercises, by which She satisfied for their faults. Then She sent one of her angels in order to draw them from purgatory and present them to her Son in heaven as his own and as the fruits of his blood and Redemption.

This happiness the Queen of heaven procured to many souls during her stay upon earth. And, as far as was made known to me, this favor is not denied in our days to those, who during their earthly life dispose themselves properly for meriting her presence. But, since it would be necessary to extend the scope of this history very much, if I were to describe how the most blessed Mary assisted many in the hour of death, I will recount only one incident, in which She freed a girl from the jaws of the infernal dragon. It is one which is so extraordinary and worthy of the attention of us all, that it would not be right to omit it in this history, or deprive ourselves of the lesson it contains.

Among the five thousand who were first converted and who received Baptism in Jerusalem, there was also a young girl of poor and humble parentage. This young woman, busying herself with her household duties, took ill and for many days She dragged on in her sickness without improvement. As happens to many other souls, she on that account fell from her first fervor and in her neglect committed some sins endangering her baptismal grace.

Lucifer, who never relaxed in his thirst for the ruin of souls, approached this woman and attacked her with fiercest cruelty, being thus permitted by God to do so for his greater glory and that of his most blessed Mother. The demon appeared to her in the form of another woman and with much cajolery told her to withdraw from those people, who were preaching the Crucified, and not to believe anything they said, because it was all falsehood; that, if she would not follow this advice, she would be punished by the priests and judges who had crucified the Teacher of that new and counterfeit religion; whereas, if she obeyed, she would live peacefully and free from danger.

The girl answered: "I will do what thou sayest; but what shall I do in regard to that Lady, whom I have seen with these men and women and who appears to be so kind and peaceful? I desire her good will very much." The demon replied: "This One, whom thou mentionest, is worse than all the rest, and Her thou must shun before all. It is most important, that thou withdraw from her snares."

Infested with this deadly poison of the ancient serpent, the soul of this simple dove was brought near to eternal death and her body, instead of being relieved, dropped into more serious illness and was in danger of a premature end. One of the seventy–two disciples, who visited the faithful, was informed of the dangerous illness of the girl; for from her neighbors he heard that one of his sect living in that house, was on the point of expiring.

The disciple entered in order to visit her and encourage her according to her necessities. But the sick girl was so ensnared by the demons, that she did not receive him or answer him one word, although he zealously sought to exhort and instruct her; she on the contrary sought to hide and stop her ears in order not to hear him.

B7C5

From these signs the Apostle saw the imminent peril of this soul, although he did not know the cause.

Eagerly he hastened to report to the Apostle Saint John who without delay visited the patient, admonishing her and speaking to her words of eternal life, if she would only listen. But she treated him in the same way as the disciple, obstinately resisting the efforts of both. The Apostle saw many legions of devils surrounding the girl and, though they retired at his approach, they failed not immediately afterward to renew the illusion with which they had filled the unhappy girl.

Seeing her obstinacy, the Apostle betook himself in great affliction to the most blessed Mary in order to ask for help. Immediately the great Queen turned her interior vision upon the sick one and She recognized the unhappy and dangerous condition, in which the enemy had drawn that soul. The kind Mother bewailed this simple sheep, thus deceived by the bloodthirsty infernal wolf; and prostrate upon the floor She prayed for her rescue.

The most blessed Mary continued for some time in this petition; but she received no answer from the Lord, in order that her invincible heart and her charity toward her neighbor might be put to the proof. The most prudent Virgin bethought Herself of what had happened to the prophet Eliseus, who had vainly sent his staff with his servant Giezi to resuscitate the boy and had found that he himself must touch and stretch himself over his body in order to restore him to life. Neither the angel nor the Apostle were powerful enough to awaken from sin and from the stupor of Satan that unfortunate girl; therefore the great Lady resolved to go and heal her in person.

This resolve She recommended to the Lord in her prayer, and, although She received no answer, She considered that the work itself was a sufficient warranty to proceed. She arose therefore to leave her room and to walk with Saint John to the dwelling of the sick woman, which was at some distance from the Cenacle. But no sooner had She taken the first steps than the holy angels, at the command of the Lord, approached to bear Her up on the way.

As God had not manifested his intention, She asked them, why they thus detained Her; to which they answered: "There is no reason why we should consent to thy walking through the city, when we can bear Thee along with greater propriety." Immediately they placed her upon a throne of resplendent clouds, on which they bore Her along and placed Her in the sick–room. The dying girl, being poor and now speechless, had been forsaken by all and was surrounded only by the demons, who waited to snatch off her soul.

But as soon as the Queen of angels made her appearance all the evil spirits vanished like flashes of lightning and as if falling over each other in their dismay. The powerful Queen commanded them to descend into hell and remain there until She should permit them to come forth, and this they were forced to do without the least power of resistance.

The kindest Mother then approached the sick woman and taking her by the hand and calling her by her name, spoke sweetest words of life. Instantly a complete change came over the girl, and she began to breathe more freely and recover herself. Then she said to the heavenly Mary: "My Lady, a woman came to me, who persuaded me to believe, that the disciples of Jesus were deceiving me and that I had better immediately separate myself from them and from Thee; otherwise, if I should accept their way of life, I should fall into great misfortune."

The Queen answered: "My daughter, she, who seemed to thee a woman, was thy enemy, the devil. I come in the name of the Most High to give thee eternal life; return then to his true faith which thou hast received, and confess Him with all thy heart as thy God and Redeemer, who, for thy salvation and that of all the world, has died upon the Cross. Adore and call upon Him, and ask Him for the pardon of thy sins."

B7C5

"All this," the patient answered, "I have believed before; but they told me, it was very bad, and that they would punish me, if I should ever confess it." The heavenly Teacher replied: "My friend, do not fear this deceit but remember that the chastisement and pains which are really to be feared are those of hell, to which the demons wish to bring thee, Thou art now very near death and thou canst avail thyself of the remedy I now offer thee, if thou wilt only believe me; and thou shalt thus free thyself of the eternal fire, which threatens thee on account of thy mistake."

Through this exhortation and the graces procured for this poor woman by Mary, she was moved to abundant tears of compunction and implored the blessed Lady further to assist her in this danger, declaring herself ready to obey all her commands. Then the loving Mother made her openly profess her faith in Jesus Christ and elicit an act of contrition in preparation for confession. At the same time She sent for the Apostles to administer the Sacraments to her. The sick girl, repeating the acts of contrition and love, and invoking Jesus and Mary, who was directing her, happily expired in the arms of her Protectress.

Death of Steven—The Creed—Departure of the Apostles

Among the saints who were especially fortunate in meriting the greater love of the Queen of heaven, there was one by the name of Stephen, who belonged to the seventy–two disciples; for from the very beginning of his following Christ our Savior, She looked upon him with an especial love, placing him first, or among the first, in her estimation.

She immediately saw, that this saint was chosen by the Master of life for the defense of his honor and his holy name, and that he was to give up his life for him. Moreover this courageous saint was of a sweet and peaceful disposition; and he was rendered much more amiable and docile to all holiness by the workings of grace. Such dispositions made him very pleasing to the sweetest Mother; and whenever She found any persons naturally of a peaceful and meek character, She was wont to say, that they resembled her divine Son.

On this account and on account of many heroic virtues of Saint Stephen She loved him tenderly, procured him many blessings, and thanked the Lord for having created, called and chosen such a one for the first–fruits of his martyrs. In consideration of his coming martyrdom, revealed to Her by her Divine Son, her heart was filled with additional affection for this great saint.

The blessed saint corresponded in most faithful and deepest reverence with the benefits conferred upon him by Christ our Savior and his heavenly Mother; for he was not only of a peaceful, but of an humble heart, and those that are so disposed in truth, are thankful for all benefits, even though they may not be so great as those conferred on saint Stephen.

He always entertained the highest conceptions concerning the Mother of mercy, and in his high esteem and fervent devotion he continued to seek her favor. He asked information on many mysterious matters; for he was very wise, full of the Holy Spirit and of faith, as is told us by Saint Luke. The great Lady answered all his inquiries, encouraged and exhorted him zealously to work for the honor of Christ.

In order to confirm him more in his strong faith. Mary forewarned him of his coming martyrdom and said: "Thou, Stephen, shalt be the first–born of the martyrs, engendered by my divine Son and Lord by the example of his death; thou shalt follow his footsteps, like a privileged disciple his master, and like a courageous soldier his captain; and at the head of the army of martyrs, thou shalt carry his banner of the Cross. Hence it is meet thou arm thyself with fortitude under the shield of faith, and be assured, that the strength of the Most High shall be with thee in the conflict."

This warning of the Queen of the angels inflamed the heart of Saint Stephen with the desire of martyrdom. As is recorded in the Acts of the Apostles, he was filled with grace and fortitude and wrought great wonders in Jerusalem. Besides the Apostles Saint Peter and Saint John, no one except he dared to dispute with the Jews. His wisdom and spirit they could not resist, because he preached to them with an intrepid heart, refuted and accused them oftener and more courageously than the other disciples.

All this Saint Stephen did with burning desire of attaining the martyrdom of which he had been assured by the great Lady. As if he were afraid of any one gaining this crown in advance of him, he offered himself before all others to engage in the disputes with the rabbis and teachers of the law of Moses, so eager was he to defend the honor of Christ, for whom he knew he would lay down his life. The infernal dragon, gradually becoming observant of the ambitions of Saint Stephen, directed his malignant attention toward him and strove to hinder his attaining public martyrdom in testimony of the faith of Christ. In order to destroy him, he incited the most incredulous of the Jews to kill Saint Stephen in secret.

But Saint Stephen did not on that account neglect preaching or arguing with the unbelieving Jews. As these Jews could not murder him in secret, nor overcome his wisdom in public, they vented their mortal hatred in seeking false testimony against him. They accused him of blasphemy against God and against Moses, of inveighing continually against the holy temple and the Law, and of asserting that Jesus would destroy as well the one, as the other.

As the witnesses loudly proclaimed their slander and the people were being roused by their falsehoods, they brought him into the hall where the priests were gathered as the judges of these accusations. The presiding judge first took the deposition of Saint Stephen before the court. The saint took occasion to prove with highest wisdom, that Christ was the true Messiah promised to them in the holy Scriptures; and in conclusion he reprehended them for their unbelief and hardness of heart so strongly, that they could find no answer and, gnashing their teeth they stopped their ears, in order not to be obliged to hear his words.

The Queen of heaven knew of the seizure of Saint Stephen; and, in order to animate him in her name for the approaching conflict, She immediately sent him one of her angels, even before he entered into dispute with the priests. Through the holy angel Saint Stephen sent Her answer, that he went with joy to confess his Master and with unflinching heart to give his life for Him, as he had always desired.

Through the same messenger, he begged Her, as his kindest Teacher and Mother, to assist him and, from her retirement, to send him her blessing, since his not having been able to obtain her parting benediction was the only regret he felt now, when he was about to lay down his life according to Her wishes.

These last words of Saint Stephen moved the maternal bosom of Mary to even greater love and esteem than hitherto; and She desired to attend upon him in person, at this hour, when her beloved disciple was to give up his life for the honor and defense of

B8C1

his God and Redeemer. But the blessed Mother hesitated at the difficulties, which would arise in her passing through the streets of Jerusalem at a time of popular excitement and also in finding an opportunity of speaking publicly to saint Stephen.

She prostrated Herself in prayer, begging the divine favor for her beloved disciple; and She presented to the Lord her desire of helping him in the last hour. The clemency of the Most High, which is always at the beck of his Spouse and Mother and which was anxious to enhance the death of his faithful disciple and servant Stephen, sent from heaven a multitude of angels, who, with those of her guard, should carry their Queen to the place where the saint then was.

And immediately the mandate of the Lord was executed: the angels placed Her upon a refulgent cloud and bore Her to the tribunal, where the highpriest was examining into the charges against Saint Stephen. The vision of the Queen of heaven was hidden from all except the Saint. He however saw Her before him, supported in the air by the holy angels in a cloud of heavenly splendor and glory.

This extraordinary favor inflamed anew the divine love and the ardent zeal of this champion of the honor of God. In addition to the joy of seeing Mary, the splendors of the Queen shone from the countenance of Saint Stephen, that it gleamed with wonderful beauty and light.

At the end of this discourse, through the intercession of the Queen and as a reward of the unconquered zeal of Saint Stephen, the heavens opened and the Savior appeared to him standing at the right hand of the Father in the act of assisting him in the conflict. Saint Stephen raised his eyes and said "Behold I see the heavens opened and its glory, and in it I see Jesus at the right hand of God himself."

But the obdurate perfidy of the Jews esteemed these words as blasphemy and they stopped their ears in order not to hear them.

As the punishment of blasphemers according to the law, was death by stoning, they passed upon him that sentence. Then they all surrounded him like wolves and dragged him from the city with great haste and noise.

At this juncture the blessed Mother gave him her benediction and speaking to him words of encouragement and endearment, She left him in charge of her angels, whom She ordered to accompany him and to remain with him until they should present his soul to the Most High. Only one of the guardian angels, in company with those that had descended from heaven as her escort to Saint Stephen, now returned with Her to the Cenacle.

From her retirement the great Lady by an especial vision saw all that happened in the martyrdom of Saint Stephen: how they led him forth from the city with great haste and violence, shouting that he was a blasphemer worthy of death; how Saul was among them, more zealous than the rest, guarding the vestments of those who had taken them off to stone saint Stephen; how the shower of stones fell upon the Saint and wounded him, some of them remaining fixed in his head and stained by his blood.

Great and tender was the compassion of our Queen at such cruel martyrdom; but still greater her joy in seeing Saint Stephen meeting it so gloriously. The kindest Mother failed him not in her tearful prayers from her oratory. When the invincible martyr saw himself near to death, he prayed: "Lord receive my spirit!" Then, on his knees, he exclaimed with a loud voice: "Lord lay not this sin to their charge!"

 In these prayers he was supported by those of the blessed Mary, who was filled with incredible joy to see the faithful disciple imitating so closely his divine Master by praying for his enemies and persecutors and commending his spirit into the hands of his Creator and Redeemer.

B8C1

Covered with wounds from the shower of stones thrown by the Jews, Saint Stephen expired, while they became still more hardened in their perfidy. Immediately the angels of the Queen bore his pure soul to the presence of God in order to be crowned with eternal honor and glory.

Saint Luke says, that on the same day on which Saint Stephen was stoned to death, a great persecution arose against the Church in Jerusalem. He mentions especially that Saul devastated it, searching through the whole city for the followers of Christ in order to seize and denounce them before the magistrates. This he did to many of the believers, who were arrested, illtreated, and killed in this persecution.

Although it was very severe on account of the hatred, which the princes and priests had conceived against the Christians, and on account of the zealous efforts of Saul in his jealous defense of the law of Moses; yet there was another cause for this severity, the effects of which they felt, though they knew not its origin.

The most prudent Mother bore in mind, that the disciples, having dispersed to preach the name and faith of Christ the Savior, had as yet no formula or express creed to guide themselves uniformly and without differences, so that all the faithful might believe one and the same express truths.

Moreover She knew that the Apostles would soon have to go forth over the whole world in order to spread and establish the Church through their preaching, and that it was proper that all should be united in their doctrine, upon which was to be founded all the perfection of a Christian life.

Therefore the most prudent Mother of wisdom wished to see all the divine mysteries, which the Apostles were to preach and the faithful to believe, reduced to a short formula. For if those truths were moulded into a few articles, they could more conveniently be brought to the mind of all, the whole Church would be united in one belief without any essential difference, and the whole spiritual edifice of the Gospel would thus rest and be built up on the same firm columns of one foundation.

In order to prepare for this work, the importance of which She recognized, She presented her wishes to the Lord, who had inspired them, and for more than forty days She persevered in this prayer with fasting, prostrations and other exercises.

In answer to her prayer for the Apostles, besides promising to assist them in preparing the symbol of the faith, the Lord informed his Mother of the very wording of the propositions or articles, of which the Creed was to be composed. Of all this the most prudent Lady was well capable; but now, when the time had arrived for executing what had been intended so long before, He wished to renew it all in the purest heart of his virgin Mother, in order that the fundamental truths of the Church might flow from the lips of Christ himself. He inspired Saint Peter his vicar and the rest with the desire of setting up a symbol of the universal faith of the Church.

Accordingly they sought conference with the heavenly Mistress concerning its opportuneness and the measures to be taken for this purpose. They resolved to fast and persevere in prayer for ten continuous days, in order to receive the inspiration of the Holy Ghost in this arduous affair.

Having completed these ten days, which were also the last ten of the forty, in which the Queen had treated with the Lord about this matter, the twelve Apostles met in the presence of Mary, and Saint Peter spoke to them as follows:

"My dear brethren, the divine mercy, in its infinite goodness and through the merits of our Savior and Master Jesus, has favored his Holy Church by gloriously multiplying its children, as we have seen and experienced in this short time. For this purpose the Almighty has multiplied miracles and prodigies and daily renews them through our ministry, having chosen us (though unworthy) as the instruments of his divine will in this work and for the glory and honor of his holy name. Together with these favors He has sent us tribulations and persecutions of the devil and of the world, in order that we may imitate our Savior and Captain, and in order that the Church, evenly ballasted, might reach more securely the port of rest and eternal felicity."

"The disciples have evaded the wrath of the chief priest and spread through the neighboring cities, preaching the faith of Christ our Redeemer and Lord. We must also soon depart and preach throughout the globe, according to the command of the Lord before ascending into heaven. Just as there is but one Baptism in which men are to receive this faith, so there must be but one doctrine, which the faithful are to believe."

"Hence it is meet that we, who are as yet gathered harmoniously in the Lord, define the truths and mysteries which we are to propound expressly to all the nations of the world, and thus, without difference of opinions, believe the same doctrines. It is the infallible promise of the Lord, that where two or three shall be gathered in his name, He shall be in their midst. Confiding in his word we firmly hope, that He will now assist us with His divine Spirit to understand and define, in his name by an unchangeable decree, the articles to be established in his holy Church as long as it shall last, to the end of the world."

All the Apostles consented to this proposal of Peter. Then he celebrated a Mass, in which he gave Communion to the most holy Mary and the Apostles whereupon they all, including the blessed Mother, prostrated themselves in prayer calling upon the Holy Ghost. After continuing their prayers for some time they heard the rumbling of thunder, as on the first coming down of the Holy Ghost upon the gathering of the faithful; at the same time the Cenacle was filled with light and splendor and all were enlightened by the Holy Spirit.

Then the most blessed Mary asked each of the Apostles to define a mystery, according as the divine Spirit should inspire them.

Thereupon saint Peter began, and was followed by the rest in the following order:

- 1. Saint Peter: I believe in God, the Father almighty, Creator of heaven and earth.
- 2. Saint Andrew: And in Jesus Christ, his only Son, our Lord.
- 3 and 4. Saint James the Greater: Who was conceived through operation of the Holy Ghost, born of the Virgin Mary.
- 5. Saint John: Suffered under Pontius Pilate, was crucified, died and was buried.
- 6 and 7. Saint Thomas: Descended into hell, arose from the dead on the third day.
- 8. Saint James the Less: Ascended into heaven, is seated at the right hand of God the Father almighty.
- 9. Saint Philip: From thence He shall come to judge the living and the dead.
- 10. Saint Bartholomew: I believe in the Holy Ghost.
- 11. Saint Matthew: In the holy Catholic Church, the Communion of saints.
- 12. Saint Simon: Forgiveness of sins.
- 13. Saint Thaddeus: The resurrection of the flesh.
- 14. Saint Mathias: Life everlasting. Amen.

This symbol, which we ordinarily call the Creed, the Apostles established after the martyrdom of Saint Stephen and before the end of the first year after the death of the Savior. Afterwards, in order to refute the Arian and other heresies, the Church, in the councils held on their account, explained more fully the mysteries contained in the Apostles' Creed and composed the one now chanted in the Mass. But in substance both are one and the same and contain the fourteen articles, which are the basis for the catechetical teaching of the Christian faith and which we are all bound to believe in order to be saved.

As soon as the Apostles had finished pronouncing this Creed, the Holy Ghost approved of it by permitting a voice to be heard in their midst saying: "You have decided well." Then the great Queen and Lady of heaven with all the Apostles gave thanks to the Most High; and She thanked also them for having merited the assistance of the divine Spirit, so as to be his apt instruments in promoting the glory of the Lord and the good of the Church.

In confirmation of her faith and as an example to the faithful, the most prudent Mistress fell at the feet of Saint Peter, loudly proclaimed her belief in the Catholic doctrine as contained in the symbol they had just now composed and formulated. This She did for Herself and in the name of all the faithful, saying to Saint Peter: "My lord, whom I recognize as the vicar of my most holy Son, in thy hands, I, a vile wormlet, in my name and in the name of all the faithful of the Church, confess and proclaim all that thou hast set down as the divine and infallible truth of the Catholic church; and in it I bless and exalt the Most High, from whom it proceeds." She kissed the hands of the Vicar of Christ and of the rest of the Apostles. Thus She was the first one thus openly to profess the Catholic faith after it had been formulated into articles.

Already a full year had passed since the death of Savior, and now the Apostles, by divine impulse, began to consider about going forth to preach the faith throughout the world; for it was time that the name of God be preached also to the heathens and that they be taught the way of eternal salvation.

In order to consult the will of God in the assignment of the kingdoms and provinces in which each one was to preach, they, upon the advice of their Queen, resolved to fast and pray for ten successive days. This practice of fasting and praying for ten days, which they had observed immediately after Ascension in disposing themselves for the coming of the Holy Ghost, they afterwards also retained in preparing themselves for the more important undertakings.

Having completed these exercises, the Vicar of Christ celebrated Mass and communicated the most blessed Mary and the eleven Apostles, as they had done in preparing the Creed. After Mass they all persevered with their Queen for some time in most exalted prayer, ardently invoking the assistance of the Holy Ghost for the manifestation of his will in this matter.

At the ending of this prayer a wonderful light descended upon the Cenacle surrounding them all and a voice was heard saying: "My vicar Peter shall point out the province, which falls to each one. I shall govern and direct him by my light and spirit."

The appointments themselves the Holy Ghost left to Saint Peter in order to confirm anew his power as head and universal pastor of the Church, and in order that the Apostles might understand, that it was to be founded throughout the world under the direction of saint Peter and his successors, to whom they were to be subject as the vicars of Christ.

They were filled with a new light and knowledge concerning the peoples and provinces assigned to them by Saint Peter, and each one recognized the conditions, nature and customs of the kingdoms singled out for him, being furnished interiorly with the most distinct and abundant information concerning each.

The Most High gave them new fortitude to encounter labors; agility for overcoming distances, although in this regard they were afterwards to be frequently assisted by the holy angels; and the fire of divine love, so that they be came inflamed like seraphim lifted far beyond the condition and sphere of mere human creatures.

The most blessed Queen was present at all these events, and the workings of the divine power in the Apostles and in Herself, were very clear to Her; for on this occasion, She experienced more of the divine influences than all of them together. As She was exalted supereminently above all creatures, so the increase of her gifts was in like proportion, transcending immeasurably those of others.

B8C1

The Most High renewed in the purest spirit of his Mother the infused knowledge concerning creatures, and especially concerning the kingdoms and nations assigned to the Apostles. She knew all that each one knew, and more than they all together, because She received a personal and individual knowledge of each person to whom the faith of Christ was to be preached; and She was made relatively just as familiar with all the earth and its inhabitants, as She was with Her oratory and all those that entered therein.

The knowledge of Mary was the knowledge of a supreme Mistress, Mother, Governess and Sovereign of the Church, which the Almighty had placed in her hands. She was to take care of all, from the highest to the lowest of the saints, and also of the sinners as the children of Eve.

As no one was to receive any blessing or favor from the hands of her Son except through that of his Mother, it was necessary that this most faithful Dispensatrix of grace should know all of her family, whom She was to guard as a Mother, and such a Mother! The great Lady therefore had not only infused images and knowledge of all this, but She actually experienced it according as the disciples and Apostles proceeded in their work of preaching.

Before Her lay open all their labors and dangers, and the attacks of the demons against them; the petitions and prayers of these and of all the faithful, so that She might be able to support them with her own, or aid them through her angels or by Herself in person; for in all these different ways did She render her assistance, as we shall see in many events yet to be described.

I wish merely to state here, that besides the knowledge derived by our Queen from infused images She had also in God himself another knowledge of things through her abstractive vision, by which She continually saw the Divinity. But there was a difference between these two different kinds of knowledge: since, when she saw in God the labors of the Apostles and of all the faithful of the Church enjoying at the same time through this vision a certain participation of the eternal beatitude, the most loving Mother was not affected with the sensible sorrow and compassion, which filled Her when perceiving these tribulations themselves through images.

In this latter kind of vision She felt and bewailed them with maternal compassion. In order that this merit might not be wanting in Her, the Lord conferred this second kind of knowledge upon Her for all the time of her pilgrimage here below. Joined with this plenitude of infused species and knowledge.

She held also absolute command of her faculties, so that She admitted no images or ideas except those that were absolutely necessary for sustaining life, or for some work of charity or perfection. With this adornment and beauty, which was patent to the angels and saints, the heavenly Lady was an object of admiration, inducing them to praise and glorify the Most High for the worthy exercise of all his attributes in Mary, his most holy instrument.

A few days after the partition of the earth among the Apostles, they began to leave Jerusalem, especially those that were allotted the provinces of Palestine, and first among them was Saint James the greater. Others stayed longer in Jerusalem, because the Lord wished the faith to be preached there more abundantly and the Jews to be called before all others, if they chose to come and accept the invitation to the marriage—feast of the Gospel; for in the blessing of the Redemption this people, although more ungrateful than the heathens, was especially favored.

Afterwards all the Apostles gradually departed for the regions assigned to them, according as time and season demanded and as obedience to the divine Spirit, the counsel of the most holy Mary, and the order of Saint Peter dictated. But before leaving Jerusalem each one visited the holy places, such as the garden, Calvary the Holy Sepulchre, the place of the Ascension, Bethany and the other memorable spots as far as possible.

B8C1

All of them showed their veneration, moved even to tears and regarding with loving wonder the very earth which the Savior had touched. Then they visited the Cenacle, reverencing the spot where so many mysteries had taken place. There, again commending themselves to her protection, they took leave of the great Queen of heaven. The blessed Mother dismissed them with words of sweetness and divine virtue.

But admirable was the solicitude and care of the most prudent Lady in showing Herself as the true Mother of the Apostles at their departure. For each of the twelve She made a woven tunic similar to that of Christ our Savior, of a color between brown and ash–gray; and in order to weave these garments She called to aid her holy angels. She furnished each of the Apostles garments the same kind and like to that formerly worn by their Master Jesus: for She wished that they should imitate Him even in their garments and thereby be known exteriorly as his disciples.

The great Lady procured also twelve crosses of the height and size of each of the Apostles and gave one to each, so that, as a witness of their doctrine and for their consolation, they might carry it along in their wanderings and their preaching. Each of the Apostles preserved and carried this cross with him to his death; and as they were so loud in praise of the Cross, some of the tyrants made use of this very instrument to torment them happily to death.

Moreover the devout Mother furnished each one of them with a small metal case, in which She placed three of the thorns from the crown of her divine Son, some pieces of the cloths in which She had wrapped the infant Savior, and of the linen with which She had wiped and caught the most precious blood of the Circumcision and Passion of the Lord.

All these sacred pledges She had preserved with the greatest care and veneration, as the Mother and the Treasure–keeper of heaven. In order to consign them to the Apostles She called them together and, with the majesty of a Queen and the tenderness of a Mother,

She told them that these remembrances, with which She would enrich them on their departure, were the greatest treasures in her possession; for in them they would carry with them vivid remembrances of her divine Son and the certain assurance, that the Lord loved them as his children and as ministers of the Most High.

Then She handed them those relics, which they received with tears of consolation and joy. They thanked the great Queen for these favors and prostrated themselves in adoration of the sacred relics. Embracing they bade farewell to each other, Saint James being the first to depart and commence his mission.

Conversion of Saint Paul

Saint Paul was distinguished in Judaism for two reasons. The one was his own character, and the other was the diligence of the demon in availing himself of his naturally good qualities. Saint Paul was of a disposition generous, magnanimous, most noble, kind, active, courageous and constant. He had acquired many of the moral virtues.

He glorified in being a staunch professor of the law of Moses, and in being studious and learned in it; although in truth he was ignorant of its essence, as he himself confesses to Timothy, because all his learning was human and terrestrial; like many Jews, he knew the law merely from the outside, without its spirit and without the divine insight, which was necessary to understand it rightly and to penetrate its mysteries.

The disposition of Saul was most noble and generous, and therefore it appeared to him beneath his dignity and honor to stoop to such crimes and act the part of an assassin, when he could, as it seemed to him, destroy the law of Christ by the power of reasoning and open justice.

He felt a still greater horror at the thought of killing the most blessed Mother, on account of the regard due to Her as a woman; and because he had seen Her so composed and constant in the labors and in the Passion of Christ. On this account She seemed to him a magnanimous Woman and worthy of veneration.

She had indeed won his respect, together with some compassion for her sorrows and afflictions, the magnitude of which had become publicly known. Hence he gave no admittance to the inhuman suggestions of the demon against the life of the most blessed Mary. This compassion for Her hastened not a little the conversion of Saul.

Neither did he further entertain the treacherous designs against the apostles, although Lucifer sought to make their assassination appear as a deed worthy of his courageous spirit. Rejecting all these wicked thoughts, he resolved to incite all the Jews to persecute the Church, until it should be destroyed together with the name of Christ.

As the dragon and his cohorts could not attain more, they contented themselves with having brought Saul at least to this resolve. The dreadful wrath of these demons against God and his creatures can be estimated from the fact, that on that very day they held another meeting in order to consult how they could preserve the life of this man, whom they had found so well adapted to execute their malice.

These deadly enemies well know, that they have no jurisdiction over the lives of men, and that they can neither give nor take life, unless permitted by God on some particular occasion; nevertheless they wished to make themselves the guardians and the physicians of the life and health of Saul as far as their power extended, namely, by keeping active his forethought against whatever was harmful and suggesting the use of what was naturally beneficial to the welfare of life and limb.

Yet with all their efforts they were unable to hinder the work of grace, when God so wished it. Far were they from suspecting, that Saul would ever accept the faith of Christ, and that the life, which they were trying to preserve and lengthen, was to redound to their own ruin and torment. Such events are provided by the wisdom of the Most High, in order that the devil, being deceived by his evil counsels, may fall into his own pits and snares, and in order that all his machinations may serve for the fulfillment of the divine and irresistible will.

Such were the decrees of the highest Wisdom in order that the conversion of Saul might be more wonderful and glorious. With this intention God permitted Satan, after the death of Saint Stephen, to instigate Saul to go to the chief priests with fierce threats against the disciples of Christ, who had left Jerusalem, and to solicit permission for bringing them as prisoners to Jerusalem from wherever he should find them.

For this enterprise Saul offered his person and possessions, and even his life; at his own cost and without salary he made this journey in order that the new Law, preached by the disciples of the Crucified, might not prevail against the Law of his ancestors. This offer was readily favored by the high–priest and his counselors; they immediately gave to Saul the commission he asked, especially to go to Damascus, whither, according to report, some of the disciples had retired after leaving Jerusalem.

He prepared for the journey, hiring officers of justice and some soldiers to accompany him. But his by far most numerous escort were the many legions of demons, who in order to assist him in this enterprise, came forth from hoping that with all this show of force and through Saul, they might be able to make an end of the Church and entirely devastate it with fire and blood.

This was really the intention of Saul, and the one with which Lucifer and his demons sought to inspire him and his companions. But let us leave him for the present on his journey to Damascus, anxious to seize all the disciples of Christ, whom he should find in the synagogues of that city.

Nothing of all this was unknown to the Queen of heaven; for in addition to her science and vision penetrating to the inmost thoughts of men and demons, the Apostles were solicitous in keeping Her informed of all that befell the followers of her Son. Long before this time She had known that Saul was to be an Apostle of Christ, a preacher to the gentiles, and a man distinguished and wonderful in the Church; for all of these things her Son informed Her.

But as She saw the persecution becoming more violent and the glorious fruits and results of the conversion of Saul delayed, and as

She moreover saw how the disciples of Christ, who knew nothing of the secret intentions of the Most High, were afflicted and somewhat discouraged at the fury and persistence of his persecution, the kindest Mother was filled with great sorrow. Considering, in her heavenly prudence, how important was this affair, She roused Herself to new courage and confidence in her prayers for the welfare of the Church and the conversion of Saul.

He permitted his blessed Mother to suffer some sensible pain and, as it were, to fall into a kind of swoon, yet her Son, could not longer resist the love which wounded his heart, consoled and restored Her by yielding to her prayers He said: "My Mother, chosen among all creatures, let thy will be done without delay. I will do with Saul as Thou askest, and will so change him, that from this moment he will be a defender of the Church which he persecutes, and a preacher of my name and glory. I shall now proceed to receive him immediately into my friendship and grace."

Thereupon Jesus Christ our Lord disappeared from the presence of his most blessed Mother leaving Her still engaged in prayer and furnished with a clear insight into what was to happen. Shortly afterward the Lord appeared to Saul on the road near Damascus, whither, in his ever increasing fury against Jesus, his accelerated journey had already brought him.

The Lord showed himself to Saul in a resplendent cloud amid immense glory, and at the same time Saul was flooded with light without and within, and his heart and senses were overwhelmed beyond power of resistance. He fell suddenly from his horse to the ground and at the same time he heard a voice from on high saying: "Saul, Saul, why dost thou persecute Me?" Full of fear and consternation he answered: "Who art Thou, Lord?" The voice replied: "I am Jesus whom thou persecutes; it is hard for thee to kick against the goad of my omnipotence."

Again Saul answered with greater fear and trembling: "Lord, what dost Thou command and desire to do with me?" The companions of Saul heard these questions and answers, though they did not see the Savior. They saw the splendor surrounding him and all were filled with dread and astonishment at this sudden and unthought of event, and they were for some time dumbfounded.

This new wonder, surpassing all that had been seen in the world before, was greater and more far—reaching than what could be taken in by the senses. For Saul was not only prostrated in body, blinded and bereft of his strength so that, if the divine power had not sustained him, he would have immediately expired; but also as to his interior he suffered more of a change than when he passed from nothingness into existence at his conception, farther removed from what he was before than from darkness, or the highest heaven from the lowest earth; for he was changed from an image of the demon to that of one of the highest and most ardent seraphim.

This triumph over Lucifer and his demons had been especially reserved by God for his divine Wisdom and Omnipotence; so that, in virtue of the Passion and Death of Christ this dragon and his malice might be vanquished by the human nature of one man, in whom the effects of grace and Redemption were set in opposition to the sin of Lucifer and all its effects.

Thus it happened that in the same short time, in which Lucifer through pride was changed from an angel to a devil, the power of Christ changed Saul from a demon into an angel in grace. In the angelic nature the highest beauty turned into the deepest ugliness; and in the human nature the greatest perversity into the highest moral perfection. Lucifer descended as the enemy of God from heaven to the deepest abyss of the earth, and a man ascended as a friend of God from the earth to the highest heaven.

And since this triumph would not have been sufficiently glorious, if the Lord had not given more than Lucifer had lost, the Omnipotent wished to add in Saint Paul an additional triumph to his victory over the demon. For Lucifer, although he fell from that exceedingly high grace which he had received, had never

B8C1

possessed beatific vision, nor had he made himself worthy of it, and hence could not lose what he did not possess.

But Paul, immediately on disposing himself for justification and on gaining grace, began to partake of glory and clearly saw the Divinity, though this vision was gradual. O invincible virtue of the divine power! O infinite efficacy of the merits of the life and death of Christ! It was certainly reasonable and just, that if the malice of sin in one instant changed the angel into a demon, that the grace of the Redeemer should be more powerful and abound more than sin, raising up from it a man, not only to place him into original grace, but into glory.

Greater is this wonder than the creation of heaven and earth with all the creatures; greater than to give sight to the blind, health to the sick, life to the dead. Let us congratulate the sinners on the hope inspired by this wonderful justification, since we have for our Restorer, for our Father, and for our Brother the same Lord, who justified Paul; and He is not less powerful nor less holy for us, than for saint Paul.

During the time in which Paul lay prostrate upon the earth, he was entirely renewed by sanctifying grace and other infused gifts, restored and illumined proportionately in all his interior faculties, and thus he was prepared to be elevated to the empyrean heaven, which is called the third heaven. He himself confesses that he did not know whether he was thus elevated in body or only in spirit. But there, by more than ordinary vision, though in a transient manner, he saw the Divinity clearly and intuitively.

Besides the being of God and his attributes of infinite perfection, he recognized the mystery of the Incarnation and Redemption, and all the secrets of the law of grace and of the state of the Church. He saw the peerless blessing of his justification and of the prayer of Saint Stephen for him; and still more clearly was he made aware of the prayers of the most holy Mary and how his conversion had been hastened through Her; and that, after Christ, her merits made him acceptable in the sight of God.

From that hour on he was filled with gratitude and with deepest veneration and devotion to the great Queen of heaven, whose dignity was now manifest to him and whom he thenceforth acknowledged as his Restorer. At the same time he recognized the office of Apostle to which he was called, and that in it he was to labor and suffer unto death.

In conjunction with these mysteries were revealed to him many others, of which he himself says that they are not to be disclosed. He offered himself in sacrifice to the will of God in all things, as he showed afterwards in the course of his life. The most blessed Trinity accepted this sacrifice and offering of his lips and in the presence of the whole court of heaven named and designated him as the preacher and teacher of the gentiles, and as a vase of election for carrying through the world the name of the Most high.

On the third day after the disablement and conversion of Saul the Lord spoke in a vision to one of the disciples, Ananias, living in Damascus. Calling him by name as his servant and friend, the Lord told him to go to the house of a man named Judas in a certain district of the city and there to find Saul of Tarsus, whom he would find engaged in prayer.

At the same time Saul had also a vision, in which he saw and recognized the disciple Ananias coming to him and restoring sight to him by the imposition of hands. But of this vision of Saul, Ananias at that time had no knowledge. Therefore he answered: "Lord, I have information of this man having persecuted thy saints in Jerusalem and caused a great slaughter of them in Jerusalem; and not satisfied with this, he has now come with warrants from the high–priests in order to seize whomever he can find invoking thy holy name. Dost thou then send a simple sheep like myself to go in search of the wolf, that desires to devour it?"

The Lord replied: "Go, for the one thou judgest to be my enemy, is for Me a vase of election, in order that he may carry my name through all the nations and kingdoms, and to the children of

Israel. And I can, as I shall, assign to him what he is to suffer for my name." And the disciple was at once informed of all that had happened.

Relying on this word of the Lord, Ananias obeyed and betook himself at once to the house, in which Saint Paul then was. He found him in prayer and said to him: "Brother Saul, our Lord Jesus, who appeared to thee on thy journey, sends me in order that thou mayest receive thy sight and be filled with the Holy Ghost."

He received Holy Communion at the hands of Ananias and was strengthened and made whole, giving thanks to the Author of all these blessings. Then he partook of some corporal nourishment, of which he had not tasted for three days. He remained for some time in Damascus conferring and conversing with the disciples in that city. He prostrated himself at their feet asking their pardon and begging them to receive him as their servant and brother, even as the least and most unworthy of them all.

At their approval and counsel he went forth publicly to preach Christ as the Messiah and Redeemer of the world and with such fervor, wisdom and zeal, that he brought confusion to the unbelieving Jews in the numerous synagogues of Damascus.

All wondered at this unexpected change and, in great astonishment, said: Is not this the man, who in Jerusalem has persecuted with fire and sword all who invoke that name? And has he not come to bring them prisoners to the chief priests of that city? What change then is this, which we see in him?

Saint Paul grew stronger each day and with increasing force continued his preaching to the gathering of the Jews and gentiles. The miraculous conversion of saint Paul took place one year and one month after the martyrdom of saint Stephen, on the twenty–fifth of January, the same day on which the Church celebrates that feast; and it was in the year thirty–six of the birth of our Lord; because saint Stephen, died completing his thirty–fourth year and one day of his thirty–fifth; whereas the conversion of saint Paul took place after he had completed one month of the thirty–sixth; and then saint James departed on his missionary journey.

Let us return to our great Queen and Lady of the angels, who by means of her vision knew all that was happening to Saul; his first and most unhappy state of mind, his fury against the name of Christ, his sudden casting down and its cause, his conversion, and above all his extraordinary and miraculous elevation to the empyrean heaven and vision of God, besides all the rest, that happened to him in Damascus.

This knowledge was not only proper and due to Her, because She was the Mother of the Lord and of his holy Church and the instrument of this great wonder; but also because She alone could properly estimate this miracle, even more so than saint Paul and more than the whole mystical body of the Church; for it was not just, that such an unheard of blessing and such a prodigious work of the Omnipotent should remain without recognition and gratitude among mortals. This the most blessed Mary rendered in all plenitude and She was the first One, who celebrated this solemn event with the acknowledgment due to it from the whole human race.

Chapter Eight

Persecution of Herod—The Will of God Made Known to Mary—Her Sojourn in Ephesus

Saint John made preparations for the journey and embarkation for Ephesus, and on the fourth day, which was the fifth of January of the year forty, Saint John notified Her that it was time to leave; for there would be a ship and all things had been arranged for the journey. The great Mistress of obedience, without answer or delay, knelt down and asked permission of the Lord to leave the Cenacle and Jerusalem; and then She proceeded to take leave of the owner of the house and its inhabitants.

It can easily be imagined, how sorrowful they were at this leave–taking; for on account of her most sweet conversation, and because of the favors and blessings received at her liberal hands, all were held captives and prisoners in love and veneration of Her, whereas now all at once they were to be deprived of her consoling presence and of this rich Treasure, the well spring of so many blessings.

All of them offered to follow and accompany Her; but as this was not opportune, they asked Her to hasten her return and not to forsake forever this house, which was entirely at her disposal. The heavenly Mother thanked them for these pious and loving wishes by expressing her own humble love, and She somewhat allayed their grief by giving them hope of her return.

Then She asked permission of Saint John to visit the holy places of our Redemption and there to worship and adore the Lord, who had consecrated them by his presence and his precious blood. With the Apostle She made these sacred stations, exhibiting incredible devotion and tears of reverent love, and saint John, deeply consoled at being permitted to accompany Her, exercised himself in heroic acts of virtue.

The most blessed Mother saw at each of the holy places the angels who had been deputed to guard and defend them; and anew She charged them to resist Lucifer and his demons, lest they destroy or profane by irreverence those sacred spots, as they desired and intended to do through the unbelieving Jews. She told the angels to drive away by holy inspirations the bad thoughts and diabolical suggestions, by which the infernal dragon sought to excite the Jews and other mortals to blot out the memory of Christ our Savior in those holy places. She charged them with this duty for all the future times, since the wrath of the evil spirits against the places and the works of the Redemption endures through all the ages. The holy angels obeyed their Queen and Mistress in all that She ordained.

Having satisfied her piety, She asked Saint John on her knees to bless her for the journey, just as She had been wont to do with her divine Son. She continued to exercise the same great virtues of obedience and humility toward the beloved disciple, His substitute. Many of the faithful of Jerusalem offered Her money, jewels, vehicles and all things necessary for her journey to the sea and to Ephesus.

The most prudent Lady humbly showed her appreciation to all, but accepted nothing. For her journey to the sea She made use of an unpretentious beast of burden, on which She was carried along as the Queen of the virtues and of the poor. She recollected the journeys and pilgrimages She had made with her divine Son and with her spouse Joseph, and these recollections together with the heavenly love, which had induced Her once more to travel, awakened in her dove–like heart tender and devout affections.

They came to the harbor and immediately embarked in the ship with other passengers. The great Queen of the world was now for the first time upon the sea. She saw and comprehended with clearness the vast Mediterranean and its communication with the great ocean. She beheld its height and depth, its length and breadth, its caverns and secret recesses, its sands and minerals, its ebb and tide, its animals, its whales and fishes of all sizes, and whatever other portentous animals it enclosed.

When this great panorama of creatures, in which were reflected, as from a most clear mirror, the greatness and omnipotence of the Creator, was presented to her faculties filled with heavenly wisdom, her spirit winged its ardent flight to the very being of God, so wonderfully reflected in those creatures, and for all of them, and in all of them, She gave praise and glory and magnificence to the Most High.

With the compassion of a most loving Mother for those who trusted their lives to the indomitable fury of the sea in navigating over its waves, She most fervently besought the Almighty to protect from its dangers all who should call upon her name and ask for her intercession.

The Lord immediately granted this petition and promised to favor whoever upon the sea should carry some image of Her, and should sincerely look upon this Star of the sea, most blessed Mary, for help in its perils. Accordingly it will be understood, that, if the Catholics and the faithful encounter ill success and perish in navigation, it is because they ignore the favors to be obtained from the Queen of the angels, or because on account of their sins they fail to remember Her in the raging storms, or fail to seek her favors with sincere faith and devotion; for neither can the word of the Lord ever fail, nor will the great Mother ever deny assistance to those endangered by the perils of the sea.

When they landed the great Queen continued to work miracles equal to those wrought upon the sea. She cured the sick and the possessed, who, as soon as they came into her presence, were set free. I will not tarry to relate all these wonders; for many books would be necessary and much time to describe all the doings of the most blessed Mary and the favors of heaven, which She dispensed as the instrument and medium of the omnipotence of the Most High. I will record only those, which are necessary for this history and which shall suffice to manifest in some measure the unknown and wonderful works of our great Queen and Lady.

In Ephesus lived some Christians, who had come from Jerusalem. There were not many, but on learning of the arrival of the Mother of Christ the Redeemer, they hastened to pay Her a visit and offer their dwellings and their possessions for her use.

But the great Queen of virtues, who sought neither ostentation nor temporal commodities, chose for her dwelling the house of a few retired and poor women, who were living by themselves free from the companionship of men. By the intervention of the angels, they lovingly and generously placed their home at the disposition of the Lady. In it they selected a very retired room for the Queen and another for Saint John, which these Two occupied during their stay in Ephesus.

The most Blessed Mary thanked the owners who were to live with Her. Then She retired to her room and, prostrate upon the ground as was usual in her prayers, She adored the immutable essence of God, offering to sacrifice Herself in his service in this city and saying: "Lord God omnipotent, by the immensity of thy Divinity Thou fillest all the heavens and the earth. I, thy humble handmaid, desire to fulfill entirely thy holy will, on all occasions, in all places, and at all times, in which thy Providence shall deign to place me; for Thou art my only Good, my being and my life, and toward thy pleasure and satisfaction tend all my thoughts, words and actions." The most prudent Mother perceived that the Lord accepted her prayer and her offering, and that He responded to her desires with divine power, ready to assist and govern Her always.

She continued her prayer for the holy Church and laid out her plans for the assistance of all the faithful. She called her angels and sent some of them to aid the Apostles and disciples, whom She knew to be too much pressed in the persecutions, raised by the demons through infidel men. In those days Saint Paul fled from

Damascus before the attacks of the Jews where he says that he was let down from the walls of the city in a basket.

To defend him from these perils and those with which Lucifer threatened him on his way to Jerusalem, the great Queen of angels sent her angels to be his guard and protection; for the wrath and fury of hell was roused against Saint Paul more than against any of the other Apostles.

This is the journey the Apostle himself refers to in his letter to the Galatians, where he says, that after three years he went to Jerusalem to visit Saint Peter. These three years are not to be counted from the time of his conversion, but from the time he had returned from Arabia to Damascus. This is to be inferred from the text itself, for after stating that he returned from Arabia to Damascus, he immediately adds, that after three years, he went up to Jerusalem. If those three years are counted from the time before his sojourn in Arabia, the text would occasion much confusion.

With greater clearness this may be proved by computing the time of the death of Saint Stephen and the journey of the most Blessed Virgin to Ephesus. For counting from the day of his Nativity, Saint Stephen died at the end of the thirty–fourth year of Christ, but counting them from the day of the Circumcision, as the Church does now, Saint Stephen died seven days before the completion of the thirty–four years, being the seven days before the first of January.

The conversion of Saint Paul happened in the year thirty–six, on the twenty–fifth of January. If he had come to Jerusalem three years afterwards, he would have found there the most holy Mary and Saint John, while he himself says, that he had not seen any one of the Apostles there, except Saint Peter and Saint James the Less, who was called Alpheus.

If the holy Queen and Saint John had at that time been in Jerusalem, Saint Paul would certainly not have missed seeing them, and he would have mentioned at least Saint John; yet he says, that he had not seen him.

The explanation is that Saint Paul came to Jerusalem in the year forty, four years after his conversion, and a little less than a month after the most Blessed Mary had departed for Ephesus. Saint Paul had entered the fifth year of his conversion and the other Apostles, except the two he saw, had already left Jerusalem and were preaching the Gospel of Christ, each one in his appointed province.

Conformably with this reckoning, we must assume that Saint Paul spent the first year after his conversion, or the greater part of it, in journeying to Arabia and preaching the Gospel there: then, the three following years, in Damascus. Hence the evangelist Luke, in the ninth chapter of his Acts of the Apostles, although he says nothing of Paul's journey to Arabia, nevertheless says that for many days after his conversion the Jews of Damascus plotted to take his life, these many days referring to the four years thus passed.

Then he adds that his disciples, aware of the plots of the Jews, on a certain night lowered him in a basket from the city walls and thus dispatched him on his journey to Jerusalem. There, although knowing of his miraculous conversion, the Apostles and the new disciples nevertheless retained a certain fear and suspicion of his not persevering, because he had been such a professed enemy of Christ, our Savior.

Hence they at first held themselves aloof from Saint Paul, until Saint Barnaby spoke to them and introduced him to Saint Peter, Saint James and the other disciples. Saint Paul prostrated himself at the feet of the Vicar of Christ, kissed them in acknowledgment of his errors and sins, and begging to be admitted as one of his subjects and as a follower of his Master, whose holy name and faith he desired to preach at the cost of his blood.

From the fear and suspicion of Saints Peter and James concerning the perseverance of Saint Paul, we can likewise deduct that he arrived in Jerusalem in the absence of the most Blessed Mary and Saint John; for he would have presented himself first of all to Her to allay suspicion against him; and the two Apostles would likewise have first asked Her, whether they could trust Saint Paul.

All of them would have been set at ease by the most prudent Lady, as She was so solicitous and attentive in consoling and instructing the Apostles, especially Saint Peter. But since the great Lady had already left for Ephesus, they had no one to assure them of the constancy of Saint Paul, until Saint Peter reassured himself of it at seeing him thus prostrate at his feet. Thereupon he was received with great joy of soul by Saint Peter and the other disciples.

All of them gave humble and fervent thanks to the Most High, and commissioned Saint Paul to preach in Jerusalem. This he gladly did to the astonishment of all the Jews who knew him. As his words were like burning arrows that penetrated into the hearts of all that heard him, they were struck with terror; and in two days all Jerusalem was roused by the news of his arrival, flocking to see him with their own eyes.

Lucifer and his demons were not asleep on this occasion, for they were visited by the Almighty with an increase of torment at the arrival of Saint Paul. The divine power, so evident in him, oppressed and paralyzed the infernal dragons. But as their pride and malice shall never be extinguished through all the eternity of their existence, they were roused to fury, as soon as they recognized this divine virtue as flowing from Paul.

Lucifer, with incredible rage, called together many legions of the demons and exhorted them anew to rouse themselves and exert all the forces of their malice for the entire destruction of Saint Paul, and not to leave any stone unturned in Jerusalem and in all the world for the attainment of this object. The demons without delay set about this work, exciting Herod and the Jews against the

Apostle, and directing their attention to the burning zeal with which he began to preach in Jerusalem.

The great Mistress of heaven perceived all this from her retirement in Ephesus; for in addition to the knowledge of all things through her heavenly science, She received information of all that happened to Saint Paul from the angels She had sent for his defense.

The Blessed Mother expected the disturbance about to be raised by the malice of Herod and the Jews, especially against Saint Paul; knowing the importance of preserving his life for the exaltation of God's name and the spread of the Gospel, the great Queen was filled with new solicitude and regret at being absent from Palestine, where She could have rendered more immediate assistance to the Apostles.

Therefore She sought to furnish it so much more abundantly from Ephesus by multiplying her prayers and petitions, her ceaseless tears and sighs, and by other measures through the hands of her holy angels. In order to allay her anxieties, the Lord one day in Her prayer, assured Her, that He would fulfill Her petitions and protect the life of Saint Paul in this danger and in these assaults of the devil.

And so He did: for one day Saint Paul, while praying in the temple, was raised to an ecstatic rapture and filled with most exalted enlightenment and understanding, wherein the Lord commanded him immediately to leave Jerusalem and save his life from the hatred of the unbelieving Jews.

Hence Saint Paul sojourned in Jerusalem at that time not more than fifteen days, as he himself says in his epistle to Galatians. After some years he turned thither from Miletus and Ephesus and was taken prisoner, and he refers to this ecstasy in the temple and to the command of the Lord to leave Jerusalem in the twenty–second chapter of the Acts.

Of this vision and command he informed Saint Peter, as the head of the apostolic college; and after consultation concerning his mortal danger, he was secretly sent to Caesarea and Tarsus with orders to preach indiscriminately to the Gentiles, which he did. The most Blessed Mary was the instrument and Mediatory of all these miraculous favours. It was through Her that her Divine Son operated them, and from Her, God received the proper thanks for the graces distributed to the whole Church.

Having thus been reassured in regard to the life of Saint Paul, the most Blessed Mother entertained the hope that through the assistance of divine Providence She might save the life of her cousin James, who was very dear to Her and who was still in Saragossa, protected by the hundred angels She had appointed for his guardians and companions at Granada. These holy angels frequently went back and forth, bringing the petitions of the Apostles to the most blessed Mary and Her counsels back to him. In this way Saint James learned of the sojourn of the great Queen in Ephesus.

When he had brought the chapel or small temple of the Pillar in Saragossa to a sufficient state of completion, he consigned it to the care of the bishop and the disciples anointed by him there as in other cities in Spain. Some months after the apparition of the Queen, he departed from Saragossa, continuing to preach through different provinces. Having come to Catalonia, he embarked for Italy, where without much delay, he pursued his journey overland always preaching until he again embarked for Asia, and ardently desiring to see there the most blessed Mary, his Mistress and Protectors.

Saint James happily attained his object and reached Ephesus. There he prostrated himself at the feet of the Mother of his Creator, shedding copious tears of joy and veneration. From his inmost heart he thanked Her for the peerless favors obtained at Her hands from the Most High during his travels and his preaching in Spain, and especially for her having visited him and conferred such blessings upon him during Her visits.

The heavenly Mother, as Mistress of humility, immediately raised him from the ground and said to him: "My Master, remember thou art the anointed of the Lord and his minister, and that I am a humble wormlet." With these words the great Lady fell on her knees and asked the blessing of Saint James as a priest of the Most High.

He remained for some days in Ephesus in the company of the most Blessed Mary and of his brother John, to whom he gave an account of all that had happened to him in Spain. With the most prudent Mother during those days he held most exalted colloquies and conferences, of which it will suffice to record the following.

When the Jews, through the conviction and conversion of Philetus and Hermogenes, saw their hope frustrated, they were filled with new anger against the apostle Saint James and they were determined to put an end to his life. For this purpose they bribed Democritus and Lysias, centurions of the Roman militia, to furnish them with soldiers for the arrest of the Apostle.

In order to hide their treachery they were to raise a feigned quarrel or disturbance on a certain day during his preaching and thus get him within their power. The execution of this wicked design was left to Abiator, the high–priest of that year and to Josias, a scribe of the same mind as the high–priest. As they had planned, so they executed their scheme; for, while the Saint was preaching to the people about the mystery of the Redemption, proving it to them with admirable wisdom from the testimonies of the ancient writings and moving his audience to tears of compunction, the priest and the scribe were roused to diabolical fury.

Giving the signal to the Roman soldiers, the priest sent Josias to throw a rope around the neck of Saint James and fell upon him, proclaiming him a disturber of the people and the author of a new religion in opposition to the Roman Empire. Democritus and

Lysias thereupon rushed up with their soldiers and brought the Apostle bound to Herod, the son of Archelaus, whose malice had been roused interiorly through the astuteness of Lucifer and exteriorly by the evil—minded and hateful Jews.

Thus doubly incited, Herod began against the disciples of the Lord, whom he abhorred, the persecution mentioned by Saint Luke in the twelfth chapter of the Acts and sent his soldiers to afflict and imprison them. He instantly commanded Saint James to be beheaded, as the Jews had asked.

Incredible was the joy of the holy Apostle at being seized and bound like his Master and at seeing himself conducted to the place, where he was to pass from this mortal life to the eternal through martyrdom, as he had been informed by the Queen of heaven. He offered most humble thanks for this benefit and publicly reiterated the open profession of his faith in Christ our Lord. Remembering the petition he had made in Ephesus, that She be present at his death, he called upon Her from his inmost Soul.

The most holy Mary from her oratory heard these prayers of her beloved Apostle and cousin; for She was attentive to all that happened to him and She helped and favored him with her own efficacious petitions. During this Her prayer, She saw a great multitude of angels and heavenly spirits of all hierarchies descending from heaven, part of them surrounding the Apostle in Jerusalem as he was led to the place of execution, while numerous others approached their Queen at Ephesus.

Presently one of them addressed Her saying "Empress of heaven and our Lady, the most high Lord and God bids you immediately to hasten to Jerusalem to console his great servant James, to assist him in his death to grant all his loving and holy desires."

This favor the most blessed Mary joyfully and gratefully acknowledged. She praised the Most High for the protection granted to those who trust in his mercy and put their lives in his hands. In the meanwhile the Apostle was led to execution and on the way thereto he wrought great miracles upon the sick and ailing and on some possessed by the demons.

There were a great number of them, because the rumor of his execution by Herod had spread about and many of the unfortunates hastened to receive his last ministrations and counsels. All that applied were healed by the great Apostle.

In the meanwhile the holy angels placed their Queen and Mistress upon a most refulgent throne, as they had done on other occasions, and on it bore Her to Jerusalem and to the place of the execution of Saint James. The holy Apostle fell upon his knees in order to offer his life to the Most High in sacrifice, and when he raised his eyes toward heaven, he saw in the air near him the Queen of Heaven, whom he had been invoking in his heart. He beheld Her clothed in divine splendors and great beauty, surrounded by multitudes of the angels.

At this heavenly spectacle the soul of James was moved to new jubilee and his heart was seized with the ardors of a divine love. He wished to proclaim the most Blessed Mary as the Mother of God and the Mistress of all creation. But one of the sovereign spirits restrained him in this fervent desire and said: "James, servant of our Creator, restrain within thy own bosom these precious sentiments and do not manifest to the Jews the presence and assistance of our Queen; for they are not worthy or capable of knowing Her, but instead of reverencing Her will only harden themselves in their hatred."

Thus advised the Apostle forebore and moving his lips in silence, he spoke to the heavenly Queen as follows: "Mother of my Lord Jesus Christ, my Mistress and Protectress, Thou consolation of the afflicted and refuge of the needy, in this hour bestow upon me, my Lady, thy so much desired blessing. Offer for me to thy Son and Redeemer of the world, the sacrifice of my life, since I am burning with desire to be a holocaust for the glory of his name. Let today thy most pure and spotless hands be the altar of my sacrifice, in order that it may become acceptable in the eyes of Him, who died for me upon the cross. Into thy hands, and through them into the hands of my Creator, I commend my spirit."

Having said these words, and keeping his eyes fixed upon the most Holy Mary, who spoke to his heart, the holy Apostle was beheaded by the executioner. The great Lady and Queen of the world received the soul of her beloved Apostle and placing it at her side on the throne, ascended with it to the empyrean heavens and presented it to her divine Son. As the most blessed Mary entered the heavenly court with this offering, She caused new joy and accidental glory to all the heavenly inhabitants and was received with songs of praise.

The Most High received the soul of James and placed it in eminent glory among the princes of his people. The most blessed Mary, prostrate before the throne of the Almighty, composed a song of praise and thanksgiving for the triumphal martyrdom first gained by one of his Apostles. On this occasion the great Lady did not see the Divinity by intuitive vision, but by an abstractive one.

The Blessed Trinity filled Her with new blessings and favors for herself and for the Holy Church, for which She had made great preparations. All the saints likewise blessed her and then the holy angels brought Her back to her oratory in Ephesus, where in the meanwhile an angel had impersonated Her. On arriving, the Heavenly Mother of virtues prostrated Herself as usual in order to give thanks to the Most High for all that had happened.

The disciples of Saint James during the following night secured his sacred body and secretly brought it to Jaffa, where by divine disposition they embarked with it for Galicia in Spain. The heavenly Lady sent an angel to guide and accompany them to the port, where according to the divine will they were to disembark. Although they did not see the angel, they felt his protection during the whole voyage and often in a miraculous manner.

Thus Spain, just as it owed its first instruction in the faith so rooted in the hearts of its people, to the protection lavished by most holy Mary upon the Apostle, now also owes to Her the possession of his sacred body for its consolation and defense. Saint James died in the year forty—one of our Lord, on the twenty—fifth of March, five years and seven months after his setting out to preach in Spain. According to this count and that which I gave above, the martyrdom of Saint James happened seven full years after the death of our Savior Jesus Christ.

The death of Saint James, and the haste of Herod in inflicting it, greatly increased the most impious cruelty of the Jews; for in the savage brutality of the wicked king they saw a valuable means of pursuing their vengeance against the followers of Christ the Lord.

Lucifer and his demons were of like opinion; they, by their suggestions, and the Jews, by their insistent flatteries, persuaded him to seize upon Saint Peter, which he readily did in order to gain the good will of the Jews for his own temporal ends. The demons stood in great awe of the Vicar of Christ on account of the power emanating from him against them; therefore they secretly sought to hasten his imprisonment. Saint Peter, bound with many chains, lay in the dungeon awaiting his execution after the holidays of the Pasch.

The dangerous crisis impending over the Church was not unknown to the heavenly Mother, for, from her retreat in Ephesus, by her clearest interior vision of all things, She saw all things that passed in Jerusalem. She likewise increased her ardent requests, her sighs, prostrations and bloody tears, supplicating the Lord for the liberation of Saint Peter and the protection of the Holy Church. These prayers of the Blessed Mother penetrated the heavens and wounded the heart of Her Son Jesus our Savior.

In response, the Lord descended in person to Her oratory, where She was lying prostrate with Her virginal face upon the ground mingling with the dust. The sovereign King entered and raised Her lovingly from the ground, saying: "My Mother, moderate thy sorrow and ask whatever thou wishest; for I shall grant it all and Thou shalt find grace in My eyes to obtain it. I desire that Thou act according to Thy wishes, using the powers I have given Thee: do or undo whatever is necessary for the welfare of my Church, and Thou mayest be sure, that all the fury of the demons will be turned toward Thee."

She thanked him for this new favor and offered to undertake the battles of the Lord for His faithful, saying: "Most High Lord, hope and life of my soul, prepared is the heart and spirit of thy servant to labor for the souls bought with thy blood and life. Although I am but useless dust, I know Thee to be infinite in power and wisdom; with the favor of thy assistance I fear not the infernal dragon. Thou wishest me to dispose and act in Thy name for the welfare of the Church, I now command Lucifer and his ministers of wickedness, who are disturbing the Church, to descend to the abyss and there to be silenced until it shall please thy Providence to permit their return to the earth."

This command of the Queen of the world in Ephesus was so powerful, that at the very moment of Her issuing it, all the demons in Jerusalem were precipitated into hell, the whole multitude descending into the eternal caverns without power of resisting the divine force exerted through the most Blessed Mary.

Lucifer and his companions knew that this chastisement proceeded from our Queen, whom they called their enemy because they dared not pronounce Her name. They remained in Hell, confounded and dismayed as on other occasions, until they were permitted to rise in order to battle against Mary, as will be related further on. During that time they consulted anew about the means of attaining this end.

Having obtained this triumph over the demons the most Blessed Mary bethought Herself of overcoming likewise the opposition of Herod and the Jews, and therefore She said to her divine Son: "Now, my Son and Lord, if it is thy will, let one of thy holy angels be sent to deliver thy servant Peter from prison." Christ Our Lord approved of her wish and, at the orders of both these Sovereigns, one of the heavenly spirits there present hastened to liberate Saint Peter from his prison in Jerusalem.

The angel executed these orders very swiftly. Coming to the dungeon, he found Saint Peter fastened with two chains, guarded by two soldiers at his side and by a number of other soldiers at the entrance of the prison. Pasch had already been celebrated and it was the night before he was to be executed according to the sentence passed upon him. But the Apostle was so little disturbed that he was sleeping with as much unconcern as his guards. When the angel arrived, he was obliged to wake him by force and while Saint Peter was still drowsy, said to him: "Arise quickly; put on thy girdle and thy shoes, take thy mantle and follow me."

Peter found himself free of the chains and, without understanding what was happening to him and ignorant of what this vision could mean, followed the angel. Having conducted him through some streets, the angel told him, that the Almighty had freed him from prison through the intercession of his most Blessed Mother, and thereupon disappeared. Saint Peter, coming to himself understood the mystery and gave thanks to the Lord for this favor.

Saint Peter thought it best first to give an account of his liberation and consult with James the Less and others of the faithful, before seeking safety in flight. Hastening his steps he came to the house of Mary, the mother of John, who was also called Mark. This was the house of the Cenacle, where many of the disciples had gathered in their affliction. Saint Peter called to them from the street, and a servant—maid, by the name of Rhode, descended to see who was calling. As She recognized the voice of Peter, She left him standing at the door outside and fled excitedly to the disciples, telling them that it was Peter.

They thought it some foolish misunderstanding of the servant; but she maintained that it was Peter; so they, far from guessing the liberation of Peter, concluded that it might be his angel. During these questions and answers Saint Peter was in the street clamoring at the door, until they opened it and with incredible joy and gladness saw the holy Apostle and Head of the Church freed from the sorrows of prison and death.

He gave them an account of all that had happened to him through the aid of the angel, in order that they might in strict secrecy notify Saint James and all his brethren. Foreseeing that Herod would search for him with great diligence, they unanimously decided that he leave Jerusalem that very night and not return, lest he should be taken in some future search. Saint Peter therefore fled, and Herod, having instituted a search in vain, chastised the guards, and was roused to new fury against the disciples. But on account of his pride and impious designs, God cut short his activity by a severe punishment, of which I shall speak in the following chapter.

In Her anxieties and in Her reliance upon the divine help, our Queen labored incessantly in prayers and tears, travailing in her clamors as I have shown on other occasions. Ever governed by her most exalted prudence, She spoke to one of the highest angels of her guard, saying: "Minister of the Most High and creature of his hands, my solicitude for the Holy Church strongly urges me to seek its welfare and progress. I beseech thee to ascend to the throne of the Most High, represent to Him my affliction; ask Him in my name, that I may be permitted to suffer instead of his faithful servants and that Herod be prevented from executing his designs for the destruction of the Church."

Immediately the angel betook himself to the Lord with this message, while the Queen of heaven, like another Esther, remained in prayer for the liberty and salvation of her people and of Herself. The heavenly ambassador was sent back by the blessed Trinity with the answer: "Princess of heaven, the Lord of hosts says, that Thou art the Mother, the Mistress and the Governess of the Church, and that Thou holdest this power while Thou art upon earth; and He desires Thee, as the Queen and Mistress of the heaven and earth, to execute sentence upon Herod."

B8C2

434—The Mystical City of God

In her humility the most blessed Virgin was somewhat disturbed by this answer, and urged by her charity, She replied to the angel: "Am I then to pronounce sentence against a creature who is the image of the Lord? Since I came forth from his hands I have known many reprobates among men and I have never called for vengeance against them; but as far as I was concerned, always desired their salvation if possible, and never hastened their punishment. Return to the Lord, angel, and tell Him that my tribunal and power is inferior to and dependent upon his, and that I cannot sentence any one to death without consulting my Superior; and if it is possible to bring Herod to the way of Salvation, I am willing to suffer all the travails of the world according to the disposition of his divine Providence in order that this soul may not be lost."

The angel hastened back with this second message of his Queen and having presented it before the throne of the most blessed Trinity, was sent back to Her with the following answer: "Our Mistress and Queen, the Most High says that Herod is of the number of the foreknown, since he is so obstinate in his malice, that he will take no admonition or instruction; he will not cooperate with the helps given to him; nor will he avail himself of the fruits of the Redemption, nor of the intercession of the saints, nor of thy own efforts, O Queen and Lady, in his behalf."

For the third time the most holy Mary dispatched the heavenly prince with still another message to the Most High, saying: "If it must be that Herod die in order to hinder him from persecuting the Church, do thou, O angel, represent to the Almighty, how in the infinite condescension of his charity, He has granted me in mortal life to be the Refuge of the children of Adam, the Advocate and Intercessor of sinners; that my tribunal should be that of kindness and clemency for the refuge and assistance of all that seek my intercession; and that all should leave it with the assurance of pardon in the name of my divine Son."

"If then I am to be a loving Mother to men, who are the creatures of his hands and the price of his life–blood, how can I now be a severe judge against one of them? Never was I charged with dealing out justice, always mercy, to which all my heart inclines; and now it is troubled by this conflict of love with obedience to rigorous justice. Present anew, O angel, this my anxiety to the Lord, and learn whether it is not his pleasure that Herod die without my condemning him."

The holy messenger ascended for the third time and the most blessed Trinity listened to his message with the plenitude of pleasure and complacency at the pitying love of his Spouse. Returning, the angel thus informed the loving Mistress: "Our Queen, Mother of our Creator and my Lady, the almighty Majesty says that thy mercy is for those mortals who wish to avail themselves of thy powerful intercession, not for those who despise and abhor it like Herod; that Thou art the Mistress of the Church invested with all the divine power, and that therefore it is meet Thou use it as is opportune: that Herod must die; but it shall be through thy sentence and according to thy order."

The most blessed Mary answered: "Just is the Lord and equitable are His judgments. Many times would I suffer death to rescue this soul of Herod, if he himself would not by his own free will make himself unworthy of mercy and choose perdition. He is a work of the Most High, formed according to his image and likeness; he was redeemed by the blood of the Lamb, which taketh away the sins of the world.

But I set aside all this and, considering only his having become an obstinate enemy of God, unworthy of his eternal friendship, by the most equitable justice of God, I condemn him to the death he has merited, in order that he may not incur greater torments by executing the evil he has planned."

This wonder the Lord wrought for the glory of his most blessed Mother and in witness of his having constituted Her as the Mistress of all creatures with supreme power to act as their Sovereign like her divine Son. I cannot explain this mystery better than in the words of the Lord in the fifth chapter of saint John, where He says of Himself: "The son cannot do anything that the Father does not; but He does the same, because the Father loves Him; and if the Father raises the dead, the son also raises whom he pleases, and the Father has given to the Son to judge all, in order that just as all honor the Father, they may also honor the Son; for no one can honor the Father without honoring the Son."

And immediately He adds: that He has given Him the power of judging, because He is the Son of man, which He is through his most blessed mother. On account of the likeness of the heavenly Mother to her Son (of which I have often spoken) the relation or proportion of the Mother with the Son in this power of judgment must be transferred to the Mother in the same manner as that of the Son from the Father.

Mary is the Mother of mercy and clemency to all the children of Adam that call upon Her; but in addition to this the Almighty wishes it to be understood that She possesses full power of judging all men and that all should honor Her, just as they honor her Son and true God. As his true Mother, He has given Her the same power with Him in the degree and proportion due to Her as his Mother and a mere creature.

Making use of this power, the great Lady sent the angel to Caesarea, where Herod then was, to take away his life as the minister of divine justice. The angel executed the sentence without delay. The evangelist Saint Luke says, that the angel of the Lord struck Herod and, eaten up by worms, the unhappy man died the temporal and eternal death. The wound of this stroke was interior and from it sprang the corruption and the worms that so miserably finished him.

From the same, text it appears that, after having beheaded Saint James and after Saint Peter had escaped, Herod descended to Caesarea in order to compose some differences that had arisen between him and the inhabitants of Sidon and Tyre. Within a few days, vested in royal purple and seated upon a throne, he haranged the people with great show of words. The people, full of vain flattery, proclaimed him as a victor and as a god; and Herod, in foolish vanity, was pleased with this adulation of the people.

Because he had not given honor to God, but usurped to himself divine honor in vain pride, the angel of the Lord struck him. Although this was his last crime, which filled the measure of his iniquity, he merited the chastisement not only for this, but for so many other crimes committed by him in persecuting the Apostles, mocking the Lord our Savior, beheading the Baptist, committing adultery with his sister—in—law Herodias, and for many other abominations.

Immediately the angel returned to Ephesus and gave an account of the execution of the sentence against Herod. The Merciful Mother wept over the loss of this soul; but praised the judgments of the Lord and gave him thanks for the benefit, which the Church would derive from his chastisement; for, as Saint Luke says, the Church grew and increased by the word of God.

This was true not only in Galilee and Judea, where the persecutor Herod was removed, but, through Saint John and the help of the most holy Mother, the Church was taking root in Ephesus. The science of the blessed Apostle was full as that of the cherubim, and the love of his heart was inflamed like that of the seraphim; and he had with him as his Mother and Teacher, the Mistress of wisdom and grace. On account of these precious advantages the Evangelist could undertake great and wonderful works for the foundation of the law of grace, not only in Ephesus, but in all neighboring regions of Asia and in the borderlands of Europe.

Arriving at Ephesus the Evangelist began to preach in the city, baptizing those whom he converted to the faith of Christ our Savior and confirming the faith by great miracles and prodigies, such as had never been witnessed by those gentiles. Since the Greek schools in those countries turned out many philosophers and men learned in what, notwithstanding the admixture of many errors, could be called human sciences, the blessed Apostle convincingly taught them the true science, making use not only of miracles and signs, but of argumentation for the credibility of the Christian faith.

All his catechumens he immediately sent to the most Holy Mary and She instructed many; as She knew the interior inclinations of all, She spoke to the heart of each one and filled it with heavenly light. She wrought prodigies and miracles for the benefit of the unfortunate, curing the possessed and the infirm, succored the poor and the needy and, by the labor of her own hands, gave assistance to the sick in the infirmaries, attending upon them in person. In her house the kindest Queen had a supply of clothes for the most poor and forsaken of her fellowmen.

She helped many in the hour of their death, gaining these souls in their last agony and bringing them safely through all the assaults of the demon to their Creator. So many souls did She draw to the path of truth and life eternal, and so numerous were the wonders She wrought for this end, that they could not be recorded in many books; for no day passed in which She did not increase the possessions of the Lord by the copious and abundant fruit of souls.

COUNCIL OF THE APOSTLES

After the death of the unhappy Herod, the primitive Church of Jerusalem enjoyed some measure of quiet and tranquillity for a considerable time. The great Lady of the world merited this favor through her maternal solicitude and care. During this time Saint Barnaby and Saint Paul preached with wonderful success in the cities of Asia Minor, Antioch, Lystra, Perge and others, as related by Saint Luke in the thirteenth and fourteenth chapter of the Acts of the Apostles and in connection with the miracles and prodigies performed by Saint Paul in those cities and provinces.

The apostle Saint Peter, after his liberation from prison, fled from Jerusalem and retired to another part of Asia not under the jurisdiction of Herod. From that place he governed the faithful accruing to the Church in Asia and those that were in Palestine. All of them acknowledged and obeyed him as the Vicar of Jesus Christ and head of the Church, believing that all he ordained and enacted upon earth was confirmed in heaven.

With this firm faith they came to him with all their doubts and difficulties as to their supreme pontiff. Among other matters they asked him to decide the questions raised by some of the Jews concerning the doings and teachings of Saints Paul and Barnaby in Jerusalem as well in Antioch, in opposition to the circumcision and the Law of Moses.

On this occasion the Apostles and disciples of Jerusalem begged Saint Peter to return to the holy city to settle these controversies and establish order, so that the preaching of the faith might not be hindered; for since the death of Herod the Jews had no one to assist them in their persecutions, and therefore the Church enjoyed greater peace and tranquillity in Jerusalem.

On the same grounds they also asked him to request the holy Mother of Jesus to come to that city; for all the faithful longed for Her with loving hearts, expected to be consoled in the Lord and hoped for the prosperity of all the affairs of the Church through her presence. On account of these appeals Saint Peter resolved to return at once to Jerusalem, and before setting out, he wrote the following letter to the most holy Queen.

Letter of Saint Peter to most Holy Mary.

"To Mary, the Virgin Mother of God:

Peter the Apostle of Jesus Christ, thy servant and the servant of the servants of God."

"Lady, among the faithful, some doubts and differences have arisen concerning the doctrine of thy Son and our Redeemer, whether the ancient Law of Moses is to be observed in conjunction with his teachings. They wish to know from us what is proper, and that we state to them what we heard from the mouth of the divine Teacher. In order to consult with my brethren, the Apostles, I am now setting out for Jerusalem and, for the consolation and by thy love for the Church, we beseech Thee likewise to come to that city, where, since the death of Herod, the Jews are more peaceful and the faithful more at ease. The multitude of the followers of Christ desire to see Thee and console themselves in thy presence. When we shall have arrived at Jerusalem, we shall notify the other cities, and with thy assistance will be established what shall be conducive to the interests of the holy faith and to the excellence of the law of grace."

I cannot restrain my wonder and confusion at the humility and obedience of the most Holy Mary in a matter of so small moment; for only her heavenly prudence could inspire Her, the Mother of God, with the thought, that it would be more humble and submissive not to read this letter of the Vicar of Christ except in the presence and under the obedience of the one to whose guidance She had submitted Herself as her superior.

Her example reproves and stigmatizes the presumption of inferiors, who try to find excuses and pretenses for evading the humility and obedience due to their superiors. But the most Holy Mary was a model and a teacher of holiness in all things, great or small. Having read the letter to Her, he asked Her, what She thought best to write to the Vicar of Christ.

But also in this She did not wish to give any appearance of her being his equal or superior, preferring to obey; and therefore She answered: "My son and master, do thou arrange what ever shall be proper; for I, as thy servant, will obey." The Evangelist replied that it seemed to him best to obey Saint Peter and return immediately to Jerusalem. "It is right and proper to obey the head of the Church," answered the purest lady; "let us prepare even now for our departure."

Thus resolved, Saint John went out to seek passage for Palestine and to prepare whatever was necessary for a speedy departure. In the meanwhile, at the request of the Evangelist, most blessed Mary called together the women who were her acquaintances and disciples in Ephesus, in order to take leave of them and instruct them in what they must do to persevere in their holy faith.

When the day of departure arrived, the Humblest of the humble asked Saint John for his blessing and they betook themselves to the ship, having remained in Ephesus two years and a half. On leaving their dwelling all her thousand angels manifested themselves in visible human forms, but all of them were armed for battle and formed into squadrons. This unwonted sight gave Her to understand that She was to be prepared to continue her conflict with the great dragon and his allies.

Before reaching the sea She saw a great multitude of the infernal legions meeting Her in various dreadful and terrific shapes; in the midst of them came a dragon with seven heads, so horrible and huge as to exceed the size of a large ship, and so fierce and abominable as to cause torment by its mere presence.

Against these formidable hosts the invincible Queen fortified Herself by the most firm faith and fervent love, repeating the words of Psalms and the sayings from the mouth of her most holy Son. She ordered her holy angels to assist Her, for those shapes naturally inspired Her with some human dread and horror. The Evangelist knew nothing of this conflict until the heavenly Lady afterwards informed him and gave him an insight into it.

Our blessed Lady embarked with the saint, and the ship's sails were set. But it had proceeded only a distance from the port, when those dragons of hell, making use of the permission given them, stirred up the sea by a tempest such as had not been seen before that time nor until now; for the Almighty wished to exalt the power of his arm and the holiness of Mary and therefore He permitted such liberty to the malice and powers of the demons in this battle.

The waves rose with terrific roarings, piling themselves upon the winds and apparently even upon the very clouds, forming with them mountains of water and foam, as if they were preparing for an onset to break the bounds of the abysses that imprisoned the ocean. The ship was lashed and battered to and fro, and it seemed a miracle that it was not shattered to splinters at each shock.

Sometimes it was hurled up into the clouds, at others sent to plow up the sand of the ocean's abysses; often its sails and masts were buried in the foaming waves. During some of the onsets of this unspeakably furious hurricane the ship was held in the air by the angels in order to save it from some of the vaster billows, which would inevitably have overwhelmed and sent it to the bottom.

The mariners and passengers perceived the effects of this assistance, but remained ignorant of the cause; in their distress they were beside themselves, bewailing their ruin, which they deemed inevitable. The demons added to their terror; for, assuming human shapes, they loudly called upon the mariners as if from neighboring ships sent to their aid and urged them to forsake their ship and save themselves in the others.

For though all the vessels suffered in this storm, yet the wrath of the demons and their power of doing harm was confined principally to the ship on which our Lady sailed and the distress and peril of the other vessels was not so great. The malicious designs of the demons were known only to the most blessed Virgin and not to the sailors, and therefore they believed these voices as of true passengers and sailors.

Thus deceived they at times gave up caring for their own ship and left it to the fury of the sea, expecting to save themselves on one of the other ships. But the angels supplied their place directing and steering it when the sailors gave it up in despair to the destruction of the waves.

In the midst of this confusion and distress the most holy Mary preserved her tranquillity, serenely borne up by the ocean of her magnanimity and virtue, but at the same time practicing all the virtues by acts heroic in proportion to the exigencies of the occasion and the dictates of her wisdom. As during this tempestuous voyage She personally experienced the dangers of navigation, which She had understood on her former voyage by divine inspiration, She was moved to new compassion for all voyagers at sea and renewed her former prayers and petitions.

The most prudent Virgin also admired the indomitable forces of the sea and was led to consider the wrath of divine justice, so well represented by this insensible creature. And passing from these considerations to that of the sins of mortals, who drew it upon themselves from the Almighty, She entered into the most ardent prayers for the conversion of the world and the increase of the Church.

For this She offered up the hardships of this voyage; since notwithstanding the tranquillity of her soul, She suffered much bodily inconvenience and still greater affliction at the thought that all her fellow–voyagers were made to suffer this persecution and tribulation of the demons on her account.

B8C3

A large share of this suffering fell to the evangelist Saint John on account of his deep solicitude for his true Mother and Mistress of the world. To this was added his own actual suffering. All was so much the more dreadful to him, because at that time he did know what was passing in the interior of the most blessed Virgin. He sought a few times to console Her and console himself by assisting and comforting Her.

Although the voyage from Ephesus to Palestine usually lasted only about six days, this one lasted fifteen, of which fourteen were tempestuous. One day Saint John was very much disheartened at the continuance of this measureless hardship and, no longer able to restrain himself, said "My lady, what is this? Are we to perish at sea? Beseech thy divine Son to look upon us with the eyes of a Father and to defend us in this tribulation."

The blessed Mother answered him: "Do not be disturbed, my son; for we must now fight the battles of the Lord and overcome his enemies by fortitude and patience." I shall beg of Him that no one who is with us shall perish, and that He sleep not, who watches over Israel; the strong ones of his courts assist us and defend us; let us suffer for Him who placed Himself upon the Cross for the salvation of all. At these words Saint John recovered the necessary courage.

Lucifer and his demons with increasing fury threatened the powerful Queen by telling Her that She would perish in this sea and not escape alive. But these and other threats were but spent arrows and the most prudent Mother despised them, not even listening to them, or looking upon the demons, or speaking to them a single word.

They themselves on the other hand could not bear even to glance at her face on account of the virtue of the Most High shining from it. And the more they strove to overcome this virtue, the weaker they became and the more were they tormented by those offensive weapons, with which the Lord had clothed his most holy Mother.

Saint Paul and Saint Barnaby were aware of the return of the Queen of heaven when they came to Jerusalem. In his ardent desire of seeing Her, Saint Paul with Saint Barnaby at once sought her presence, and they cast themselves at her feet, shedding abundant tears of joy. Not less was the joy of the heavenly Mother at meeting these Apostles, toward whom She bore an especial love in the Lord on account of their zealous labors for the exaltation of God's name and the spread of the faith.

The Mistress of the humble desired them to present themselves first to Saint Peter and the rest, and last to Her, judging Herself to be the least of all creatures. But they, preserving the proper order in their reverence and love, thought that none should be preferred to Her who was the Mother of God, the Mistress of all creation and the beginning of all our happiness.

The great Lady prostrated Herself before Saint Paul and Barnaby, kissed their hands and asked for their blessing. On this occasion Saint Paul was favored with a wonderful ecstatic abstraction, in which were revealed to him great mysteries and prerogatives of this mystical City of God, the Blessed Mary, and he saw Her as it were completely invested with the Divinity.

Saint Peter, as the head of the Church, had called upon the Apostles and disciples then in and around Jerusalem, and convoked them to a meeting in the presence of the Mistress of the world. In order that the most prudent Virgin, in her profound humility, might not absent Herself from this council, saint Peter had interposed his authority as Vicar of Christ.

All of them being gathered, Saint Peter said: "My brethren and children in Christ our Savior, it was necessary that we meet in order to solve the difficulties and decide upon the affairs which our most beloved brethren Paul and Barnaby have brought to our notice, and to determine other matters touching the increase of the holy faith. For it is proper that we engage in prayer to obtain the assistance of the Holy Ghost and we shall persevere therein for ten days as is our custom. On the first and the last day we shall celebrate the sacrifice of the Mass, by which we shall dispose our hearts to receive the divine light."

All of them approved of this arrangement. In order to celebrate the first Mass on the next day the Queen prepared the hall of the Cenacle, cleaning and decorating it with her own hands and holding all in readiness for the Communion for Herself together with the Apostles and disciples during those Masses. Saint Peter alone celebrated, observing all those rites and ceremonies which I have described, when speaking of the Masses on other occasions.

The other Apostles and disciples communicated at the hands of Saint Peter; then the most blessed Mary, taking the last place. Many angels descended to the Cenacle. All those present saw them and at the time of the consecration the Cenacle was filled with a wonderful light and fragrance, through which the Lord wrought wonderful effects in their souls.

Having celebrated the first Mass, they agreed upon certain hours, in which they were to persevere together in prayer, as far as they could without neglecting the necessary ministry of souls. The great Lady retired to a place, where She remained alone and motionless for those ten days without eating or speaking to any one. During that time She experienced such hidden mysteries as to move the angels to astonishment; and I find myself unable to describe what has been manifested to me concerning them. I will briefly indicate a small part of these mysteries, for to state all is impossible.

The heavenly Mother having received Holy Communion on the first of the ten days and retired to pray alone, at the command of the Lord, was immediately raised up by her angels and others there present to the empyrean heavens. Since She was taken up body and soul, one of the angels took her shape in order that the Apostles in the Cenacle might not become aware of her absence.

They bore Her up with the splendor and magnificence described by me on other occasions, and on this occasion it was even greater on account of the designs of the Lord. When Mary arrived in a region of the air far removed from the earth, the almighty Lord commanded Lucifer and all his hellish hosts to come into the presence of the Queen into those higher regions.

Immediately all of them came before Her and She saw them and knew them all just as they were and the condition they were in. The sight was somewhat painful to her, because the demons are so abominable and disgusting; but She was armed with divine virtue, so that She could not be harmed by this horrible and execrable sight.

Not so the demons; for the Lord gave them to understand by an especial insight the greatness and superiority of that Woman, whom they were persecuting as their Enemy. They were made to perceive how foolishly presumptuous they had been in their attempts against Her. To their still greater terror they saw that She carried in her bosom the sacramental Christ and that the whole Divinity held Her as it were enveloped in its Omnipotence for their humiliation, overthrow and destruction.

The demons moreover heard a voice proceeding from the Deity itself, saying: "With this shield of my powerful arm, invincible and strong, I shall always defend my Church. This Woman shall crush the head of the ancient serpent, and shall forever triumph over its haughty pride for the glory of my holy name." All these and other mysteries of the most holy Mary the demons perceived and understood while they were gathered around Her in dismay.

So great was the despair and crushing pain which they felt, that they, with loudest clamors, said: "May the power of the Almighty cast us immediately into hell, and let it not keep us in the presence of this Woman, who torments us more than the fire. O invincible and strong Woman! Recede from us, since we ourselves cannot fly from thy presence, where we are bound by the chains of the Almighty. Why dost Thou also torment us before our time?"

"Thou alone of all human nature art the instrument of the Omnipotent against us; and through Thee men can acquire the eternal blessings we have lost. Those that have sunk into despair of ever seeing God eternally, are now rewarded for the accredited good works of their Redeemer by the vision of Thee, which in our hate is to us a torment and chastisement. Release us, almighty Lord and God; let this new punishment, in which Thou renewest that of our fall from heaven, cease; for in it Thou executest the punishment Thou hast threatened us with in this wonder of thy powerful arms."

During these and other lamentations of despair the demons were held spellbound in the presence of the Queen for a long time, and although they made the most violent efforts to fly, they were not permitted to do it as fast as their fury urged them on.

In order that the terror of the most Holy Mary might strike them so much the deeper and become the more notorious, the Lord ordained, that She herself should use her authority as Mistress and Queen in permitting them to leave. At the instant in which She did this, all of them cast themselves, with all the swiftness in their power, from the upper regions into the abyss.

They gave forth dreadful howls, terrorizing all the damned souls with new punishments, and, full of dismay and torments in not being able to deny their defeat, they proclaimed in their presence the power of the Almighty and of his holy Mother. Having won this triumph the most serene Empress proceeded on her way to the empyrean heaven, where She was received with new and admirable jubilee, remaining there for twenty–four hours.

She prostrated Herself before the throne of the blessed Trinity and adored It in the unity of its undivided nature and majesty. She prayed for the Church, in order that the Apostles might understand and resolve what was proper for the establishment of the evangelical law and the termination of the Law of Moses.

In answer to these petitions She heard a voice from the throne, by which the three divine Persons, One after the Other and each One for Himself, promised to assist the Apostles and disciples in declaring and establishing the truth, assuring Her, that the Father would direct its establishment by His Omnipotence, the Son, as head of the Church, assist it by His Wisdom, and the Holy Ghost, as its Spouse, by His Love and His enlightening gifts.

Then the heavenly Mother saw, that the most holy humanity of her Son presented to the Father the prayers and petitions, which She Herself had offered for the Church, and how, approving of them, He proposed the reasons why they should be fulfilled, in order that the faith of the Gospel and his entire holy law might be established in the world in accordance with the decrees of the divine will and mind.

Immediately, in execution of this will and proposal of Christ our Savior, the Lady saw issuing forth from the Divinity and immutable essence of God the form of a temple or Church, beautiful, clear and resplendent as if built of diamond or the sparkling crystal, adorned with many enamels and reliefs to enhance its beauty. The angels and saints saw it and in astonishment exclaimed: "Holy, holy, holy and powerful art Thou, Lord in thy works".

This Church or temple the most blessed Trinity placed in the hands of the most holy humanity of Christ, and, in a manner which cannot be described in words, He united it with Himself. Thereupon He turned it over to the holy Mother and as soon as Mary received it, She was filled with new splendor. She annihilated Herself within Herself and then saw the Divinity, clearly and intuitively, by eminent and beatific vision.

The great Queen remained in this joy for hours. What She experienced and received surpasses created thought or capacity; Her love was directed with new fervor toward the Church consigned to Her under the above symbol. Enriched by these favors, She was borne back by the angels to the Cenacle, having in her hands the mystical temple She had received from her divine Son.

She remained in prayer during the other nine days without motion and without interrupting the acts, in which She had been left by the beatific vision. They fall not within human thought, and can much less be indicated by human words. Among other things which She did, was to distribute the treasures of the Redemption among the children of the Church. Commencing with the Apostles and going through the different ages, She applied them separately to the just and the saints, according to the secret disposition of eternal predestination.

The execution of these decrees her divine Son had consigned to the most holy Mary, giving Her dominion over the whole Church and the dispensation of all the graces, that each one earn through the merits of the Redemption. Regarding a mystery so exalted and hidden, I cannot say more than this.

On the last of the ten days Saint Peter celebrated the other Mass and all received Holy Communion as in the first. Then, all being gathered in the name of the Lord, they invoked the Holy Ghost and began to consult about the solution of the difficulties that had arisen in the Church.

Saint Peter, as the head and the highpriest, spoke first, then Saint Paul and Barnaby, and Saint James the Less, as is related by Saint Luke in the fifteenth chapter of the Acts. The first decision of this council was that the exact law of the circumcision and the Law of Moses should not be imposed upon the baptized; since eternal salvation was given through Baptism and faith in Christ.

Although Saint Luke principally mentions this decision, yet there were others, which defined certain matters concerning the government and the ceremonies of the Church, in order to stop some abuses introduced by the indiscreet piety of some of the faithful. This is held to be the first council of the Apostles.

Couched in these terms the decision of the council was sent by letter to the faithful and to the churches of Antioch, Syria and Cilicia; and they remitted these letters through the hands of Saint Paul and Barnaby and of other disciples. In order that the approbation of the Lord might not be wanting, it happened, that, both in the Cenacle at coming to their decision, and in Antioch when the letters were read before the faithful, the Holy Ghost descended in visible fire, so that all the faithful were consoled and confirmed in the Catholic truth.

The most holy Mary gave thanks to the Lord for the blessings thus bestowed upon the Church. She immediately despatched Saints Paul and Barnaby with the rest and for their consolation She gave them as relics part of the clothes of Christ our Lord and some objects She had still left of the Passion. Offering them her protection and prayers, She sent them filled with new consolation and spiritual force upon the labors still awaiting them.

During all these days of the council, on account of the terror with which most holy Mary had inspired him, Lucifer and his ministers could not come near the Cenacle; yet they prowled about in the distance, without being able to execute any of their malice against its members.

THE GOSPELS

I have described, as far as I was permitted, the exalted state of the great Queen and Lady after the first council of the Apostles, and also her victories over the infernal dragon and his demons. Although the wonderful works which She accomplished during these times and at all times, cannot be recorded in a history, nor even summed up, I was nevertheless given special light for the purpose of describing the beginnings of the Gospels and the call of the Evangelists to undertake their writing, the part which Mary bore in their being written, her care for the absent Apostles, and the miracles She wrought for them.

In the second part, and on many occasions I have stated, that the heavenly Mother had a positive knowledge of all the mysteries of grace, of the Gospels and other holy writings, which were to serve for the confirmation of the new Law. In this knowledge She was confirmed many times, especially on the day of her ascension with her divine Son into heaven.

From that day on, without forgetting anything, She often prostrated Herself in prayer before the Lord, asking Him to send his divine light upon the Apostles and holy writers and to order them to write, when the opportune should have come.

Afterwards, when the Queen returned from heaven was put in charge of the Church, the Lord made known to Her that the time for beginning to write the holy Gospels had arrived and that She should make her arrangements for this purpose as the Mistress and Instructress of the Church. But in her profound humility and discretion She obtained the consent of the Lord, that this should be attended to by Saint Peter, his vicar and the head of the Church; and that he should be especially assisted by divine enlightenment for a matter of such importance.

All this was granted by the Most High when the Apostles met in the council mentioned by saint Luke in the fifteenth chapter of the Acts, after they had settled the doubts about circumcision, as I described in the sixth chapter, saint Peter proposed to them all the necessity of recording in writing the mysteries of the life of Christ our Savoir and Teacher, so that they might be preached to all the faithful in the Church without variation or difference, thus doing away with the old Law and establish the new.

Saint Peter had already consulted with the Mother of wisdom; and all the council having approved of his proposal, they called upon the Holy Ghost to point out the Apostles and disciples who should write the life of the Savior. Immediately a light was seen descending upon Saint Peter and a voice was heard saying: "The high priest and head of the Church shall assign four for recording the works and the teachings of the Savior of the world." Saint Peter and all present prostrated themselves, giving thanks to the Lord for this favor.

When all of them had again risen, Saint Peter spoke: "Matthew our beloved brother, shall immediately begin to write his Gospel in the name of the Father, the Son and the Holy Ghost. Mark shall be the second, who shall likewise write the Gospel in the name of the Father, the Son and the Holy Ghost. Luke shall write the third, in the name of the Father, the Son and the Holy Ghost. Our most beloved brother John shall be the fourth and last to write the mysteries of our Savior and Teacher in the name of the Father, the Son and the Holy Ghost." This decision the Lord confirmed by permitting the heavenly light to remain until these words were repeated and formally accepted by all those appointed.

Within a few days saint Matthew set about writing the first Gospel. While praying in a retired room of the Cenacle and asking to be enlightened for the inception of his history, the most blessed Mary appeared seated on a throne of great majesty and splendor, the doors of the room still remaining closed. The great Lady told him to arise, which he did, asking for her benediction.

Then She spoke to him and said: "Matthew, my servant, the Almighty sends me with his blessing, in that with it thou begin the writing of the Gospel thou hast the good fortune to be entrusted with, thou shalt have the assistance of the Holy Ghost and I shall beg it for thee with all my heart.

But concerning myself it is not proper, that thou write anything except what is absolutely necessary for manifesting the Incarnation and other mysteries of the Word made man, for establishing his faith in the world as the foundation of his Church. This faith being established, the Almighty will find other persons, who, when the times arrive in which it shall become necessary, shall reveal to the faithful the mysteries and blessings wrought by his powerful arm in me."

Saint Matthew signified his willingness to obey the mandate of the Queen; and while he conferred with Her about composing his Gospel, the Holy Ghost came down upon him in visible form; and in the presence of the Lady he began to write the words as they are still extant in his Gospel. The blessed Mary then left him and Saint Matthew proceeded in his history, finishing it in Judea. He wrote it in the Hebrew language in the year forty–two of our Lord.

The Evangelist Mark wrote his gospel four years later, in the forty–sixth year after the birth of Christ. He likewise wrote it in Hebrew and while in Palestine. Before commencing he asked his guardian angel to notify the Queen of heaven of his intention and to implore her assistance for obtaining the divine enlightenment for what he was about to write.

The kind Mother heard his prayer and immediately the Lord commanded the angels to carry Her with the usual splendor and ceremony to the Evangelist, who was still in prayer. The great Queen appeared to him seated on a most beautiful and resplendent throne. Prostrating himself before Her, he said: "Mother of the Savior of the world and Mistress of all creation, I am unworthy of this favor, though I am a servant of thy divine Son and of Thyself."

The heavenly Mother answered: "The Most High, whom thou servest and lovest, sends me to assure thee, that thy prayers are heard and that his Holy Spirit shall direct thee in the writing of the Gospel, with which He has charged thee." Then She told him not to write of the mysteries pertaining to Her, just as She had asked Saint Matthew.

Immediately the Holy Ghost, in visible and most refulgent shape, descended upon Saint Mark enveloping him in light and filling him with interior enlightenment; and in the presence of the Queen he began to write his Gospel.

At that time the Princess of heaven was sixty—one years of age. Saint Jerome says that saint Mark wrote his short Gospel in Rome, at the instance of the faithful residing there; but I wish to call attention to the fact, that this was a translation or copy of the one he had written in Palestine; for the Christians in Rome possessed neither his nor any other Gospel, and therefore he set about writing one in the Roman or Latin language.

Two years afterwards, in the year forty—eight and of the Virgin the sixty—third, Saint Luke wrote his Gospel in the Greek language. To him also, as to the others, Mary appeared when he was about to begin it. Having represented to the heavenly Mother, that, in order manifest the Incarnation and life of her divine Son, it was necessary to touch upon the manner of the conception of the Word made man and upon other things concerning her dignity as the natural Mother of Christ, and having received orders from Her to pass over in silence the other mysteries and wonders connected with her dignity as Mother of God, saint Luke obtained her permission to write somewhat more freely of the heavenly Mary in his Gospel.

The Holy Ghost descended upon him and in the presence of the great Queen he began to write his Gospel, drawing his information principally from direct inspiration of her Majesty. Saint Luke continued a most devoted servant of the Lady and permitted the image of the sweetest Mother seated on the throne of majesty, as he had seen Her on this occasion, to be effaced from his mind. Thenceforward he lived continually in her presence. Saint Luke was in Achaia, when this apparition happened to him, and there also he wrote his Gospel.

The last of the four Evangelists who wrote the Gospels, was the apostle Saint John in the year fifty–eight of the Lord. He wrote his in the Greek language, during his stay in Asia Minor after the glorious transition and assumption of the most blessed Mary. His Gospel was directed against the heresies and errors which the devil, immediately after the transition of the Virgin Mother, began to sow for undermining the faith in the Incarnation of the divine Word.

For as Lucifer had been humiliated and vanquished by this mystery, he at once directed the onslaught of heresy against it. For this reason the evangelist Saint John writes so sublimely and adduces so many arguments for the true and undoubted Divinity of Christ our Savior, far surpassing the other Evangelists in this regard.

Although when the Evangelist was about to begin his Gospel the most blessed Mary was already in heaven, She descended in person, resplendent with ineffable glory and majesty and surrounded by thousands of angels of all choirs and hierarchies.

Appearing to Saint John She said: "John, my son and servant of the Most High, now is the proper time for writing the life and mysteries of my divine Son, so that all mortals may know Him as the Son of the eternal Father, as true God and at the same time as true man. But it is not yet the opportune time for recording the mysteries and secrets which thou know of me; nor shall they as yet be manifested to a world so accustomed to idolatry, lest Lucifer abuse them for disturbing those who are to receive the faith in their Redeemer and in the blessed Trinity. The Holy Ghost will assist thee and I desire thee to begin writing in my presence." The Evangelist worshipped the great Queen of heaven and was filled with the divine Spirit as the others had been. Assisted by the kind Mother, he immediately set about writing his Gospel.

Before she departed to the right hand of her divine Son, She gave him her benediction and promised him her protection for all the rest of his life. Such were the beginnings of the sacred Gospels, all of them having been commenced with the assistance and by the intervention of the most blessed Mary, giving the Church to understand, that all these benefits have been vouchsafed at her hands. After having thus anticipated the history of the Evangelists, in order to account for the beginning of the Gospels, we shall now return to our narrative.

In proportion as the most blessed Lady after the council of the Apostles was exalted by her divine knowledge and the abstractive vision of God, so her care and solicitude for the welfare of the Church increased; for the faith was now spreading out over the earth day by. As a true Mother and Teacher, She lavished her special attention upon the Apostles, whose names and whose welfare She bore written in her heart.

All of them, except Saint John and saint James the less, immediately after the termination of the council, left Jerusalem for the field of their labors, and the kindest Mother was deeply concerned at the thought of the hardships and difficulties connected with their preaching. She looked upon them with tender pity in their peregrinations, and held them in highest veneration on account of their holiness and dignity as priests, as Apostles of her divine Son, founders of the Church, preachers of his doctrine, and as the elect of the divine Wisdom chosen for such high ministries to the glory of the Most High.

It was truly necessary that the most blessed Lady and Mistress, in order to attend to and take care of so many matters throughout the holy Church, should be raised to the state which She now held: for in any lower condition She could not have so easily and properly attended to so many duties and at the same time maintain that interior tranquility and peace, which her soul enjoyed.

Besides her own knowledge and solicitude for the whole Church, the most holy Mother again charged her angels to take care of all the Apostles and disciples, to console them in all their tribulations and to haste to their aid in all their difficulties. For by the subtlety of their spiritual nature they could attend to all this without losing sight of the face of God and enjoying beatific vision.

She thus charged them because it was so important to establish the Church and because they were the ministers of the Most high and the works of his hand. She told them also to inform Her of all that the Apostles and disciples were doing, and especially when they were in need of any clothing; for to this matter the watchful Mother wished to attend in particular, in order that they might go about clothed in a uniform manner, such as they wore when they departed from Jerusalem.

By this prudent foresight, the Apostles showed no difference in their garments as long as the great Lady was alive; but all of them wore clothes of the same form and color, similar to that worn by her divine Son. Assisted by the holy angels, She wove with her own hand the tunics for this purpose and sent them through the angels to the Apostles on their journeys. In thus making it possible for them to wear vestments similar to those which had been worn by Christ our Savior, the great Mother provided that even in their exterior appearance the Apostles preached his doctrines and his most holy life. In regard to the other necessities of life, such as food, She left them to begging and to the labor of their hands, or to the alms which were offered to them.

At the orders of the Queen the angels frequently assisted the Apostles in their travels and tribulations and in the persecutions as well of the gentiles and the Jews, as of the demons, who continually excited evil–minded men against the preachers of the

Gospel. The angels often visited them in visible shapes, conversing with them and consoling them in the name of the most blessed Mary.

At other times they performed the same office interiorly without manifesting themselves; sometimes they freed them from prison; sometimes they warned them of dangers and snares; sometimes they accompanied them on their way or carried them from one place to another where they were to preach, or informed them of what they were to do according to the circumstances peculiar to certain place; or peoples.

Of all these things they also kept their blessed Lady informed; for She took care of all of them and labored with them more than all of them together. It is not possible to enumerate the cares, solicitudes and diligent doings of this kindest Mother; for not a day or a night passed, in which She did not perform many miracles for the Apostles and for the Church. Besides all this She wrote to them many times, animating them with heavenly exhortations and doctrines, and filling them with consolation and strength.

Her Devotion to the Passion of Christ and Holy Eucharist—How She Celebrated the Immaculate Conception and Other Feasts

Without ever failing in her attention to the exterior government of the Church, the most blessed Mary in secret practiced other exercises and good works, by which she merited innumerable gifts and blessings from the Most High, as well for the common benefit of all the faithful, as for myriads of particular souls in furtherance of their salvation.

As far as I can in these last chapters, I shall for our instruction and admiration and for the glory of the most blessed Mother, write of these hidden and unknown works. First of all I will state, that notwithstanding the many privileges which the great Queen of heaven enjoyed, She constantly kept present in her memory the doings and the mysteries of the life of her divine Son; for besides the abstractive vision, by which She these last years continually saw the Divinity and knew all things, the Lord had from her Conception conceded to Her the privilege of never forgetting what She once had known or understood; for in this regard She enjoyed the privilege of an angel.

I also stated in the second part that the blessed Mother felt in her body and purest soul all the pains and torments of our Savior Jesus, so that none of them were hidden to Her or without the corresponding suffering in her own self. All the images or impressions of the Passion remained imprinted in her interior just as She had received them; for She had made this request of her Lord.

Hence She ordered all her occupations in such a manner, that She might at all times preserve in her heart the image of her divine Son, afflicted, outraged, wounded and disfigured by the torments of his Passion, and within Herself She beheld this image as in a most clear mirror. She heard the injuries, outrages, affronts and blasphemies against Him, with all the circumstances of time and place, and She beheld the whole Passion as one living and penetrating vista.

Throughout the day this sorrowful vision excited Her to most heroic acts of virtue and stirred her sorrow and compassion: but her most prudent love did not content itself with these exercises. During stated hours and times She engaged in other exercises with her holy angels, especially with those I have mentioned in the first part as bearing the tokens or the escutcheons of the instruments of the Passion. These in the first place, and then the other angels, She engaged as assistants in the following exercises.

For each kind of the wounds and sufferings of Christ our Savior She recited special prayers and salutations, in order to give them special adoration and worship. For each of the contemptuous and insulting words of the Jews and his other enemies, which had been spoken either in envy or in fury or vengeance, for each of the blasphemies uttered, She composed special hymns of veneration and honor to make up for their attempts at diminishing it.

For the insulting gestures, mockeries and personal injuries, She practiced most profound humiliations, genuflections and prostrations, and in this manner She sought continually to make up for the affronts and injuries heaped upon her divine Son in his life and his passion; and thus She confessed his Divinity, his humanity, his holiness, his miracles, his works and his doctrines. For all She gave him glory and magnificence; and in all the holy angels joined Her, and corresponded with Her full of admiration of such wisdom, fidelity and love united in a mere creature.

Even if the most blessed Mother during her whole life had engaged in no other occupation than these exercises, She would have accomplished and merited more than all the saints in all that they have done or suffered for God. By the force of love her sorrow in these exercises was equal to martyrdom many times over; and

many times would She have died in them, if the divine power had
not sustained her life for still greater merit and glory.

And if, as is true, She in her immense charity offered all these
works for the Church let us consider how much we are in her debt
as faithful children for thus increasing the treasures of help, which
She left at the disposal of us unfortunate children of Eve. And in
order that our meditation may not be half–hearted and lukewarm,
I will say, that the effects of her contemplations were often
astounding; many times She wept tears of blood, which covered
her whole face; at other times in her agony She was not only
bathed in perspiration, but in a bloody sweat, running from Her
even to the ground.

What is more, sometimes her heart was wrenched from its natural
position by the violence of her grief; and when She was in such
extremes, her divine Son came from heaven, furnishing Her with
new strength and life to soothe her sorrow and heal the wounds
caused by love of Him, and in order that by such assistance and
comfort, She might continue the exercises of her compassion.

The Lord however wished Her to lay aside these sorrowful
sentiments and affections on the days in which She
commemorated the mystery of his Resurrection, as I will speak of
later on, in order that there might be maintained the proper
relation between cause and effect. For some of these sorrows were
incompatible with the favors overflowing in their effects upon the
body, yet excluding pain.

But She never lost sight of his sufferings and therefore felt other
effects of her compassion by uniting with her joys, the gratitude
for what the Lord endured. Thus in the sweetness of all the favors
of the Lord his Passion entered as a mixture of bitterness. She
obtained also the consent of the evangelist Saint John to remain
retired in her oratory for celebrating the death and burial of her
divine Son on Friday of each week.

On those days Saint John remained in the Cenacle to receive those who called upon Her and allowed none to disturb Her; and whenever he could not attend to this duty, it was performed by some other disciple. The most blessed Mary retired for this exercise at five o'clock on Thursday and did not reappear until toward noon of Sunday.

In order that during these three days no important matter pertaining to the government of the Church might be neglected, the great Lady appointed one of her angels to take her shape and briefly dispatch what would suffer no delay, so provident and attentive was She in all affairs of charity touching her children and domestics.

To describe or comprehend what happened with our heavenly Mother during the exercises of these three days can never be within our capacity; the Lord alone, who was the Author of them, shall one day manifest it to us in the light of the saints. Also what I myself have come to know of it, I am unable to describe; I will only say that beginning with the washing of the feet, the most blessed Mary commemorated all the mysteries up to that of the Resurrection; and in each hour and moment She renewed in Herself all the movements, actions, works and sufferings as they had happened in her divine Son.

She repeated the same prayers and petitions as He himself had made. Anew the most pure Mother felt in her virginal body all the pains endured by Christ our Savior. She carried the Cross and placed Herself upon it. In short, I will say, that as long as She lived, the whole passion of her divine Son was renewed in Her week for week. Through this exercise the great Queen gained great favors and blessings for those who devoutly bear in mind the Lord's passion; and hence the powerful Queen has promised to all such souls, especial assistance and participation in the treasures of the Passion; for She desired from her inmost heart, that the Church should continue and preserve its commemoration.

In virtue of her wishes and prayers the Lord ordained, that afterwards many persons in the holy Church should follow these exercises of the Passion, imitating his most blessed Mother, who was the first one to teach and practice such an exalted profession.

In these exercises the great Queen sought especially to celebrate the institution of the most Blessed Sacrament by new hymns of praise, of thanksgiving and fervent love. She was solicitous to invite for this purpose her own angels and many others from the empyrean heaven, in order to assist and accompany in these praises of the Lord.

It was a wonder worthy of his Omnipotence, that the Most High should send from heaven multitudes of angels to view this prodigy of Christ's remaining sacramentally present in her heart from one Communion to the other and to incite them to give glory and praise for the wonderful effects of his sacramental presence in this Creature, whom they beheld more pure and more holy than the angels and seraphim and the like of which they had not seen or would ever see in all the rest of creation.

It was not less wonderful to them (just as it ought to be to us) to see, that though the great Queen worthy of preserving within Herself the sacred species as in a tabernacle, She was so solicitous in preparing Herself anew by the most fervid exercises and devotions every time She was again to receive Holy Communion; and this She did nearly every day except on those in which She remained in her oratory.

She first offered up for this purpose her weekly exercises of the Passion and besides this, whenever She retired at nightfall before the day of Communion, She began other exercises such as prostrations in the form of a cross, genuflections, prayers, and adorations of the immutable essence of God. She asked permission of the Lord to speak to Him and to permit Her, in spite of her earthly lowliness to partake of his Son in the holy Sacrament; She appealed to his infinite bounty and to his love toward the Church in thus remaining sacramentally present, as a reason that She should be favored with this blessing.

She offered to Him his own Passion and Death, the worthiness with which He had communicated Himself, the union of his human nature with the divine, all his works from the moment of his conception in the virginal womb, all the virtue of the angelic nature and its works, of all the just in past, present and future times. Then she made most intense acts of humility, professing Herself but dust and ashes in comparison with the infinite being of God, to which the highest creatures are so inferior and unequal.

In the contemplation of what She was to receive sacramentally, She was so affected and so deeply moved, that it is impossible describe it in words; for She raised Herself and transcended above the choirs of seraphim and cherubim; and as, in her own estimation, She considered Herself the lowest of all creatures, She called upon her guardian angels and upon all the other angels, asking them, with incomparable humility, to supplicate the Lord to dispose and prepare Her for receiving Him worthily, since She was but an inferior and earthly creature. The holy angels, obeying Her in joyful admiration, assisted and accompanied Her in these petitions, in which She persevered for the greater part of the night preceding her Communion.

As the wisdom of the great Queen, although in itself finite, is for us incomprehensible, we can never worthily understand to what height rose her virtues and works of love on these occasions. But they were often of such a kind as to oblige the Lord to respond by personal visit, in which He gave Her to understand with what pleasure He came to dwell sacramentally in her heart and to renew in Her the pledges of his infinite love.

When the hour of her Communion arrived, She first heard the Mass usually celebrated by the Evangelist. In these Masses, although the Epistles and Gospels, being not yet written, were not read, the consecration was always the same as now, and to it were added other rites and ceremonies with many psalms and orations.

At the end of Mass the heavenly Mother approached, making there
most profound genuflections; all inflamed with love She received
her Son in the Sacrament, welcoming in her purest bosom and
heart that same God, to whom She had given the most sacred
humanity in her virginal womb. Having communicated, She
retired, and, unless some very urgent need of her fellowmen
demanded otherwise, remained alone for three hours. During
these hours the Evangelist was often privileged to see rays of light
darting forth from Her as from the sun.

The prudent Mother also provided that for the celebration of the
unbloody sacrifice of the Mass the Apostles and priests be clothed
in ornate and mysterious vestments, different from those they
wore in ordinary life. Accordingly, with her own hands, She
provided ornaments and sacerdotal vestments for its celebration,
thus originating the ceremonious observances in the Church.
Although these vestments were not quite of the same form as
nowadays; yet they were not materially different in appearance
from those which in the course of time came into use in the
Roman Church.

The material was more alike; for She made them of linen and rich
silks, purchased with the alms and presents made to Her.
Whenever She worked at these vestments, sewing or fitting them,
She remained on her knees or on her feet, and She would not
entrust them to other sacristans than the angels, who assisted and
helped Her in all these things; likewise She kept these ornaments
and all that pertained to the service of the altar in incredible order
and cleanliness; and from such hands as hers, all came forth with a
celestial fragrance, which enkindled the spirit of the ministers.

From many kingdoms and provinces, where the Apostles were
preaching, numbers of converts came to Jerusalem in order to visit
and converse with the Mother of the Redeemer of the world, at the
same time offering rich gifts. Among others, four sovereign
princes, who were royal governors of provinces, visited Her and

brought many valuable presents, which they placed at her disposal for her own use and for the Apostles and disciples.

The great Lady answered that She was like her Son, and that the Apostles likewise were in imitation of their Master; that hence these riches were not appropriate to the life they professed. They begged Her to console them by accepting their gifts for the poor or for the divine worship. On account of the persistent requests She received part of what they offered, and from the rich silks She made some ornaments for the altar; the rest She distributed among the indigent and the infirmaries.

For She was accustomed to visit such places and often served and washed the poor with her own hands, performing such services, as well as distributing the alms, on her knees. Wherever it was possible She consoled the needy and assisted the sick in their last agony. Nor did She ever rest from works of charity, either actually engaging in them, or pleading and praying for others in her retirement.

During these last years the Queen ate or slept very little; and this little only, because Saint John asked Her to rest for at least a small portion of the night. But this sleep was only a slight suspension of the senses, lasting no longer than a half hour, during which, in the manner above described, She lost not the vision of the Divinity. Her food was a few mouthfuls of ordinary bread and sometimes a little fish, taken at the of the instance of the Evangelist and in order to keep him company; in this, as in other privileges, Saint John was thus fortunate, not only eating with Her from the same table but having the food prepared for him by the great Queen and administered to him as from a mother to her son, and moreover being obeyed by Her as a priest and a substitute of Christ.

Very well could the great Queen get along without even this sleep or nourishment, which seemed more a ceremony than the sustenance of life; but She partook of them not from necessity, but in order to practice obedience and humility and thus pay some tribute to human nature; for in all things She was most prudent.

B8C5

All the offices and titles of honor, which the most blessed Mary held in the Church, that of Queen, Mistress, Mother, Governess and Teacher, and all the rest, were given to her by the Omnipotent not as empty and fruitless names, but were accompanied by the superabundant plenitude of grace which is proper and which the Almighty can communicate to each.

This plenitude consisted in this, that as Queen She knew all that concerned her reign and its extent; as Mistress She knew the measure of her power; as Mother She knew all the children and dependents of her household, without excepting anyone through all the ages of the Church until the end; as Governess She knew all that were subject to Her; and as Teacher, She possessed the wisdom and science through which the holy Church, by her intercession, was to be instructed and guided, while enjoying the presence and the influence of the Holy Ghost until the end of the world.

Hence our great Queen had a clear knowledge not only of all the saints that preceded or followed Her in the Church, of their lives, their works, their deaths, and rewards in heaven; but also of all the rites, ceremonies, decisions, and festivities of the Church in course of the ages, and of all the reasons, motives, necessities and opportunities, in and for which they were established with the assistance of the Holy Ghost. For He gives us our spiritual nourishment in proper time for the glory of the Lord and the increase of the holy Church.

From her full knowledge and her corresponding holiness, there arose within the heavenly Instructress a certain thankful eagerness, to introduce into the Church militant the worship, veneration and festivities observed by the holy angels in the triumphant Jerusalem, and thus imitate, as far as was possible, what She had so often seen done in heaven for the praise and glory of the Most High.

In this more than seraphic spirit She commenced to practice by Herself many of the ceremonies, rites and exercises, which were afterwards introduced in the Church; and these She also inculcated and impressed upon the Apostles, in order that they might introduce them as far as the circumstances then allowed. She not only invented the exercises of the Passion, but many other customs and ceremonies which were later on received in the churches, in the congregations and religions.

For whatever She knew as pertaining to the worship of the Lord or the practice of virtue, She performed, and in her wisdom She was ignorant of nothing that ought to be known. Among these exercises and rites was the celebration of the feasts of the Lord and of Herself, in order to renew the memory of the benefits for which She stood indebted, as well the benefits relating in general to the human race, as those especially referring to Herself, striving thus to give thanks and adoration for all.

Although She had spent her whole life in this pursuit without relaxation or forgetfulness, yet, when She entered upon this new mysterious phase of her life, She prepared to signalize these feast days by celebrating them with exercises founded on a deeper insight. As I will speak of the other festivals in the following chapters, I will describe here only how She celebrated her Immaculate Conception and Nativity, the first mysteries of her life. These commemorations or feasts She had begun to celebrate since the Incarnation of the Word; but She celebrated them more particularly after the Ascension, and especially in these last years of her life.

On the eighth day of December of each year She celebrated her Immaculate Conception with a jubilee and gratitude beyond all human words; for this privilege was for the great Queen of the highest importance and value. She imagined Herself altogether incapable of ever acknowledging it with sufficient gratitude. She commenced her exercises on the evening before and spent the whole night in admirable devotions, shedding tears of joy, humiliating Herself, prostrating Herself and singing the praises of the Lord.

She deeply reflected, that She was formed of the same earth and descended from Adam according to the common order of nature; that She was preserved and exempted from the weight of the same guilt and conceived with such a plenitude of graces and gifts only because She was set apart and snatched from the rest by the Almighty.

She invited her own angels to help Her to return proper thanks, and in union with them She alternated new songs of praise. Then She asked the same favor of the rest of the angels and saints in heaven; but during all this time the divine love so inflamed Her, that the Lord was obliged to strengthen Her, lest all her natural forces be consumed and death ensue.

After She had spent the whole night in these exercises, Christ descended from heaven and the angels raised Her to his royal throne in heaven, where the celebration of the feast was continued with new glory and accidental joy of the courtiers of the heavenly Jerusalem. There the blessed Mother prostrated Herself and adored the most holy Trinity, again giving thanks for the benefit of her immunity from sin and her Immaculate Conception.

Then She again took her place at the right hand of Christ her Son and the Lord himself as it were acknowledged the goodness of the eternal Father in having given Him a Mother so worthy and so full of grace, exempt from the common guilt of Adam. Anew the three divine Persons confirmed upon Her this privilege, as it were ratifying and approving it and pleasing Themselves in thus having distinguished Her among all the creatures.

In order to give repeated testimony to this truth, a voice proceeded from the throne in the name of the Father, saying: "Beautiful are thy footsteps, O prince's Daughter, conceived without sin." Another in the name of the Son, said: "Altogether pure and without contact of guilt is my Mother, who gave Me human form to redeem men." And in the name of the Holy Spirit: "All fair art thou, my Spouse, all fair art thou and without stain of the universal guilt."

In between these voices were heard the choirs of all the angels and saints, singing in sweetest harmony: "Most holy Mary, conceived without original sin. To all these honors the most prudent Mother answered by thanksgiving, worship and praise of the Most High, rendered with such profound humility that it passed all angelic understanding. In order to conclude the solemnity She was raised to the intuitive and beatific vision of the most holy Trinity; and after enjoying this glory for some hours, She was brought back by the angels to the Cenacle. This was the manner in which her Immaculate Conception was solemnized after the Ascension of her divine Son.

Saint Gabriel Brings Notice of the Death of the Virgin Mary

In writing of what still remains of the history of our Lady, of our only and heavenly Phoenix, the blessed Mary, it is no more than right that our hearts be filled with tenderness and our eyes with tears at the sweet and touching marvels of the last years of her life. I should wish to exhort the devout faithful not to read of them nor consider them as past and absent, since the powerful virtue of faith can make these truths present to the mind; and if we look upon them with the proper piety and Christian devotion, without a doubt we shall gather the sweetest fruit, and our hearts shall feel the effects and rejoice in the good, which our eyes cannot see.

The most holy Mary had arrived at the age sixty–seven years without having tarried in her career, ceased in her flight, mitigated the flame of her love, or lessened the increase of her merits from the first instant of her Conception.

As all this had continued to grow in each moment of her life, the ineffable gifts, benefits and favors of the Lord had made Her entirely godlike and spiritual; the affectionate ardors and desires of her most chaste heart did not allow Her any rest outside the centre of her love; the bounds of the flesh were most violently irksome; the overwhelming attraction of the Divinity to unite Itself with Her with eternal and most close bonds, had attained the summit of power in Her; and the earth itself, made unworthy by the sins of mortals to contain the Treasure of heaven, could no longer bear the strain of withholding Her from her true Lord.

The eternal Father desired his only and true Daughter; the Son his beloved and most loving Mother; and the Holy Ghost the embraces of his most beautiful Spouse. The angels longed for their Queen, the saints for their great Lady; and all the heavens mutely awaited the presence of their Empress who should fill them with glory, with her beauty and delight. All that could be alleged in favor of Her still remaining in the world and in the Church, was the need of such a Mother and Mistress, and the love, which God himself had for the miserable children of Adam.

But as some term and end was to be placed to the career of our Queen, the divine consistory conferred upon the manner of glorifying the most blessed Mother and established the kind of loving reward due to Her for having so copiously fulfilled all the designs of the divine mercy among the children of Adam during the many years in which She had been the Foundress and Teacher of his holy Church.

The Almighty therefore resolved to delight and console Her by giving Her definite notice of the term still remaining of her life and revealing to Her the day and hour of the longed for end of her earthly banishment. For this purpose the most blessed Trinity despatched the archangel Gabriel with many others of the celestial hierarchies, who should announce to the Queen when and how her mortal life should come to an end and pass over into the eternal.

The holy prince descended with the rest to the Cenacle in Jerusalem and entered the oratory of the great Lady where they found Her prostrate on the ground in the form of a cross, asking mercy for sinners. But hearing the sound of their music and perceiving them present, She rose to her knees in order to hear the message and show respect to the ambassador of heaven and his companions, who in white and refulgent garments surrounded Her with wonderful delight and reverence.

All of them had come with crowns and palms in their hands, each one with a different one; but all of them represented the diverse premiums and rewards of inestimable beauty and value to be conferred upon their great Queen and Lady.

Gabriel saluted Her with the Ave Maria, and added thereto: "Our Empress and Lady, the Omnipotent and the Holy of the holy sends us from his heavenly court to announce to Thee in his name the most happy end of thy pilgrimage and banishment upon earth in mortal life. Soon, O Lady, is that day and hour approaching which, according to thy longing desires, Thou shalt pass through natural death to the possession of the eternal and immortal life, which awaits Thee in the glory and at the right hand of thy divine Son, our God. Exactly three years from today Thou shalt be taken up and received into the everlasting joy of the Lord, where all its inhabitants await Thee, longing for thy presence."

The most holy Mary heard this message with ineffable jubilee of her purest and most loving spirit, prostrating herself again upon the earth, She answered in the same words as at the incarnation of the Word: "Ecce ancilla Domini, fiat mihi secundum verbum tuum." "Behold the handmaid of the Lord, be it done according to thy word". Then She asked the holy angels and ministers of the Most High to help Her give thanks for this welcome and joyful news.

The blessed Mother alternately with the seraphim and other angels sang the responses of a canticle that lasted for two hours. Although by their nature and supernatural gifts the angelic spirits are so subtle, wise and excellent, they were nevertheless excelled in all this by their Queen and Lady, as vassals are by their sovereign; for in Her, grace and wisdom abounded as in a Teacher, in them, only as in disciples.

Having finished this canticle and humiliating herself anew, She charged the supernal spirits to beseech the Lord to prepare Her for her passage from mortal to eternal life, and to ask all the other angels and saints in heaven to pray for the same favor. They offered to obey Her in all things, and therewith Saint Gabriel took leave and returned with all his company to the empyrean heaven.

The great Queen and Lady of all the universe remained alone in her oratory, and amid tears of humble joy prostrated Herself upon the earth, embraced it as the common mother of us all, saying:

"Earth, I give thee thanks as I ought, because without my merit thou hast sustained me sixty–seven years. Thou art a creature of the Most High and by his will thou hast sustained me until now. I ask thee now to help me during the rest of my dwelling upon thee, so that, just as I have been created of thee and upon thee, I may through thee and from thee be raised to the blessed vision of my Maker."

She addressed also other creatures, saying: "Ye heavens, planets, stars and elements, created by the powerful hands of my Beloved, faithful witnesses and proclaimers of his greatness and beauty, you also I thank for the preservation of my life; help me then from today on, that, with the divine favor, I may begin anew to perfect my life during the time left of my career, in order that I may show myself thankful to my and your Creator."

The devout Queen resolved to take leave of the holy places before her departure into heaven, and having obtained the consent of Saint John She left the house with him and with the thousand angels of her guard. Although these sovereign princes had always served and accompanied Her in all her errands, occupations and journeys, without having absented themselves for one moment since the instant of her birth; yet on this occasion they manifested themselves to Her with greater beauty and refulgence, as if they felt special joy in seeing themselves already at the beginning of her last journey into heaven.

The heavenly Princess, setting aside human occupations in order to enter upon her journey to the real and true fatherland, visited all the memorable places of our Redemption, marking each with the sweet abundance of her tears, recalling the sorrowful memories of what her Son there suffered, and fervently renewing its effects by most fervent acts of love, clamors and petitions for all the faithful, who should devoutly and reverently visit these holy places during the future ages of the Church.

On Calvary She remained a longer time, asking of her divine Son the full effects of his redeeming Death for all the multitudes of souls there snatched from destruction. The ardor of her ineffable charity during this prayer rose to such a pitch, that it would have destroyed her life, if it had not been sustained by divine power.

The Queen asked also the angels of the sanctuaries and the Evangelist to give Her their blessing in this last leave–taking; and therewith She returned to her oratory shedding tears of tenderest affection for what She loved so much upon earth. There She prostrated Herself with her face upon the earth and poured forth another long and most fervent prayer for the Church; and She persevered in it, until in an abstractive vision of the Divinity, the Lord had given Her assurance that He had heard and conceded her petitions at the throne of His mercy.

In order to give the last touch of holiness to her works, She asked permission of the Lord to take leave of the holy Church, saying: "Exalted and most high God, Redeemer of the world, head of the saints and the predestined, Justifier and Glorifier of souls, I am a child of the holy Church, planted and acquired by thy blood. Give me, O Lord, permission to take leave of such a loving Mother, and of all my brethren, thy children, belonging to it."

She was made aware of the consent of the Lord and therefore turned to the mystical body of the Church, addressing it in sweet tears as follows:

"Holy Catholic Church, which in the coming ages shall be called the Roman, my mother and Mistress, true treasure of my soul, thou hast been the only consolation of my banishment; the refuge and ease of my labors; my recreation, my joy and my hope ; thou hast sustained me in my course; in thee have I lived as a pilgrim to the Fatherland and thou hast nourished me after I had received in thee my existence in grace through thy head, Christ Jesus, my Son and my Lord. In thee are the treasures and the riches of his infinite merits; thou shalt be for his faithful children the secure way to the promised land, and thou shalt safeguard them on their dangerous and difficult pilgrimage. Thou shalt be the mistress of the nations to whom all owe reverence; in thee are the rich and inestimable jewels of the anxieties, labors, affronts, hardships, torments, of the cross and of death, which are all consecrated by those of my Lord, thy Progenitor, thy Master, thy Chief, and are reserved for his more distinguished servants and his dearest friends."

" Thou hast adorned and enriched me with thy jewels in order that I might enter in the nuptials of the Spouse; thou hast made me wealthy, prosperous and happy, and thou containest within thee thy Author in the most holy Sacrament. My happy Mother, Church militant, rich art thou and abundant in treasures! For thee have I always reserved my heart and my solicitude; but now is the time come to part from thee and leave thy sweet companionship, in order to reach the end of my course."

"Make me partaker of thy great goods; bathe me copiously in the sacred liquor of the blood of the Lamb, preserved in thee as a powerful means of sanctifying many worlds. At the cost of my life a thousand times would I bring to thee all the nations and tribes of mortals, that they might enjoy thy treasures. My beloved Church, my honor and my glory, I am about to leave thee in mortal life; but in the eternal life I will find thee joyful in an existence which includes all good. From that place I shall look upon thee with love, and pray always for thy increase, thy prosperity and thy progress".

This was the parting of the most blessed Mary from the mystical body of the holy Roman Catholic Church, the mother of the faithful, in order that all who should hear of Her, might know by her sweet tears and endearments, in what veneration, love and esteem She held that holy Church. After thus taking leave, the great Mistress, as the Mother of Wisdom, prepared to make her testament and last Will.

When She manifested this most prudent wish to the Lord, He deigned to approve of it by his own royal presence. For this purpose, with myriads of attending angels, the three Persons of the most blessed Trinity descended to the oratory of their Daughter and Spouse, and when the Queen had adored the infinite

Being of God, She heard a voice speaking to Her: "Our chosen Spouse, make thy last will as thou desirest, for We shall confirm it and execute it entirely by our infinite power."

The most prudent Mother remained for some time lost in the profoundness of her humility, seeking to know first the will of the Most High before She should manifest her own. The Lord responded to her modest desires and the person of the Father said to Her: "My Daughter, thy will shall be pleasing and acceptable to Me; for thou art not wanting in the merits of good works in parting from this mortal life, that I should not satisfy thy desires."

The same encouragement was given to her by the Son and the Holy Ghost. Therewith the most blessed Mary made her will in this form:

"Highest Lord and eternal God, I, a vile wormlet of the earth, confess and adore Thee with all the reverence of my inmost soul as the Father, the Son and the Holy Ghost, three Persons distinct in one undivided and eternal essence, one substance, one in infinite majesty of attributes and perfection. I confess Thee as the one true Creator and Preserver of all that has being."

" In thy kingly presence I declare and say, that my last will is this: Of the goods of mortal life and of the world in which I live, I possess none that I can leave; for never have I possessed or loved anything beside Thee, who art my good and all my possession. To the heavens, the stars and planets, to the elements and all creatures in them I give thanks, because according to thy will they have sustained me without my merit, and lovingly I desire and ask them to serve and praise Thee in the offices and ministries assigned to them, and that they continue to sustain and benefit my brethren and fellowmen."

"In order that they may do it so much the better, I renounce and assign to mankind the possession, and as far as possible, the dominion of them, which thy Majesty has given me over these irrational creatures, so that they may now serve and sustain my fellowmen. Two tunics and a cloak, which served to cover me, I leave to John for his disposal, since I hold him as a son."

" My body I ask the earth to receive again for thy service, since it is the common mother and serves Thee as thy creature; my soul, despoiled of its body and of all visible things, O my God, I resign into thy hands, in order that it may love and magnify Thee through all thy eternities. My merits and all the treasures, which with thy grace through my works and exertions I have acquired, I leave to the holy Church, my mother and my mistress, as my residuary heiress, and with thy permission I there deposit them, wishing them to be much greater."

"And I desire before all else they redound to the exaltation of thy holy name and procure the fulfillment of thy will earth as it is done in heaven, and that all the nations come to the knowledge, love and veneration of Thee, the true God."

"In the second place I offer these merits for my masters the Apostles and priests, of the present and of the future ages, so that in view of them thy ineffable clemency may make them apt ministers, worthy of their office and state, filled with wisdom, virtue and holiness by which they may edify and sanctify the souls by thy blood."

"In the third place I offer them for the spiritual good of my devoted servants, who invoke and call upon me, in order that they may receive thy protection and grace, and afterwards eternal life. In the fourth place I desire that my services and labors may move Thee to mercy toward all the sinning children of Adam, in order that they may withdraw from their sinful state. From this hour on I propose and desire to continue my prayers for them in thy divine presence, as long as the world shall last. This, Lord and my God, is my last will, always subject to thy own."

At the conclusion of this testament of the Queen, the most blessed Trinity approved and confirmed it; and Christ the Redeemer, as if authorizing it all, witnessed it by writing in the heart of his Mother these words: "Let it be done as thou wishest and ordainest."

If all we children of Adam, and especially we who are born in the law of grace, had no other obligation toward the most blessed Mary than this of having been constituted heirs of her immense merits and of all that is mentioned in this short and mysterious testament, we could never repay our debt, even if in return we should offer our lives and endure all the sufferings of the most courageous martyrs and saints.

THE GLORIOUS TRANSITION OF THE VIRGIN MARY

And now, according to the decree of the divine will, the day was approaching in which the true and living Ark of the Covenant was to be placed in the temple of the celestial Jerusalem, with a greater glory and higher jubilee than its prophetic figure was installed by Solomon in the sanctuary beneath the wings of the cherubim.

Three days before the most happy Transition of the great Lady the Apostles and disciples were gathered in Jerusalem and in the Cenacle. The first one to arrive was Saint Peter, who was transported from Rome by the hands of an angel. At that place the angel appeared to him and told him that the passing away of the most blessed Mary was imminent and the Lord commanded him to go to Jerusalem in order to be present at that event.

Thereupon the angel took him and brought him from Italy to the Cenacle. Thither the Queen of the world had retired, somewhat weakened in body by the force of her divine love; for since She was so near to her end, She was subjected more completely to love's effects.

The great Lady came to the entrance of her oratory in order to receive the Vicar of Christ our Savior. Kneeling at his feet She asked his blessing and said: "I give thanks and praise to the Almighty, that He brought to me the holy Father for assisting me in the hour of my death." Then came Saint Paul, to whom the Queen showed the same reverence with similar tokens of her pleasure at seeing him.

The Apostles saluted Her as the Mother of God, as their Queen and as Mistress of all creation; but with a sorrow equal to their reverence, because they knew that they had come to witness her passing away. After these Apostles came the others and the disciples still living. Three days after, they were all assembled in the Cenacle.

The heavenly Mother received them all with profound humility, reverence and love, asking each one to bless Her. All of them complied, and saluted Her with admirable reverence. By orders of the Lady given to Saint John, and with the assistance of Saint James the less, they were all hospitably entertained and accommodated.

Some of the Apostles, who had been transported by the angels and informed by them of the purpose of their coming, were seized with tenderest grief and shed abundant tears at the thought of losing their only protection and consolation. Others were as yet ignorant of their approaching loss, especially the disciples, who had not been positively informed by the angels, but were moved by interior inspirations and a sweet and forcible intimation of God's will to come to Jerusalem.

They immediately conferred with Saint Peter, desirous of knowing the occasion of their meeting; for all of them were convinced, that if there had been no special occasion, the Lord would not have urged them so strongly to come. The apostle Saint Peter, as the head of the Church, called them all together in order to tell them of the cause of their coming, and spoke to the assembly: "My dearest children and brethren, the Lord has called and brought us to Jerusalem from remote regions not without a cause most urgent and sorrowful to us. The Most High wishes now to raise up to the throne of eternal glory his most blessed Mother, our Mistress, our consolation and protection.

His divine decree is that we all be present at her most happy and glorious Transition. When our Master and Redeemer ascended to the right hand of his Father, although He left us orphaned of his most delightful presence, we still retained his most blessed Mother and our light now leaves us what shall we do? What help or hope have we to encourage us on our pilgrimage? I find none except the hope that we all shall follow Her in due time."

Saint Peter could speak no farther, because uncontrollable tears and sighs interrupted him. Neither could the rest of the Apostles answer for a long time during which, amid copious and tenderest tears, they gave vent to the groans of their inmost heart. After some time the Vicar of Christ recovered himself and added: "My children, let us seek the presence of our Mother and Lady. Let us spend the time left of her life in her company and ask Her to bless us." They all betook themselves to the oratory of the great Queen and found Her kneeling upon a couch, on which She was wont to recline for a short rest. They saw Her full of beauty and celestial light, surrounded by the thousand angels of her guard.

The natural condition and appearance of her sacred and virginal body were the same as at her thirty–third year; for, as I have already stated, from that age onward it experienced no change. It was not affected by the passing years, showing no signs of age, no wrinkles in her face or body, nor giving signs of weakening or fading, as in other children of Adam, who gradually fall away and drop from the natural perfection of early man or womanhood.

This unchangeableness was the privilege of the most blessed Mary alone, as well because it consorted with the stability of her purest soul, as because it was the natural consequence of her immunity from the sin of Adam, the effects of which in this regard touched neither her sacred body nor her purest soul. The Apostles and disciples, and some of the other faithful occupied her chamber, all of them preserving the utmost order in her presence. Saint Peter and Saint John placed themselves at the head of the couch.

The great Lady looked upon them all with her accustomed modesty and reverence and spoke to them as follows: "My dearest children, give permission to your servant to speak in your presence and to disclose my humble desires." Saint Peter answered that all listened with attention and would obey Her in all things; and He begged Her to seat Herself upon the couch, while speaking to them. It seemed to Saint Peter that She was exhausted from kneeling so long and that She had taken that position in order to pray to the Lord, and that in speaking to them, it was proper She should be seated as their Queen.

But She, who was the Teacher of humility and obedience unto death, practiced both these virtues in that hour. She answered that She would obey in asking of their blessing, and besought them to afford Her this consolation. With the permission of Saint Peter She left the couch and, kneeling before the Apostle, said to him: "My lord, I beseech thee, as the universal pastor and head of the holy Church, to give me thy blessing in thy own and in its name. Pardon me thy handmaid for the smallness of the service I have rendered in my life. Grant that John dispose of my vestments, giving them to the two poor maidens, who have always obliged me by their charity."

She then prostrated Herself and kissed the feet of Saint Peter as the vicar of Christ, by her abundant tears eliciting not less the admiration than the tears of the Apostle and of all the bystanders.

From Saint Peter She went to Saint John, kneeling likewise at his feet, said: "Pardon, my son and my master, my not having fulfilled toward thee the duties of a Mother as I ought and as the Lord had commanded me, when from the Cross He appointed thee as my son and me as thy mother. I humbly and from my heart thank thee for the kindness which thou hast shown me as a son. Give me thy benediction for entering into the vision and company of Him who created me."

The sweetest Mother proceeded in her leave—taking, speaking to each of the Apostles in particular and to some of the disciples; and then to all the assembly together; for there were a great number. She rose to her feet and addressed them all, saying: "Dearest children and my masters, always have I kept you in my soul and written in my heart. I have loved you with that tender love and charity, which was given to me by my divine Son, whom I have seen in you, his chosen friends. In obedience to his holy and eternal will, I now go to the eternal mansions, where I promise you as a Mother I will look upon you by the clearest light of the Divinity, the vision of which my soul hopes and desires in security.

I commend unto you my mother, the Church, the exaltation of the name of the Most High, the spread of the evangelical law, the honor and veneration for the words of my divine Son, the memory of his Passion and Death, the practice of his doctrine. My children, love the Church, and love one another with that bond of charity which your Master has always inculcated upon you. To thee, Peter, holy Pontiff, I commend my son John and all the rest."

The words of the most blessed Mary, like arrows of a divine fire, penetrated the hearts of all the Apostles and hearers, and as She ceased speaking, all of them were dissolved in streams of tears and, seized with irreparable sorrow, cast themselves upon the ground with sighs and groans sufficient to move to compassion the very earth.

All of them wept, and with them wept also the sweetest Mary, who could not resist this bitter and well–founded sorrow of her children. After some time She spoke to them again, and asked them to pray with Her and for Her in silence, which they did. During this quietness the incarnate Word descended from heaven on a throne of ineffable glory, accompanied by all the saints and innumerable angels, and the house of the Cenacle was filled with glory.

The most blessed Mary adored the Lord and kissed his feet. Prostrate before Him She made the last and most profound act of faith and humility in her mortal life. On this occasion the most pure Creature, the Queen of the heavens, shrank within Herself and lowered Herself to the earth more profoundly than all men together ever have or ever will humiliate themselves for all their sins.

Her divine Son gave Her His blessing and in the presence of the courtiers of heaven spoke to Her these words: "My dearest

Mother, whom I have chosen for my dwelling–place, the hour is come in which thou art to pass from the life of this death and of the world into the glory of my Father and Mine, where thou shalt possess the throne prepared for thee at my right hand and enjoy it through all eternity.

And since, by my power and as my Mother have caused thee to enter the world free and exempt from sin, therefore also death shall have no right or permission to touch thee at thy exit from this world. If thou wishest not to pass through it come with Me now to partake of my glory, which thou hast merited."

The most prudent Mother prostrated Herself at the feet of her Son and with a joyous countenance answered: "My Son and my Lord, I beseech Thee let thy mother and thy servant enter into eternal life by the common portal of natural death, like the other children of Adam. Thou, who art my true God, hast suffered death without being obliged to do so; it is proper that as I have followed Thee in life, so I follow Thee also in death."

Christ the Savior approved of the decision and the sacrifice of his most blessed Mother, and consented to its fulfillment. Then all the angels began to sing in celestial harmony some of the verses of the Canticles of Solomon and other new ones. Although only Saint John and some of the Apostles were enlightened as to the presence of Christ the Savior, yet the others felt in their interior its divine and powerful effects; but the music was heard as well by the Apostles and disciples, as by many others of the faithful there present.

A divine fragrance also spread about, which penetrated to the street. The house of the Cenacle was filled with a wonderful effulgence, visible to all, and the Lord ordained that multitudes of the people of Jerusalem gathered in the streets as witnesses to this new miracle.

When the angels began their music, the most blessed Mary reclined back upon her couch or bed. Her tunic was folded about her sacred body, her hands joined and her eyes fixed upon her divine Son, and She was entirely inflamed with the fire of divine love. And as the angels intoned those verses of the second of the Canticles: "Surge, propera, amica mea," that is to say: "Arise, haste, my beloved, my dove, my beautiful one, and come, the winter has passed," etc., She pronounced those words of her Son on the Cross: "Into thy hands, O Lord, I commend my spirit." Then She closed her virginal eyes and expired.

The sickness which took away her life was love, without any other weakness or accidental intervention of whatever kind. She died at the moment when the divine power suspended the assistance, which until then had counteracted the sensible ardors of her burning love of God. As soon as this miraculous assistance was withdrawn, the fire of her love consumed the life—humors of her heart and thus caused the cessation of her earthly existence.

Then this most pure Soul passed from her virginal body to be placed in boundless glory, on the throne at the right hand of her divine Son. Immediately the music of the angels seemed to withdraw to the upper air; for that whole procession of angels and saints accompanied the King and Queen to the empyrean heavens.

The sacred body of the most blessed Mary, which been the temple and sanctuary of God in life, continued to shine with an effulgent light and breathed forth such a wonderful and unheard of fragrance, that all the bystanders were filled with interior and exterior sweetness. The thousand angels of her guard remained to watch over the inestimable treasure of her virginal body.

The Apostles and disciples, amid the tears and the joy of the wonders they had seen, were absorbed in admiration for some time, and then sang many hymns and psalms in honor of the most blessed Mary now departed. This glorious Transition of the great Queen took place in the hour in which her divine Son had died, at three o'clock on a Friday, the thirteenth day of August, she being seventy years of age, less the twenty—six days intervening between the thirteenth day of August, on which She died, and the eighth of September, the day of her birth.

The heavenly Mother had survived the death of Christ the Savior twenty–one years, four months and nineteen days; and his virginal birth, fifty–five years. This reckoning can be easily made in the following manner: when Christ our Savior was born, his virginal Mother was fifteen years, three months and seventeen days of age. The Lord lived thirty–three years and three months; so that at the time of his sacred Passion the most blessed Lady was forty–eight years, six months and seventeen days old; adding to these another twenty–one years, four months and nineteen days, we ascertain her age as seventy years, less twenty–five or twenty–six days. (Age at death, 69 years, 11 months, 5 or 6 days.)

Great wonders and prodigies happened at the precious death of the Queen; for the sun was eclipsed and its light was hidden in sorrow for some hours. Many birds of different kinds gathered around the Cenacle, and by their sorrowful clamors and groans for a while caused the bystanders themselves to weep.

All Jerusalem was in commotion, and many of the inhabitants collected in astonished crowds, confessing loudly the power of God and the greatness of his works. Others were astounded and as if beside themselves. The Apostles and disciples with others of the faithful broke forth in tears and sighs. Many sick persons came who all were cured. The souls in purgatory were released.

But the greatest miracle was that three persons, a man in Jerusalem and two women living in the immediate neighborhood of the Cenacle, died in sin and impenitent in that same hour, subject to eternal damnation; but when their cause came before the tribunal of Christ, His sweetest Mother interceded for them and they were restored to life.

They so mended their conduct, that afterwards they died in grace and were saved. This privilege was not extended to others that died on that day in the world, but was restricted to those three who happened to die in that hour in Jerusalem.

BURIAL AND ASSUMPTION OF THE VIRGIN MARY

In order that the Apostles, the disciples, and many others of the faithful might not be too deeply oppressed by sorrow, and in order that some of them may not die of grief caused by the passing away of the blessed Mary, it was necessary that the divine power, by an especial providence, furnish them with consolation and dilate their heart for new influences in their incomparable affliction.

For the feeling, that their loss was irretrievable in the present life, could not be repressed; the privation of such a Treasure could never find recompense; and as the most sweet, loving and amiable interactions and conversation of their great Queen had ravished the heart of each one, the ceasing of her protection and company left them as it were without the breath of life. But the Lord, who well knew how to estimate the just cause of their sorrow, secretly upheld them by his encouragements and so they set about the fitting burial of the sacred body and whatever the occasion demanded.

Accordingly the holy Apostles, on whom this duty specially devolved, held a conference concerning the burial of the most sacred body of their Queen and Lady. They selected for that purpose a new sepulchre, which had been prepared mysteriously by the providence of her divine Son. As they remembered, that, according to the custom of the Jews at burial, the deified body of the Master had been anointed with precious ointments and spices and wrapped in the sacred burial cloths; they thought not of doing otherwise with the virginal body of His most holy Mother.

Accordingly they called the two maidens, who had assisted the Queen during her life and who had been designated as the heiresses of her tunics, and instructed them to anoint the body of the Mother of God with highest reverence and modesty and wrap it in the winding–sheets before it should be placed in the casket.

With great reverence and fear the two maidens entered the room, where the body of the blessed Lady lay upon its couch; but the refulgence issuing from it barred and blinded them in such a manner that they could neither see nor touch the body, nor even ascertain in what particular place it rested.

In fear and reverence still greater than on their entrance, the maidens left the room; and in great excitement and wonder they told the Apostles what had happened. They, not without divine inspiration, came to the conclusion, that this sacred Ark of the Covenant was not to be touched or handled in the common way. Then Saint Peter and Saint John entered the oratory and perceived the effulgence, and at the same time they heard the celestial music of the angels who were singing: "Hail Mary, full of grace, the Lord is with thee." Others responded: "A Virgin before childbirth, in childbirth and after childbirth."

From that time on many of the faithful expressed their devotion toward the most blessed Mary in these words of praise; and from them they were handed down to be repeated by us with the approbation of the holy Church. The two holy Apostles, Saint Peter and Saint John, were for a time lost in admiration at what they saw and heard of their Queen; and in order to decide what to do, they sank on their knees, beseeching the Lord to make it known. Then they heard a voice saying: "Let not the sacred body be either uncovered or touched."

Having thus been informed of the will of God they brought a bier, and, the effulgence having diminished somewhat, they approached the couch and with their own hands reverently took hold of the tunic at the two ends. Thus, without changing its posture, they raised the sacred and virginal Treasure and place it on the bier in the same position as it had occupied on the couch. They could easily do this, because they felt no more weight than that of the tunic.

On this bier the former effulgence of the body moderated still more, and all of them, by disposition of the Lord and for the consolation of all those present, could now perceive and study the beauty of that virginal countenance and of her hands. As for the rest, the omnipotence of God protected this His heavenly dwelling, so that neither in life nor in death anyone should behold any other part except what is common in ordinary conversation, her most inspiring countenance, by which She had been known, and her hands, by which She had labored.

So great was the care and solicitude for His most blessed Mother, that in this particular He used not so much precaution in regard to his own body, as that of the most pure Virgin. In her Immaculate Conception He made Her like to Himself; likewise at her birth, in as far as it did not take place in the common and natural manner of other men. He preserved Her also from impure temptations and thoughts.

But, as He was man and the Redeemer of the world through his Passion and Death, He permitted with his own body, what He would not allow with Hers, as that of a woman, and therefore He kept her virginal body entirely concealed; in fact the most pure Lady during her life had herself asked that no one should be permitted to look upon it in death; which petition He fulfilled.

Then the Apostles consulted further about her burial. Their decision becoming known among the multitudes of the faithful in Jerusalem, they brought many candles to be lighted at the bier, and it happened that all the lights burned through that day and the two following days without any of the candles being consumed or wasted in any shape or manner.

In order that this and many other miracles wrought by the power of God on this occasion might become better known to the world, the Lord himself inspired all the inhabitants of Jerusalem to be present at the burial of his most blessed Mother, so that there was scarcely any person in Jerusalem, even of the Jews or the gentiles, who were not attracted by the novelty of this spectacle.

The Apostles took upon their shoulders the sacred body and the tabernacle of God and, as priests of the evangelical law, bore the Propitiatory of the divine oracles and blessings in orderly procession from the Cenacle in the city to the valley of Josaphat. This was the visible accompaniment of the dwellers of Jerusalem.

In the midst of this celestial and earthly accompaniment, visible and invisible, the Apostles bore along the sacred body, and on the way happened great miracles, which would take much time to relate. In particular all the sick, of which there were many of the different kinds, were entirely cured. Many of the possessed were freed from the demons; for the evil spirits did not dare to wait until the sacred body came near the persons thus afflicted.

Greater still were the miracles of conversions wrought among many Jews and gentiles, for on this occasion were opened up the treasures of divine mercy, so that many souls came to the knowledge of Christ our Savior and loudly confessed Him as the true God and Redeemer, demanding Baptism. Many days thereafter the Apostles and disciples labored hard in catechizing and baptising those, who on that day had been converted to the holy faith.

The Apostles in carrying the sacred body felt wonderful effects of divine light and consolation, which the disciples shared according to their measure. All the multitudes of the people were seized with astonishment at the fragrance diffused about, the sweet music and the other prodigies. They proclaimed God great and powerful in this Creature and in testimony of their acknowledgment, they struck their breasts in sorrow and compunction.

When the procession came to the holy sepulchre in the valley of Josaphat, the same two Apostles, Saint Peter and Saint John, who had laid the celestial Treasure from the couch onto the bier, with joyful reverence placed it in the sepulchre and covered it with a linen cloth, the hands of the angels performing more of these last rites than the hands of the Apostles.

They closed up the sepulchre with a large stone, according to custom at other burials. The celestial courtiers returned to heaven, while the thousand angels of the Queen continued their watch, guarding the sacred body and keeping up the music as at her burial. The concourse of the people lessened and the holy Apostles and disciples, dissolved in tender tears, returned to the Cenacle. During a whole year the exquisite fragrance exhaled by the body of Queen was noticeable throughout the Cenacle, and in her oratory, for many years. This sanctuary remained a place of refuge for all those that were burdened with labor and difficulties; all found miraculous assistance, as well in sickness as in hardships and necessities of other kind. After these miracles had continued for some years in Jerusalem, the sins of Jerusalem and of its inhabitants drew upon this city, among other punishments, that of being deprived of this inestimable blessing.

Having again gathered in the Cenacle, the Apostles came to the conclusion that some of them and of the disciples should watch at the sepulchre of their Queen as long as they should hear the celestial music, for all of them were wondering when the end of that miracle should be.

Accordingly some of them attended to the affairs of the Church in catechizing and baptizing the new converts; and others immediately returned to the sepulchre, while all of them paid frequent visits to it during the next three days. Saint Peter and Saint John, however, were more zealous in their attendance, coming only a few times to the Cenacle and immediately returning to where was laid the treasure of their heart.

If on this account the glory even of the least of the saints is ineffable, what shall we say of the glory of the most blessed Mary, since among the saints She is the most holy and She by Herself is more like to her Son than all the saints together, and since her grace and glory exceed those of all the rest, as those of an empress or sovereign over her vassals?

This truth can and should be believed; but in mortal life it cannot be understood, or the least part of it be explained; for the inadequacy and deficiency of our words and expressions rather tend to obscure than to set forth its greatness. Let us in this life apply our labor, not in seeking to comprehend it, but in seeking to merit its manifestation in glory, where we shall experience more or less of this happiness according to our works.

Our Redeemer Jesus entered heaven conducting the purest soul of his Mother at his right hand. She alone of all the mortals deserved exemption from particular judgment; hence for Her there was none; no account was asked or demanded of Her for what She had received; for such was the promise that had been given to Her, when She was exempted from the common guilt and chosen as the Queen privileged above the laws of the children of Adam.

For the same reason, instead of being judged with the rest, She shall be seated at the right hand of the Judge to judge with Him all the creatures. If in the first instant of her Conception She was the brightest Aurora, effulgent with the rays of the sun of the Divinity beyond all the brightness of the most exalted seraphim, and if afterwards She was still further illumined by the contact of the hypostatic Word, who derived his humanity from her purest substance, it necessarily follows that She should be His Companion for all eternity, possessing such a likeness to Him, that none greater can be possible between a Godman and a creature.

In this light the Redeemer himself presented Her before the throne of the Divinity; and speaking to the eternal Father in the presence of all the blessed, who were ravished at this wonder, the most sacred humanity uttered these words: "Eternal Father, my most beloved Mother, thy beloved Daughter and the cherished Spouse of the Holy Ghost, now comes to take possession of the crown and glory, which We have prepared as a reward for her merit. She is the one who was born as the rose among thorns, untouched, pure and beautiful, worthy of being embraced by Us and being placed upon a throne to which none of our creatures can ever attain, and to which those conceived in sin cannot aspire."

"This is our chosen and our only One, distinguished above all else, to whom We communicated our grace and our perfections beyond the measure accorded to other creatures; in whom We have deposited the treasure of our incomprehensible Divinity and its gifts; who most faithfully preserved and made fruitful the talents, which We gave Her; who never swerved from our will, and who found grace and pleasure in our eyes."

"My Father, most equitous is the tribunal of our justice and mercy, and in it the services of our friends are repaid in the most superabundant manner. It is right that to my Mother be given the reward of a Mother; and if during her whole life and in all her works She was as like to Me as is possible for a creature to be, let Her also be as like to Me in glory and on the throne of our Majesty; so that where holiness is in essence, there it may also be found in its highest participation."

This decree of the incarnate Word was approved by the Father and the Holy Ghost. The most holy soul of Mary was immediately raised to the right hand of her Son and true God, and placed on the royal throne of the most holy Trinity, which neither men, nor angels nor the seraphim themselves attain, and will not attain for all eternity.

This is the most exalted and supereminent privilege of our Queen and Lady, that She is seated on the throne with the three divine Persons and holds her place as Empress, while all the rest are set as servants and ministers to the highest King. To the eminence and majesty of that position, inaccessible to all other creatures, correspond her gifts of glory, comprehension, vision and fruition; because She enjoys, above all and more than all, that infinite Object, which the other blessed enjoy in an endless variety of degrees. She knows, penetrates and understands much deeper the eternal Being and its infinite attributes; She lovingly delights in its mysteries and most hidden secrets, more than all the rest of the blessed.

Just as little can be explained, the extra joy which the blessed experienced on that day in singing the new songs of praise to the Omnipotent and in celebrating the glory of his Daughter, Mother and Spouse; for in Her He had exalted all the works of his right hand. Although to the Lord himself could come no new or essential glory because He possessed and possesses it immutably infinite through all eternity; yet the exterior manifestations of His pleasure and satisfaction at the fulfillment of his eternal decrees were greater on that day.

On the third day after the most pure soul of Mary had taken possession of this glory never to leave it, the Lord manifested to the saints His divine will, that She should return to the world, resuscitate her sacred body and unite Herself with it, so that She might in body and soul be again raised to the right hand of her divine Son without waiting for the general resurrection of the dead.

The appropriateness of this favor, its accordance with the others received by the most blessed Queen and with her supereminent dignity, the saints could not but see; since even to mortals it is so credible, that even if the Church had not certified it, we would judge those impious and foolish, who would dare deny it. But the blessed saw it with greater clearness, together with the determined time and hour as manifested to them in God himself.

When the time for this wonder had arrived, Christ our Savior himself descended from heaven bringing with Him at His right hand the soul of his most blessed Mother and accompanied by many legions of the Angels, the Patriarchs and ancient Prophets. They came to the sepulchre in the valley of Josaphat, and all being gathered in sight of the virginal temple, the Lord spoke the following words to the saints.

"My Mother was conceived without stain of sin, in order that from Her virginal substance I might stainlessly clothe Myself in the humanity in which I came to the world and redeemed it from sin. My flesh is her flesh; She co–operated with Me in the works of the Redemption; hence I must raise Her, just as I rose from the dead, and this shall be at the same time and hour. For I wish to make Her like Me in all things."

All the ancient saints of the human race then gave thanks for this new favor in songs of praise and glory to the Lord. Those that especially distinguished themselves in their thanksgiving were our first parents Adam and Eve, Saint Anne, Saint Joachim and Saint Joseph, as being the more close partakers in this miracle of his Omnipotence.

Then the purest soul of the Queen, at the command of the Lord, entered the virginal body, reanimated it and raised it up, giving it a new life of immortality and glory and communicating to it the four gifts of clearness, impassibility, agility and subtlety, corresponding to those of the soul and overflowing from it into the body.

Endowed with these gifts the most blessed Mary issued from the tomb in body and soul, without raising the stone cover and without disturbing the position of the tunic and the mantle that had enveloped her sacred body.

It is sufficient to say, that just as the heavenly Mother had given to her divine Son in her womb the form of man, pure, unstained and sinless, for the Redemption of the world, so in return the Lord, in this resurrection and new regeneration, gave to Her a glory and beauty similar to his own. In this mysterious and divine interchange each One did what was possible: most holy Mary engendered Christ, assimilating Him as much as possible to Herself, and Christ resuscitated Her, communicating to Her of his glory as far as She was capable as a creature.

Then from the sepulchre was started a most solemn procession, moving with celestial music through the regions of the air and toward the empyrean heaven. This happened in the hour immediately after midnight, which also the Lord had risen from the grave; and therefore not all of the Apostles were witness of this prodigy, but only some of them, who were present and watching at the sepulchre.

The saints and angels entered in the order in which they had started; and in the last place came Christ our Savior and at his right hand the Queen, clothed in the gold of variety, and so beautiful that She was the admiration of the heavenly court. All of them turned toward Her to look upon Her and bless Her with new jubilee and songs of praise.

Thus were heard those mysterious eulogies recorded by Solomon: Come, daughters of Sion, to your Queen, who is praised by the morning stars and celebrated by the sons of the Most High. Who is She that comes from the desert, like a column of all aromatic perfumes? Who is She, that rises like the aurora, more beautiful than the moon, elect as the sun, terrible as many serried armies? Who is She that comes up from the desert resting upon her Beloved and spreading forth abundant delights? Who is She in whom the Deity itself finds so much pleasure and delight above all other creatures and whom He exalts above them all in the heavens! O novelty worthy of the infinite Wisdom! O prodigy of his Omnipotence, which so magnifies and exalts Her!

Amid this glory the most blessed Mary arrived body and soul at the throne of the most blessed Trinity. And the three divine Persons received Her on it with an embrace eternally undissoluble. The eternal Father said Her: "Ascend higher, my Daughter and my Dove." The incarnate Word spoke: "My Mother, of whom I received human being and full return of my work in thy perfect imitation, receive now from my hand the reward thou hast merited." The Holy Ghost said: "My most beloved Spouse, enter into the eternal joy, which corresponds to the most faithful love;

do Thou now enjoy thy love without solicitude; for past is the winter of suffering for Thou hast arrived at our eternal embraces."

There the most blessed Mary was absorbed in the contemplation of the three divine Persons and as it were overwhelmed in the boundless ocean and abyss of the Divinity, while the saints were filled with wonder and new accidental delight.

THE CORONATION OF THE MOTHER OF GOD

We call that the throne of the Divinity, from which God manifests Himself to the saints as the principal cause of their glory and as the infinite, eternal God, independent of all things and on whose will all creatures depend, from which He manifests Himself as the Lord, as the King, as the Judge and Master of all that is in existence. This dignity Christ the Redeemer possesses, in as far as He is God, essentially, and as far as He is man, through the hypostatic union, by which He communicates his Godhead to the humanity.

Hence in heaven He is the King, the Lord and supreme Judge; and the saints, though their glory exceeds all human calculation, are as servants and inferiors of this inaccessible Majesty. In this the most holy Mary participates in a degree next inferior and in a manner otherwise ineffable and proportionate to a mere creature so closely related to the Godman; and therefore She assists forever at the right hand of her Son as Queen, Lady and Mistress of all creation, her dominion extending as far as that of her divine Son, although in a different manner.

After placing the most blessed Mary on this exalted and supereminent throne, the Lord declared to the courtiers of heaven all the privileges She should enjoy in virtue of this participation in his majesty. The Person of the eternal Father, as the first principle of all things, speaking to the angels and saints, said to them: "Our Daughter Mary was chosen according to our pleasure from amongst all creatures, the first one to delight Us, and who never fell from the title and position of a Daughter, such as We had given Her in our divine mind; She has a claim on our dominion, which We shall recognize by crowning Her as the legitimate and peerless Lady and Sovereign."

The incarnate Word said: "To my true and natural Mother belong all the creatures which were created and redeemed by Me; and of all things over which I am King, She too shall be the legitimate and supreme Queen." The Holy Ghost said: "Since She is called my beloved and chosen Spouse, She deserves to be crowned as Queen for all eternity."

Having thus spoken the three divine Persons placed upon the head of the most blessed Mary a crown of such new splendor and value, that the like has been seen neither before nor after by any mere creature. At the same time a voice sounded from the throne saying: "My Beloved, chosen among the creatures, our kingdom is Thine; Thou shalt be the Lady and the Sovereign of the seraphim, of all the ministering spirits, the angels and of the entire universe of creatures. Attend, proceed and govern prosperously over them, for in our supreme consistory We give Thee power, majesty and sovereignty. Being filled with grace beyond all the rest, Thou hast humiliated Thyself in thy own estimation to the lowest place; receive now the supreme dignity deserved by Thee and, as a participation in our Divinity, the dominion over all the creatures of our Omnipotence."

"From thy royal throne to the centre of the earth Thou shalt reign; and by the power We now give Thee Thou shalt subject hell with all its demons and inhabitants. Let all of them fear Thee as the supreme Empress and Mistress of those caverns and dwelling–places of our enemies. In thy hands and at thy pleasure We place the influences and forces of the heavens, the moisture of the clouds, the growths of the earth; and of all of them do Thou distribute according to thy will, and our own will shall be at thy disposal for the execution of thy wishes."

'Thou shalt be the Empress and Mistress of the militant Church, its Protectress, its Advocate, its Mother and Teacher. Thou shalt be the special Patroness of the Catholic countries; and whenever they, or the faithful, or any of the children of Adam call upon Thee from their heart, serve or oblige Thee, Thou shalt relieve and help them in their labors and necessities."

"Thou shalt be the Friend, the Defender and the Chieftainess of all the just and of our friends; all of them Thou shalt comfort, console and fill with blessings according to their devotion to Thee. In view of all this We make Thee the Depositary of our riches, the Treasurer of our goods; we place into thy hands the helps and blessings of our grace for distribution; nothing do We wish to be given to the world, which does not pass through thy hands; and nothing do We deny, which Thou wishest to concede to men. Grace shall be diffused in thy lips for obtaining all that Thou wishest and ordainest in heaven and on earth, and everywhere shall angels and men obey Thee; because whatever is ours shall be thine, just as Thou hast always been ours; and Thou shalt reign with Us forever."

In the execution of this decree and privilege conceded to the Mistress of the world, the Almighty commanded all the courtiers of heaven, angels and men, to show Her obedience and recognize Her as their Queen and Lady. There was another mystery concealed in this wonder, namely, it was a recompense for the worship and veneration, which, as is clear from this history, the most blessed Mary, notwithstanding that She was the Mother of God, full of grace and holiness above the angels and saints, had bestowed upon the saints during her mortal pilgrimage.

Although during the time when they were comprehensors and She yet a pilgrim, it was for her greater merit, that She should humble Herself beneath them all according to the ordainment of the Lord; yet now, when She was in possession of the kingdom, it was just, that She should be venerated, worshipped and extolled by them as her inferiors and vassals.

This they also did in that most blessed state, in which all things are reduced to their proper proportion and order. Both the angelic spirits and the blessed souls, while rendering their adoration to the Lord with fear and worshipful reverence, rendered a like homage in its proportion to His most blessed Mother; and the saints who were there in their bodies prostrated themselves and gave bodily signs of their worship.

All these demonstrations at the coronation of the Empress of heaven redounded wonderfully to her glory, to the new joy and jubilee of the saints and to the pleasure of the most blessed Trinity. Altogether festive was this day, and it produced new accidental glory in all the heavens. Those that partook more especially therein were her most fortunate spouse Saint Joseph, Saints Joachim and Anne and all the other relatives of the Queen, together with the thousand angels of her guard.

Within the glorious body of the Queen, over her heart, was visible to the saints a small globe or monstrance of singular beauty and splendor, which particularly roused and rouses their admiration and joy. It was there in testimony and reward of her having afforded to the sacramental Word an acceptable resting–place and sanctuary, and of her having received holy Communion so worthily, purely and holily, without any defect or imperfection, and with a devotion, love and reverence attained by none other of the saints.

In regard to the other rewards and crowns corresponding to her peerless works and virtues, nothing that can be said could give any idea; and therefore I refer it to the beatific vision, where each one shall perceive them in proportion as his doings and his devotion shall have merited.

ZONON BOOKS
Cincinnati, Ohio

www.ingramcontent.com/pod-product-compliance
Lightning Source LLC
Chambersburg PA
CBHW032051090426
42744CB00005B/167